Reading Instruction
in America

Reading Instruction in America

BARBARA RUTH PELTZMAN

McFarland & Company, Inc., Publishers
Jefferson, North Carolina

LIBRARY OF CONGRESS CATALOGUING-IN-PUBLICATION DATA

Peltzman, Barbara R., 1946–
 Reading instruction in America / Barbara Ruth Peltzman.
   p.   cm.
 Includes bibliographical references and index.

 ISBN 978-0-7864-3524-1 (softcover : acid free paper) ∞
 ISBN 978-1-4766-2013-8 (ebook)

  1. Reading—United States. 2. Reading—History—United States. I. Title.
 LB1050.P375 2015
 428.40973—dc23   2015028107

BRITISH LIBRARY CATALOGUING DATA ARE AVAILABLE

© 2015 Barbara Ruth Peltzman. All rights reserved

No part of this book may be reproduced or transmitted in any form or by any means, electronic or mechanical, including photocopying or recording, or by any information storage and retrieval system, without permission in writing from the publisher.

Front cover image © 2015 iStock/Thinkstock

Printed in the United States of America

McFarland & Company, Inc., Publishers
 Box 611, Jefferson, North Carolina 28640
 www.mcfarlandpub.com

To the memory of
my beloved mother, Norma Miln Peltzman (1909–2003),
my beloved father William Morris Peltzman (1916–2014) and
my beloved brother Stephen Arthur Peltzman (1947–2007).
They were scholars who inspired hard work, dedication,
and reaching a goal. We will not see their like again.

"Death and life and the written word that binds them....
The hand of bone and sinew and flesh achieves its immortality
in taking up a pen. The hand on a page wields a greater
power than the fleshly hand ever could in life."
—Laurie R. King. *A Letter of Mary.*
New York: St. Martin's, 1997.

Acknowledgments

Many kind and supportive people have assisted in the completion of this book in countless ways. Professor Lois Cherepon, reference librarian at the Loretto Memorial Library, St. John's University, always found hard to locate material and provided expert advice. Erin Cushing, a librarian at the International Reading Association, was generous with time, advice, and material.

Beth Puffer and Andrea Wilk of the Bank Street Book Store are master detectives who locate out of print and obscure sources. They suggest material, listen and care.

Theresa A. Trimarco and Michael Capobianco, friends and colleagues, gave generously of their time, wisdom and support.

Thank you Maryann Cornacchio for always listening. Many thanks to Ann Lieberman for continued help and encouragement. Thank you John and Roseann Kaczoroski for excellent long distance research assistance.

Joan Robelen did a masterful job of word processing, proofreading, and page design. She is truly an expert in ciphers because she was able to translate handwritten material into a professional looking manuscript. There are dozens of reference librarians and archivists who were voices on the telephone and who provided help and advice.

All these people and many others deserve thanks and, to paraphrase Lawrence Cremin, credit for whatever worth this book may have. I, however, am responsible for its faults.

Table of Contents

Acknowledgments	vi
Preface	1
Introduction	3
Noah Webster, Jr. (1758–1843)	7
William Holmes McGuffey (1800–1873)	17
The Joplin Plan	24
Grouping for Instruction	29
Basal Readers	41
Arthur Irving Gates (1890–1972)	50
William Scott Gray, Jr. (1885–1960)	56
Fernald Technique	62
The Gillingham-Stillman Approach and the Orton-Gillingham Approach	83
The Language Experience Approach	97
The Individualized Reading Approach	108
Readability	117
Oral Reading	129
Miscue Analysis	135
Initial Teaching Alphabet—ITA	144
Words in Color	147
The Linguistic Approach	155
Emergent Literacy	164
Story Grammar	168
Reading Recovery Program	175

Phonemic Awareness	183
The Whole Language Approach	188
Literature Circles	196
Literature-Based Reading Approaches	202
Readers' Theater	225
The Four Blocks Framework	231
Cloze Procedure	246
Question-Answer Relationship Strategy	254
Alternative Assessment Techniques	259
Reading-Writing Workshop	266
Index	275

Preface

This work grew out of my frustration with bibliographies in other books. I always want to know "about" a source. Just finding a bibliographic citation is not enough for me. I want to know what is in the source and if it will be useful for my purpose. I decided that other researchers and practitioners might benefit from an annotated bibliography following a discussion of a method or technique of reading instruction. This would certainly have saved me a great deal of money spent on sources that "might" help.

I also wanted to provide a reference work that examined reading instruction methods by explaining them and then telling how scholars in the field viewed the technique. The more information provided for the researcher and practitioner the better able they are to understand the technique being discussed.

I am always trying to better understand what I read. I want to say as Dewey did, "now I understand that!" In order to do this I need as much information as possible.

It is hoped that this reference work will provide enough information about each technique of reading instruction to give the reader a clear understanding of it. The more we know, the more effectively we can implement a method for the benefit of students.

I enjoy knowing the origins of the teaching methods I use. An historical perspective provides a view of what has led to what we do now and helps me explain to my students the origin and use of a method. I always want to know the source of what I use. Where did it come from and how did it start?

This curiosity led me to dig and hunt for the origins of the methods of instruction included here to give researchers as much information as I would want.

∽

"Birth of an Alchemist"
from Better Than Life *by Daniel Pennac, translated by David Homee (Portland, ME: Stenhouse Publishers, 1999). Editions Gallimard, 1992.*

Then one day ... he contemplated the silent flowering of the word on white paper, there, before his eyes: *Mommy*.... Then, suddenly, he understood *"Mommy!"*

His triumphant cry celebrated the culmination of the greatest intellectual voyage ever, a sort of first step on the moon, the movement from an arbitrary set of lines to the most emotionally charged meaning. Little bridges, circles, and slanted sticks ... and you could say "Mommy!" ... a magical transformation infinitely more eloquent than the most faithful photographic likeness built from nothing but little circles and sticks and bridges that have now suddenly—and forever—become more than scratches on paper.... They have become her presence ... that wholeness, so intimately absolute, and so absolutely foreign to what is written there....

Lead into gold.
Nothing less.
He had turned lead into gold.

This is learning to read—this is true alchemy.

Introduction

According to *Teaching Reading in Today's Elementary Schools*, reading instruction takes up a large part of every school day. Most schools require a reading block every morning to ensure uninterrupted, extended instruction time. Content area reading and reading/study techniques are also a vital part of everyday instruction.

Educators need to understand a variety of reading methods to help every student learn. Effective instruction across the curriculum requires teachers to be well informed in order to make independent decisions. Educators need information about a variety of strategies and materials to provide options that best fit the needs of each student. The diverse student population presents educators with many challenges.

According to Roe and Smith, "there is no one correct way to teach reading because some methods ... work better for some students than others. All students are individuals who learn in their own ways.... Some methods also work better for some teachers than they do for others. Teachers need to be acquainted with a variety of methods ... so that they can help all of their students." Each method has its own merits.

This book examines a variety of reading methods to help educators become informed decision makers to meet the diverse needs of their students. Teachers are individuals too and should develop a repertoire of teaching strategies in which they have confidence. Research indicates that educators are influenced by current fads and trends in reading instruction that burn hot and fade away quickly. Robinson suggests that the rich history of the field be reviewed because "educators of the past have struggled and reflected ... about many of the same dilemmas and problems faced by reading educators today."

This book examines reading methods in America from the 19th to the 21st century. Methods are arranged chronologically to show progress in the field. Selected biographies of researchers provide a description of the researcher's contributions and a discussion of the significance of the researcher's work with the response and acceptance of the educational community. Each discussion is followed by an annotated bibliography; in the biographical chapters it is divided into primary and secondary sources. Primary sources are arranged in chronological order and secondary sources are arranged in alphabetical order according to the author's name. Sources include books, journal articles, obituaries, biographical references, and dissertations.

More than 30 instructional methods are described in this book. Highlights from selected entries provide an overview of several significant methods.

The basal reading approach or core reading series (1930s–1970s) was for a very long time the most widely used approach in American elementary schools. Schools purchased a series which provided materials for every grade level starting with pre-reading. Each series provided teachers with materials for the presentation and practice of strategies for every grade level. A teacher's manual provided useful suggestions for teaching, questions to ask, suggestions for guided and independent practice, assessment techniques, and suggestions for differentiating instruction. Preparation time for each lesson was lessened because the teacher's guide provided valuable, useful, and realistic suggestions for teaching. Schools were able to provide students with continuity because teachers were aware of what had been taught in previous grades. Teachers were given structure with room to add and elaborate on suggestions provided. Research has also pointed to problems and misuses of the basal reading approach such as stereotypical portrayals of people, limited vocabulary, and stories that did not have literary merit.

The individualized reading approach (1950s) enables each student to make progress at his or her own pace using material that he or she has selected rather than being part of a group or using material presented by the teacher. The approach provides students with personalized help to develop independence. Students select material from a variety of books based on interest and readability and read at their own pace. Teacher-pupil conferences provide opportunities for assessment of progress. This approach requires a great deal of teacher preparation before starting. The approach is also more effective with upper elementary grades rather than beginning readers.

The language experience approach (1960s) connects all of the language arts using the student's experiences as the foundation for reading material. Students tell or write a story about an experience they have had as an individual or in a group. These stories become the material from which skills are taught. The stories are meaningful to the students and reflect their language. Since the student's own experiences are the source for written language the student has enough preexisting knowledge to understand the story and develop a knowledge structure that shows that written words have meaning. The approach has been used for many years in the early childhood grades. It is useful for students for whom English is a second language and also for older students and adults who are non or poor readers.

The whole language approach (1980s–1990s) is considered a professional and theoretical perspective based on a set of beliefs about learning, teaching, how language develops, curriculum, and the social community. Research on the writing process, sociolinguistics, psycholinguistics, and emergent literacy form the bases for the approach. It is a movement whose major advocates are classroom teachers. The approach is based on the belief that all parts of the language arts are connected and should not be taught as separate skills. Strategies are taught in a meaningful context. Authentic assessment procedures of each student's progress are used. Research states whole language is a set of beliefs, a perspective not a practice. Language always occurs in a context critical to meaning making. Language must be kept whole and authentic and children should use language in ways that relate to their cultures and everyday lives. The classroom is child centered and students enjoy learning because they believe what they are learning has meaning and is relevant to them. The right answer is not what is important rather the process of learning is the important part.

The preceding highlights of entries provide an overview of significant trends in the field of reading. This book is an attempt to illuminate the history of reading methods. As you will see there is a great deal of material in this volume. Research was intensive and required a great deal of time. To paraphrase H.M. Chadwick and N.K. Chadwick in the Preface to *Growth of Literature*, "if I had read more widely I should never have completed this book." As Mary Stewart stated in the *Merlin Trilogy*, "if I had ever known how much there was to read I would never have dared to start writing at all." I agree!

References

Altwerger, B., Edelsky, C., and Flores, B. "Whole Language: What's New?" *Reading Teacher* 27 (1987): 144–154.

Chadwick, H. Munro., and Chadwick, Nora K. *Growth of Literature*. Cambridge, England: Cambridge University Press, 1932–1940, 1968. "Preface," Volume 1.

Harris, Theodore L., and Hodges, Richard, eds. *The Literacy Dictionary: The Vocabulary of Reading and Writing*. Newark, DE: International Reading Association, 1995.

Robinson, Richard D. *Classics in Literacy Education: Historical Perspectives for Today's Teachers*. Newark, DE: International Reading Association, 2002.

Roe, Betty D., and Smith, Sandy H. *Teaching Reading in Today's Elementary Schools*. Belmont, CA: Wadsworth, 2012.

Steward, Mary. *Merlin Trilogy*. New York: William Morrow, 1980.

Tierney, Robert J., and Readence, John E. *Reading Strategies and Practices: A Compendium*. Boston: Pearson, 2005.

Noah Webster, Jr. (1758–1843)

Webster was born on October 16, 1758, in West Hartford, Connecticut, to Noah and Mercy (Steele). He started at Yale College at age 16 and graduated in 1778. He was the founder of the *American Minerva*, a New York City newspaper, and was elected to the Connecticut legislature and the Massachusetts legislature. Webster was a founder and president of the board of trustees of Amherst College. Webster died on May 28, 1843, in New Haven, Connecticut, according to Monaghan (1983), Shoemaker (1936), Ford (1912), Warfel (1936), and Unger (1998).

Webster wanted to read law, but the devaluation of paper money after the Revolution made that impossible until he could earn money. Unger (1998), Ford (1912), Monaghan (1983) and Shoemaker (1936) state that the only job Webster could hope for was teaching because most communities had problems finding teachers. Salaries were low and conditions were difficult. Webster applied to Glastonbury, Connecticut, where he had spent a summer during his junior year at Yale. He was given the post in 1778 and discovered, Unger (1998) and Shoemaker (1936) state, that he liked teaching. Webster was frustrated by the poor facilities and not enough books for his students.

Webster (1787) wrote about the state of American education describing the conditions, lack of teacher education, and overcrowding and the "absolute impossibility of obtaining books." Webster (1787) states that the worst misuse of the economy is not providing adequate funding for the education of children because the only way to reform society is to start with its children. "Education should, therefore, be the first ... article in the code of political regulations."

In 1782 Webster accepted a teaching job in Goshen, New York, determined, he said, according to Monaghan (1983), Unger (1998), and Rollins (1989), "to undertake an employment which gave a complexion to my whole future life. This is the compilation of books for the instruction of youth in schools." Webster began writing a spelling book. Webster was able to demand payment in silver for his teaching because his reputation preceded him. During his time in Goshen he found that speech was as essential to education as spelling, reading, and writing. Unger (1998), Monaghan (1983), and Rollins (1989) state that Webster believed that only a uniform way of speaking and a common language would ensure the unity Americans needed to govern themselves and stay a peaceful united nation.

Webster found that the way students were taught pronunciation was a disaster. Webster, in Rollins (1989) and Unger (1998), states that he decided to do away with provincial dialects which cause ridicule and difficulty of communication. Unger (1998) and Monaghan (1983) state that Webster's decision to teach spelling and grammar with reading selections from the writings of American patriots to teach all American students to read, write, and speak in a uniform way was extraordinary. Webster believed that in order for all Americans to become literate a new method of instruction was necessary. Monaghan (1983), Cremin (1979), Rosenberg (1967), and Unger (1998) state that Webster examined the available spellers and grammars and the way the most widely used words were spelled. He found that the spellers did not teach pupils to spell, but were intended to teach reading using spelling as a secondary method. Students were taught, Monaghan (1983), Unger (1998), and Rosenberg (1967) state, to spell out words in syllables as a method of pronunciation. This method was called the alphabet method. According to Monaghan (1983) and Unger (1998) this method of decoding can be traced as early as the work as William Kempe's 1588 *The Education of Children in Learning.* Unger (1998), Monaghan (1983) and Rosenberg (1967) state that spelling books before Webster consisted of the alphabet, a syllabarium or a list of syllables in alphabetical order such as ba, be, bi, bo, bu, by, and a list of words starting with one syllable words of two, three, and four letters and progressing in difficulty to multi-syllable words. The word lists ended with a reading selection made up of the words taught in each list. The book most widely used when Webster taught was Thomas Dilworth's *New Guide to the English Tongue,* published in 1771. Dilworth presented six short lessons at the end of each word list. The first lesson ended with:

No man may put off the Law of God.
The Way of God is no ill Way.
My joy is in God all the Day.
A bad man is a Foe of God.

Monaghan (1983), Unger (1998), and Rosenberg (1967) state that Samuel Johnson believed that when students could "pronounce words without spelling and proceed without hesitation in an intelligible way one is said to read." Unger (1998), Monaghan (1983), and Rosenberg (1967) state that students would pronounce the first line of this passage by saying "En, O No; emm, ai, en, man; emm, ai, wy, may; pee, you, tee, put; o, double eff, off; tee, aitch, ee, the; ell, ai, double you, Law; o, eff, of; gee, o, dee, God."

Webster recognized the difficulty of learning to read in this way. Monaghan (1983), Rosenberg (1967), and Unger (1998) report that Webster found Dilworth's book contained contradictory rules for spelling and pronunciation. Words were often spelled in several ways such as "might and mite." Punctuation and pronunciation rules did not match spoken language. In 1783 Webster said that the wide variety of local pronunciation throughout America caused the vowels and consonants to have four or five different sounds. Webster (1783) reported that dictionary authors complained that it was not possible to organize and standardize the English language. He proposed a national language that would ensure standardized pronunciation orally and standard spelling in writing. Webster (1787) proposed a national language as part of the new national government for the new country.

Webster developed a new speller because be believed that the speller influenced the language of a country. Webster consulted the President of Yale University who suggested he title his book *The Grammatical Institute of the English Language*. It was published in 1783 under that name, but in 1787 Webster retitled the book *The American Spelling Book*, a name it would be known by for the next forty years according to Unger (1998) and Monaghan (1983). The new speller used methods Webster applied to his classroom teaching. The book, Unger (1998), Monaghan (1983) and Warfel (1936) state, was small and easy to hold and at first look was the same as other spellers. Rosenberg (1967), Monaghan (1983), and Unger (1998) state that the difference in Webster's speller was the way the words in each list were grouped. Webster grouped words according to the way they were pronounced instead of the way they were spelled. This new idea was a true innovation. Students enjoyed rhymes and Webster discovered that they learned and remembered rhyming words quickly. Rosenberg (1967), Monaghan (1983), and Unger (1998) state that Lesson I used cap, gap, lap, map, tap and by Lesson XII students learned, be, pea, sea.

Monaghan (1983) states that Webster's most important new approach was a "description of the sounds represented by different letters" in the language. No other book had provided such an "accurate attempt to describe, categorize and compare the phonemic value of different letters." Webster provided a word for each letter as an example of the sound to be heard. Rosenberg (1967), Monaghan (1983), and Unger (1998) provide examples: "H is only an aspiration of breathing and is often silent, as in hour. The following have the first sound of th as in thick, thin."

The lists of words and lessons proceeded in a logical way from one syllable to two syllables and on through six syllable words. Webster used words that American students would recognize because these words were part of their spoken vocabulary. He used "superiority, impossibility, and divisibility" as multi-syllable words. Webster used the names of fruits, animals, and household objects in his word lists Unger (1998) and Monaghan

(1983) state. Webster made learning to read easy by classifying the sounds of English and providing an easy way to teach and learn American English. Unger (1998) states that Webster's speller "represented a giant step in the history of education and the spread of literacy."

Unger (1998), Monaghan (1983), Rosenberg (1967) and Warfel (1936) state that Webster included a geography section which listed the capitals of the American states, other towns and cities, and a list of foreign countries and their capitals. Webster included a chronological history of America from 1492 to the end of the Revolutionary War. Webster was also helpful to the teacher by providing an easy strategy for describing sounds for students. Examples such as "The consonant c is hard like k before a, o, u, l, r, and at the end of words such as cup, crop, public but is always soft like s before e, i, y as cellar, civil, cypress. G is always hard before a, o, u as gat, got, gum."

Monaghan (1983), Unger (1998), Rosenberg (1967), and Warfel (1936) state that Webster was the first author to help the teacher teach. He classified sounds of vowels and vowel combinations such as "sky, lie, eye" and used a new more natural division of words that was closer to the way the words were said. Students were able to see written words as they were really pronounced with the accent on the first syllable such as "bish-op, clus-ter." This was the first teacher-student friendly speller. Webster continued to revise the speller based on suggestions from other educators and the speller was published in many editions.

Unger (1998), Monaghan (1983), and Rosenberg (1967) state that Webster presented a very important and very controversial change in pronunciation of the suffixes "cion, sion, and tion." Samuel Stanhope Smith, who became President of the College of New Jersey at Princeton, suggested that Webster teach the suffix as two syllables rather than three or four syllables so that nation was pronounced na-tion instead of na-ti-on and salvation was pronounced "sal-va-tion instead of sal-va-ti-on."

Webster included reading selections in the speller that Unger (1998), Monaghan (1983), and Carpenter (1963) state were intended to inspire patriotism and develop the moral character of students. Selections included fables, stories, and dialogues. Warfel (1936), Shoemaker (1936), Monaghan (1983), and Rosenberg (1967) state that George Washington's virtuous character was used as an example for students and Webster also provided direct character instruction through advice such as:

> Be good child; mind your book; love your school; and strive to learn. Tell no tales, call no ill names; you must not lie, swear, nor cheat nor steal.
>
> A good child will not lie nor steal. He will be good at home, and ask to read his book; when he gets up, he will wash his hands and face clean; he will comb his hair, and make haste to school; he will not play by the way as bad boys do.
>
> Happy is the man that finds wisdom. She is of more value than rubies.

Monaghan (1983), Unger (1998), Shoemaker (1936), and Rosenberg (1967) state that Webster's work became a three text system of education divided into a speller, a grammar, and a reader. These books were uniquely American. Before Webster published these texts American schools only had texts printed and developed in England. American educators had no choice of books or method. Webster urged Americans to declare their independence in all ways including language.

Monaghan (1983), Unger (1998), Rosenberg (1967), Warfel (1936), and Ford (1912) state that Webster's speller and system of education were a success in the classroom. Parents and students were pleased by the rapid pace of learning and the joy of learning they felt for the first time. Webster believed that his system was useful and should be published. He also realized that he needed to protect his work with a copyright. The British copyright laws no longer protected the independent United States. Webster went to the Continental Congress in 1782 with letters from parents and students to ask for an American copyright for his speller.

Monaghan (1983), Unger (1998), Carpenter (1963), and Johnson (1917) state that Webster traveled to all the states to promote his books and to keep his rights as an author. In 1783 Massachusetts passed a copyright law and the Continental Congress recommended that the states grant a fourteen year copyright to authors and publishers of new and previously unpublished books; however, Webster needed protection in ten more states. Webster was frustrated because he had to finance the publication of more copies of his book with a loan.

Unger (1998) states that Webster's *Blue-Back Speller* "not only changed the course of education in the United States, it eventually changed the English language as no other book had or ever would. It made every previous speller obsolete and gained ... a monopoly in American classrooms for more than a century." The speller ensured that Americans learned to speak alike.

Webster's contribution to reading instruction was to write a spelling book that would standardize and Americanize spelling and pronunciation. Johnson (1917) states that Webster set the "American standard for spelling and brought order out of chaos." Millions of people remembered the old *Blue-Back Speller*, so called because it was bound in inexpensive blue cardboard according to Monaghan (1983).

According to Monaghan (1983) and Carpenter (1963), Webster's book became the foundation for the American Spelling Bee which was a staple in every schoolhouse during the 19th and early 20th centuries. Johnson (1917) states that spelling became a national obsession as a result of Webster's book because before Webster, spelling was rarely taught, but after Webster's book appeared it "absorbed a large share of pupil interest and enthusiasm."

Webster's aim was to provide an inexpensive textbook that would introduce students to letter sound correspondence according to Monaghan (1983), and Rosenberg (1967). Tebbel (1972) states that reviews indicate that Webster accomplished this aim. Webster not only compiled a speller, he marketed it by making 18th century book tours across the new country. He was also, Monaghan (1983), Unger (1998), and Morgan (1975) state, the father of the American copyright law. He fought for the rights of authors to profit from their books.

Sales of the *American Spelling Book* continued until the 1930s and as recently as 1987 a facsimile edition was published by the Noah Webster Foundation.

Unger (1998), and Monaghan (1983) state that Webster believed that the freedom and independence of America must be built on the adoption of an American language and culture. Webster was not only the author of a speller, but the business agent and chief of publicity. His reforms in spelling were adopted by subsequent authors and a truly American orthography emerged. Webster's *Blue-Back Speller* taught Americans to read and spell. His diacritical marks were innovative. He advocated the use of standard type in the printing of the Speller. Monaghan (1983) calls Webster the "father of royalties" for authors. He became the promoter of his own books and made them known to parents, school boards, and children through marketing ideas that were new in his time.

Webster's contribution to reading instruction was his personal commitment to a truly American language which led to the standardization of spelling and pronunciation through his *Blue-Back Speller*.

Annotated Bibliography

Primary Sources in Chronological Order

The First Part of a Grammatical Institute of the English Language Containing the Rudiments of the English Language for the use of Schools in the United States. Hartford, CT: Hudson & Goodwin, 1787.

An American Selection of Lessons in Reading and Speaking. Calculated to Improve the Minds and Refine the Taste of Youth. Being the Third Part of a Grammatical Institute of the English Language. Hartford, CT: Hudson & Goodwin, 1789.

    This is the first American textbook to describe the history of the new nation starting with its formation. "Rules for reading and speaking" are provided along with "narration" which includes short stores about moral virtues such as honesty, modesty, and piety. "The discovery and settlement of North-America" includes a chronology of events and a discussion of each of the original 13 states. "Geography" describes the "Explanation of the Terms in Geography" defining and explaining geographic features of America. "Lessons in Speaking" include famous American speeches, dialogues and poetry. Everything in the book was uniquely American by American authors about the new country.

A Collection of Essays and Fugitive Writings. Boston, MA: I. Thomas and E.T. Andrews, 1790.

    A collection of essays intended to inspire the citizens of the new United States to take their freedom seriously and become responsible for the new nation. Webster included essays on Moral, Historical, Political, and Literary subjects. In the essay "On the Education of Youth in America" Webster states "Americans, unshackle your minds and act like independent beings. You now have an interest of your own to augment and defend—you have an empire to raise and support by your own exertions, and a national character to establish and extend by your wisdom and virtue." There is an essay called "On the Education of Females" stating that the education of women is important and women should be taught useful subjects. Women should have a good education because they are responsible for raising children who will become future citizens. Webster lists the subjects women should learn as Americans.

The Little Reader's Assistant. Hartford, CT: Elisha Babcock, 1790.

A collection of: (1) Stories from American History; (2) English Grammar; (3) A Federal Catechism which is an essay on the constitution, and (4) General Principles of Government.

A Grammatical Institute of the English Language; Comprising an Easy, Concise and Systematic Method of Education. Designed for the Use of English Schools in America. In Three Parts. Part Second: Containing a Plain and Comprehensive Grammar, Grounded on the True Principles and Idioms of the Language. Hartford, CT: Hudson & Goodwin, 1800.

See: *A Grammatical Institute of the English Language Part II: A Facsimile Reproduction with an Introduction by Charlotte Downey, R.S.M.* Delmar, New York: Scholars' Facsimiles & Reprints, 1980.

This is the first American published grammar. This did not have the popularity of the Speller, but was a most important publication. Webster revised material after research for subsequent editions and provides an American English grammar book that was a guide for students. Webster called grammar a science rather than an art because grammar as a science deals with the connection between ideas and words "which are the signs of ideas, and develops the principles which are common to all languages." This is a guide to usage and punctuation.

Elements of Useful Knowledge. Volume I Containing a Historical and Geographical Account of the United States. Hartford, CT: Hudson and Goodwin, 1802; *Volume II Containing History and Geography for Use in School.* 1804. *Volume III Containing a Historical and Geographical Account of the Empires and States of Europe, Asia and Africa and Their Colonies.* New Haven, CT: Bronson, Walter & Co., 1806.

These volumes are an early encyclopedia discussing history, geography of America, Asia, Europe and Africa, natural science and the history and geography of America.

The American Spelling Book Containing the Rudiments of the English Language for the Use of Schools in the United States. Middletown, CT: William H. Neles, 1831.

This is the famous Speller which was Webster's attempt to Americanize and standardize spelling and pronunciation. **See:** *Noah Webster's American Spelling Book. With an Introductory Essay by Henry Steele Commager.* New York: Bureau of Publications, Teachers College, Columbia University, 1958. Provides an introductory biography and discussion of Webster's work and reprint of the 1831 edition of the Speller. Most useful.

The Little Franklin: Teaching Children to Read What They Daily Speak and to Learn What They Ought to Know. New Haven, CT: S. Babcock, 1836.

Lessons and anecdotes such as "The Whistle" by Ben Franklin. This is a textbook of reading selections.

The Teacher. New Haven, CT: S. Babcock, 1836.

A supplement to the spelling book. This is an early teachers' guide.

A Manual of Useful Studies for the Instruction of Young Persons of Both Sexes in Families and Schools. Hartford, CT: S. Babcock, 1839.

An encyclopedia-like book with material from *The Teacher* and lessons on a variety of topics. This is a textbook of math, science, social studies, and language arts. It is an attempt by Webster to provide teachers with the material of instruction.

Secondary Sources in Alphabetical Order

Babbidge, Homer D., Jr., ed. *Noah Webster: On Being American. Selected Writings, 1783–1828.* New York: Prager, 1967.

    A selection of Webster's work on a variety of subjects related to the development of an American national spirit. This includes the introduction to the Speller. These essays present a view of Webster's ideas on a variety of subjects related to his devotion to America as a united country. Babbidge provides an introduction and an afterward with biographical information and a brief Biographical Note. Provides valuable primary sources in one volume.

Belok, Michael V. *Forming the American Minds: Early School-Books and Their Compilers (1783–1837).* Moti Katra, Agra-U.P., India: Stish Book Enterprises, 1973, pp. 95–126.

    Presents an analysis of Webster's contribution to education. States that Webster taught for a short time but, spent the rest of his life instructing in many ways. A brief bibliography is included.

Benton, Joel. "An Unwritten Chapter in Noah Webster's Life-Love and the Spelling Book." *Magazine of American History* 10 (1883): 52–56.

Benton, Joel. "The Webster Spelling-Book: Its Centennial Anniversary." *Magazine of American History* 10 (1883): 299–306.

    These are 19th century views of Webster's contributions to education.

Bugbee, Bruce W. *Genesis of American Patent and Copyright Law.* Washington, D.C.: Public Affairs Press, 1967.

    Traces the history of copyright law mentioning Webster's role in the process.

Bynack, Vincent Paul. "Language and the Order of the World: Noah Webster and the Idea of an American Culture." Ph.D. diss., Yale University, 1978.

    Examines Webster's idea of a national language through a discussion of ontological and epistemology theory. Provides a brief biography, a history of an American National language, and a discussion of a national culture and American literature. Extensive bibliography.

Carpenter, Charles. *History of American Schoolbooks.* Philadelphia: University of Pennsylvania Press, 1963, pp. 95–98, 148–155.

    Presents a discussion of the origins of textbooks in America with a description of Webster's speller and grammar.

Carpenter, Edwin H., Jr., ed. *A Bibliography of the Writings of Noah Webster.* New York: New York Public Library, 1958.

    Presents a comprehensive, chronological, well organized bibliography of Webster's writings. This is the starting place for a view of Noah Webster's work. A most valuable resource.

Cole, Gary R. "Noah Webster, Journalist, 1783–1803." Ph.D. diss., University of Southern Illinois, 1971.

    Traces Webster's career as a journalist providing a view of his work outside of education.

Colton, A.M. "Our Old Webster's Spelling Book." *Magazine of American History* 24 (1890): 465–466.

    A remembrance of Webster's speller.

Commager, Henry S. *Noah Webster's American Spelling Book.* New York: Teachers College, Columbia University, 1962.

    Commager presents a comprehensive introduction to a reprint of *The American Spelling Book.* Provides biographical information and a good overview of the development of the Speller. Commager calls the Introduction "Schoolmaster to America" borrowing Harry R. Warfel's title to a biography of Webster. Commager provides a good summary of Webster's influence.

Cremin, Lawrence A. *American Education: The Colonial Experience, 1607–1783.* New York: Harper and Row, 1970, pp. 373, 568–569.

Cremin, Lawrence A. *American Education: The National Experience, 1783–1876.* New York: Harper and Row, 1979, pp. 261–270, 565–566.

    The Colonial Experience has a brief discussion of Webster's work. The *National Experience* presents a biography, a discussion of Webster's work and educational thought. Both volumes provide excellent "Bibliographical Notes." Both are clearly written and interesting.

Curti, Merle. *The Social Ideas of American Educators.* Totowa, NJ: Littlefield, Adams, 1968.

    In Chapter 1, "Colonial Survival and Revolutional Promises, 1620–1820," Webster's educational contribution to post-revolutionary America is discussed. Describes the Speller.

Elson, Ruth. *Guardians of Tradition: American Schoolbooks of the Nineteenth Century.* Lincoln: University of Nebraska Press, 1964.

    Presents a brief discussion of Webster's impact on subsequent textbooks.

Evans, Charles. *American Bibliography.* Chicago: Privately Printed, 1903–1959.

    A comprehensive index of books written in America from the 17th century.

Ford, Emily Ellsworth Fowler. *Notes on the Life of Noah Webster.* 2 volumes. New York: Privately Printed, 1912; New York: Burt Franklin, 1971.

    Memories by Webster's granddaughter provides a biography with diary entries and a "Check List of the Writings of Noah Webster." An incomplete bibliography of works cited is included.

Johnson, Clifton. *Old-Time Schools and School Books.* New York: Macmillan, 1917, pp. 167–184.

    Presents an in-depth discussion of the Speller with biographical information about Webster. Johnson analyzes the importance of the Speller concluding that "the Old Blue-Back stands unrivalled among American books in circulation and length of life."

Monaghan, E. Jennifer. *A Common Heritage: Noah Webster's Blue-Back Speller.* Hamden, CT: Archon Books, 1983.

    This is an in-depth study of Webster's Speller using Webster's papers. Provides a biography of Webster and the history of the Speller with reference to the linguistic and orthographic theories on which it was based. This is the comprehensive history of the Speller. Excellent bibliography, chapter notes and appendices showing Webster's sales and number of editions. Provides a conclusion and epilogue.

Morgan, John S. *Noah Webster.* New York: Mason/Charter, 1975.

    A biography that used the resources of the Noah Webster Foundation; however, the bibliography is brief.

Moss, Richard J. *Noah Webster.* Boston: Twayne Publishers, 1984.

    Presents a biographical sketch followed by chapters that address specific topics such as "Politics," "Language," and "Schoolbooks, Schoolhouses, and Moralisms" ending with an "Epilogue." A bibliography of Primary and Secondary sources is included along with a chronology of Webster's life.

Mott, Frank L. *Golden Multitudes: The Story of Best Sellers in the United States.* New York: Macmillan, 1947.

    Presents a discussion of books in America that are best sellers for various reasons. This is an interesting look at why books become popular.

Nietz, John. *Old Textbooks. Spelling, Grammar, Reading, Arithmetic, Geography, American History, Civil Government, Physiology, Penmanship, Art, Music—As Taught in the Common Schools from Colonial Days to 1900.* Pittsburgh: University of Pittsburgh Press, 1961.

    Provides a brief discussion of Webster's texts in spelling, grammar, and reading with sample pages. No bibliography is included.

Reeder, Ralph R. *The Historical Development of School Readers and of Methods of Teaching Reading.* New York: Macmillan, 1900.

    An early–20th century examination of the history of reading texts in America.

Rollins, Richard M. *The Long Journey of Noah Webster.* Philadelphia: University of Pennsylvania Press, 1980.

A biography showing the change in Webster's outlook on life from optimistic to pessimistic critic of society. A very different type of biography.

Rollins, Richard M., ed. *The Autobiographies of Noah Webster from the Letters and Essays, Memoir, and Diary.* Columbia: University of South Carolina Press, 1989.

Contains Webster's autobiography, letters and essays. Rollins provides an introduction that views Webster's life in the context of the times in which he lived and his own view of himself. A chronology of Webster's life, illustrations, and a bibliography of primary and secondary sources are included. This is a very interesting view of Webster by Webster.

Rosenberg, William A. "The Influence and Contribution of Noah Webster Upon Language Arts Teaching in the Nineteenth Century." Ph.D. diss., University of Connecticut, 1967.

Discusses Webster's influence on reading and language instruction in America. Presents information on the Speller and changes in the method of teaching reading as a result of its publication. A very useful resource.

Rusche, Dennis Patrick. "An Empire of Reason: A Study of the Writings of Noah Webster." Ph.D. diss., University of Iowa, 1975.

An examination of Webster's published works. Provides an extensive bibliography.

Scudder, Horrice E. *Noah Webster.* Boston: Houghton-Mifflin, 1883.

An early biography providing insights from a 19th century perspective.

Shoemaker, Erwin C. *Noah Webster: Pioneer of Learning.* New York: Columbia University Press, 1936.

This biography emphasizes Webster's contributions to education. A good view of Webster's impact on American education.

Skeel, Emily Ellsworth Ford. *A Bibliography of the Writings of Noah Webster.* Ed. Edwin H. Carpenter, Jr. New York: New York Public Library, 1958; New York: Arno Press, 1971, reprint.

A well-organized, complete bibliography of Webster's writings. This is a very important resource for the publication history of Webster's published works.

Snyder, K. Alan. *Defining Noah Webster: Mind and Morals in the Early Republic.* Lanham, MD: University Press of America, 1990.

Examines Webster's life in relation to his concern for the intellectual life and morals of people and the new nation. Discusses Webster's view of the world and its impact on his work.

Tebbel, John. *A History of Book Publishing in the United States, Volume I: The Creation of an Industry, 1630–1865.* New York: R.R. Bowker, 1972.

Discusses Webster's place in the creation of the American publishing business, his marketing methods, and his role in creating American copyright laws.

Unger, Harlow Giles. *Noah Webster: The Life and Times of an American Patriot.* New York: Wiley and Sons, 1998.

This biography examines Webster's many roles in American history. Provides a detailed picture of Webster the educator. Unger used Webster's letters, paper, and diaries. An excellent bibliography is included.

Warfel, Harry R. *Noah Webster: Schoolmaster to America,* New York: Macmillan, 1936; New York: Octagon, 1966, reprint

This is considered the most definitive biography of Webster with special emphasis on his contributions to education.

Warfel, Harry R., ed. *Letters of Noah Webster.* New York: Library Publishers, 1953.

An interesting view of Webster's life in his own words through his letters.

William Holmes McGuffey (1800–1873)

McGuffey was born in Washington County, Pennsylvania, on September 23, 1800, to Alexander and Anna (Holmes). In 1802 the family moved to Turnbull County in the Ohio territory. McGuffey's early education was conducted by his mother at home. He attended Greersburg Academy in Pennsylvania and in 1826 graduated from Washington College in Pennsylvania. Before he could afford to attend college, McGuffey earned money by teaching in rural subscription schools. In subscription schools parents paid the teacher a fixed sum for a specific period of time. When the teacher had enough pupils (subscriptions) the term started.

McGuffey taught at Miami University in Oxford, Ohio, from 1826 to 1832. He was elected president of Cincinnati College in 1836. In 1837 McGuffey became president of Ohio University after financial problems forced Cincinnati College to close. From 1843 to 1845 McGuffey taught at Woodward High School in Ohio. In 1845 he became professor of philosophy at the University of Virginia.

McGuffey died on May 4, 1873, in Charlottesville, Virginia.

McGuffey's contribution to reading instruction was to create a series of readers that suited the needs of the new settlers in the West. Westerners, says Wright (1955), developed a regional self-consciousness that caused them to reject New England school books and to seek books more suitable to their own lives. The new settlers in the West, Sullivan (1994) states, needed textbooks that reflected their multiethnic and pioneering lifestyle. McGuffey's pioneer childhood led him to believe that stories and poetry about farm animals, pets, nature, and a strict but benevolent God would appeal to the children of the West. McGuffey's books were planned and designed specifically for pioneer children, presenting material with which they could identify.

The method McGuffey used to teach reading was very different from the prevailing method of the time. The most widely used method was to teach spelling for a long period of time before the pupil was allowed to read words in context. Rather than teach spelling as a prerequisite to reading, McGuffey taught the alphabet first and went straight to reading using spelling as a way to learn new words. Minnich (1936) states that McGuffey promoted self-help as part of all lessons and taught "spelling with reading all the time." McGuffey accelerated the reading process and did not put primary importance on spelling. Nietz (1961) states that McGuffey presented a systematic way to help students learn to read using words in context related to pictures. Lessons on correct enunciation, a guide to articulation, definitions of key words, and comprehension questions for the teacher were included in the third, fourth, and fifth readers.

All stories had a lesson for the reader. According to Nietz (1961), McGuffey selected stories that had "human interest appeal" to help students not only learn to read, but to develop those character traits necessary to endure the pioneer life. McGuffey's original 1836–1837 readers were designed to help students master the skills needed to read with fluency and to help them build a strong moral character. McGuffey's early experience as a teacher and his vocation as a Presbyterian minister are reflected in the stories included in the first edition of the readers.

Subsequent editions of the *McGuffey Readers* were compiled by a group of editors. The most frequently remembered editions are these later ones. Sales from 1836 to 1920 were estimated at over 122 million copies, making the *McGuffey Readers*, as Quick (1925) states, "the most influential volumes ever published in America."

Annotated Bibliography

Primary Sources in Chronological Order

"General Education." *The Western Monthly Magazine* 2 (March 1834): 30–35. Cincinnati, OH: Taylor and Tracy.

The McGuffey Museum, Miami University, Oxford, Ohio, has a collection of 146 letters written to and by William Holmes McGuffey.

    McGuffey advocates a "revised system of public instruction, and faithful, competent, enthusiastic and persevering instructors to carry it into complete effect." Only after such educational reforms are made will "every department of civil society (be) conducted by competent—and if morality and religion keep pace with intelligence—honest men." This is a plea for equality of educational opportunity for rich and poor citizens. States that the citizens of America need a good general education, to ensure that everyone can do what is necessary for the functioning of our democratic society.

"James Kirrwood: A True Narrative" and "Seth Bushnell: A Yankee Trick." *The Western Monthly Magazine* 2 (March 1834): 424–429.

    Tells the story of two young men who travel to Cincinnati to become lawyers. Kirrwood arrives in style from Virginia and makes many social connections, neglecting his law practice to become popular. He "paid the price for his great popularity. He was to be found everywhere, except in bad company and in his office." His business declined and he had to return to Virginia to manage the family estate and never mentioned his career nor did he prepare his sons for the law.

Seth Bushnell arrived in Cincinnati at the same time as Kirrwood only he walked and was more modest. He asked questions about the West and tried to learn all he could about Cincinnati. Bushnell was careful about his remarks and did not intrude on the distinguished lawyers. Everyone spoke well of him and he did not frequent public bars. Bushnell helped a judge with some work in his office and secured a job which led to a successful practice. McGuffey concluded that a degree of common sense teachers that "the only way to conquer is to obey. And that self-esteem not compatible with the means of a sound and lasting popularity." These two selections are similar to the moral tales McGuffey would include in his Readers two years later. This is an early example of the material the Readers became famous for.

"Reverie." *The Western Monthly Magazine* 2 (March 1834): 113–119. Cincinnati, OH: Taylor and Tracy.

McGuffey discusses cause and effect in the context of the Master Plan of the Creator. Stating that "we have attempted ... to deduce the original character of the effect, from the known and necessary attributes of the cause ... the primitive condition of the Creator's words must have been that of perfection...." When everything worked as it should the Creator rejoiced "matter accurately obeyed the laws which were imposed upon it; and mind by a species of moral gravitation was voluntarily retained in its proper relation to the great center of the moral system. Alas! that it did not so continue." States that this perfection is found in the laws of astronomy in the instincts of animals, but "becomes barely discoverable in the still splendid ruins of our moral nature."

McGuffey is using his training as a clergyman to speculate about the causes of good and evil in the world. This is an interesting example of his mental exercise or "Reverie" which would later be used to select material for his Readers.

The Eclectic First Reader, for Young Children. Consisting of Progressive Lessons in Reading and Spelling in Easy Words of One and Two Syllables. Cincinnati, OH: Truman and Smith, 1836.

Consists of 45 lessons and a "Good Bye" to the readers telling them that if "you have been a good child and have learned your lessons well, you many now have the Second Readers."

The Eclectic Primer: for Young Children. Designed to Precede Wm. H. McGuffey's Eclectic Readers. Cincinnati, OH: Truman and Smith, 1836.

Begins with the alphabet and presents a series of eighteen lessons proceeding from words in isolation to sentences and finally to stories.

The Eclectic Second Reader Consisting of Progressive Lessons in Reading and Spelling for the Younger Classes in Schools with Engravings. Cincinnati, OH: Truman and Smith, 1836.

Consisting of 85 lessons containing stories and questions with "Suggestions to Teachers" on strategies for teaching. Stories include: "About Using Profane Language" and "The Ten Commandments" stating that "each little boy and girl should know these Ten Commandments and be careful to obey them." Lists the Commandments, a vocabulary list, and teacher questions for the lesson. There are fewer illustrations in this 240 page volume.

"Lecture on the Relative Duties of Teachers and Parents." *Transactions of the Fifth Annual Meeting of the Western Literary Institute and College of Professional Teachers Held in Cincinnati, October 1835.* Cincinnati, OH: The Executive Committee, 1836, pp. 129–150.

Discusses "the necessity and practicability of general education..." stating that the reasons for educating "the whole community..." are to ensure "universal intelligence among the citizens ... to protect their own interests and ... prevent the suspicions and temptation to which popular ignorance must always expose the better informed portions of the community." The aim of the lecture is "to point out some of the respective and relative duties of teachers and parents; in order that they may the more successfully cooperate in, their mutual work of training, to intelligence and virtue the future citizens of our happy republic."

Describes in detail the duties of teachers and parents, many of which sound very contemporary. For example he states "there must be an increase of teachers. Not more than thirty pupils ought ordinarily be committed to the care of a single instructor at any one time." Provides a very good argument for the value and importance of teaching as a profession. Provides a case for free public education for all Americans. One of McGuffey's lifelong commitments was to establish quality public school systems for all children.

"Remarks on the Study of the Classics." *Transactions of the Fifth Annual Meeting of the Western Literary Institute and College for Professional Teachers Held in Cincinnati, October 1836.* Cincinnati, OH: The Executive Committee, 1836, pp. 203-208.

McGuffey discusses the study of the Classics by students providing advice stating their importance in education.

The Eclectic Third Reader; Containing selections from the Best American and English Writers, with Plain Rules for Reading, and Directions for Avoiding Common Errors. Cincinnati, OH: Truman and Smith, 1837.

Consists of 63 lessons some with prereading instructions to the pupil, all with a prereading rule and teacher questions. Selected prose include: "The Importance of Well Spent Youth"; "The Goodness of God"; and "How to Guard Against Temptation." the Poetry selections include: "The Skylark"—Mrs. Hemans; "The Moss Covered Bucket"—Woodworth; and "Ode to the 19th Psalm"—Addison. There are no illustrations in this volume.

"Report on the Most Efficient Methods of Conducting Examinations in Common Schools, High Schools and Academies." *Transactions of the Sixth Annual Meeting of the Western Literary Institute and College of Professional Teachers Held in Cincinnati, October 1836,* ed. D.L. Talbott. Cincinnati, OH: The Executive Committee, 1837, pp. 240-243.

Presents the reasons why "examinations should be so conducted as to serve as a stimulus to all concerned in their results; and to this end, should be fair, rigid, protracted and thoroughly accurate."

The Eclectic Fourth Reader: Containing Elegant Extracts in Prose and Poetry, from the Best American and English Writers, with Copious Rules for Reading, and Directions for Avoiding Common Errors. Cincinnati, OH: Truman and Smith, 1838.

Contains a Preface discussing strategies for instruction and giving advice to teachers and a series of 129 lessons. The prose lessons include: "Paine's Age of Reason"—Erskine and "Capturing the Wild Horse"—W. Irving. The poetry lessons include: "Apostrophe of Light"—Milton; Divine Providence"—Bible; and "Anthony's Oration Over Caesar's Dead Body"—Shakespeare. Each lesson is preceded by a Rule and followed by questions and a discussion of Errors. The book is 422 pages long concluding with "American-National Hymn" Mason's Sacred Harp.

"Conversations in a School Room." *Monthly Chronicle of Interesting and Useful Knowledge* (March 1839): 147-149.

Consists of two conversations between a teacher and several pupils. Conversation number one is designed to teach that "one should study words in their connection, and you will understand them much better than by learning their definitions from a dictionary, or an expositor ... you will find ... that almost every word has a variety of shades of meaning ... some of which ... are not entirely correct in their application." Conversation number two asks "How is teaching like training?" Concludes that "you see of what importance it is to have the right kind of training, for our character will certainly be such as our habits have been."

These conversations demonstrate the Socratic or dyadic method of teaching which McGuffey used and suggested in the Preface of the *Third Reader.*

McGuffey's Newly Revised Eclectic Primer with Pictorial Illustrations. Cincinnati, OH: Winthrop B. Smith, 1849.

Presents the alphabet, a series of pictures for each letter and 88 lessons with spelling words, sentences, and stories. There are black and white pictures with each lesson.

Secondary Sources in Alphabetical Order

Byington, Jean Gregory, and Powys, Alyse Gregory. "An Inside Story of the McGuffey Readers." *Elementary English* 40, no. 7 (November 1963): 743–747.

  Written by the granddaughters of Dr. Thomas Stone Pinneo who edited and revised the Third and Fourth McGuffey Readers from 1843 to 1862. The information is taken from material found in an attic trunk providing insight into Dr. Pinneo's life and work. This article provides another dimension to the McGuffey Readers and a man whose name is mentioned briefly in historical accounts of the Readers.

Cameron, W.J. "The Mind of McGuffey." Delivered at Memorial Exercises Honoring Dr. William Holmes McGuffey, Miami University, Oxford, OH: July 1937.

  Cameron discusses the importance of McGuffey's contributions to education through the character development lessons in his Readers. States that the values of kindness, magnanimity, honor, truth, dependability, manliness, moral courage, reverence, and chivalry were an intentional part of the McGuffey Readers. Reading and spelling were considered a vehicle for the development of character. Examples from each Reader are given. States that McGuffey's training in the classics (Latin and Greek) is reflected in the selection of material and in the organization of the Readers which are not separate but "parallel lines of growth" building on each other. What is introduced in the First Reader continues in the Second and Third with added moral and social elements. The moral of each story deals with reality and a central truth. The material is timeless, Cameron states, and can be understood by children in any time in our history. Cameron believes that the truth remains unchanging and carries the same message without moralizing.

Carpenter, Charles. *A History of American Schoolbooks*. Philadelphia: University of Pennsylvania Press, 1963, pp. 79–92.

  Describes the McGuffey Readers providing brief biographical information and a discussion of the development and revisions of the Readers. Describes Alexander McGuffey's contributions as the compiler of the Fifth and Sixth Readers. Compares the McGuffey Readers to other series in use at the same time. Provides an annotated bibliography.

Crawford, Benjamin. *William Holmes McGuffey: The Schoolmaster to Our Nation*. Delaware, OH: Carnegie Church Press, 1963.

  Describes the founding of the McGuffey Society of Columbus, Ohio, and the development of the Federation of McGuffey Societies. Provides biographical information about the McGuffey family and a chronology of McGuffey's life. There is no bibliography or list of sources consulted. Provides an analysis of the 1879 revision of the *McGuffey Readers*.

Havighurst, Walter. *The Miami Years*. New York: Putnam's Sons, 1958–1969.

  Discusses the ten productive years McGuffey spent at Miami University describing the town of Oxford, Ohio, and the University. A bibliography is included.

Lindberg, Stanley W. *The Annotated McGuffey's Selections from the McGuffey Eclectic Readers, 1836–1920*. New York: Van Nostrand Reinhold, 1976.

  Lindberg traces the changes in the contents of the Readers with each revision. Provides an introduction with biographical information and a history of the Readers. There is a brief bibliography. The selections from the Readers with commentary about each selection are most valuable in understanding the origins of the material and the purpose of the lessons included.

Lively, Louise Robinson. "The McGuffey Readers." M.A. thesis, Western Kentucky State Teachers College, 1945.

  Provides a discussion of the people, education, and books of the Ohio Frontier a biography of McGuffey and a history of the Readers; an evaluation of the interest, comprehension factor, content, methods of instruction, and mechanical construction of the Readers. Concludes with an analysis of the value of the Readers. A bibliography is included.

Livengood, W.W. *Our Heritage: Being a Brief History of the American Book Company and an Account of Sundry Textbooks and Their Authors. An Address Delivered to the Entire*

Agency Force of American Book Company, January 4, 1947. At the Sinton Hotel, Cincinnati, Ohio: Cincinnati, OH: American Book Co., 1947.

    Describes various kinds of textbooks including The McGuffey Readers stating that "one set of Readers alone would establish our prestige in this field: McGuffey." Gives sales figures from 1836 to 1920, a brief biography of McGuffey, an anecdote about the fame of the Readers, concludes by stating that "at any rate after 110 years, we have a living heritage in the McGuffey's Readers that no other publishing house can match by miles; and it is doubtful if McGuffey will or can ever be equaled."

Minnich, Harvey C. *William Holmes McGuffey and His Readers.* New York: American Book Co., 1936.

    This is an analysis of the content of the Readers with a complete list of collections of the various editions of the Readers. Includes a bibliography of primary and secondary sources, biographical information, a discussion of the content and illustrations of the Readers, and compares the Readers to other series. The list of collections of the Readers is the most complete.

Murphy, Anna, and Cullen Murphy. "Onward, Upward with McGuffey and Those Readers," *The Smithsonian* 15 no. 8 (November 1984): 182–207.

    Discusses the use of the McGuffey Readers in the 1980s by various schools throughout the United States and the reasons for their adoption. Gives a brief history of the Readers describing the content and speculating that the reason for their longevity is that several editors and publishers revised them to reflect the changes in society. Biographical material is included along with many contemporary opinions of the value and weaknesses of the Readers. There is no bibliography.

Nietz, John A. *Old Textbooks.* Pittsburgh: University of Pittsburgh Press, 1961, pp. 70–80.

    An analysis of the strengths and weaknesses of the McGuffey Readers with biographical information and a publishing history of the Readers. There is no bibliography, but complete footnotes are included. This provides a good overview of the life of McGuffey and the Readers.

Parker, Franklin. "Ideas That Shaped American Schools," *Phi Delta Kappa* 62, no. 5 (January 1981): 314–319.

    Presents ten books that represent major turning points in American education between 1906 and 1981, during the 75 years that *Phi Delta Kappa* has been published. Among these influential books Parker lists the McGuffey Readers because they presented moral and inspirational ideas that educated generations of Americans. The Readers did more than teach reading and spelling skills they are an important part of our cultural heritage presenting the values that helped shape the American culture.

Quick, Herbert. *One Man's Life.* Indianapolis: Herbert Quick, 1925.

    This is a good examination of the life and work of McGuffey.

Reeder, Rudolph Rex. "The Historical Development of School Readers and of Methods in Teaching Reading. *Columbia University Contributions to Philosophy, Psychology, and Education* 8, no. 2 (May 1900): 109–16. New York: Macmillan.

    This is a history of readers in America providing a brief discussion of the McGuffey Readers praising their content. Includes a brief bibliography.

Revzin, Milton R. *McGuffey Readers Update.* Homesite Edition. Youngstown, OH: Scott Press, 1975.

    Provides biographical material, selected lessons, and pictures from the readers with comments and praise for McGuffey's contribution to Education. This is a tribute to McGuffey. A short bibliography is included.

Rugges, Alice McGuffey. *The Story of the McGuffeys.* New York: American Book Co., 1950.

    The foreword states that the book is a story of a family not a documented history. It is written by Alexander Hamilton McGuffey's granddaughter. Discusses Alexander's contribution to the series of Readers and provides many family pictures.

Scully, James Arnold. "A Biography of William Holmes McGuffey." Ed.D. diss., University of Cincinnati, 1967.

Provides an in-depth biography with a scholarly analysis of the Readers including a discussion of McGuffey's social and educational philosophy. Gives an interpretation of McGuffey as a person and an educator providing an extensive bibliography of primary and secondary sources.

Sullivan, Dolores P. *William Holmes McGuffey: Schoolmaster to the Nation.* Rutherford, NJ: Fairleigh Dickinson University Press, 1994.
   A complete biography of McGuffey with an excellent analysis of the influence of the Readers; comparison with present day readers; a publishing history; an appraisal of the strengths and weaknesses of the McGuffey Readers and a bibliography of primary and secondary sources.

Sutton, Walter. *The Western Book Trade: Cincinnati as a Nineteenth Printing and Book Trade Center.* Columbus, OH: Ohio State University Press for the Ohio Historical Society, 1961, pp. 166-189.
   Discusses the McGuffey Readers as part of a discussion about its publishers and other textbooks. Gives statistics on sales and tells about marketing. The bibliography includes special collections, books and periodicals, and Cincinnati newspapers.

Svobodny, Dolly, ed. *Early American Textbooks, 1775-1900: A Catalog of 1/ic Titles held by the Educational Research Library.* Washington, DC: United States Government Printing Office, 1978, pp. 92-95.
   Provides a list of the McGuffey Readers included in the library's collection with a paragraph describing the "firsts" provided by the readers. Calls the Readers "highly nationalistic and religious," designed "to teach morality and acceptable social conduct describing real human situations."

Vail, Henry. H. *A History of the McGuffey Readers.* Cleveland, OH: Burrows Brothers, 1911.
   Written by one of the editors and a partner in the Winthrop B. Smith and Company publishing firm, the book is the first complete history of the Readers. There is no bibliography. Vail provides biographical information about the publishers of the 1836 edition and evaluates the importance of the Readers. This is a very short book, only 72 pages long.

Venezky, Richard L. "A History of the American Reading Textbook." *The Elementary School Journal* 87, no. 3 (January 1987): 247-265.
   Venezky traces the 300 year history of readers starting with the *New England Primer.* Discusses the history, content, and popularity of the McGuffey Readers. States that there are two features that are common among all the readers examined. They (1) build reading instruction around a group of passages or stories and (2) present a limited conservative picture of society and the child's role in it. Also states that readers have changed in response to changing attitudes about society toward children and in response to society's changing impression of itself.

Westerhoff, John H., III. *McGuffey and His Readers: Piety, Morality and Education in Nineteenth Century America.* Nashville, TN: Abingdon, 1978; Milford, MI: Mott Media, 1982.
   Discusses McGuffey's educational philosophy, his place in the history of education, and his contributions providing biographical information and examples from lessons in the first edition of the Readers. Shorter than his dissertation and aimed at teachers.

Westerhoff, John H., III. "William Holmes McGuffey: Studies on World-View and Value System in the First Editions of the *Eclectic First, Second, Third and Fourth Readers.*" Ed.D. diss., Teachers College, Columbia University, 1975.
   Presents a detailed analysis of the value system and world-view McGuffey expressed in the first edition of his Readers. Biographical information, content analysis, and a discussion of the historical significance of the McGuffey Readers is provided. Extensive bibliography of primary and secondary sources.

Wright, Louis B. *Culture on the Moving Frontier.* Bloomington: Indiana University Press, 1955.
   Discusses the cultural elements that influenced the development of the United States. The McGuffey Readers and their effect on the lives of the pioneers are discussed in a chapter called "Instruments of Civilization: Secular Agencies" which provides an overview of the textbooks and systems of education found on the Western frontier.

The Joplin Plan

The Joplin Plan grouped students in grades four, five and six according to reading ability. Each group consisted of students from different grades who read at the same level. One teacher worked with each group.

According to Harris and Sipay (1985) schools developed many plans for homogeneously grouping pupils only for reading instruction. Factors such as test results and teacher judgment were used to separate students into reading classes with as narrow a range of reading ability as possible.

Cushenbery (1967) and Newport (1967) state that these inter-class ability groups were developed to group students for the best educational results.

Newport (1967), Cushenbery (1967), and Harris and Sipay (1985) stated that after Tunley's (1957) article in the *Saturday Evening Post* the inter-class ability grouping plan used in the Joplin, Missouri, schools gained national attention. Cushenbery (1967) reports that basal readers selected by each teacher were the material of instruction. The workbooks were not used by the students, but only as teacher references. It was suggested that teachers develop their own practice material suited to the needs of the students with whom they worked. In addition to the groups, 20 minutes a day was devoted to recreational reading within the student's homeroom. Cushenbery (1967) states that this provided the opportunity for wide reading based on interest and ability in a relaxed atmosphere.

In order to assess achievement, Cushenbery (1967) reports that a variety of standardized and informal techniques were used. Careful recording of progress in word attack skills, reading for different purposes, and summarized different reading materials was made. A special Reading Report Card was developed, Cushenbery (1967) states, that rated pupils in four areas: Oral Reading, Silent Reading, Word Skills, and Recreatory and Supplementary Reading. Pupils were rated on fluency, reading rate, use of voice, and regard for punctuation in the oral reading section. In the silent reading section Cushenbery (1967) states that reading rate; understanding of what is read; the ability to remember and relate what was read; concentration and understanding; adjusting rate to the material; stating the main idea of a paragraph, and interpreting implied meaning were rated. In the word skills section pupils were rated on the ability to: understand and use most word attack skills; guess at words instead of applying word attack skills; use the dictionary; and acquire the vocabulary needed at the present level of achievement. In the recreatory and supplementary reading section, Cushenbery (1967) states that the number of books read during a nine week period; the amount of reading with meaning on a variety of subjects; interest in independent reading; and problems with a narrow variety of materials, lack of interest and more use of the library were rated. Teachers used a check to indicate the areas that applied to each student along with comments and suggestions written in narrative form.

Newport (1967) and Cushenbery (1967) report on research studies that compared inter and intra-class grouping done between 1946 and 1964. They state that only two studies, Morgan and Stucker (1960) and Green and Riley (1963), favored inter-class grouping, one study done by Powell (1964) favored intra-class grouping and five studies Russell (1946), Hull (1958), Kierstead (1963), Moorhouse (1964), and Carson and Thompson (1964) reported that inter and intra-class grouping were equally effective.

Cushenbery (1967) states that the advantages of the Joplin Plan outnumber the disadvantages "particularly when the procedures are introduced in a careful, systematic manner...." He also cautions that these narrow inter-class groups are not homogeneous. "The Plan is merely a grouping method employed to narrow the range of reading abilities and thus allow the teacher time to concentrate on the needs of pupils whose strengths and limitations are similar in nature." Within these narrow groups there are individual differences which must be provided for.

Slavin (1987) examined research on in-class ability grouping and between class ability grouping concluding that ability grouping for specific subjects such as the Joplin Plan seems to be most effective. Slavin also states that students should remain in heterogeneously group classes for most of the instructional day.

Powell (1962) examined reading achievement in self-contained classrooms with reading achievement in a Joplin Plan Program and found no significant difference in pupil achievement. Powell did find that the pupils in the Joplin Plan were encouraged to do more recreational reading than pupils in the self-contained classroom. It was also concluded that student achievement in reading is affected more by the type of learning activities that take place rather than the classroom organizational plan used. Powell suggests that more studies are needed with more diverse student populations to determine whether a particular type of school organization will affect reading achievement.

Annotated Bibliography

Bralow, David. "An Evaluation of the Joplin Plan in School A Compared to a Traditional Program with Literature Supplement in School B." Unpublished doctoral dissertation, Temple University, 1970.

Studied the reading growth made by pupils in a Joplin Plan program and students in a supplemental literature program with consideration given to grade, sex and intelligence as factors. Broken homes, working mothers, and economic status were also considerations.

Carson, Roy M., and Thompson, Jack M. "The Joplin Plan and Traditional Reading Groups." *The Elementary School Journal* 65 (Oct. 1964): 38-43.

Compared the reading growth of 129 4th, 5th, and 6th graders in a Joplin Plan program with 121 students in a three group in-class reading program. States that test results indicate more than one year of growth for both groups of students. The majority of parents of students in the Joplin Plan group favored the continued use of the Plan.

Cushenbery, Donald C. "The Joplin Plan and Cross Grade Grouping." In *Organizing for Individual Differences*. W.Z. Ramsey, ed. Newark, DE: International Reading Association, 1967, pp. 33-46.

Presents the history of the Joplin Plan, an explanation of the Plan, and a discussion of research studies using the Plan. Discusses the advantages and limitations of the Joplin Plan. Provides a summary and extensive list of references.

Green, D., and Riley, H. "Inter-Class Grouping for Reading Instruction." *The Journal of Experimental Education* 31 (1963): 273-278.

Reports that the Joplin Plan is not new because Russell (1946) conducted a study using an ability grouping plan called circling. States that inter-class grouping is a useful organizational plan. Reports on a one year inter-class grouping plan in grades 4-6 sampling 420 students in matched pairs for reading.

Harris, Albert J., and Sipay, Edward R. *How to Increase Reading Ability: A Guide to Developmental and Remedial Methods*, New York: Longman, **1985**, 1987, 1988, pp. 106-110.

A brief definition and description of the Joplin Plan as part of a discussion of various organizational plans of grouping for reading instruction. Includes a useful bibliography.

Hull, J. "Multigrade Teaching." *The Nation's Schools* 62 (1958): 33-36.

Reports on teacher enthusiasm for a new inter-class plan for reading instruction. The first two year study of grades one through six reported that progress in reading was related to teacher enthusiasm. In the second one year study done at the same school system with many of the same teachers and pupils who participated in the first study, Hull found that the results in the second study was not as significant as those in the first study. Hull concluded that enthusiasm for the Plan lessened over time.

Kierstead, Reginald. "A. Comparison and Evaluation of Two Methods of Organization for the Teaching of Reading." *The Journal of Educational Research* 56 (Feb. 1963): 317-321.

Reports on a study conduced in 1959 in Vermont with two groups of students in grades three through eight. One group was taught within the classroom in small groups, the second group was grouped according to reading ability and teacher observation rather than grade level. Group two was sent to reading classrooms outside their regular classroom. The results of the study indicated that there was no significant difference in vocabulary and comprehension skills between the two groups based on the Iowa Test of Basic Skills. Kierstead also reported that ability grouping did not replace the need to attend to the individual needs of students and that parents of both groups accepted ability grouping when communication was established between the parents and the school.

Miller, Wilma, H. "The Joplin Plan—Is It Effective for Intermediate—Grade Reading Instruction?" *Elementary English* 66, no. 7 (Nov. 1969): 951-954.

Questions the effectiveness of the Joplin Plan with intermediate grade students. Discusses instructional purposes, materials and methods of instruction.

Miller, Wilma, H. "Some Less Commonly Used Forms of Grouping." *Elementary English* 48, no. 8 (Dec. 1971): 989-992.

Discusses less frequently used plans for grouping pupils for reading instruction. Provides a description of each plan including the Joplin Plan.

Moorhouse, W.F. "Inter-class Grouping for Reading Instruction." *The Elementary School Journal* 64 (1964): 280–286.

    Reports on a two and one half year study of 338 pupils in grades four to six. After one semester Moorhouse found that reading gains and interest favored the inter-class grouping plan. Samples at the end of three and five semesters indicated lower reading gains, and lower teacher and student interest in the inter-class groups. These lower results were sometimes less than the reading level gains and interest in the graded classes. It was concluded that inter-class grouping produced growth early in the program, but the program did not provide continued or lasting growth in reading.

Morgan, Elmer, and Stucker, Gerold. "The Joplin Plan of Reading vs. Traditional Method." *Journal of Educational Psychology* 51 (April 1960): 69–73.

    Reports on a one year study of ninety matched pairs of 5th and 6th grade students designed to find out if the Joplin Pan would produce significantly better results in reading if teachers had been randomly assigned to the Joplin Plan and the self-contained classroom and initial reading ability method, sex, and measured intelligence were controlled. Students were given the Durrell-Sullivan and California Achievement tests as pre and post-tests. It was concluded that the Joplin Plan is a more effective way to group students for reading than the plan used in self-contained classrooms where there were wide ranges of reading ability.

Newport, John F. "The Joplin Plan: The Score." *The Reading Teacher* 21, no. 2 (Nov. 1967): 158–162.

    Describes the Joplin Plan and presents research evidence from many studies to discuss the effectiveness of the Plan. Presents evidence about the acceptance of the Joplin Plan by teachers, parents, and pupils and provides a brief history of inter-class grouping.

Powell, William R. "A Comparative Evaluation of the Joplin Plan." Unpublished doctoral dissertation, Indiana University, 1962.

    Reports research done in Joplin Plan reading groups and self-contained classrooms in two public schools in Indianapolis, Indiana, focusing on 4th, 5th and 6th grade students. The study was started in October 1961 and ended in March 1969. Extensive data was collected. It was concluded that the Joplin Plan did not produce significant differences in reading achievement, or pupil performance in content areas. The Joplin Plan encourages wider reading and can encourage higher teacher enthusiasm, but this finding is not as important as the type of learning activities which happen in the classroom. The extensive bibliography and statistical tables are included.

Powell, William R. "The Joplin Plan: An Evaluation," *The Elementary School Journal* 65 (1964): 387–392.

    This is a journal article based on Powell's dissertation which presents a more concise view of his study.

Ramsey, Wallace. "An Evaluation of a Joplin Plan of Grouping for Reading Instruction." *Journal of Educational Research* 55 (Aug. 1962): 567–572.

    Reports a study conducted in Logansport, Indiana, from 1958 to 1960 to evaluate the results of using the Joplin Plan in two schools of different sizes. Students in grades 4, 5, and 6 were given the Stanford Achievement Test early in October 1958 and 1959 to group students from two schools into seven different reading level classes. It was concluded that the data indicates that inter-grade grouping was effective and expected growth at all three grade levels was shown. It was also found that students with higher intelligence levels showed more growth in reading than students with lower intelligence levels. Teachers and students in both groups reported unanimous satisfaction for the Joplin Plan.

Russell, D.H. "Inter-Class Grouping for Reading Instruction in the Intermediate Grades." *Journal of Experimental Research* 39 (1946): 462–470.

    Studied inter-class grouping for two years with 526 4th, 5th, and 6th graders and found that inter-class grouping did not result in greater growth in reading.

Slavin, Robert E. "Ability Grouping and Student Achievement in Elementary Schools: A Best—Evidence Synthesis." *Review of Educational Research* 57, no. 3 (Fall 1987): 292–336.

    Presents a review of research comparing between class and within class ability grouping for reading. Concludes that the most effective use of ability grouping is when students stay in heterogeneously grouped classrooms for most of the day and are grouped for specific content area subjects. Cross-grade grouping for specific subjects may result in greater growth.

Tunley, Roul. "Johnny *Can* Read in Joplin." *Saturday Evening Post*, Oct. 26, 1957, pp. 108, 110.

    The popular magazine article that drew national attention to the Joplin Plan. Describes in layman's language what the Plan is and how it was implemented. Tells about the support for the Plan by principals and teachers in Joplin, Missouri. No research data is present.

Grouping for Instruction

Students are grouped for instruction because classrooms consist of students with a range of proficiency levels. In order to differentiate instruction for the benefit of students, teachers grouped children with similar needs and abilities together for instruction.

Harris and Sipay (1988) state that "the range of individual differences in reading proficiency is wide at every age level and increases as children get older. One way of dealing with these differences is to group for reading instruction." Burns, Roe, and Smith (2002) state that teachers group students to deal with the wide range of reading levels and as a compromise between individualized instruction and whole class instruction. Harris and Sipay (1988) and Burns, Roe, and Smith (2002) identify several types of groups for instruction. Students can be grouped according to achievement or reading ability, special skills or needs groups, interest, project or research or committees, friendship, and pairs or partners. Activities within these groups may be carried out by the teacher or another adult, a student leader or self-directed by students. Grouping for instruction is an effective use of instructional time according to Harris and Sipay (1988) and Burns, Roe, and Smith (2002). Students, teachers, and situations differ and one plan does not fit every situation. Harris and Sipay (1988) state that "whatever the grouping plans, it should be remembered that grouping for reading instruction is a means for facilitating learning; it is not an end in itself."

Flood, Lapp, Flood, and Nagel (1992) state that students learn from the teacher, independently, and from peers. Students have many opportunities in one day to work in various types of groups that change for different purposes, formats, and kinds of materials used. The reasons for groups could be skill development or common interest, the format may be student or teacher led with changing numbers of members, and materials may be different based on themes or reading levels. Salinger (1996) believes that students should be able to move in and out of flexible groups as needs and interests of members change. Burns, Roe, and Smith (2002) describe achievement grouping and Harris and Sipay (1988) call this type of organization general level of reading ability or ability-level groups. Usually achievement or ability groups are created based on the difficulty level of the material students can read for instructional purposes or levels of reading ability. Teachers organized three or four such groups and Burns, Roe, and Smith (2002) state these groups read basal readers because basal readers came as a package with a teacher's manual and workbooks that provided a skills-based reading program. Teachers continuously assessed pupil progress and made changes based on slower or more rapid progress. The teacher was advised to keep the groups flexible so that students could move up or down a level or even two levels. Harris and Sipay (1988) advised teachers to place a student whose exact level was not clear in the lower of the two groups considered because "this usually ensures successful participation, and … is psychologically more sound to move a child from a lower to a higher group than to 'demote'…"

Another kind of group is based on special skills or special needs. Harris and Sipay (1988) and Burns, Roe, and Smith (2002) state that special needs groups are temporary groups formed after assessment shows deficiency in a particular skill or reading strategy. These students need help with the same problem regardless of their placement within an ability level group. Students from high, middle, and low ability groups might all become members of the same special needs group. Once the purpose for the group is accomplished students are reassessed and if the students can apply the skill or strategy for which they received intensive care the group is disbanded. A new group focusing on another skill for other students is then formed. Teachers present mini lessons and students apply the skill or strategy after each mini lesson. Any classroom can have several special needs groups containing one or more students meeting at one time until the students have gained competence in the skill.

Interest groups, Harris and Sipay (1988) and Burns, Roe, and Smith (2002) state, are based on students' shared interests and it is suggested that they meet to explore topics through reading, writing and literature. These groups need not meet frequently and membership is voluntary. Students who have a special interest in a particular subject can usually read material at a higher level than they usually read because of the built in motivation the topic generates. Students are encouraged to meet, research, discuss, and report to the rest of the class. These groups can be part of content area studies.

Project, research groups or committees are groups based on classroom projects related to a unit under study in one or more of the content areas. These groups contain members of various abilities who work together to study a topic, gather and merge their information for a presentation to the rest of the class. Each group member contributes to the final presentation, according to Harris and Sipay (1988) and Burns, Roe, and Smith (2002).

Friendship groups, Burns, Roe, and Smith (2002) state, are formed based on specific friendship and work very well for a specific purpose for a given period of time. These groups are successful because of the basis for formation.

Students can also work very successfully, Burns, Roe, and Smith (2002) state, as partners who meet to read orally, revise or edit a piece of writing, correspond through a journal, or help one partner perfect a reading skill.

Paratore and Indrisano (2003) state that research has focused on the effects of grouping on students' success or failure in reading throughout the history of reading research. During the 1960s, 1970s, and 1980s the research focused on ability grouping, peer tutoring (student partners) and cooperative learning. A number of syntheses and meta-analyses have been done by Cohen, Kulik, and Kulik (1982), Good and Marshall (1984), Johnson, Marvyama, Johnson, and Nelson (1981), Kulik and Kulik (1984), Lou, Abrami, Spence, Paulsen, Chambers and d'Apollonia (1996), and Slavin (1980, 1987, 1990). These works have helped to make sense out of the overwhelming "mountains of research evident" about grouping practices according to Oakes (1985).

Hiebert (1983) examined the relation between students' group membership, self-concept and attitude toward reading for students placed in the lower ability groups. It is not clear whether a negative attitude toward reading is caused by a lack of interest in reading that may cause a student to be placed in a lower group or if lower group placement contributes to negative attitude and negative self concept.

Good and Marshall (1984) examined observational studies with specific research designs tracking across different variables such as peer effects, teacher behavior and attitude, and content of instruction. They focused on between-class grouping. It was concluded that there was evidence that students in lower groups suffered consistent deprivation. There is a difference between students in heterogeneous small groups and students in homogeneous small groups. Students in achievement groups do not do well. They show consistently low performance according to Good and Marshall (1984), Oakes (1985), Slavin (1987). Procedures differ in terms of follow-up assignments and highly structured assignments between high achievement groups and low achievement groups according to Borko, Shavelson and Stern (1981) and Shavelson and Stern (1981). Slavin (1990) found that ability grouping does not affect learning at different levels in different ways. Students do not read better when placed in groups with others like themselves. Learning is not accelerated and they do not complete elementary or secondary school faster than average students, Kulik and Kulik (1984) conclude. It was also found by Allington (1984) and Hiebert (1983) that the material used with students in the high, middle and low groups was different in difficulty, interest, and motivation. Also Allington (1984) and Hiebert (1983) found that teaching differs among groups. The teachers spent more time with the high achieving group, teachers allowed fewer interruptions when they worked with the higher achieving groups, lower achieving groups were often allowed less time to answer questions, often were not as involved in assignments, and teachers had to spend more time on negative behavior and attention problems in lower groups, Hiebert (1983) found. Webb (1982) found that patterns of interaction between students and teacher influence learning. Teacher attention to individual group members and attitude toward the group can affect participation and self concept. Barr and Deeben (1991), Dweck (1986), Eder (1983), and Swanson (1985) found that students in low achievement groups have low self-concepts and poor attitudes toward reading and learning.

Braddock and Dawkins (1993) and Oakes (1985) found that low ability groups had many more students from racial and ethnic minority groups than did the high achievement groups.

Lou, Abrami, Spence, Paulsen, Chambers and d'Apollonia (1996) found that ability grouping produced more positive results about attitude and self-concept than did situations in which teachers did not group for instruction, but taught the whole class as one group.

Cohen, Kulik, and Kulik (1982) found that peer tutoring or partners can help both members to succeed better. The person who is tutoring and the one receiving the help succeed only when what they are doing is highly structured and specific and was evaluated by a test that was highly correlated to the skill on which the students worked.

Studies in the 1980s and 1990s related to the findings about heterogeneous groupings within classrooms influenced teachers' instruction planning. Some teachers adopted whole class teaching, Paratore and Indrisano (2003) state, as a response to the whole language philosophy. Other teachers implemented multiple heterogeneous small groups, while others used large or small groups that changed based on the material presented, similar to special needs groups, and other teachers employed large groups and small groups for part of the day.

Paratore and Indrisano (2003) report that teachers and administrators in some schools were concerned about changing to heterogeneous groups. Juel's (1990) research offered support by finding that first grade students needed careful monitoring when learning basal reader words and learned to read when the material is carefully matched to individual reading levels. The question of the lowest achieving students' success has been asked again and Paratore and Indrisano (2003) report that these students who have the lowest success rates may not be learning to read at all, but are learning to listen to material that is read to them. Allan (1991) and Renzulli and Reis (1990) asked if the most able students were being challenged enough.

Stevens, Madden, Slavin, and Farnish (1987) examined the cooperative integrated reading and composition, approach which includes basal related activities, direct teacher instruction in reading comprehension and integrated language arts and writing. The teacher introduced a new skill, vocabulary, and story ideas in reading level groups. Students then practiced the skills in heterogeneous teams. Once a week students were given direct instruction in comprehension skills followed by team practice sessions. Process writing instruction was part of language arts projects and writing was part of daily language arts instruction. Students read trade books and practiced in teams. Students read for 20 minutes at home with parents supervising this and students presented a book report every two weeks.

The effectiveness of the approach was studied in two investigations. The first with eleven third and fourth grade classes in a suburban district with ten control classes using traditional methods and materials. Special needs students were included in the experimental and control classrooms. During twelve weeks the teachers all allocated the same length of time for reading and language arts. No significant difference was found on total reading score; however, language arts scores were higher for the experimental group on four of the five standardized tests including reading comprehension. The experimental group did well on language expression and spelling and there was a significant difference in writing. No difference for language mechanics. "No significant ability-by-treatment interactions on any posttest measures" were found, Stevens, Madden, Slavin and Farnish (1987) state.

The second study also looked at third and fourth grade classes in a suburban district but studied the groups for 24 weeks rather than 12 weeks. Posttest results found that the experimental group performed significantly better on all measures. The study was extended by Stevens and Slavin (1995) over a two year period in grades two through six with 1299 students in a suburban district. Posttest results in the first and second year indicated that the experimental groups performed significantly better than the control groups. Special needs students were included; however, their data were analyzed separately. It was found that the experimental group test results had significant differences on reading, vocabulary and comprehension for both years.

This technique, CIRC, uses ability groups for reading but uses heterogeneous cooperative learning practice groups. Jenkins, Jewell, Leicester, O'Connor, Jenkins, and Troutner (1994) used an adapted type of CIRC eliminating ability groups and used the same materials for all students. To help students who had problems with grade level material they added three practices to help students with problems: cross-age and peer tutoring, special decoding lessons, taught in a 12 to 20 minute daily limited pull-out program, and in class help from specialists. During the year long study data was collected from two schools, one in the experimental model and a comparison school. At least two classes on each grade level and all students including those with special needs were studied. Posttest results were mixed finding that experimental schools showed superior growth on reading vocabulary, total reading and language on the Metropolitan Achievement Test with marginally significant growth on reading comprehension. No significant differences were found between the experimental and comparison schools on the Gates MacGinitie Reading Test, the Reading subtest of Basic Academic Skills Samples, and Passage Reading Test. The growth pattern favored the experimental groups on these tests.

Cunningham, Hall and Defee (1991), using the Four Blocks Model, set up non ability grouped multilevel teaching in a first grade classroom. Equal time for each of four blocks of teaching was given using basal readers, self-selected reading, writing, and working with words. Comparison was not made to a control group, but achievement levels by grade level standards were compared with students' expected achievement in ability grouped classes. Students who would have been in the lowest group at the end of the first year were reading at grade level or above. Middle level groups were on or above grade level and top level students read above grade level. Hall and Cunningham (1995) worked for six years with first and second graders in multilevel, multi-method teaching and reported that there was a lack of a control group but results of achievement were consistent.

Turpie and Paratore (1995) studied reading of four students who were reading below the 48th percentile on a readiness test and were identified as at risk for poor performance. The four were in a first grade of 25 students with flexible grouping using heterogeneous whole-class lessons and needs based small groups. Turpie and Paratore (1995) used a multi-baseline, single case design focused on the effects of repeated readings on word accuracy, fluency, self-correction, and reading comprehension. Results indicated that students improved reading accuracy, fluency and self correction based not on memorization but on attention to graphemic-phonemic cues, and reading comprehension also indicated growth.

Paratore and Indrisano (2003) state that even though there were few studies that focused on alternative forms of grouping for reading, there were many different models of instruction. The results of these studies were consistent indicating that when ability grouping is replaced with other ways of grouping achievement is higher for vocabulary, comprehension, and fluency. In studies done by Cunningham and Hall (1995) and Turpie and Paratore (1995) students taught in heterogeneous groups have better opportunities to read, reread, write and practice words. Students identified as low performing learn the word identification skills needed to read grade level material.

Studies of the Book Club program looked at the ways students talk about what they read when they meet in heterogeneous groups. These alternative grouping ideas found in literature based programs are an effort to broaden the ways reading success is defined and examine changes in the ways students talk about books.

Studies examined the limitations of ability grouping and the effects of ability grouping on student self-concept, teacher expectations, and the use of poor curriculum for low achieving students. Elbaum, Schumann and Vaughn (1997) examined third, fourth and fifth grade students in three large urban schools using closed and open ended questions administered during class time with two researchers present. Students reported: mixed ability groups and pairs of students rated higher than whole class lessons, whole class lessons rated higher than same ability pairs of students, and same ability pairs of students rated higher than same ability groups according to Paratore and Indrisano (2003). Student perceptions of characteristics of groupings indicated: mixed ability groups were described as more cooperative and better for learning; in mixed ability groups good readers can help poor readers; mixed ability groups are more fair than same ability groups because they can help poor readers; same ability groups do not frustrate good readers because they are not slowed down by poor readers; and student responses about enjoyment in various groups were evenly split between same and mixed ability groups. Elbaum, Schumann, and Vaughn (1997) state that students responding to the questions in some instances had little experience with several grouping types and responses were based on expectations not experience with the grouping types, and even when students had experience with the type of groups no definition or explanation of the activities that went on in the grouping types was made.

Paratore and Indrisano (2003) conclude that the research evidence available from a few teams of investigators is worth considering to help teachers make decisions about reading instruction. Two conclusions can be made from this research: (1) when students are grouped not by ability they achieve higher scores on achievement tests or informal reading inventories; students of all abilities do better on vocabulary, comprehension, and fluency than students in same ability groups; (2) students in heterogeneous groups show better understanding through group decisions and the ways they assume leadership during decisions on non-traditional evaluations of reading achievement. Heterogeneous grouping appears to be more effective for teaching reading.

Paratore and Indrisano (2003) state that the studies of flexible groupings they reviewed indicated that "in no case did the instructional model represent a 'one-size-fits-all' framework…" and help was provided in various ways for students struggling with reading. It is also indicated that the models described in the studies show strength, but also weakness. Success is not the result of the nature of flexibility and heterogeneity specifically. The students studied were taught in flexible, heterogeneous groups with successful opportunities to read and write.

Paratore and Indrisano (2003) state that alternatives to ability grouping provide teachers with other ways to teach students to read; however, more research is needed to provide evidence about effective ways to help individuals with special needs and effective practices for all students.

Annotated Bibliography

Allan, S.D. "Ability Grouping Research Review: What Do They Say About Grouping and the Gifted?" *Educational Leadership* 48 (1991): 60–65.
    Very useful review of the research on ability grouping asking if the most able students were being challenged enough even in the highest group.
Allington, R.L. "Content Coverage and Contextual Reading in Reading Groups." *Journal of Reading Behavior* 16 (1984): 85–96.
    States that student performance and behavior is linked to the ability group in which he/she is placed and the teacher's attitude toward the group.
Anderson, Linda M., Evertson, Carolyn M., and Brophy, Jere E. "An Experimental Study of Effective Teaching in First Grade Reading Groups." *Elementary School Journal* 79 (March 1979): 193–223.
    Presents effective techniques for working with groups from a study of first grade reading groups.
Anderson, Gary, Higgins, Diana, and Wurster, Stanley R. "Differences in Free-Reading Books Selected by High, Average, and Low Achievers." *Reading Teacher* 39 (December 1985): 326–330.
    Descries the effects of interest groups on student achievement.
Barr, Rebecca. "Classroom Reading Instruction from a Sociological Perspective." *Journal of Reading Behavior* 14, no. 4 (1982): 375–389.
    Reports on ways in which teachers determine group size and the effects of group size on pupil learning.
Barr, Rebecca, and Deeben, R. *How Schools Work*. Chicago: University of Chicago Press, 1991.
    Describes student performance and attitude toward school and reading focusing on those placed in lower ability groups.
Borko, Hilda, Shavelson, Richard J., and Stern, Paula. "Teacher's Decisions in the Planning of Reading Instruction." *Reading Research Quarterly* 16, no. 3 (1981): 449–466.
    Presents conclusions about how teachers form reading groups.
Bozzomo, Lawrence E. "Does Class Size Matter?" *The National Elementary Principal* 57 (January 1978): 78–81.
    States that class size does not influence student achievement.
Braddock, J.H., and Dawkins, M.P. "Ability Grouping Aspirations and Attainments: Evidence from the National Educational Longitudinal Study of 1988." *Journal of Negro Education* 62 (1993): 324–336.
    Reports on the ethnic composition of high and low ability groups based on a longitudinal study. Twenty-two sources are cited.
Brophy, Jere E. "Teacher Behavior and Student Learning." *Educational Leadership* 37 (October 1979): 33–38.
    Describes the effects of teacher behavior on student behavior. A most interesting perspective on classroom dynamics and climate.
Brown, Ann L., Palincsar, Annemarie, and Armbruster, Bonnie. "Instructing Comprehension." In *Theoretical Models and Processes*, 4th edition. Robert Ruddell, Martha Rapp Ruddell, and Harry Singer, eds. Newark, DE: International Reading Association, 1994, pp. 757–787.
    Discusses the importance of training in comprehension skills for at risk students and the quality of teaching for low ability reading groups.

Burns, Paul C., Roe, Betty D., and Smith, Sandy H. *Teaching Reading in Today's Elementary School.* Boston: Houghton-Mifflin, 2002, pp. 472–481.
    A textbook overview of grouping practices. This is a good starting point.

Cazden, Courtney B. "Contexts for Literacy: In the Mind and in the Classroom." *Journal of Reading Behavior* 14, no. 4 (1982): 413–427.
    Examines individual differences, class size and number of groups used to understand success or failure in reading.

Cohen, P.A., Kulik, J.A., and Kulik, C.L.C. "Educational Outcomes in Tutoring: A Meta-Analysis of Findings." *American Educational Research Journal* 19 (1982): 237–248.
    A meta-analysis that concludes peer tutoring can help students achieve success in reading for both tutor and student only when the tasks required are structured and explicit.

Cunningham, P.M., Hall, P.D., and Defee, M. "Non-ability Group Multilevel Instruction: A Year in a First Grade Classroom." *Reading Teacher* 44 (1991): 566–576.
    This study provides the foundation for the Four Block Model describing its use over the course of a whole year of instruction.

Durrell, Donald D. *Improvement of Basic Reading Abilities.* New York: World Book, 1940.
    Suggested the number of reading groups for effective instruction. A classic in the field.

Durrell, Donald D. *Improvement of Reading Instruction.* New York: Harcourt, Brace & World, 1956.
    Suggests a varied structure of classroom organization using whole class, individualized, and heterogeneous group activities for better reading instruction.

Durrell, Donald D., ed. "Adopting Reading Instruction to the Learning Needs of Children in the Intermediate Grades." *Journal of Education* 42 (December 1959): 1–78.
    A report of a practice using team learning in groups of three to five students for successful learning in the intermediate grades.

Dweck, C.S. "Motivational Processes Affecting Learning." *American Psychologist* 41 (1986): 1040–1048.
    Examined attitudes toward learning and reading of students in low ability groups.

Eder, D. "Ability Grouping and Students' Academic Self-Concept: A Case Study." *Elementary School Journal* 84 (1983): 149–161.
    Examined self-concept and attitude toward learning of students in low ability groups.

Elbaum, E.B., Schumann, J.S., and Vaughn, S. "Urban Middle Elementary Students' Perceptions of Group Formation for Reading Instruction." *Elementary School Journal* 97 (1997): 475–500.
    A study of 3rd and 4th grade student's perceptions from a questionnaire in three large urban school districts about instructional methods of grouping.

Flood, James, Lapp, Diane, Flood, Sharon, and Nagel, Greta. "Am I Allowed to Group? Using Flexible Patterns for Effective Instruction." *Reading Teacher* 45 (April 1992): 608–616.
    Describes various opportunities to use different kinds of groups for different purposes to increase success.

Gambrell, Linda. "Creating Classroom Cultures that Foster Reading Motivation." *Reading Teacher* 50 (September 1996): 14–25.
    States that teachers need to motivate students by creating an environment that encourages students to read. Provides guidelines to help teachers.

Good, T.L., and Marshall, S. "Do Students Learn More in Heterogeneous or Homogeneous Groups.?" In *The Social Context of Instruction: Group Organization and Group Processes.* P.L. Peterson, L.C. Wilkinson, and M. Hallinan, eds. New York: Academic Press, 1984, pp. 15–38.
    Examined the effects of both types of grouping plans on student achievement in reading.

Hall, Dorothy, and Cunningham, Patricia M. "Becoming Literate in First and Second Grades: Six Years of Multi-Method, Multi-Level Instruction." In *Literacy for the 21st Century:*

Research and Practice: 45th Yearbook of the National Reading Conference. D.J. Leu, C.K. Kinger, and K.H. Hinchman, eds. Chicago: National Reading Conference, 1996. pp. 195–204.

    A follow-up study of the four block multi-level, multi-method approach over a six year period.

Hall, Dorothy, Prevatte, Connie, and Cunningham, Patricia. "Eliminating Ability Grouping and Reducing Failure in Primary Grades." In *No Quick Fix.* Richard Allington and Sean Walmsley, eds. Newark, DE: International Reading Association, 1995, pp. 137–158.

    Examines the use of a multi-level, multi-material four block plan on student achievement in the primary grades.

Harris, Albert J., and Sipay, Edward. *How to Increase Reading Ability: A Guide to Developmental and Remedial Methods.* New York: Longman, 1985, 1987, **1988**, pp. 103–132.

    A classic textbook and a good place to start locating information on any topic in the field. Contains a good chapter on adapting instruction to individual differences describing types of groups, materials, and scheduling in the classroom. Describes practice based on research.

Hiebert, Elfrieda H. "An Examination of Ability Grouping in Reading Instruction." *Reading Research Quarterly* 18 (Winter 1983): 231–255.

    Provides an examination of student behavior and performance in ability groups. This is an important study in the field referred to frequently.

Jenkins, J.R., Jewell, M., Leicester, N., O'Connor, R., Jenkins, L.M., and Troutner, N.M. "Accommodations for Individual Differences Without Classroom Ability Groups: An Experiment in School Restructuring." *Exceptional Children* 60 (1994): 344–358.

    Examines an adapted type of CIRC eliminating ability groups and used the same material for all students helping special needs students with special decoding lessons and a limited pull-out program.

Johnson, D.W., Marvyama, G., Johnson, R., and Nelson, D. "Effects of Cooperative, Competitive, and Individualistic Goal Structures on Achievement: A Meta-Analysis." *Psychological Bulletin* 89 (1981): 47–62.

Juel, C. "Effects of Reading Group Assignments on Reading Development in First and Second Grade." *Journal of Reading Behavior* 22 (1990): 233–254.

    States that first graders need careful monitoring when learning vocabulary in basal readers to be successful. Students learn best when the books they read match individual reading levels.

    A meta-analyses of studies of student achievement in various grouping types.

Knight, Jenny. "Learning in a Community." *Reading Teacher* 47 (March 1994): 498–499.

    Describes members in a community of learners and the role each plays.

Kulik, J.A., and Kulik, C.L.C. "Effects of Accelerated Instruction on Students." *Review of Educational Research* 54 (1984): 409–425.

    Describes the effects of ability grouping focusing on the higher level groups.

Lou, Y., Abrami, P.C., Spence, J., Paulsen, C., Chambers, B., and d'Apollonia, S. "Within Class Grouping: A Meta-Analysis." *Review of Educational Research* 66 (1996): 423–458.

    A meta-analysis of grouping and non-grouping studies and the effects on student self-concept, achievement, and, attitude toward learning.

McKenzie, Gary R. "Personalize Your Group Teaching." *Instructor Magazine* 85 (August/September 1975): 57–59; also in A. Harris and E. Sipay, eds., *Reading on Reading Instruction.* New York: Longman, 1984, pp. 177–180.

    Suggests ways to personalize group teaching and involve all students in responding non-verbally to questions.

Meints, Donald W. "The Task System in an Individualized Reading Class." *Journal of Reading* 20 (1977): 301–304.

    Explains how to adopt learning stations to high school reading.

Oakes, J. *Keeping Track: How Schools Structure Inequality.* New Haven, CT: Yale University Press, 1985.

Examines the effects of placement in low ability groups on self-concept and expectations on students.

Palmer, Barbara, Codling, Rose Marie, and Gambrelle, Linda. "In Our Own Words: What Elementary Students Have to Say About Motivation to Read." *Reading Teacher* 48 (October 1994): 176–178.

Students explain what motivates them to read.

Paratore, Jeanne R., and Indrisano, Roselmina. "Grouping for Instruction in Literacy." In *Handbook of Research on Teaching the English Language Arts*. James Flood, Diane Lapp, James Squire, and Julie M. Jensen, eds. Mahwah, NJ: Erlbaum, 2003, pp. 566–572.

An overview of research on grouping practices with an excellent bibliography.

Pikulski, John J., and Kirsch, Irwin S. "Organization for Instruction." In *Teach Reading in Compensatory Classes*. R. Calfee and P. Drum, eds. Newark, DE: International Reading Association, 1979, pp. 187–191.

Recommends more flexibility in grouping suggesting two kinds of grouping plans.

Renzulli, J.S., and Reis, S.M. "The Reform Movement and the Quiet Crises in Gifted Education." *Gifted Child Quarterly* 35 (1990): 26–35.

Questions the use of heterogeneous groups as unfair to high performing and gifted students.

Salinger, Terry S. *Literacy for Young Children*. Englewood Cliffs, NJ: Merrill, 1996.

Advocates flexible grouping structures so that students can move among groups based on changing needs and interests.

Shavelson, Richard J., and Stern, Paula. "Research on Teachers Pedagogical Thoughts, Judgements, Decisions, and Behaviour." *Review of Educational Research* 51 (Winter 1981): 455–498.

Describes the effects of group placement on student and teacher behavior.

Slavin, R.E. *Ability Grouping and Student Achievement in Elementary School: A Best Evidence Synthesis*. Baltimore, MD: Johns Hopkins University Center for Research on Elementary and Secondary Schools, 1987.

A review of research and a discussion of the effects of ability grouping on student success.

Slavin, R.E. "Ability Grouping in Middle Grades: Achievement Effects and Alternatives." *Review of Educational Research* 60 (1990): 471–499.

A continued look at and update of research on ability grouping and its effects on student success.

Slavin, R.E. "Cooperative Learning." *Review of Educational Research* 50 (1980): 315–342.

Describes research on cooperative learning and reading achievement.

Smith, Mary Lee, and Glass, Gene V. "Meta-Analysis of Research on Class Size and Its Relationship to Attitudes and Instruction." *American Educational Research Journal* 17 (Winter 1980): 419–433.

Examines the effects of class size on achievement, attitude toward instruction, attitude toward students, classroom climate, and student self-concept. States smaller classes lead to better achievement, attitude, and class climate.

Stevens, R.J., Madden, N.A., Slavin, R.E., and Farnish, A.M. "Cooperative Integrated Reading and Composition: Two Field Experiments." *Reading Research Quarterly* 22 (1987): 433–454.

Examines the effects of the comprehensive cooperative learning technique on reading and writing skills of 3rd and 4th grade students over a 12 week period.

Stevens, R.J., and Slavin, R.E. "Effects of a Cooperative Learning Approach to Reading and Writing on Academically Handicapped and Non-handicapped Students." *Elementary School Journal* 95 (1995): 241–262.

Examined grades two to six in 31 experimental and 32 control groups over a two year period analyzing the data for remedial and special needs students separately to study the cooperative learning approach.

Swanson, B.B. "Listening to Students about Reading." *Reading Horizons* 25 (1985): 123–128.
   Describes the negative effects of ability grouping.

Thompson, Richard A., and Merritt, King, Jr. "Turn On to a Reading Center." *Reading Teacher* 28 (January 1975): 384–388.
   Describes practical suggestions for implementing reading stations.

Tierney, Robert J., and Pearson, P. David "A Revisionist Perspective on Learning from Text: A Framework for Improving Classroom Practice." In *Theoretical Models and Processes of Reading*, 4th edition. Robert Ruddell, Marth Rapp Ruddell, and Harry Singer, eds. Newark, DE: International Reading Association, 1994, pp. 514–519.
   A social view of learning to read and the importance of teachers modeling ways to work through learning situations for students.

Turner, Julianne, and Paris, Scott. "How Literacy Tasks Influence Children's Motivation for Literacy." *Reading Teacher* 48 (May 1995): 662–673.
   Describes how the kinds of literacy jobs students do influences motivation. Suggests ways teachers can help students.

Turpie, J., and Paratore, J.R. "Using Repeated Readings to Promote Reading Success in a Heterogeneously Grouped First Grade." In *Perspectives on Literacy Research and Practice. 44th Yearbook of the National Reading Conference.* K.A. Hinchman, D.J. Leu, and K. Kinger, eds. Chicago: National Reading Conference, 1995, pp. 255–264.
   A study of four first grade students and the importance of flexible grouping on success.

Vacca, Jo Anne L., and Vacca, Richard T. "Learning Stations: How to in the Middle Grades." *Journal of Reading* 19 (April 1979): 563–567.
   Describes using a combination of learning stations with middle grade students for success in reading.

Webb, Noreen M. "Student Interaction and Learning in Small Groups." *Review of Educational Research* 52 (Fall 1982): 421–445.
   Describes the ways in which students in a group influence one another, the teacher, and the learning that takes place in the group.

Wiggins, Robert. "Large Group Lesson/Small Group Follow Ups: Flexible Grouping in a Basal Reading Program." *Reading Teacher* 47 (March 1994): 450–460.
   Describes the long-term effects of group placement and the quality of teaching with low groups.

Wilkinson, Louise C., and Calculator, Steven. "Requests and Responses in Peer-Directed Reading Groups." *American Educational Research Journal* 19 (Spring 1982): 107–120.
   A study of peer-directed groups concluding that they are less effective for lower ability students.

Wilson, Robert, and Ribovich, Jerilynn K. "Ability Grouping? Stop and Reconsider." *Reading World* 13 (December 1973): 84–91.
   Suggests open grouping where students meet with any group they select in addition to their own.

Basal Readers

The basal reading approach or core reading series was the most widely used approach for many years. Schools purchased a series which provided materials for every grade level. Each series provided materials for the presentation and practice of strategies at each grade level.

According to Harris and Sipay (1985) basal reader programs are "preplanned, sequentially organized, detailed materials and methods to teach developmental reading skills systematically." For more than 75 years most basal reader series were eclectic in the attempt to provide a balanced developmental program with varied and broad objectives. Most series used the whole-word approach to teach work recognition skills. Chall and Conrad (1984) state that the whole word approach provided fast introduction to meaningful sentences and stories. "Before the mid 1960s, decoding skills were introduced very gradually, mainly in second and third grade readers. Since then, there has been a trend toward more and earlier emphasis on decoding skills."

Goodman et al. (1988), Shannon (1992), and Betts (1946) state that basal readers represent a package of materials that were purchased together. Chall (1996) states that publishers attempted to "give teachers and pupils a 'total reading program' embodying a system of teaching reading (in the teacher's manuals), a collection of stories and selections for pupils to read (the readers), and exercises for additional practice (the workbooks)." Harris and Sipay (1985) and Chall (1996) state that series started with a pre-reading program consisting of one, two, or three reading readiness books for kindergarten and/or grade one students. When these books are completed the graded readers are presented. Usually, Spache and Spache (1986), Chall (1996) and Harris and Sipay (1985) state, three or more preprimers that are paperback books are followed by the primer which is the first hardcover book. Then the first reader is presented. In the first grade, five or six books are used and children advance from one book to the next at different rates. The basal series usually provided a book for each half of grade two, calling them 2–1 and 2–2. The same arrangement is used in grades three through six. Consumable paperback workbooks with practice exercises accompany each reader. Every reader has a teacher's manual which tells the teacher how to teach reading using the readers. Detailed material on lesson plans for each story in the reader, activities for enrichment and slow readers, and suggestions for teaching skills and meeting the needs of all the students are provided. Supplementary materials such as charts, content area books, pictures, and duplicable worksheets are also provided by publishers.

Harris and Sipay (1985) and Spache and Spache (1986) state that frequently readers were given a level number rather than a grade number to refute the idea that a specific book had to be used in a specific grade. Therefore, the first pre-primer could be labeled Level 3 because it was used after the two readiness books. Spache and Spache (1986), Chall (1996), and Harris and Sipay (1985) state that teachers used the parts of a basal series as a package developing instructional strategies and using materials provided by the publisher.

According to Chall (1996) and Chall and Squire (1991) basal reading series were written by a team whose leader was usually a well known authority in the field of reading. Several of the large publishing companies employed a permanent staff of writers. Some series were planned and supervised by a lead author with the other team members responsible for different tasks. Some publishers employed classroom teachers and writers to adapt stories for the readers and to develop the teacher's manual and the workbook activities. Chall (1996) states that all the teams worked cooperatively with each other and the editors. No one person was completely responsible for a series because a series was such a large enterprise involving authors, editors, consultants with expertise in reading, child development, linguistics and literature, and illustrators. The readers and manuals were composites. Reading series were also very expensive and production could take as long as five years.

Chall (1996) and Burns, Roe, and Ross (1988) state that basal reader lessons centered on a story. The teacher's manual provided guidance in teaching the story. Generally the lesson consisted of preparation or pre-reading activities, presentation of new words to be found in the story, guided reading and interpretation of the story, and follow-up activities to be done after reading the story. The Directed Reading Activity (DRA), according to Burns, Roe, and Ross (1988), is a teaching strategy used with basal readers and other materials to reinforce students' reading abilities. The steps in the DRA are:

1. Motivation and development of background;
2. Directed story reading—both silent and oral;
3. Skill-building activities;
4. Follow-up practice;
5. Enrichment activities.

These steps correspond to the lesson guidelines Chall (1996) identifies. Both start with motivation by establishing interest and building background for the story. Background is drawn from student experiences and is established by teacher questions, pictures, or reference to previous stories. DRA presents the new vocabulary in step one whereas the lesson guidelines use a separate step for presenting new words. Some basal guidebooks suggest presenting new words several days before reading the story so that the students will not have difficulty comprehending the story. Guided reading and directed story reading both present purpose questions and a variety of comprehension questions for each part of the story to ensure that pupils understand what they read. The DRA suggests both oral and silent reading to help students understand and retain what is read.

McCallum (1988) states that basal readers were the most widely used materials for teaching reading. Gates (1935) stated that the basal reading programs provided the teacher with the freedom to select other reading materials and to provide guidance for students as part of the total reading program. Reutzel and Cooter (1992) state that basal readers such as the Scott Foresman series *Dick and Jane New Basic Readers* were widely used throughout the United States during the 1940s through the 1960s. Shannon (1992) states that teachers used basal readers as standardized products to ensure that all children received similar instruction. Bohning (1986) states that the rate at which new vocabulary was introduced in basal readers was carefully controlled.

Many of the features and reasons for the packaged basal reader systems, Shannon (1992) believes, came from the problem of the early 20th century when a large increase in the number of school age children required more teachers who were, unfortunately, not always well trained. The concern that all students should have similar instruction, Betts (1946) states, resulted in packaged sets of graded reading material to ensure adequate instruction.

Roe, Smith, and Burns (2005) state that basal series have been the most widely used tool for reading instruction in the United States. Newer basal readers are useful because they provide, according to Cullinan (1992), literature such as poems, plays, nonfiction material and a more integrated thematic approach to teaching reading. Wiggins (1994) states that basal reader programs provide teachers with help in organizing systematic teaching and re-teaching of skills and strategies; scope and sequence skill charts that tell which strategies are taught at which grade levels; suggestions for assessing student progress; and a view of what students have been taught already.

Roe, Smith, and Burns (2005) state that "much of the criticism of basal readers has focused on less than desirable use of the materials. Teachers have a responsibility to plan the use of all materials in their classrooms, including the basal readers, regardless of the presence or absence of guiding suggestions accompanying the materials." This stems from the myth that if teachers used a basal series they need not prepare or think about lessons because all they needed to do was read the teacher's manual. Teachers did not individualize skills instruction based on student need, but assigned material because it was the next lesson listed in the manual. The way the basal materials were used (not the materials themselves) has, Roe, Smith, and Burns (2005) state, been a major question about basal series. If teachers think of a basal series as a complete reading program they may "fail to provide the variety of experiences that children need in a balanced program. Basals can never provide all of the reading situations a student needs to encounter."

Much has been written by Auckerman (1981), Goodman, Shannon, Freeman and Murphy (1988), Shannon and Goodman (1994), Chall (1996), Shannon (1982) and others about the problems associated with basal readers. Burns, Roe, and Ross (1988) present a summary of the weaknesses of basal readers stating that the most frequently listed weaknesses are:

1. Controlled vocabularies result in dull, repetitive stories with little literary merit.
2. The sentence structure found in most basal readers is not like that used by children who read them. It is too stiff and formal, devoid of the contractions and sentence fragments used in normal conversation.
3. Settings and characters tend to be familiar to middle-class suburban white children from intact families, but not to other racial and socioeconomic groups or to groups from rural or urban backgrounds.
4. The characters tend to be presented in stereotyped male/female roles and situations.
5. Basal series are often advertised as *total* reading programs. If teachers accept this assertion, they may fail to provide the variety of experiences that children need for a balanced program.
6. Teachers are often led to believe that if they do not carry out *all* the suggestions in the teacher's manuals, they will fail to provide adequate instruction. By trying to do everything suggested, they use up valuable time with inappropriate activities for some groups of children, leaving no time for appropriate ones. Basal readers should not be used from front to back in their entirety without considering the special needs of particular children in the class.

These weaknesses are based on research done by Fry and Sakiey (1986), Durkin (1984), Sorenson (1985), Egan (1983), Bridge, Winograd, and Haley (1983), and Britton, Lumpkin and Britton (1984).

There has been much effort to overcome these weaknesses. Hoffman and McCarthey (1995) found that five publishers completely revised and renovated the readers and the accompanying materials. "The new materials have less vocabulary control, more diversity of genre, minimal adaptations, higher literary quality, increased predictability, and decreased decodability." Roe, Smith and Burns (2005) found that the newer basal readers provide integrated reading and language instruction and frequently included varied practice activities that go beyond worksheets. The new basal readers have answered many of the criticisms and provide, according to Roe, Smith, and Burns (2005): stories with higher quality; limited vocabulary and extensive repetition; unaltered folktales in some of the early readers; other good quality, unadapted literature; more content area or nonfiction material; more natural and conversational language in stories; more diverse characters including people from various racial and ethnic groups, the elderly, and people with disabilities depicted in less stereotyped ways; and presentation of women in many roles. These changes demonstrate that publishers have implemented research findings in ways that respond to the pressures classroom teachers face. Changes include diagnosis of reading problems, reading appreciation, and suggestions for guided practice and instructional strategies according to Roe, Smith and Burns (2005).

Burns, Roe, and Ross (1988) list the strengths that basal readers are reported to have. More recent research by Wiggins (1994), Cullinan (1992), Weiss (1987), and Chall and Squire (1991) suggests that the advantages of basal readers need to be enhanced by using strategies from current research to ensure that the strengths benefit all students. Strengths can become weaknesses when they are taken for granted. Teachers need to be very active participants, selective users of materials, and evaluators of what is best for their class.

The strengths Burns, Roe and Ross (1988) identified were:

1. The books are carefully graded in difficulty. The vocabularies of most series are carefully controlled so that children do not meet too many unfamiliar words in a single lesson, and repetition of words is planned so that children have a chance to fix them in their memories.
2. The teacher's manuals have many valuable suggestions about teaching reading lessons, and thus can save much lesson preparation time.
3. Most basal reader series deal with all phases of the reading program, including word recognition, comprehension, oral reading, silent reading, reading for information, and reading for enjoyment. This comprehensive coverage helps a teacher avoid over-emphasis or under-emphasis of any aspect.
4. The series provide for systematic teaching of skills and systematic review.

Basal readers are one tool that teachers can use to teach reading. Many approaches and tools are needed to help all students reach their potential. Teachers, Roe, Smith and Burns (2005) suggest, should not use basal readers in their entirety, but select what they use based on the needs of their students. Using activities that directly relate to the story read, the skills taught and the abilities of students is an effective way to use basal materials. Teacher judgment is the most important factor in reading instruction. Any material can be good or bad used well or misused if informed judgment is not used to select what suits the needs of students.

Annotated Bibliography

Apple, Michael W. *Teachers and Texts: A Political Economy of Class & Gender Relations in Education.* New York: Routledge & Kegan Paul, 1988.

    Discusses changes in teacher control over materials and content in the classroom.

Aukerman, Robert C. *The Basal Reader Approach to Reading.* New York: Wiley & Sons, 1981.

    Presents a description of the basal reading approach, an analysis of 15 series, and a discussion of the approach in the 1980s.

Austin, Mary C., and Morrison, Coleman. *The First R: The Harvard Report on Reading in the Elementary Schools.* New York: Macmillan, 1963, pp. 54–69.

    A classic investigation on the state of reading instruction in the United States. Discusses the responses from 795 questionnaires sent to American teachers asking about basal readers, workbooks, teachers manuals, curriculum guides, and worksheets.

Baumann, James F., Hoffman, James V., Duffy-Hester, Ann M., and Ro, Jennifer Moon. "The First R Yesterday and Today: U.S. Elementary Reading Instruction Practices Reported by Teachers and Administrators." *Reading Research Quarterly* 35, no. 3 (July/August/September 2000): 338–377.

    A discussion of late-20th century reading instruction as a follow-up to the 1963 Harvard study done by Austen and Morrison. Using the same survey technique this report compares the results of the two studies to describe practices in the 1990s. Describes changes and practices that have remained the same. A most valuable companion to the original study.

Beck, Isabel L., McKeown, Margaret G., and McCaslin, Ellen S. "Does Reading Make Sense? Problems of Early Readers." *Reading Teacher* 34 (April 1981): 780–785.

    Discusses the problems young readers face especially the limited vocabulary in basal reader stories which causes comprehension problems. Suggest ways to improve comprehension through teacher questioning and prediction strategies.

Beck, Isabel L., et al. "Improving the Comprehensibility of Stories: The Effects of Revisions that Improve Coherence." *Reading Research Quarterly* 19 (Spring 1984): 263–277.

    Describes ways to revise basal reader stories to make them easier to understand.

Betts, Emmett Albert. *Foundations of Reading Instruction. With Emphasis on Differentiated Guidance.* New York: American Book Co., 1946.

    A classic textbook discussing the use of basal reading programs from kindergarten through the elementary grades. Discusses: readiness, vocabulary development; directed reading activities; and levels of differentiation. A very early discussion of the practice of differentiated instruction 60 years ago.

Bohning, Gerry. "The McGuffey Eclectic Readers: 1836–1986." *Reading Teacher* 40 (1986): 253–289.

    Discusses the vocabulary control practice in basal readers citing the early *McGuffey Readers* as a start of this practice.

Bridge, C.A., Winograd, N.P., and Haley, D. "Using Predictable Materials vs. Preprimers to Teach Beginning Sight Words." *Reading Teacher* 36 (1983): 884–891.

    Compares the two types of materials as tools for teaching early sight words.

Britton, Gwyneth, Lumpkin, Margaret, and Britton, Ester. "The Battle to Improve Citizens for the 21st Century." *Reading Teacher* 37 (April 1984): 724–733.

    Discusses the development of basal reading series and how they are planned, organized, and used.

Brown, Chares, M. "Whether Basal Readers?" *Education* 82 (September 1961): 3–5.

    Evaluates basal readers and individualized instruction. Recommends continued use of basals. Based on a research study from 1958 to 1960.

Burns, Paul C., Roe, Betty D., and Ross, Elinor. *Teaching Reading in Today's Elementary Schools.* Boston: Houghton-Mifflin, 1988, pp. 280–311.

    A textbook providing a solid overview of the basal reading approach with excellent references.

Cairney, Trevor H. "The Purpose of Basal Readers: What Children Think." *Reading Teacher* 41, no. 4 (1988): 420–428.
   This is a discussion of student impressions about the reason for basal readers.
Chall, Jeanne S. *Learning to Read: The Great Debate*. New York: Harcourt Brace, 1996, 3d ed., pp. 187–262.
   A classic history of teaching students to read. A report of a three year study on methods of beginning reading from 1910 to 1965. A valuable resource.
Chall, Jeanne S., and Conrad, Sue S. "Resources and Their Use for Reading Instruction." In *Becoming Readers in a Complex Society. 83rd Yearbook of the National Society for the Study of Education Part I*. A. Purvis and O. Niles, eds. Chicago: University of Chicago Press, 1984, pp. 209–232.
   Describes methods and materials used to teach reading.
Chall, Jeanne S., and Squire, James R. "The Publishing Industry and Textbooks." In *Handbook of Reading Research, Volume II*. Rebecca Barr, Michael L. Kamil, Peter Mosenthal, and P. David Pearson, eds. New York: Longman, 1991, pp. 120–146.
   Describes the history of textbook publishing and the development of curriculum and instruction methods in reading.
Combs, Marth. *Readers and Writers in Primary Grades. A Balanced and Integrated Approach K-4*. Upper Saddle River, NJ: Pearson, 2006, pp. 396–426.
   Describes basal reading/language arts series and how these new programs integrate reading and the language arts. Presents a brief history of basal readers and the challenge for creating better materials.
Crawley, Sharon J. "Readabilities of the New Basal Programs." *The New England Reading Association Journal* 10, no. 3 (1975): 35–38.
   Discusses the leveling and difficulty of basal readers as designated by publishers and the reality of difficulty in the classroom.
Cullinan, Bruce. "Whole Language and Children's Literature." *Language Arts* 69 (October 1992): 426–430.
   Discusses the reading selections included in newer basal readers commenting on their literary value.
Durkin, Doloris. "Is There a Match Between What Elementary Teachers Do and What Basal Manuals Recommend?" *Reading Teacher* 37 (April 1984): 734–744.
   Discusses how teachers use the suggested activities in basal reader manuals stating that teachers use questions more frequently than instructional suggestions.
Durkin, Doloris. "Reading Comprehension Instruction in Five Basal Reader Series." *Reading Research Quarterly* 16, no. 4 (1981): 515–544.
   Research describing the attention to comprehension assessment and directions for providing instruction in the manuals of five reader series.
Egan, Owen. "In Defense of Traditional Language: Folktales and Reading Texts." *Reading Teacher* 37 (December 1983): 228–233.
   States that reader publishers have so badly rewritten folktales that they are unrecognizable. Recommends using the complete folktale in readers.
Fry, Edward, and Sakiey, Elizabeth. "Common Words Not Taught in Basal Reading Series." *Reading Teacher* 39 (January 1986): 395–398.
   States that only 50–59 percent of the most common English words are taught in basal readers. Recommends teachers supplement this with additional vocabulary instruction.
Gates, Arthur Irving. *The Improvement of Reading*. New York: Macmillan, 1935.
   A classic textbook on reading instruction. Gates states that basal readers have the advantage of providing prepared material that allows teachers to make decisions about the use of supplementary materials.
Goodman, Kenneth S., Shannon, Patrick, Freeman, Yvonne S., and Murphy, Sharon. *Report Card on Basal Readers*. Katonah, NY: Owen, 1988.
   An examination of basal readers presenting a history, reasons why basals are used,

how they are produced, alternatives to basal readers and recommendations. A critique of basal readers.

Green, Frank. "Professional Materials: Report Card on Basal Readers." *Reading Teacher* 42, no. 8 (1989): 650.
   This is a review of the Goodman, Shannon, Freeman, and Murphy book *Report Card on Basal Readers*.

Greenlinger-Harless, Carol S. "Updated Cross Referenced Index to U.S. Reading Materials, Grades K–8." *Reading Teacher* 37 (March 1984): 613–625; *Reading Teacher* 37 (May 1984): 871, 878–879 [errata].
   This useful tool identifies the reading levels of K-8 reading materials.

Harris, Albert J., and Jacobson, Milton. *Basic Reading Vocabularies*. New York: Macmillan, 1982.
   Describes the vocabulary included in basal readers and why the number of words used increased.

Harris, Albert J., and Sipay, Edward R. *How to Increase Reading Ability: A Guide to Developmental and Remedial Methods*. New York: Longman, 1985, 1987, 1988.
   This classic textbook is a good place to start locating information on any topic in the field.

Hoffman, James V., and McCarthey, Sara J. "Ongoing Research: Teachers' Practices and New Basals." *NRRC News* (May 1995): 6–7.
   A study comparing old and new first grade reading materials from five publishers.

Mason, Jana M. "An Examination of Reading Instruction in Third and Fourth Grades." *Reading Teacher* 36 (May 1983): 906–913.
   Reports on the instructional strategies that teachers use and notes that the lessons seen did not follow suggestions and lacked order.

McCallum, Richard D. "Don't Throw the Basals Out with the Bathwater." *Reading Teacher* 42, no. 3 (1988): 204–209.
   Presents a history and discussion of the use of basal readers. Suggests that there are some advantages to using basal readers.

Ollila, Lloyd O., and Nurss, Joanne B. "Beginning Reading in North America." In *Beginning Reading Instruction in Different Countries*. Lloyd Ollila, ed. Newark, DE: International Reading Association, 1981, pp. 26–55.
   Describes methods and materials used to teach reading in America highlighting the strengths and weaknesses of the basal approach.

Osborn, Jean. "The Purpose, Uses, and Content of Workbooks and Some Guidelines for Publishers." In *Learning to Read in American Schools: Basal Readers and Content Texts*. R. Anderson, J. Osborn, and R.J. Tierney, eds. Hillsdale, NJ: Erlbaum, 1984, pp. 45–111.
   Describes and critiques workbooks, skills sheets, practice books, mastery lessons and materials for student use. Discusses the purpose, function, use and guidelines for improving these materials

Osborn, Jean. "The Purpose, Uses and Contents of Workbooks and Some Guidelines for Teachers and Publishers." *Reading Education Report No. 27*. Champaign: Center for the Study of Reading, University of Illinois, August 1981.
   Describes the content and use of workbooks that are part of basal programs.

Osborn, Jean. "Workbooks That Accompany Basal Reading Programs." In *Comprehension Instruction: Procedures and Suggestions*. G.D. Duffy et al., eds. New York: Longman, 1984, pp. 163–186.
   Discusses the relationship between workbooks and student comprehension skills.

Pearson, P. David. "A Context for Instructional Research on Reading Comprehension." In *Promoting Reading Comprehension*. J. Flood, ed. Newark, DE: International Reading Association, 1984, pp. 1–15.
   Discusses the comprehension problems created for students because of the limited vocabulary used in many instructional materials including basal readers.

Reutzel, D. Ray, and Cooter, Robert B., Jr. *Teaching Children to Read: From Basals to Books*. New York: Merrill-Macmillan, 1992.

A textbook that examines the transition to a more holistic approach to language arts and reading instruction.

Roe, Betty D., Smith, Sandy H., and Burns, Paul C. *Teaching Reading in Today's Elementary School.* Ninth edition, Boston: Houghton-Mifflin, 2005, pp. 266–277.

A textbook which presents a good clear overview of the basal reading approach including research findings.

Rosecky, Marion. "Are Teachers Selective When Using Basal Guidebooks?" *Reading Teacher* 31 (January 1978): 381–384.

Discusses teacher decisions about guidebook suggestions for basal reader lessons. States that frequently follow-up and enrichment activities are not used.

Shannon, Patrick. "A Retrospective Look at Teachers' Reliance on Commercial Reading Materials." *Language Arts* 59 (November/December 1982): 844–853.

Describes the use of reading materials by classroom teachers. Traces the history of using basal readers.

Shannon, Patrick, ed. *Becoming Political: Reading and Writing in the Politics of Literacy Education.* Portsmouth, NH: Hunemann, 1992.

A collection of readings by different authors on the politics of reading and writing instruction.

Shannon, Patrick, and Goodman, Kenneth S., eds. *Basal Readers A Second Look.* Katonah, NY: Owen, 1994.

Twelve chapters written by several authors discuss concerns about changes needed in basal readers. Topics include: manuals, Canadian readers, writing process, testing, literature, pictures and basal readers.

Sorenson, Nancy. "Basal Reading Vocabulary Instruction: A Critique and Suggestions." *Reading Teacher* 39 (October 1985): 80–85.

A critical look at the vocabulary instruction suggestions in basal reader manuals.

Spache, George D., and Spache, Evelyn, *Reading in the Elementary Schools.* Boston: Allyn and Bacon, 1986, pp. 45–87.

A textbook describing the methods, materials, and research of basal reading series. A good starting point for understanding the basal reading approach.

Spiegel, Dixie Lee. "Six Alternatives to Directed Reading Activity." *Reading Teacher* 34 (May 1981): 914–920; also in A.J. Harris and E. Sipay, eds., *Readings on Reading Instruction.* New York: Longman, 1984, pp. 391–396.

Discusses different ways to organize reading lessons using basal readers.

Staiger, Ralph C. "How Are Basal Readers Used?" *Elementary English* 35 (January 1958): 44–46.

Report of a study surveying 474 teachers in 48 states and Hawaii on the way teachers use basal readers.

Swaby, Barbara. "Varying the Way You Teach Reading with Basal Stories." *Reading Teacher* 35 (March 1982): 676–680.

Suggests strategies for presenting basal reader stories in innovative ways.

Weiss, Maria J. "Who Needs a Teacher's Guide?" *Reading Teacher* 41 (October 1987): 119–120.

Describes ways to supplement the suggested activities in the basal reader teacher's guide suited to the needs of individual students. Encourages student choices about activities and student participation in decision making.

Wiggins, Robert C. "Large Group Lessons/Small Group Follow-Up: Flexible Grouping in a Basal Reading Program." *Reading Teacher* 47 (March 1994): 450–460.

Suggests teachers find alternative ways of providing skills practice rather than using the basal reader workbook exactly as suggested. Provides ideas for other ways to reinforce skills.

Arthur Irving Gates
(1890–1972)

Gates was born on September 2, 1890, in Red Wing, Minnesota, to William P. and Lenore (Gaylord) Gates. He received a B.L. in 1914, and an M.A. in 1915, from the University of California at Berkeley. Gates took a position as a teaching assistant in experimental psychology at Columbia University. He was awarded a Ph.D. in psychology from Columbia University in 1917 and accepted a position at Teachers College, Columbia University. Gates taught at Teachers College until he retired in 1956. Gates authored over 300 books, articles, and readers for children and became an authority on translating research findings into classroom practice, according to Thorndike (1973), Vance (1985), and Tostberg (1971). Gates died on August 24, 1972, in Montrose, New York.

Gates used his interest in psychological research and his work in education to start research in reading that would become the main interest of his career according to Thorndike (1973), Tostberg (1971), and Vance (1985). The early research done in 1922 studied reading and spelling problems. Gates (1922) concluded that reading and spelling problems had multiple causes and that remediation was complex and required a variety of approaches. This early research led Gates to conclude that better diagnostic and remedial procedures were needed along with better ways to teach reading so that skills would develop and problems would be avoided, according to Thorndike (1973), Vance (1985), Russell (1957), Gates (1971), and Tostberg (1971). Gates (1928) suggested instructional strategies and that the identification of reading problems be done through research. Instructional materials such as readers, workbooks, and teacher's guides, Gates (1928) stated, should provide organized, graded practice to help students master skills with authentic, interesting materials. Gates (1928) called his approach the Intrinsic Method, stating that basic reading strategies and potential problems were to be identified through research studies. Instructional materials should be organized to provide systematic, graded practice. Gates (1928) stated that when a valid analysis of skills was complete and teaching materials were ingeniously prepared, the materials alone with occasional teacher assistance would lead students to develop the necessary perceptual skills, word analysis skills, and comprehension skills for deriving meaning from a text.

Thorndike (1973), Vance (1985), and Tostberg (1971) state that when Gates reviewed his method and materials in 1970 he found that he had anticipated programmed instruction consistent with the work of Thorndike and Skinner. Programmed instruction based on Thorndike's and Skinner's advice sought to organize instructional materials into manageable steps to insure that practice of a skill will be through and successful. Students should be able to develop skills they will need and be rewarded by a knowledge of their own success or by the teacher for the correct responses.

Research convinced Gates that the acquisition of reading strategies that led to success should not be left to maturation or chance, Thorndike (1973), and Vance (1985) state. Gates stated that techniques to effectively diagnose individual differences in reading so that appropriate remedial strategies could be applied as well as more effective ways to teach beginning reading became the focus of his lifelong research. Gates believed that the diagnosis of problems, appropriate remedial help, and better teaching strategies do not happen on their own. Intervention from research was essential to ensure success in reading.

Donald Durrell (1935), Miles A. Tinker (1932), and William McAndrew (1930) reviewed Gates's research and writing, concluding, according to Tostberg (1971), that Gates's work has "added substantially and significantly to the literature on reading research and instruction." McAndrew (1930) states "among the helpers this age is giving us in remarkable numbers I think you will put Arthur Gates in the front rank. He has a genius for selecting facts that are pertinent and for putting them into form adapted for the schoolman's immediate use." Tinker (1932) reviewed *Interest and Ability in Reading* stating that "the development of a program of research dealing with materials and methods of reading by Dr. A.I. Gates and his associates ... has resulted in contributions that may be classified as among the most important appearing during the past decade.... Dr. Gates gives an outline of what promises to become one of the most effective methods[s] of teaching reading." Durrell (1935) reviewed *The Improvement of Reading* stating that "this book is without question the best treatment of diagnosis and correction of defects in reading that has yet appeared."

Tostberg (1971) states that proof of Gates's status is that his research has been discussed in "major longitudinal reviews of research on reading and reading instruction."

Russell (1957) states:

> The desire to get at the facts has characterized most of Arthur Gates's professional work, a career marked by wide-ranging interests and tremendous productivity in general psychology and educational psychology as well as in the study of reading

problems.... In the field of reading instruction Gates's original research and wide ranging writing have made him one of the most influential figures in the United States and throughout the world.... His (intrinsic) method, with some later variations, has become standard practice in most American schools.... It is no exaggeration to say that [Gates's] books largely changed reading from an isolated and mechanical exercise to a series of consecutive, meaningful, and zestful activities.

Gates received the First World Congress in Reading Award in 1968 from the International Reading Association for "his distinguished service and many contributions to a better understanding of the reading process and to reading instruction throughout the world" according to Staiger and Andersen (1969).

Tostberg (1971) states that "not only has he contributed substantially to answering questions about reading, but he has been instrumental in forming the fundamental questions to which students of reading have addressed themselves for over half a century." Gates's publications, according to Tostberg (1971), "provide both a history of the study of reading and a register of the persons who made that history..." and made him a dominant figure in reading research and instruction. Gates's work at Teachers College, Columbia University, during the period of its greatest success with a faculty of eminent American educators, association with colleagues, and his membership in many professional organizations including the American Psychological Association (President of Educational Psychology section 1948–1949), American Educational Research Association (President 1940–1942), and American Association for the Advancement of Science (Chair and Vice-President of Section Q, Education, 1925) spread his research and ideas.

Tostberg (1971) states that Gates used his research "to provide a better knowledge base for the teaching of reading, a set of abilities that he has considered fundamental to all formal education and ... fundamental to enhancing the quality of living..."

Thorndike (1973) states that Gates's "pragmatic and empirical approach to research programs and teaching strategies recognized the need for a continued up-dating of both to match changing circumstances." He believed that evidence should be "adapted to the changing realities of the present conditions" not only on universal psychological principles. Gates believed, according to Thorndike (1973), in the empirical scientific approach to solving problems in the field of education, but held that research must not be removed from the reality of the classroom. Research findings were more likely to be applied if research "was closely related to the educational task than from artificial laboratory studies..." Thorndike (1973) states. Gates encouraged research that would produce "practical maxims" that could be synthesized for the classroom teacher because education would move forward on the results of empirical research.

Thorndike (1973) states that Gates was strongly convinced that the one important problem in education was

> how best to help children learn.... His concern was always to seek out the usable principle and its practical application by unspectacular, but rigorous inquiry.... He came to stand for what was best in the empirical and scientific method applied to educational problems and functioned more as an educational statesman than an educational prophet.

Robinson (2002) states that Gates's work

> still has important implications for today's reading teachers ... his beliefs about reasons for the teaching of reading ... the role of the reading teacher ... and easy answers to reading instruction are as current as if they had been written yesterday.... Gates saw the reading process as one unique to the individual reader and most importantly, that it was the effective classroom teacher who needed to build on his knowledge of each student's abilities.

Russell (1957) states that Gates's research in

> reading ... spelling, handwriting, vocabulary, and with handicapped children have many implications for teaching methods.... His influence on reading instruction has been due not only to his research, his critical appraisals of practice, and his writings, but to his impact as a person on thousands of colleagues and students who transmit his ideas in most parts of the world.

Annotated Bibliography

PRIMARY SOURCES IN CHRONOLOGICAL ORDER

This is a brief selection from the more than 300 primary sources Dr. Gates produced.

The Psychology of Reading and Spelling with Special Reference to Disability. New York: Teachers College, Columbia University, 1922.
    A study of reading and spelling difficulties in a private school. Concludes that there were many kinds of reading and spelling problems with multiple causes. Suggests that remediation strategies were complex and must be different for each problem. Reports research which led to later work in diagnosis, and remediation.
"Problems in Beginning Reading." *Teachers College Record* 26 (1925): 572–591.
    Examines problems that can occur in the early stages of reading instruction.
"Gates Primary Reading Tests." *Teachers College Record* 28 (1926): 146–178.
    A discussion of what became an important test of early reading ability.
With Walter H. MacGinitie. "Gates MacGinitie Primary Reading Tests," 1969.
The Improvement of Reading: A Program of Diagnostic and Remedial Methods. New York: Macmillan, 1927, rev. 1935, 1947.
    A classic reference in the field of reading which helped start the new field of remedial reading.
New Methods in Primary Reading. New York: Bureau of Publication, Teachers College, Columbia University, 1928.
    Introduces the "intrinsic" method which emphasizes visual strategies for comprehension and questions emphasis on the phonics approach.

Interest and Ability in Reading: A Report of Investigations. New York: Macmillan, 1930.
    A report of experimental studies dealing with reading interests. Includes a discussion of materials and strategies to use with primary grade students. Studies in vocabulary control included in this book influenced the preparation and use of reading materials by many other authors.

"Recent Developments in Diagnostic and Remedial Training in Reading." Washington, DC: *American Educational Association Annual Report*, February 1935, pp. 83–91.
    Reports innovations in the new field. Provides a good historical view of the beginnings of an important branch of reading.

"An Experimental Evaluation of Reading-Readiness Tests." *Elementary School Journal* 39 (1939): 497–508.
    Report of research on the use of tests to evaluate student's readiness to begin formal reading instruction.

With G.L. Bond and D.H. Russell assisted by Andrew Halpin and Kathryn Horan. *Methods of Determining Reading Readiness.* New York: Bureau of Publications, Teachers College, Columbia University, 1939.
    This is intended as a guide to testing students for readiness to begin formal reading instruction.

Teaching Reading. Washington, DC: Department of Classroom Teachers and American Educational Research Association, 1953, rev. 1962, 1967.
    The first in a series of studies called "What Research Says to the Teacher" intended to help classroom teachers understand and use research.

"An Autobiography." In *Leaders in American Education Seventieth Yearbook of the National Society for the Study of Education Part II.* Robert J. Havighurst, ed. Chicago: University of Chicago Press, 1971, pp. 189–221.
    Gates reflects on his life and work providing biographical details in a lively manner. Includes a selected bibliography of primary sources.

SECONDARY SOURCES IN ALPHABETICAL ORDER

American Educational Research Association, *Newsletter* 15, No. 2 (1964): 6.
    Reports Gates's honor for Distinguished Contributions to Educational Research printing the citation on the plaque presented to Dr. Gates.

Beck, Robert H. "Educational Leadership, 1906–1956." *Phi Delta Kappan* 37 (1956): 159–165.
    A discussion of distinguished leaders in education describing their contributions during 50 years.

Durrell, Donald D. "A Review of the Improvement of Reading," *Education* 56 (1935): 58.
    Praises Gates's book as a valuable contribution to the literature.

Freeman, Frank N. "Introduction." *The Scientific Movement in Education, Thirty-Seventh Yearbook of the National Society for the Study of Education, Part II.* Bloomington, IL: Public School Publishing Co., 1938, p. 2.
    A discussion of the impact of the scientific movement in education during the 20th century.

McAndrew, William. "Psychology That Beats the Morning Paper," *School and Society* 32 (1930): 779.
    Praises Gates's *Psychology for Students of Education* and his contributions to research.

Robinson, Richard D. *Classics in Literacy Education. Historical Perspectives for Today's Teachers.* Newark, DE: International Reading Association, 2002, pp. 47–59.
    Provides excerpts from Gates's writings, a brief discussion of Gates's contributions, and selected primary references.

Russell, David H. "Pioneers in Reading II: Arthur Irving Gates." *Elementary English* 34 (October 1957): 397–398.
    Presents a brief biography providing Gates's contribution to the field of reading

instruction. States that Gates's influence on reading instruction was not only because of his research, but because of his personal contacts with students and colleagues.

Staiger, Ralph, and Andersen, Oliver, eds. *Reading: A Human Right and a Human Problem.* Newark, DE: International Reading Association, 1969.

Discusses Gates's contributions to reading education on the occasion of his award from the International Reading Association. Contains Gates's acceptance speech.

Thorndike, Robert L. "Arthur I. Gates (1890–1972) A Biographical Memoir." Washington, DC: National Academy of Education, 1973.

A discussion of the life and work of Gates presented by the son of a colleague, Edward L. Thorndike. Thorndike provides an analysis of Gates's research, teaching, and contribution to the field of reading. Includes a selected bibliography of primary sources.

Tinker, Miles A. "Review of Interest and Ability in Reading." *Journal of Educational Psychology* 23 (1932): 73–74.

A review of Gates's book discussing its value to the field.

Tostberg, Robert E. "Biographical Essay on Arthur I. Gates." In *Leaders in American Education. Seventieth Yearbook of the National Society for the Study of Education, Part II.* Robert J. Havighurst, ed. Chicago: University of Chicago Press, 1971, pp. 222–230.

Comments on Gates's autobiographical essay in the same volume. Evaluates Gates's contributions to psychology and reading in the time and setting in which his work was done.

Vance, Ellen Ruth. "Classroom Reading and the Work of Arthur Gates: 1921–1930." Ed.D. diss., Teachers College, Columbia University, 1985.

An attempt to present a clear definition of reading by examining the early research and contribution to classroom practice made by Gates. Provides an extensive bibliography of primary and secondary sources. Presents an in-depth view of Gates's research and its impact on reading instruction.

William Scott Gray, Jr. (1885–1960)

Gray was born on June 5, 1885, in Coatsburg, Illinois, to William Scott Gray and Annie Letitia (Gilliland). He graduated from high school in 1904 and taught in a one-room school in Adams County, Illinois. Gray served as principal and teacher in Fowler, Illinois, from 1905 to 1908. He was awarded a diploma from Illinois State Normal University in 1910. Gray served as principal and supervised student teachers at the Normal University Training School from 1910 to 1912 and published twelve articles about teaching geography based on Herbartian principles in *School Century*. Gray died on September 8, 1960, in Wolf, Wyoming, after a riding accident, according to Mavrogenes (1985), Gilstad (1985), Moore (1961), and Gates (1960).

Gray continued his education and received a B.S. from the University of Chicago in 1913, an M.A. from Teachers College, Columbia University, in 1914, and a Ph.D. in 1916 from the University of Chicago. Gates (1960), Mavrogenes (1985), Stevenson (1985), and Moore (1961) state that Gray became an instructor at the University of Chicago in 1915, Dean of the College of Education in 1917, and a full professor in 1921. Gray served as dean until 1931 when the College of Education was dissolved. He continued to serve as executive secretary of the All-University Committee on the Preparation of Teachers until 1945 and after he retired in 1950, Gray served as director of research in reading.

Gray helped establish the International Reading Association and served as the first president from 1955 to 1956. After he retired in 1950, Gray continued to actively participate in research, conference, and writing. Chall (1967) states that Gray was the "acknowledged leader of, and spokesman for, reading experts for four decades." Mavrogenes (1985) states that Gray was so successful because he had practical experience as a classroom teacher and was able to combine the humanistic and scientific approaches in all his work. Gray became interested in the scientific study of learning as a master's degree student at Teachers College, Columbia University under the guidance of Edward L. Thorndike. Gray's thesis, "A Tentative Scale for Measuring Oral Reading," was expanded into his doctoral dissertation and later became the widely used

"Gray's Standardized Oral Reading Paragraphs." Mavrogenes (1985), Gilstad (1985), and Moore (1961) state that the "Gray's Oral" was revised several times and not only used standardized statistical results, but was developed to take into account the comfort level of the students and teachers using the test. It was based on an analysis of the student's oral reading errors which helped the teacher develop a diagnosis of the student's reading difficulties. This diagnosis assisted in the development of a remediation plan. Mavrogenes (1985) states that the "Gray Oral" provided information about the nature of reading problems, the process of reading and also created interest in the field of reading. In 1922, according to Mavrogenes (1985), Gilstad (1985), Gates (1960), and Moore (1961), Gray and his colleagues Delea Kibbe, Laura Lucas, and Lawrence Miller published *Remedial Cases in Reading: Their Diagnosis and Treatment*. This was a landmark book based on real case studies which aimed at identifying specific causes of reading problems and providing teachers with assistance in how to plan individualized instruction. The book used research that the authors carried out in schools and Mavrogenes (1985) states was instrumental in the development of specialists in remedial reading.

Gray had the uncanny ability to summarize material easily. He began publishing an annual *Summary of Reading Investigations* in 1925 and continued every year until 1960. The International Reading Association continued to publish similar summaries of research on reading after Gray's death. Gray inaugurated an Annual Conference on Reading at the University of Chicago and published the *Proceedings* of these conferences. He wrote summaries of reading research for the *Encyclopedia of Educational Research* in 1941, 1950, and 1960 and edited three Yearbooks for the National Society for the Study of Education in 1925, 1937, and 1948 about reading research.

Gray's work influenced the inclusion of research on readers' attitudes towards reading, and students' problem solving abilities in reading from the elementary school through adulthood. Gray's main interest was in how to improve reading instruction at all levels.

Mavrogenes (1985), Stevenson (1985), Gilstad (1985), and Moore (1961) state that Gray's work made an impact on the field of reading because his approach was practical, covered all the information completely, and was based on solid information. Gray was not famous for being an originator, but for being an interpreter who explained and clarified research. Guthrie (1984) states that Gray was "the preeminent reading educator." Gates (1960) states that "Dr. Gray labored to improve the teaching of reading for a longer period of time (more than half a century), with greater singleness of purpose, and in a wider variety of enterprises than anyone else in history. His contributions are enormous both in number and importance.... He was a quiet but determined crusader. He waged a lifelong campaign to improve education with unrelenting effort." According to Guthrie (1984) Gray was devoted to helping teachers find new insights and renewed enthusiasm from research on reading. Gray recommended reforms in reading instruction at all levels from kindergarten to college.

Chall (1984) describes Gray as an "investigator, teacher, and curriculum developer...." Gray reviewed research on reading, trained reading specialists and teachers, and wrote the famous Dick and Jane reading series for Scott Foresman and Company through the 1950s. Mavrogenes (1985) states Gray insisted that the readers contained stories that were interesting "and ... presented a gradual increase in vocabulary, sentence structure, and plot complexity." In a 1932 letter to Nila Banton Smith, Director of the Reading Institute at New York University, Gray describes the Dick and Jane Readers, according to Mavrogenes (1985), as having "an attractive, well-organized content of first-class authorship, amply provided with modern study-helps and well illustrated by many well known artists." The reading series was a best seller and was used by over 86,000 schools at the height of its influence, teaching reading to several generations of children, Mavrogenes (1985), Moore (1961), and Stevenson (1985) state.

According to Chall (1984) Gray believed that "the objective study of reading ... would ultimately lead to a better guide for reorganizing and improving instruction. For Gray ... research and instruction were one and that the health of one would be tied to the health of the other." Gray was a meticulous reporter of research who was, Chall (1984) states, the first teacher educator, researcher and curriculum developer in reading. Gray believed in the importance of applying research for the improvement of reading instruction and for literacy social policy. He was, Chall (1984) believes, enthusiastic and optimistic about the importance of research. "Gray opted for using the knowledge of the past to understand the present and future."

Gray retired in 1950 with over 400 publications to his credit. Moore (1961) states that Gray took advantage of his retirement to write 100 more publications. He became internationally known as a result of his work with UNESCO. Moore (1961), Mavrogenes (1985), and Stevenson (1985) state Gray evaluated reading methods and worldwide literacy in *The Teaching of Reading and Writing: An International Survey* published in 1956.

Mavrogenes (1985) and Willis et al. (1960) summed up Gray's influence by stating that "during his lifetime he was the leader in the improvement of reading instruction. Through his efforts reading was recognized as a series of complex mental activities, skills involved in many types of reading were identified, growth in reading was seen as a continuous process during the period of formal education and afterwards, appropriate guidance came to be considered necessary to facilitate the acquisition of reading competencies, reading programs were expanded, content area reading was promoted, an increased need for critical reading was recognized." Gray was in the right place at the right time," Mavrogenes (1985) states; he attended the right universities and entered the field of reading at the time when standardized tests made diagnosis and remediation of reading problems possible and a new field was born. Gray was solid rather than brilliant. Hilgard (1964) states that to be effective education needs "both pure and applied research, both theory and application, both Einstein's and Edison's." Mavrogenes (1985) states that Gray was an Edison. Thorndike (1912) said that education will "always need its poets, its artists, and its craftsmen, as well as its managers and men of science." Mavrogenes (1985) calls Gray "a master craftsman, an efficient manager, and a sometime man of science." The International Reading Association named Gray "Mr. Reading" for his outstanding contributions to the field. According the Guthrie (1984) Gray "anticipated trends for research synthesis as a basis for reasoned generalizations." He inspired the establishment of national conferences at the University of Chicago, making it the center of research on reading. Gray was a professional and intellectual leader in his field, Guthrie (1984) states, who was eminently qualified to review research. Chall (1984) calls Gray the widely accepted leader in his field. Gray was, Moore (1961) states, "the most influential figure in the field of reading..." but was also "first and foremost a teacher" whose pupils attained prominence and leadership in reading education.

Annotated Bibliography

PRIMARY SOURCES IN CHRONOLOGICAL ORDER

This is a brief selection from the more than 500 primary sources Dr. Gray produced.

With Kibbe, D., Lucas, L., and Miller, L.W. *Remedial Cases in Reading: Their Diagnosis and Treatment*. Chicago: University of Chicago Press, 1922.
    This work is based on case studies and was intended to identify the specific causes of reading difficulties and provide assistance in planning individualized instruction. This work used research done in schools and became the basis for the development of remedial reading specialists. This work was the first in the field to examine the actual problems of pupils in a school setting.

Standardized Oral Reading Paragraphs, Grades 1-8. Bloomington, IL: Public School Publishing Co., 1915.
    This early edition of a classic test of oral reading ability was revised a number of times and is still used for diagnostic purposes. It was based on an analysis of reading errors and was the first instrument to provide information on the source of reading problems and the reading process.

Annual Summary of Reading Investigations
Elementary School Journal
February/March/April/May 1926
February/March 1927
February/March/April 1928
February/March 1929
February/March 1930
March/April 1931
February/March/April 1932

Journal of Educational Research

February 1933	February 1946
April 1934	February 1947
February 1935	February 1948
February 1936	February 1949
April 1937	February 1950
February 1938	February 1951
March 1939	February 1952
March 1940	February 1953
February 1941	February 1954
February 1942	February 1955
February 1943	February 1956
February 1944	February 1957
February 1945	February 1958

These summaries provided researchers and teachers with annotated bibliographies and discussions of research. The contributions to *The Elementary School Journal* summarized practice oriented articles while those that appeared in *Journal of Educational Research* focused on more research oriented articles. Nine summaries from 1931 to 1940 appeared as longer research summaries in *Review of Educational Research*.

Each summary presented current topics in reading providing clear information for students and teachers giving a broad view of teaching reading organized into categories.

And Whipple, Gertrude. *Improving Instruction in Reading: An Experimental Study*. Educational Monograph No. 40. Chicago: University of Chicago, 1933.

Presents a view of instructional strategies emphasizing systematic guidance and helpful leadership by administrators.

With Holms, Eleanor. *The Development of Meaning Vocabularies in Reading: An Experimental Study*. Publication of Lab School University of Chicago, No. 6. Chicago: University of Chicago, 1938.

Discussed content area reading instruction strategies.

On Their Own in Reading: How to Give Children Independence in Attacking New Words. Chicago: Scott, Foresman 1948; 1960.

Presents strategies for word-attack skills in elementary and high schools. Discusses the history of word-attack strategies and practical applications for classroom use.

The Teaching of Reading and Writing: An International Survey. Monographs on Fundamental Education X. UNESCO, Paris, 1956. Chicago: Scott, Foresman.

A discussion of world literacy instruction suggesting that a variety of strategies are necessary. This is a survey of instructional strategies used for teaching children and adults.

Secondary Sources in Alphabetical Order

Chall, Jeanne S. "Foreword." In *Reading William S. Gray: A Research Retrospective, 1881–1941*. John T. Guthrie, ed. Newark, DE: International Reading Association, 1984, pp. viii–xii.

Discuses Gray's monograph and his contributions to the field of reading.

Chall, Jeanne S. *Learning to Read the Great Debate*. New York: Harcourt Brace, 1967, 1983, 1996.

Gates, Arthur I. "William Scott Gray, 1885–1960." *Reading Teacher* 14 (November 1960): 73.

An obituary tribute to Gray from a friend and colleague.

Gilstad, June R. "William S. Gray (1885–1960): First IRA President." *Reading Research Quarterly* 20 (Summer 1985): 509–511.

An obituary including an evaluation of Gray's contributions to reading education. A bibliography is included.

Guthrie, John T., ed. *Reading William S. Gray: A Research Retrospective, 1881–1941*. Newark DE: International Reading Association, 1984, Preface pp. v–vii.

This is a reprint of Gray's review of reading research that appeared in *The Encyclopedia of Educational Research* in 1941. Gray's monograph discusses eleven topics in reading that provide a review of important trends in the field. A bibliography of works by Gray and secondary sources is included. This is a classic work. Guthrie provides a "Preface" that discusses Gray's life and work.

Hilgard, E.R. "A Perspective on the Relationship Between Learning Theory and Educational Practice." In *The Sixty-Third Yearbook of the National Society for the Study of Education*. E.R. Hilgard, ed. Chicago: University of Chicago, 1964, pp. 402–415.

Discusses the relationship between theory and its application in practice to educational settings. Differentiates between pure theory and the adjustments in response to the necessity of practice.

Luke, Allan. "Making Dick and Jane: Historical Genesis of the Modern Basal Reader." *Teachers College Record* 89, no. 1 (Fall 1987): 91–116.

Discusses the history of the basal reader and how Gray helped shape the Scott Foresman readers. Provides a discussion of Gray's background and influence in the field of reading.

Mavrogenes, Nancy Ashby. "William Scott Gray: Leader of Teachers and Shaper of American Reading Instruction." Ph.D. diss., University of Chicago, 1985.

A detailed biography and evaluation of Gray's work in reading. An extensive bibliography of primary and secondary sources including unpublished sources is included. This is, so far, the only in-depth work about Gray.

Moore, Walter J. "Pioneers in Reading, I: William Scott Gray." *Elementary English* 34 (1957): 326–328.

A discussion of Gray's life and work while he was still an active contributor to the field.

Moore, Walter J. "William S. Gray, 1885–1960" *Elementary English* 38 (1961): 187–189.

An extensive obituary presenting Gray's life and work from the perspective of a colleague.

Pelosi, P.L. "The Roots of Reading Diagnosis" in H.A. Robinson, ed., *Reading and Writing Instruction in the United States: Historical Trends*. Newark, DE: International Reading Association, 1977, pp. 69–75.

Describes Gray's contributions to the development of the field of diagnosis of reading difficulties.

Stevenson, Jennifer A., ed. *William S. Gray: Teacher, Scholar, Leader*. Newark, DE: International Reading Association, 1985.

This booklet discusses Gray's life and work divided into the categories of teacher, scholar, and leader telling about his contributions in each category. Includes a complete bibliography of Gray's work which is most valuable.

Thorndike, Edward L. "The Measurement of Educational Products." *The School Review* 20 (1912): 289–299.

Discusses the different ways to evaluate educational outcomes stating that a variety of methods and types of evaluators are needed for this important task.

Willis, B.C., McCaffrey, F.S., Gray, W.S., and Scott, W.H. *After Fifty Momentous Years Education Looks Ahead: Honoring William S. Gray on the Occasion of the Fiftieth Anniversary of the Basic Reading Program*. Chicago: Scott Foresman, 1960.

A tribute to Gray's contribution as senior author to the Dick and Jane readers describing his achievements in the field of reading.

Fernald Technique

The Fernald technique is a multisensory approach to assist students with reading difficulties to master decoding and comprehension.

In 1921 The Clinic School was opened at the University of California, Los Angeles to develop diagnostic, remedial, and preventive techniques to help students adjust to their environment, according to Myers and Hammill (1969). Students included in the program had normal intelligence and extreme reading disability. Students were grouped, Myers and Hammill (1969) state, according to the type of problem and attended classes daily from 9 a.m. to 3 p.m. for eight months to one year. Detailed records were kept and parents agreed to allow the students to remain in the program until they were ready to return to a regular classroom.

Grace M. Fernald (1943) conducted research in the program and believed that "the first thing the child needs for satisfactory adjustment to life is successful achievement along those lines which fit him to meet the demands that will be made upon him." School, which children are forced to attend, makes the most important demands for continuous adjustment, Fernald (1943) states. Students cannot succeed in school unless they master the fundamental subjects of reading, writing, spelling, and arithmetic. Without mastery of these skills students will not only fail in school, but in later life because job opportunities will be limited. Fernald (1943) believed that children fail to learn for a variety of reasons, but those with average or high intelligence learn to compensate for emotional, physical, or school problems if diagnosis and remediation are found and used. If possible remediation should be used before the student has failed and emotional problems develop. Once students experience extreme failure negative emotional reactions to all activities and people associated with the failure develop. Students, Fernald (1943) believes, either withdraw from the group or compensate for the failure by becoming disruptive. The failure "is the cause not the result of the emotion which is so serious a part of our problem in remedial work." Children begin to hate or fear school when they continue to meet only failure. The natural desire to learn is suppressed by continued failure at "the very things he dreamed of doing when at last he could enter school," according to Fernald (1943).

Detailed case histories kept by Fernald for each student indicate that most of the students with learning difficulties did not have emotional problems before they entered school. Fernald (1943) describes two ways of handling these emotional problems, the Analytical Method and the Reconditioning Method. In using the Analytical Method it is necessary to discover all the factors that have caused the student's emotional problem and then to "focus the patient's attention on those past experiences which have been associated with the ideas involved in the complex." When the student is able to express these ideas verbally or in some other way the blocking is relieved and the student is able to start "constructive voluntary activities" which alleviate the frustration.

The Reconditioning Method is the opposite of the Analytical Method. First, Fernald (1943) states the situation that caused the negative emotion which is to be modified is avoided. Second, "provide some substitute stimulus connected with a positive emotion. After this second stimulus has been well established, we introduce the object for which we wish a new conditioning." This process is repeated until the object causes a new emotion. This method diverts the student's attention away from everything connected with the undesirable emotion. Case history information is used to avoid stimulating the negative reaction.

Fernald (1943) states that the Clinic School method allows a student to start with successful learning on the very first day. "No one sympathizes with the non-reader or even talks things over…" or calls attention to what the student does not know. Students find that they are capable of learning any word regardless of length or complexity. Fernald (1943) states that the success of the emotional and social reconstruction occurs because the start of the process is very quick and the student experiences the positive emotional reactions connected to success before he/she knows what has happened. The student who feared or hated reading and writing becomes eager to learn and use these skills.

Fernald (1943) cautions that if remedial intervention is to provide steady progress, the following conditions must be avoided:

1. "Calling attention to emotionally loaded situations"—do not urge the student to try harder to please his/her family;
2. "Use of methods by which individual cannot learn"—do not send the child back to the regular classroom too soon expecting the child to use the method that would reestablish the original negative emotional reaction;
3. "Child subjected to conditions which cause him to feel embarrassed or conspicuous"—do not return the student to the regular classroom and expect him/her to use a method that is different from the one

the rest of the class uses. The technique that would provide success becomes negative because the student refuses to use it. Students were not sent back to the regular classroom until he/she achieved a level of success that allowed him/her to compete with the rest of the class;
4. "Child's attention directed to what he is unable to do rather than his progress"—do not point out the student's errors or slower pace.

Fernald (1943) believed that there were many students who had normal sight, hearing, and intelligence and no physical disabilities, but still did not learn to read by any methods that were used. These students can be placed in two categories: students with total or extreme disability and students with partial disability. The cases of total disability were Fernald's first target. Cases of partial disability also were treated after Fernald refined the method. Both types of cases benefited from Fernald's method which she called the hand-kinesthetic method. She states that for students to succeed in reading they must perceive a group of words as a unit. Students must see words that are taken together as having a certain meaning, as a single object not as a set of unrelated words. Because the meanings of words vary with the group in which they occur, word-by-word reading is not only slow but meaningless when compared to "reading in which the apperceived unit is the word group. Throughout the entire history of education we find various methods of teaching used to accomplish this result," Fernald (1943) states. She describes various reading methods stating that the kinesthetic methods would help beginning readers because "these methods may be eye, lip-throat or hand kinesthetic, the last being the one that most completely represents the word in terms of the individual's movements." Fernald (1943) praises the Montessori Method of tracing as a very effective method in learning letter and word forms. "The ease with which children learn the formal characters they trace shows the importance of kinesthetic elements in learning.... In the Montessori method letters and words were traced with direct finger contact." Fernald (1943) believed that the hand-kinesthetic method "served to build up an adequate appreciative background which makes if possible for the child to use effectively such sensory cues as he has" so that visual or auditory cues are supplemented by the tracing and writing of words.

Fernald (1943) discusses the prevalence of reading disability stating that failure to learn to read occurs in most schools. The degree of failure ranges from complete non readers to cases who fail to achieve adequate rate of reading and level of comprehension. Fernald (1943) states that attention was given to cases of word-blindness for many years, but "even as late as 1921, when our first study was published, the supposition that there could be children of normal intelligence who had been unable to learn to read was considered absurd by many educators." The work done by Arthur I. Gates, Marion Monroe, W.F. Dearborn, Emmett Betts, and William S. Gray, Fernald (1943) states, confirms that the problem of reading disability is widespread and serious. All of the researchers stated that there were numerous causes of reading disability that varied from case to case. Fernald (1943) stated that her research indicated that there was not "one specific disorder ... responsible for the seeming inability of some individuals to learn to read."

Fernald (1943) states that the method she developed, the hand-kinesthetic method, consists of: "(1) the discovery of some means by which the child can learn to write words correctly, (2) the motivating of such writing, (3) the reading by the child of the printed copy of what he has written, (4) extensive reading of materials other than own compositions." The method starts when the clinician explains to the student that "we have a new way of learning words we want him (her) to try. We explain ... that many bright people have had the same difficulty ... in learning to read and have learned easily by this new method which really is as good as any other way," Fernald (1943) states. The student may choose any word to learn regardless of length and it is taught by stage one of the hand-tracing method. The student is allowed as much time as is necessary to learn the word. Fernald (1943) states that as soon as the student finds out that he/she can learn to write words story writing begins. At first the student writes about any topic of interest, but as skill is gained school projects are worked on. The student writes and then after the material is typed, reads what he/she has written. Each word is written by the student and learned before it becomes part of the story.

The Stages of the Hand-Kinesthetic Method

Stage 1—*Child learns by tracing a word*

The student selects a word to learn. According to Fernald (1943) and Myers and Hammill (1969), the word is written for the child with crayon in plain, blackboard-sized script or print. The child traces the word with his finger and says each part of the word as he traces it. The process is repeated until the word can be written by the child without his looking at the copy. The pupil is allowed as much time as necessary.

The word is written on a scrap of paper first, and then it is incorporated into a story which the child composes. The story is typed, and the child reads his printed story to the teacher. The child places the word or words that have been learned by tracing in a word-file. This file is arranged alphabetically, and the child learns the alphabet incidentally. The practice is excellent training for learning how to use the dictionary as well as for learning the letters of the alphabet. In cases of extreme disability every word used in the first composition may have to be learned by tracing. Usually the child soon gains enough skill and progresses into the second stage.

Fernald (1943) and Myers and Hammill (1969) state that pertinent points relative to stage one are:

1. Direct finger contact in tracing. Fernald (1943) notes that the child may use one or two fingers in tracing. She found, however, that learning takes place more quickly when the child uses direct finger contact in tracing rather than when he uses a pencil or stylus.
2. Writing the traced word from memory. Fernald (1943) emphasizes that the child should never copy the words which he has traced. Looking back and forth from the copy to the word he is writing tends to break the word into fragmentary, meaningless units. In copying, Fernald (1943) believes that the flow of the hand in writing is interrupted, and the eyes move back and forth instead of fixing as they should on the word being written. Fernald (1943) stated that the habit of copying words interferes with the correct writing or spelling, and with the recognition of words already written.
3. Writing words as units. The word must be learned and written as a whole rather than by sounds or syllables. If a child is unsuccessful in his attempt to write a word after tracing it, the incorrect form is taken away. The child begins the tracing process again and attempts to write the word as a whole. Erasing or correcting single words, letters, or syllables is *not* permitted, since Fernald (1943) believed that such procedures break the word into a jumbled, meaningless entity which does not represent the correct form of the word.
4. Using words in context. By always using words in context, the child experiences them in meaningful groups, which helps to give exact meaning to all of the words. The child usually has a speaking vocabulary large enough to express those things that interest him/her. When a child has a limited vocabulary, he should start learning to write and read words which he already uses in speech.

Stage 2—Same as Stage 1 except that tracing is no longer necessary.

Fernald (1943) and Myers and Hammill (1969) state: "tracing is no longer necessary in stage two of the technique. The child has developed enough skill to learn words by looking at the word in script, saying the word over to himself as he looks at it, and then writing the word without copying. The child continues to write freely and to read the printed copy of his work. Writing becomes easier, and stories become longer and more interesting. The child is allowed to write on any subject that is of interest."

Fernald (1943) and Myers and Hammill (1969) state that the important connection between stages one and two is that the child continues to vocalize the word being learned. The child must establish the connection between the sound of a word and its form so that visual stimulation will immediately stimulate a vocal recall. Vocalization of the word should be natural and not a stilted or distorted sounding out of letters or syllables, which results in the loss of the word as a whole. The sounds of each letter are never said separately and are never overemphasized. In a longer word such as *important*, the student says *im* while tracing the first syllable, *por* while tracing the second syllable, and *tant* as he finishes the word. In writing the word, the student again pronounces each syllable as he writes it. After some practice, the two activities, writing and speaking, seem to occur simultaneously without effect.

Fernald (1943) suggests no arbitrary limit for the length of time needed for tracing because the student usually stops tracing gradually. A decrease in the number of tracings needed to learn a new word is observed first; then a few short words are learned without tracing. Eventually tracing is no longer necessary. The average tracing period lasts from two to eight months.

Material should not be simplified to a point below the intelligence level of the child, either in terms of vocabulary range or complexity of subject matter. According to Fernald (1943), the student is more highly motived when reading and writing somewhat difficult material that he can understand rather than when given material that is below his mental level. Once the child discovers that he has learned a technique by which even long and difficult words can be learned, he takes delight in learning. The longer and more difficult words are easier to recognize on later presentation. When tracing is no longer necessary, a small word box file is substituted for the larger word box. The words now are written in ordinary-sized script. According to Fernald (1943) and Myers and Hammill (1969),

Stage 3—*Same as Stage 2 except that the child is able to learn from the printed word by looking at it and saying it before writing it.*

The child learns directly from the printed word in stage three. He/she looks at the word and is able to write the word without vocalizing or copying. In this stage books are presented; the student is permitted to read from them and is told the words he/she does not know. When he/she is through reading the article, the new words are reviewed and the words then are written from recall. A check is made later to determine if the words have been retained.

Stage 4—*Ability to recognize new words from their similarity to words or parts of words already learned.*

According to Fernald (1943) and Myers and Hammill (1969), the fourth stage begins when the student can generalize and recognize new words from their resemblance to known words. The student's interest in reading increases with his/her reading skill. Fernald (1943) states that the student is *never read to* either at home or at school until he/she has achieved normal reading skill.

Fernald does not object to reading to the student after he/she has developed normal reading skill, because by this time the student prefers to read by himself/herself. Usually he/she finds that reading for himself/herself is faster, easier, and more pleasant.

In reading difficult material, the student is encouraged to glance over a paragraph for words he/she does not know. These new words are learned before reading so that the paragraph is read as a unit. At first, the new words are retained better if the student pronounces the word as he/she writes them. He/she repeats the words, turns the paper over, and rewrites the word. Eventually the child gains enough skill to retain the word and its meaning if the word is identified for him/her. The teacher records the word for later review so that it may be determined whether words learned in this manner are being retained.

These four stages are the instructional method designed by Fernald (1943) for use with cases of total or partial reading disability. During each stage a child is continually evaluated to discover whether he/she retains the words he/she has learned. If the retention rate decreases, the teacher returns the pupil to an earlier stage of learning, according to Myers and Hammill (1969). In discussing the phonics approach to teaching reading, Fernald (1943) comments that the child should never sound out words and that the teacher should never sound out words for the child except in rare cases where the child, because of previous training, wants to sound out a word. Then the child is allowed to sound out a word if he/she does it before he/she reads. Many people believe that phonics must be taught if a student is to develop the ability to recognize new words from their similarity to words that have been experienced in other combinations. Fernald (1943) says that the student will learn to understand word combinations after the development of a varied reading background. The average individual after several years of extensive reading develops a complex appreciative background and a larger reading vocabulary than either his/her spoken or written vocabulary.

The length of reading instruction needed to help a child with a reading disorder to reach his/her optimal reading level depends upon the individual and upon the educational age desired. Fernald (1943) states the younger child is ready to return to regular classes when the reading achievement level of his/her regular class group is reached. The older child should remain in the remedial group until he/she (1) can recognize new words, (2) has established an adequate reading vocabulary, and (3) has developed the necessary conceptual background to make it possible for the reader to perceive the meaning of word groups in many new contexts.

Fernald (1943) states many failures occur because the individual does not have the wealth of reading experience necessary for intelligent, rapid reading. Enough skill must be achieved before the student can read with speed and comprehension materials suitable to his/her age and intellectual level.

Certain bodily adjustments are necessary and skills are needed in order to acquire the particular coordination which characterizes the reading process. Fernald (1943) discusses some of the conditions that may affect reading, such as farsightedness, nearsightedness, astigmatism, muscle imbalance, aniseikonia, and lack of visual acuity. Fernald (1943) and Myer and Hammill (1969) state that poor eye coordination is not the reason a child fails to learn to read; some people with monocular vision, nystagmus, and spastic imbalance learn to read with a fair degree of speed and comprehension provided the eye can provide a clear retinal image. Most good readers, however, develop the ability to move across each line of print with a series of sweeps and fixations. Fast readers make few fixations and only occasional regressions while reading familiar material. A slow reader makes many stops with many regressions.

In 1947 Grace Fernald answered a critique of her hand-kinesthetic method by Helen M. Robinson. "Appraisal of Current Practices Relating to Poor and Disabled Readers: Appraisal of Methods of Teaching Nonreaders and Pupils who Make Slow Progress in Learning to Read in the Primary Grades" appeared in *The Appraisal of Current Practices in Reading* edited by William S. Gray. Fernald (1947) states that "it seems to the writer that part of the criticism is based on a spotty reading of our publications in some cases and on our failure to publish certain of our findings with reference to our investigations in others." Fernald (1947) presents material from her published work in answer to specific points and describes experiments not published at the time. The following critique was made by Robinson:

1. The method does not promote the development of necessary skills. It does not provide a comparison of likeness and difference in sounds of words and their printed form. The technique does not teach phonetic elements or make use of contextual clues. This makes the student dependent on the teacher for help in recognizing unknown words;
2. The method makes no direct contribution to a "wider perceptual span or regular eye-movements" except where a student may make this adjustment as a result of recognizing a word immediately. Students are not helped to acquire reasonable speed of reading except indirectly;
3. Since students learn words in a written form they have problems recognizing the printed forms of words and letters;
4. There are students who do not want to retrace words as often as needed in the beginning stage of the technique. This causes students to become bored and the rate of learning to decrease;

5. Kottmeyer (1945) states that there are first the "ideational methods which emphasize a direct connection between printed symbol and the thought of idea presented by it";
6. Students are never allowed to correct errors or to erase parts of words; and
7. Many students quickly reach a limit in their association between word forms and meanings. Students become overwhelmed by the increasing flow of words and cannot distinguish the likenesses and differences between them. Students fail to perceive phonetic principles and do not recognize enough words to use context clues correctly. Students confuse monosyllabic words that have similar patterns and cannot deal with multi-syllabic words. Students soon become discouraged with their own helplessness when they struggle with increasingly difficult reading material that they make little effort to learn.

In response to the first point, Fernald (1947) stated "on page 93 of our book is the following: Sufficient Reading to Make It Possible to Recognize New Words." It is often believed that this can only be accomplished by teaching some form of phonics. It is not necessary to put like objects side by side to have one suggest the other. Many experiences with different words that have similar combinations will lead to recognition of the part of a new word that has the same letter grouping. If the student has experienced most of the syllables of a new word in various other words the whole new word will be recognized. If the student has, for example, learned many words at different times with the "h" sound, such as him, hot, hear, and also has learned many words with the "and" sound such as and, sand, when the student sees the new word hand for the first time he/she "recognizes" it immediately although the words having the common sound have been learned as parts of meaningful wholes rather than as separate phonetic units or as words strung along in meaningless "families" or "groups." Fernald (1947) states that when students begin the remedial program at the clinic they are not able to pass the simplest phonics test. Where these students complete the remedial program they pass any phonics test even though they have never been taught phonics, words grouped by sound. They have only been taught words in context. "The more the individual reads, the more complex is his perceptive background for new words." Students can gain "an adequate sensory basis for the perception of even a long word as a whole, provided the word is one he uses in speech or understands when he hears it" if most of the word is supplied from experiences with words that have similar sounds.

Fernald (1947) states that she is puzzled by the remark that her technique does not use context clues. Students begin to generalize and figure out new words from their resemblance to known words as soon as they are able to learn from print. If the case is carefully handled, the student becomes eager to read. Students are permitted to read as much as they want about any topic of interest. Some students are motivated to learn from books and magazines while others are more interested in stories. In either case students should be allowed to read whatever is of interest so that they continue to read in order to find out what they want to know. "Because the children always write about things that interest them, and because their first reading is the printed form of what they have written, they develop a reading vocabulary not only of the more commonly used words, but also words connected with particular subjects. Finally the children want to find out more about these topics and begin to read." Since students have written many of the words they find in articles about a topic of interest they read even difficult material well.

Fernald (1947) cites page 39 of her book which states "words should always be used in context. It is important that the child should know the meaning of all words that he learns. It is also important that he should experience the words in meaningful groups. He usually has a sufficiently extensive speaking vocabulary to express himself in words with reference to those things which interest him." Even if the student's vocabulary is limited it is better to start with words the student uses in speech.

In response to Robinson's second point, Fernald (1947) explains that the "amount of reading the individual must do before he is considered a completed case will depend upon the educational age he must reach." Younger students will continue reading in connection with school work, and home activities need to reach the reading level of the class he/she will go into at the end of the remedial intervention. Older students need more time and help to achieve the needed level. Upper grade students must develop the complex concepts needed to perceive words as groups. This may be, Fernald believes, difficult because many students reach the first stage of remediation with enthusiasm, but teachers return pupils to the regular classroom too soon. Many do not have the flexible, immediate recognition of many word groups. "It is certain that the failures reported ... are due to the failure to give the individual the wealth of experience necessary for intelligent and rapid reading." Frequently too many students return to the classroom at the stage when they still read new material slowly and if left alone read word by word. "In all our cases the remedial work is continued until the individual is able to go back into his proper age group and read well enough to make satisfactory progress there ... the work must be continued until sufficient skill has been achieved to make it possible ... to read with speed and comprehension any material suited to ... (the student's) age and intelligence," Fernald (1947) states.

Regarding reading speed, Fernald (1947) states that no direct instruction in speed methods is given. Speed increases indirectly for all students. Before students are ready to return to the regular classroom all students have achieved adequate speed. "Our records show that this speed has been developed easily, especially in those cases in which this has been accomplished indirectly." Fernald adds that it seems better to increase speed without using speed exercises. Fernald used speed up methods only when needed in very few cases.

In response to Robinson's third point, Fernald (1947) states that words are written in script, but there is no reason why words could not be written in manuscript. Fernald lists the following reasons for using script:

(a) words are written as a unit, the flow of the hand is not interrupted by tracing separate letters, the word remains a meaningful whole,

(b) script is as much like print as manuscript writing,

(c) script is easier than manuscript, which can be laborious, and often during the slow process of printing the word is lost;

(d) no difficulty has been found in the transfer from script to print for any of the students. Students write stories and they are printed (typed) for them to read;

(e) nothing prevents students from using manuscript if they wish. Fernald (1947) reports data on transfer stating that "at present we have over 90 percent retention. Our percentage of word recognition is from 85 to 90 on words that have been written in individual self-expression.... Out of 5,980 words learned by 18 children, 94 percent were recognized on rereading and out of 20,870 words written in four rooms, 17,658 or 85 percent were recognized on re-check. That is, the recognition of the word after it has been written in script as a part of meaningful context is as satisfactory as the above percentages would indicate." She states that recall was an average of 92 percent with some students' recall as high as 99 percent, and the transfer from script to print was made with no difficulty. Students who were the most disabled used difficult words in the first stories they wrote and later were able to recognize 85 to 95 percent of these words.

Robinson's fourth point attributed a decrease in the rate of learning to boredom. Our students do not get bored because they understand that tracing is only the initial stage of learning and will soon become unnecessary. Students develop big word files during the tracing stage and small files where tracing is no longer used. Students make the transition to writing some words without tracing within two to three weeks. If students become bored something must be wrong with the application of the method. Some reasons for this could be:

(a) the student continues tracing too long;
(b) the student does not connect the sound with the tracing and writing of the word, but traces mechanically,
(c) the student sounds out the word distorting it so that the word is no longer in his/her mind;
(d) the student is not writing something of interest.

Tracing should be set up as part of the method to continue only as long as it is needed. Perhaps, Fernald (1947) states, the tracing method is wrong for the bored student who would learn better by another method. Students who, Fernald (1947) states, have failed to learn by other methods learn rapidly as soon as they get reinforcement of the kinesthetic factors. Students trace words only as long as they cannot learn any other way and "we do not have any trouble with the interest in tracing or the learning that goes with it." Perhaps, Fernald (1947) states, tracing for the bored student is done as a chore in a room where no one else is using the method. Students who need tracing, Fernald (1947) states, discover that it is a way to learn easily. These students want to learn and have found they can learn by tracing. In 1986 Adelman and Taylor discuss the motivational context of Fernald's technique stating that Fernald emphasized the newness of the technique when it was introduced and presented it as special in a positive way. "She then moved on quickly to embed the method in what she called 'story writing' and 'special projects'; today these strategies are widely known as language experience and discovery approaches." Fernald introduced the tracing within the context of student interests and offered it. Adelman and Taylor (1986) state, "as an aid to students as they pursue some chosen activity ... rather than being limited by a specific technique's power to mobilize a student's interest, we ... capitalize on a wide range of substantive and popular activities ... in efforts to facilitate motivational readiness." Fernald (1947) states that once a student has learned a word it is placed in a file. When the student wants to write or read the word he/she has already learned it is found in the file. If the student does not have a word in his/her file, the teacher will write it for the student to learn. Fernald states that students are not forced to retrace words because "they do this of their own accord as part of the successful learning process ... we just let them do it."

Fernald (1947) responded to Robinson's fifth point by stating she is pleased that her method is called one that "emphasizes a direct connection between printed symbol and the thought ... represented by it" because "we can see no aim in reading except to have the printed symbol call up as quickly and directly as possible the thought or idea for which it stands." Fernald explains why students are never allowed to correct mistakes or erase parts of words. Where an error is made it is covered and the student starts again to write the word. "The word is never patched up by erasing the incorrect part and substituting the correction. The reason for this procedure is that the various movements of erasing, correcting single letters or syllables ... break the word up into a meaningless total which does not represent the word." Once the student goes through the process of correcting a mistake the word becomes part of "fumbled associations that occur as the word is being patched together, he fails to recognize the word when it is presented ... in correct form." Corrections are made by retracing and rewriting the word as a whole.

In response to Robinson's comment that children reach a limit in associating words with their meaning, Fernald (1947) states that the more students read the more meaningful associations become. Students learn to distinguish between monosyllabic words such as "when," "where," "saw" and "was" after they have written these words several times in context. Fernald (1947) states "in fact the rapidity with which this type of confusion is cleared up is quite amazing. New and difficult longer words are recognized more quickly than is usually the case with children who have been taught through "phonetic principles...." Fernald (1947) cites Leonard Ayres' "Measurement of Ability in Spelling" to justify the writing of "the 10 commonest words in English. These are probably "the," "and," "of," "to," "I," "a," "in," "that," "you," "for." With their repetitions they constitute more than one-fourth of all the words we write. Save for the personal pronouns, they are essential in writing about any subject ... from Aaron through Zythum." Fernald states that students' writing is made up of the 50 most common words which are so frequently repeated that they make up half of all the words students write. Students do not encounter a mass of new words, but repeat the same words many times with only certain new words used as new topics are introduced. If students have learned the 1,000 words Ayres identifies as repetitions in any writing project, students are reading and writing these same words continually no matter what they write about.

Fernald (1947) discusses the importance of the kinesthetic factor citing several reasons why learning increases as soon as the kinesthetic tracing part of the technique is introduced:

1. "In our cases of extreme and total reading disability, 60 to 1 of the cases are males (less than 2 percent females). It is probable that the male is more dynamic in his learning"...
2. Students who seem to need the kinesthetic cue in reading need it for other subjects as well. Fernald's experiments indicate that students using Braille and mazes "were superior to the control groups in learning and accuracy (and) ... in transportation of material, as in the rotated maze."

3. In work with cases of acquired alexia as a result of brain injury, persons who lost the ability to read that they once had "were still able to recognize words if they trace them (use kinesthetic cues)."
4. Those who need the kinesthetic cues need them for everything they do and depend on these cues. "In doing mental tests, children do such tests as orientation, enclosed boxes, etc., by using kinesthetic cues quite obviously."

Fernald (1947) concludes her response by stating that too much emphasis has been placed on the visual methods of reading instruction at the expense of the kinesthetic method. It is also suggested that writing and reading should be taught together instead of teaching reading first then writing. Fernald states that more boys have reading problems and need the kinesthetic approach, but most of the teachers are females and "are less dynamic than men in learning." More boys than girls need to write as well as read. These students, Fernald (1947) states, "need the feel of making the word at the same time they say and see it. These children have the same need in all their learning processes. The most direct expression of the word in terms of the individual's own movements is to write it." If the student, Fernald (1947) continues, is learning foundation words whose meaning they already know, they do not need to define the word, see a picture of what the word represents, or act the word out. "The most direct representation of the word is the writing or printing of the word itself. Yet this is omitted in many of our systems of reading." It is often taken for granted that the student can first develop perception of the word from visual stimuli alone with a little auditory reinforcement. Only later is the student permitted to learn to write and by that time the words "have become vague, meaningless objects."

Myers (1978) presents a review of the literature of the Fernald technique reporting on the distinguishing features of the technique and research data. A table reports the success of the Fernald technique in fifteen research reports. Myers (1978) concludes that while "there is no conclusive evidence which totally supports or rejects Fernald's method," more research is needed to define who can benefit most from the method and it should be used only when needed and when it will be most effective. "Dr. Grace Fernald may not have developed a flawless method," Myers (1978) states, "but perhaps she was the prototype of the precision teacher who clinically evaluates a child's learning position and then tries to teach from there." N. Dale Bryant (1965) listed five principles of remedial instruction. Bryant was concerned with the dyslexic child who has "specific, severe disability in word recognition (dyslexia) ... usually resistant to standard remedial procedures.... Dyslexia cases can learn to read, but only if the teacher recognizes the nature and extent of the child's difficulties and uses procedures appropriate for dealing with those difficulties." Bryant's principles are an application of principles of learning to the specific problems experienced by cases of reading disability. These principles can also be used with students who are not dyslexic. These learning principles, Bryant (1965) states "are not a method of remediation, but are, instead, a partial framework on which effective remediation can be built. Several principles are common to all efficient learning. They are emphasized … because the learning difficulties of dyslexic children necessitate close adherence to general learning principles."

Close examination of Bryant's principles of remediation reveals that 44 years after Fernald developed her technique Bryant provides validation of her procedures. Bryant's (1965) remedial principles are:

1. "Remediation should initially, focus on the simplest, most basic perceptual-associational elements in reading: perception of details within the Gestalt of words and association of sounds with the perceived word elements." The student with dyslexia does not easily make generalizations. The remediation must focus on the student's problems and simplify the work to avoid confusion and basic perceptions and associations are over-learned. One of the problems the student has is perceiving and remembering a detailed picture of a word. Students use minimal cues such as the general shape of the word, its length or its first letter. "Calling attention to the details within a word is an important aspect of remedial teaching. Writing or even tracing the word is useful not only because of possible kinesthetic-tactile facilitation of memory, but perhaps more important, because the child's attention is called to each letter then the word." A second problem is associating sounds with letters and perceiving word parts. "The letter should be presented as part of a word and the sound should be quickly blended to produce the word." The child should, therefore, practice with words rather than individual letters. "Every word that is written should be pronounced aloud so that the student practices sound symbol association." "Always the pronunciation should be correct, aloud (so you know it is correct), and immediate. If the child ever falters, the word should be pronounced for him."

2. "Perceptual and associational responses should be over learned until they are automatic." The student needs to develop quick, appropriate responses and not need to consciously try to find the appropriate response. The student needs to over learn the basic skills and practice with complex words. "The teacher should not encourage laborious sounding out." Easy tasks should be used initially so that recognition becomes fast. As the student makes progress more diffi-

cult tasks should be introduced until the student can make the associations quickly in even very difficult words.
3. The teacher should plan the experiences and adjust the presentation of instructional tasks and materials based on student performance so that "the child is correct in nearly all of his responses" whether they are made silently or aloud. "Incorrect responses can produce negative learning and confusion, as well as damage the confidence and motivation of the student." Learning is based on stages of correct responses with immediate knowledge that the answer is right. "Any remedial session in which the child is allowed to make ... incorrect responses, particularly when he thinks even for a minute that they may be correct is damaging to the child."
4. When two associations are mutually interfering, one of the associations should be over learned to the automatic level; the second association should then be over learned to the automatic level; the first association should be reviewed; the two associations should be integrated using tasks that show the difference between the two; and the teacher should gradually help the student automatically associate and discriminate the interfering associations. For example several vowel sounds associated with a letter can cause problems. "If the teacher can stabilize the discrimination of each letter and the correct association of a short vowel sound with the appropriate sound, most of the confusion can be eliminated." The student can process the skill he/she knows well and go on to learn situations when the vowels have long or short sounds. Review the short "a" vowel sounds so the student knows that a word will have a short "a" vowel sound, then go on to short "o" to establish both associations.

"Once basic skills are stabilized at an automatic level, routine remedial procedures using small steps and lots of reading will take a dyslexic child the rest of the way to adequate reading achievement."
5. "There should be frequent reviews of basic perceptual, associational, and blending skills, and as rapidly as possible these reviews should involve actual reading." It is suggested that frequent assessment of student problems and progress be made so that teaching can be adjusted to student needs.

Fletcher (1960) states that when the Fernald technique is used students do not have comprehension problems because students select words they already know and use orally. When book reading begins students need emphasis on word meaning.

Bond, Tinker, and Wasson (1979) describe methods of treating reading disability including the Fernald technique, stating that clinicians report moderate success with the Fernald technique with cases of extreme disability. "When used by experienced clinicians, the Fernald method is undoubtedly successful. In the early stages it tends to be time consuming.... But other methods require long periods of instruction also when dealing with extreme disabilities. So the time factor hardly can be termed a drawback." Fernald attributed the success of the method to the kinesthesis, but there are other important features which lead to success when the method is implemented by an experienced clinician:

> The Fernald technique teaches left to right direction of word perception, the visual form of words, skill in phonics (including syllabication and the equivalent of consonant substitution) and use of context clues for identification and recognition of words (without phonics instruction). Add to this, the child is strongly motivated by working with materials interesting to him. Although the kinesthetic aspect of this method may be very important for certain visually handicapped and neurologically impaired children and certain children with visual-perceptual or visual-processing difficulties, it should be noted that ... [the other by-product skills] are inherent to the method when properly taught. It is doubtful that kinesthesis alone is responsible for the success of the method, but rather kinesthesis in combination with a sound, well-balanced program for teaching word perception in remedial instruction.

Students not only learn word recognition because the Fernald technique, Bond, Tinker, and Wasson (1979) state, "stresses vocabulary and concept development, and comprehension."

Adelman and Taylor (1986) state that "throughout all ... phases the emphasis is on (a) clarifying intrinsic reasons for pursuing learning activities and overcoming problems, (b) providing meaningful opportunities for learners to make personal and active choices from among a variety of options, and (c) involving learners in evaluating how well their intrinsic objectives are being met." Adelman and Taylor (1986) also describe the value of the Fernald technique by stating that the steps Fernald developed "provide a framework for working out novel and personalized learning and practice activity. They demonstrate ways to provide structure (support and guidance) and feedback to maximize the type of learning and feelings of satisfaction and increased competence that are prerequisites to maintaining what is learned."

Johnson (1966) states that one characteristic of dyslexia is the difficulty associating meanings and associating spoken words with printed words. Roberts and Coleman (1958) state that tracing and kinesthetic techniques have helped severely disabled readers successfully overcome blocks to reading. Roberts and Coleman (1958), Johnson (1963), and Morris (1958) state that this type of approach provides students with multi-sensory (visual-auditory, kinesthetic-tactile) stimulation in a highly structured approach which helps them attend to and complete the task they are presented with. The approach provides students with a most helpful setting for concentration on and attention to learning. Students master print which represents the student's own language, ideas and interests. Students progress from something they know and can deal with effectively to learning something new, the association with the printed form of ideas and oral vocabulary. Johnson (1966) states that once students have started "on their paths to mature reading through tracing words in order to learn them, many nonreaders have moved gradually on to become quite facile, mature readers." Johnson (1966) describes the refinements of Fernald's technique for use with dyslexic or severely disabled readers, stating that specific tracing (VAKT) and kinesthetic (VAK) techniques are the results of the refinement. No change was made in Fernald's original approach or in the learning activities but "the specific steps to be followed have been clarified and certain modifications made in terms of repeated experience with the technique." For example the dyslexic student with severe problems starts with the VAKT experiences. The less severely disabled student who cannot make or remember associations only by visual-auditory activities will start with the VAK experiences. Johnson (1966) describes the learning principles involved in the technique; the sequence of language development which occurs; the multi-sensory stimulation which is inherent in the technique; the development of a positive self concept for the students as a result of the technique; and the learning outcomes which result from the technique. Johnson (1966) concludes that "VAKT and VAK correctly used can help the dyslexic child move from failure to success in dealing with visual language symbols. As he does so, he loses the operational characteristics of a dyslexic and develops at least the "outward appearance" of a normal reader." Success replaces failure. The student is guided "toward better thinking, organization of ideas … and no longer sees himself as a failure … he loses his fear of setting goals…—goals which involve academic achievement … and ultimately he is able to learn and retain words in the way others have been doing all along."

Annotated Bibliography

Adelman, Howard S., and Taylor, Linda. *An Introduction to Learning Disabilities*. Glenview, IL: Scott Foresman, 1986, pp. 282–298.
    This text defines and discusses learning disabilities. "Fernald's Techniques in their Motivational Context" describes the technique and explains how student motivation is maintained to maximize learning.

Anderson, Rose G. "A Note on a Case of Spelling Disability." *Journal of Applied Psychology* 22 (April 1938): 211–214.
    Reports on the use of the Fernald technique as highly effective when used for a student with spelling problems. An early report of the use of the technique outside of Fernald's Clinic School.

Ayers. J. "Tactile Functions, Their Relation to Hyperactive and Perceptual-Motor Behavior." *American Journal of Occupational Therapy* 6 (1964): 6–11.
    Discusses the two cutaneous systems that function in humans, stating that tactile

discrimination may counteract some of the hyperactivity caused by the protective system. Perhaps this may explain why Fernald found success with hyperactive students.

Ayres, Leonard P. *Measurement of Ability in Spelling: Educational Monograph.* New York: Russell Sage Foundation, 1915.

   Discusses a project to identify commonly used words and evaluate success in spelling through writing.

Baker, Georgia Pitcher, and Raskin, Larry M. "Sensory Integration with the Learning Disabled." *Journal of Learning Disabilities* 6 (December 1973): 645–649.

   Describes case studies using the Fernald technique, stating that the rate of learning increased when tracing was used.

Blair, Glenn Myers. *Diagnostic and Remedial Teaching: A Guide to Practice in Elementary and Secondary Schools.* New York: Macmillan, 1968.

   Describes the Fernald Technique, stating it is used with considerable success in cases of spelling disorders. States that the tracing and pronouncing insures appropriate associations. Cites case studies stating that learning rate increases with the use of tracing.

Bond, Guy L., Tinker, Miles A., and Wasson, Barbara B. *Reading Difficulties: Their Diagnosis and Corrections.* Englewood, NJ: Prentice-Hall, 1979.

   This text on reading problems describes the Fernald Technique, evaluating its effectiveness and stating why it is successful. A good starting point for a study of the Fernald Technique.

Bryant, N. Dale. "Some Principles of Remedial, Instruction for Dyslexia." *Reading Teacher* 18, no. 7 (April 1965): 567–572.

   Lists and discusses five learning principles for effective remedial instruction for dyslexic students. States this is not the description of an approach, but the basis on which to build effective instruction. This validates Fernald's Technique.

Cawley, J.F., Goldstein, H.A., and Burrow, W.H. *The Slow Learner and the Reading Problem.* Springfield, IL: Charles C. Thomas, 1972.

   Describes the Fernald Technique and discusses its use.

Chale, Jeanne S. *Learning to Read: The Great Debate*, New York: Harcourt-Brace, 1996.

   Describes the Fernald Technique, presenting a discussion of experimental studies that show the effectiveness of the technique in using oral language to teach written language using writing and tracing.

Charuk, John M. "The Effects of Visual-Haptic Training on Reading Achievement." Unpublished Ph.D. diss., University of South Carolina, 1973.

   Studied the effectiveness of multi-sensory or inter-modal training and conventional approaches over a six week period with 72 fourth grade disabled readers. Concluded that the multi-sensory approach was beneficial resulting in significant differences in all skills areas.

Fernald, Grace M. "Certain Points Concerning Remedial Reading as It Is Taught at the University of California." *Education* 67 (March 1947): 442–458.

   Fernald responds to a critique of the technique by Helen M. Robinson providing details of the technique's use.

Fernald, Grace M. *Remedial Techniques in Basic School Subjects.* New York: McGraw-Hill, 1943; Austin, TX: Pro-Ed, 1988.

   This is the detailed discussion of the Fernald Technique and its use for reading, spelling, arithmetic, and writing problems. Case studies and materials are presented. This is the source book for the Technique.

Fernald, Grace M., and Keller, Helen B. "The Effects of Kinesthetic Factors in the Development of Word Recognition in Cases of Non-Readers." *Journal of Educational Research* 4 (December 1921): 355–377.

   Describes the kinesthetic method used with students who were unable to recognize words after one or more years of classroom teaching. This is an early discussion of the Fernald Technique.

Fletcher, Lillian G. "Methods and Materials for Teaching Word Perception in Corrective and

Remedial Cases." In *Sequential Development of Reading Abilities (Supplementary Education Monograph No. 90)*. Helen M. Robinson, ed. Chicago: University of Chicago Press, 1960, pp. 46–50.

Describes methods of word recognition, stating that when Fernald's method is followed students do not have comprehension problems because words are learned in story writing and students select the words they want to learn.

Frierson, Edward C. "Clinical Education Procedures in the Treatment of Learning Disabilities." In *Educating Children with Learning Disabilities*. Edward C. Frierson and Walter B. Barbe, eds. New York: Appleton-Century-Crofts, 1967, pp. 478–488.

Describes the Fernald Technique, stating that the learning disabled student often benefits from a multimodality approach.

Gates, Arthur I. *The Improvement of Reading: A Program of Diagnostic and Remedial Methods*. New York: Macmillan, 1947.

Describes the Fernald Technique, presenting the advantages and disadvantages if the technique is correctly used. Calls the technique highly successful.

Gillepsie-Silver, Patricia. *Teaching Reading to Children with Special Needs: An Ecological Approach*. Columbus, OH: Bell and Howell, 1979, pp. 343–346.

Describes the Fernald Technique, citing research supporting its effectiveness and success. This is a textbook providing a good review of the technique.

Hamilton, Andrew. "They Think with Their Hands." *The Rotarian* 74 (April 1949): 32–34.

Praises the Fernald Technique after viewing a demonstration. A lay person's perspective.

Hewlett, Frank M. "A Hierarchy of Educational Tasks for Children with Learning Disabilities." *Exceptional Children* 31, no. 4 (December 1964): 207–214.

Describes the Fernald Technique as a program organized at an exploratory level in which students are given highly reinforcing means for learning words which provides visual, auditory, and kinesthetic cues. States that the Fernald is a highly successful approach for students with learning disabilities.

Johnson, G.O. *Education for the Slow Learners*. New Jersey: Prentice-Hall, 1963.

A discussion of methods for slow learners praising the use of a multi-sensory approach which helps students concentrate, stay on task because it is highly structured.

Johnson, Marjorie Seddon. "Tracing and Kinesthetic Techniques." In *The Disabled Reader*. John Money, ed. Baltimore: Johns Hopkins University Press, 1966, pp. 147–160.

Discusses tracing and kinesthetic techniques to help dyslexic students. Describes the Fernald Technique and discusses the adaptation VAKT and VAK approaches. Provides references to research.

Kaluger, G. and Kolson, C.J. *Reading and Learning Disabilities*. Columbus, OH: Merrill, 1969, pp. 263–267.

A text that describes the Fernald Technique.

Kottmeyer, William. *Appraisal of Current Methods of Direct Promoting Growth in Word Perception in Elementary Grades*. Chicago: University of Chicago Press, 1945.

Presents a brief critique of the Fernald Technique. This is a difficult to find and little known reference.

McCarthy, William, and Oliver, Joan. "Some Tactile-Kinesthetic Procedures for Teaching Reading to Slow Learning Children." *Exceptional Children* 31 (April 1965): 419–421.

States the Fernald Technique helps students overcome negative emotional reactions to reading instruction and books. Refers to research done by Cruickshank, Strauss and Lehtinen using kinesthetic techniques with brain injured students.

Meyers, C.A. "Reviewing the Literature on Fernald's Technique of Remedial Reading." *Reading Teacher* 31 (1978): 614–619.

This is a review of studies describing the effectiveness of the Fernald Technique.

Morris, J. "Teaching Children to Read." *Educational Research* (1958): 38–39.

Discusses the structured nature of multi-sensory approaches which help students concentrate and attend to the reading task.

Myers, Patricia I., and Hammill, Donald D. *Methods for Learning Disorders.* New York: John Wiley and Sons, 1969, pp. 152–161.

    This textbook presents a detailed description of the Fernald Technique citing research, advantages and disadvantages of the technique. A good starting point for an understanding of Fernald's work.

Ofman, L., and Schalwitz, M. "The Kinesthetic Method in Remedial Reading." *Journal of Experimental Education* 31 (1963): 319–320.

    Discusses the use of the kinesthetic approach with cases of reading disability. Describes the approach and its application.

Roberts, R.W., and Coleman, J.C. "Investigation of the Role of Visual and Kinesthetic Factors in Reading Failure." *Journal of Educational Research* 51 (1958): 445–451.

    States the approach is highly successful for severely disabled readers, but is not recommended for general classroom use. The use of tracing and kinesthesis helps students overcome blocks to learning to read.

Robinson Helen M. "Appraisal of Current Practices Relating to Poor and Disabled Readers: Appraisal of Methods of Teaching Non Readers and Pupils Who Make Slow Progress in Learning to Read in the Primary Grades." In *The Appraisal of Current Practices in Reading.* William S. Gray, ed. Chicago: University of Chicago Press, 1946, pp. 130–149.

    Presents a critique of the kinesthetic method describing Fernald's approach listing its disadvantages. Ends by stating that in spite of its limitations, the method is different from other methods usually used and students who fail with other methods "will be encouraged" when they find they can learn some words.

    See Fernald's response above.

Smith, D.E., and Carrigan, P.M. *The Nature of Reading Disability.* New York: Harcourt Brace and World, 1959.

    A text on reading problems that gives an overview of causes and remediation.

Note: Little biographical material about Grace Maxwell Fernald (1879–1950) can be found; however, here are several sources:

1. Barchas, Cecile. "Grace Fernald as Remembered by Cecile Barchas 55 Years Later." *History of Reading News* 21, no. 2 (Spring, 1998).
2. Barchas, Jack D. "Grace Fernald: A Remembrance by a Student." *History of Reading News* 21, no. 2 (Spring, 1998).
3. Irving, Paul. "Grace Maxwell Fernald (1879–1950): A Biographical Sketch." *Journal of Special Education* 4 (Summer/Fall 1970): 258–259.
4. Sullivan, Ellen, B. Dorcus, Roy M. Allen, M. Bennet, and Louis K. Koontz. "Grace Maxwell Fernald, Psychology: Los Angeles." University of California: In Memoriam, 1950.

The Gillingham-Stillman Approach and the Orton-Gillingham Approach

The Orton-Gillingham approach is a multi-sensory method designed to help students with language disabilities gain success in decoding and comprehension.

The Gillingham-Stillman Approach is based on the work of neuropathologist Samuel Torrey Orton (1879–1948) who Myers and Hammill (1969) state studied the "effects of brain injury on language function in adults and applied his findings to the study of developmental language disorders in children." Orton described a specific reading disability found in children with average or above average intelligence who had very poor auditory and visual memory but with normal visual and auditory acuity. These students, Orton (1929, 1937) states, had not suffered a brain injury but showed symptoms similar to adults who suffered a loss of language. These students do not establish hemispheric dominance in particular brain areas and have developmental language disabilities such as reading disability. Masland (1989) states that "Orton observed a disorder, or rather a peculiarity, of cerebral dominance leading to interference in left-right discrimination in many dyslexic children. Furthermore, family histories often revealed unusually large numbers of relatives with mixed cerebral dominance, left-handedness, or various forms of language disability. Because of the frequency of poorly established cerebral dominance associated with disturbances of left-right discrimination and sequencing problems, developmental variations in hemisphere preponderance were thought to be underlying causes in many cases."

Orton did not agree with Hinshelwood's (1917) theory that word-blindness was the result of a congenital malformation of the left angular gyrus or the word storage area of the brain. Masland (1989) states that evidence at the turn of the last century indicated that "the two hemispheres of the brain were identical at birth and were equally capable of normal language function." Myers and Hammill (1969) state that Orton based his theory on brain research done in the late 19th century by Broca and Bouillard. Orton (1937) stated that one side of the brain controls all the language processes and the same side is dominant for manual skills. Orton also believed that reading was a complex activity that involved several areas of the brain. Orton (1929, 1937) lists:

(a) confusion of lower case letters
(b) difficulty reading short palindromical words such as "was" and "saw"
(c) reversal of parts of words or whole syllables
(d) ability to read from the mirror and often the ability to do mirror writing. Orton used the information about brain injured adults to explain similar symptoms found in children who had language disabilities. These children, Orton (1937) stated, displayed "motor intergrading" or mixture of left and right sidedness for hand, eye and foot preference. If they showed confused dominance in motor function they also had a comparable mixture in the language areas of the brain. Orton (1937) states that there was no straightforward evidence, however, that this mixed dominance is caused by "transmission of a better brain structure ... due to size and is probably dependent more on numbers of nerve cells, richness of their interconnections, and abundance of blood supply." This superiority can be transmitted to one complete hemisphere, to one or more areas of one hemisphere or to the cortex of one hemisphere and to other areas of the other hemisphere "leading to difficulty in establishing a complete unilateral superiority in function or a use."

Myers and Hammill (1969) state that Orton explained the symptoms observed in alexic children stating that reversals and mirror reading occur because where associations of written words and their meaning are stored in the dominant brain hemisphere, mirror copies are stored in the non-dominant hemisphere. Orton (1928, 1929) states that:

> if these opposite engrams are not elided through establishment of consistent selection from one hemisphere, we would expect ... errors or confusion in direction.... The immediately successive linkage between sensory stimulus (printed word) and its meaning (concept) which constitutes reading could not take place. Reading disability is probably dependent on failure of constant selection of either the right or the left sensory record in the brain.

Myers and Hammill (1969) state that Orton's theory explaining reading difficulty is open to question. Masland (1989) states that late 20th century research produced three discoveries that strengthen Orton's concept and also make it necessary to modify them. The first discovery is that while

> the left cerebral hemisphere is "dominant" for handedness, language, and similar special activities, the right hemisphere is superior in pattern recognition orien-

tation, and other functions requiring parallel processing. These findings ... strengthen Orton's concepts since the establishment of an association between the visual stimulus, most effectively analyzed in the right hemisphere and the linguistic counterpart, stored in the left hemisphere, could easily be seen to predispose to uncertainty of cerebral dominance, especially if the language function were poorly established in the left or if the spatial skills in the right hemisphere were strongly developed.

The second discovery stems from the work done by Geshwind and Levitsky (1968) who found "significant structural asymmetries" in the human brain. Masland (1989) states "specifically, the planum temporale—that area most directly involved in the analysis of auditory input—is ordinarily much more highly developed on the left than on the right. These findings establish a structural basis for the physiological asymmetry noted by Orton." The third and most important finding from work done by Galaburda and Kemper (1979), Galaburda (1993), Geshwind and Galaburda (1984) is that "anatomically observable irregularities occur in the development of the brains of dyslexic individuals." In a sense, these findings support the view of Hinshelwood that dyslexia is attributable to a developmental anomaly. On the other hand, they also support the view of Orton, that "other areas would be competent to assume the function." Masland (1989) states that the significance of Galaburda's and Kemper's findings is

> not the presence of minor irregularities of development on the left side, but rather the evidence of compensatory over growth on the right. As a result, instead of the usual asymmetry, the planum temporale on the two sides is more likely to be equal in the brains of dyslexic individuals. This finding provides anatomical support for Orton's thesis of confusion of cerebral dominance. It provides similar support for his observation that many individuals who are deficient in language skills are superior in other areas of intelligence. These new findings highlight the fact that the brilliant insights presented by Orton as a result of his meticulous case studies are still illuminating the discoveries of those who continue his work.

Gearheart (1973) states that Orton related hemispheric dominance to the "quality of the brain structure, meaning number of brain cells and abundance of blood supply to the brain not brain size." Ansara (1982) lists the premises on which Orton based his neurological ideas about developmental dyslexia that resulted in diagnostic and educational practices:

1. Orton (1937) believed that language was an evolutionary function of the human brain;
2. He believed that brain functions were related to the structure of the brain;
3. Orton (1937) believed that one hemisphere of the brain became dominant for language functions;

4. Orton (1928) stated that while the two hemispheres of the brain work together "at the first and second levels of cortical elaboration, at the third or associative level, there is an important difference between them";
5. Orton (1937) believed that information learned about cases of acquired alexia provided evidence that auditory and visual association at the third cortical level was essential for reading to take place;
6. Orton (1930, 1937) stated that evidence from cases with speech and language disabilities where a genetic link was found showed that there was "a neurological basis for the variations" in growth and development that showed up as reading and other language disabilities.

Children with severe reading, spelling, and writing disabilities, Orton (1928 and 1928) states, had severe problems in the ability to recognize and remember the spatial orientation and sequencing of letters in syllables and words which was the result of an innate problem in the associative process. These students also had reversal and sequencing problems and mixed left right laterality in motor behavior.

Ansara (1982) states that Orton's twenty-five years of research in specific language disabilities resulted in the following:

(a) a neurological explanation of the disabilities that rejected the earlier views that they were caused by an obscure brain defect or brain damage; (b) a view of specific reading disability as a maturational deviation in language development; (c) the identification of developmental reading disability (dyslexia) as differentiated from a reading disability caused by mental deficiency, brain damage, or primary emotional disturbance; (d) the identification of distinct syndromes in specific language disabilities; (e) principles of diagnosis and remediation for the disabilities.

The Gillingham-Stillman Approach or Orton-Gillingham-Stillman Approach is often called the Alphabetic method. Orton (1937) cautioned teachers that there was no general formula that can be applied to all students with learning problems because factors such as heredity, environment, emotional reactions, educational needs, and neurological status influence each individual. Orton (1937) stated that it cannot be emphasized enough that each student is an individual and must be treated as such. He also stated that this is difficult because "we are all prone to search for a simplified and universally applicable formula, but no such general 'method' can be defined ... and any attempt to apply such a blanket prescription without thorough diagnosis of the individual case would assuredly lead to error or misguided effort." Orton stressed the use of an approach for remediation to be used judiciously based on the needs of the individual student. Orton (1937) states "we have tried to avoid over standardization lest the procedure become too inflexible and be looked upon as a routine method applicable to all cases ... which would be clearly unwise in view of the wide variation of symptomatology and hence in training needs which these children exhibit."

Orton studied 1000 students from preschool to college age in public, private, and parochial schools in a ten year period. The approach was developed as a result of these case studies. The research and practice that form the basis of the approach are described in the *Gillingham Manual: Remedial Training for Students with Specific Disability in Reading, Spelling, and Penmanship* by Anna Gillingham and Bessie W. Stillman that first appeared in 1936 at Orton's request. Gillingham had been a teacher, administrator, and school psychologist in the 1920s at the Ethical Culture Schools in New York. She took a leave of absence, Myers and Hammill (1969) report, to become a Research Fellow at the Neurological Institute at Columbia-Presbyterian Medical Center to work with Orton. Gillingham was asked to develop teaching procedures for students with learning disabilities. Gillingham consulted with her colleague Bessie W. Stillman to develop the teaching manual to "organize remedial techniques consistent with his working hypothesis..." according to Gillingham (1960). In 1936 Gillingham and Stillman traveled to Honolulu, Hawaii, to develop a teaching program based on their manual. The Orton-Gillingham-Stillman Approach is intended for students in grades three through six with a supplementary section for working with students in high school and with adults.

Orton's research identified the problems faced by dyslexic student as: spatial orientation in reading and writing; memory instability for symbols; sound-symbol association; and sequencing. Gillingham and Stillman (1997) stated that the approach starts with the individual sounds and uses them to build words. This approach also

> builds a close association or link between what the student sees in print (visual), what the student hears (auditory), and what the student feels as he or she makes the sounds of the letters and writes (kinesthetic—large muscle movements, and tactile—sensations in the mouth and on the fingertips). Each phonogram (representation of a sound) is presented through each association (visual, auditory, and kinesthetic), and each association is linked and presented simultaneously. The individual pathway makes an imprint on the brain and thus strengthens the learning process.

Ansara (1982) summarizes the approach by stating that in the Orton-Gillingham Approach

> the building of the visual-auditory (grapheme-phoneme) associations and fixing them firmly in memory is constantly reinforced kinesthetically in the initial learning stage through speech and movement (tracing and/or writing). The pupil sees, hears, says, traces and writes. He produces the sound for the letter he sees or the letter for the sound he hears. He reads, he spells, he writes.

The phoneme and grapheme is given to or said for the student and the student is not asked to select or analyze similarities or differences within a group of sounds or words. Students do not segment words on their own. Ansara (1982) states that the Orton-Gillingham Approach provides dyslexic students who cannot locate the distinctive features of written language, with awareness of these language features which will help them develop the ability to detect these distinctions and eventually learn to decode words easily.

Gillingham (1960) stated that phonics should help students learn the structure of language for reading and writing and lessons should provide lively, fun activities. Gillingham (1960) believed that students need to build the letter sounds into words as if building a wall of bricks. She advised that the teacher "begin at the beginning" to follow the steps in the procedure because they are "a series of logical sequences, the omission of any one of which will jeopardize the complete success of the procedure." Gillingham (1960), Myers and Hammill (1969), and Gearheart (1973) state that there are six basic patterns for the integration of associations. These patterns are:

1. V-A Translation of visual symbols into sounds, either vocalized or not vocalized
2. A-V Translation of auditory symbols into visual images
3. A-K Translation of auditory symbols into muscle response for speech and writing
4. K-A Movement of a passive hand with help to produce a letter form to lead to the naming or sounding of the letter
5. V-K Translation of a visual symbol into muscular action of speech and writing
6. K-V The muscular "feel" of the speaking or writing of a letter to lead to the association with the appearance of the letter.

A language triangle is a visualization of the technique. The associations are linked and presented at the same time. "The individual pathway makes an imprint on the brain and strengthens the learning process."

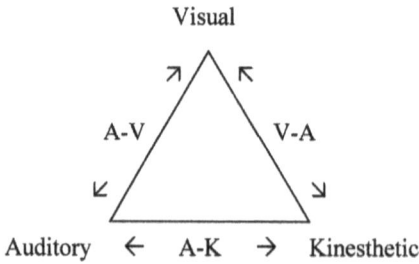

Very specific materials are used: phonics drill cards for reading and spelling, phonetic word cards, graded phonetic stories, and syllable exercises. Letters are always introduced by a key word which the student must say whenever the letter is shown such as:

a	apple	t	top	i	itchy
b	bay	h	hat	j	jam
k	kite	m	man	p	pan
f	fish				

Students then learn to recognize and explain the differences between vowel and consonant sounds. Consonants are printed on white cards and vowels are printed on salmon cards. Writing is taught in a very specific way for all the letters. Gearheart (1973), Gillingham (1960), and Myers and Hammill (1969) explain that the writing procedure includes the use of cursive writing rather than manuscript. The steps in writing are:

1. The teacher writes the letter;
2. The student traces the letter;
3. The student copies the letter;
4. The student writes the letter without the copy;
5. The student writes the letter with eyes averted {/NL}

Cursive writing helps prevent letter reversals and makes writing quicker and easier because the letters are linked together. Handwriting is a separate subject.

Spelling, Gillingham (1960), Myers and Hammill (1969), and Gearheart (1973) state, should be taught several days after sound blending in reading has been started. Gillingham (1960) calls the spelling procedure a Fourpoint Program because each point helps establish visual-auditory-kinesthetic associations Orton suggested. Saying the name of each letter out loud as it is written reinforces Orton's idea. This procedure is oral with written spelling done at the same time. Gillingham (1960) called this S.O.S. or Simultaneous Oral Spelling to teach sound and letter form connections. S.O.S. is used to teach non-phonetic words by impressing letter sequences and is suggested as a procedure during the entire remedial program. The spelling sequence consists of the teacher saying the word slowly overemphasizing the phonetic parts and making sure the pupil hears all the letters in the word. After the word is said a second time, the student

1. Repeats the word;
2. Names the letters in the word;
3. Writes the word, naming each letter as it is written; and
4. Reads the word that has just been written.

Once students have learned to read and write three-letter phonetic words, Gillingham (1960) suggests that sentence and story writing should start. The first stories are composed of three-letter words learned by the student, but Gillingham (1960) states that these early stories do not inhibit the student's writing. The teacher assists when asked to sound out words the student has problems with.

The concept of syllables is taught as detached syllables such as **pel** and **vil** before teaching read words separated into syllables. Gillingham (1960) states that three or four times a week the syllable concept is taught in the following way:

1. Teach the recognition of nonsense syllables printed on orange cards;
2. Pupils read multi-syllable real words printed with syllables separated;
3. Words are typed with syllables separated far apart and then the syllables are cut out. Words are built using these parts. As part of spelling, students learn that words of one syllable ending in **f, l** or **s** after one vowel usually end in double **f, l** or **s**. These words are written on yellow cards. Students place the accent on each syllable of a word in succession and decide which trial produces a word he/she recognizes.

Gillingham (1960) emphasizes that reading is taught by using Drill Cards that form a word be placed on a table. The student is asked to provide the sounds of the letters repeating the sounds again and again to increase speed and smoothness. Help is given if necessary. Yellow word cards are turned over one at a time by the teacher and the student reads them as fast as possible. Correctly read words are put in one pile and incorrectly read words are put in another pile. The teacher does not correct the student and self-correction is not encouraged yet. The schedule of a lesson, according to Gillingham (1960) consists of

1. Daily review of Drill Cards;
2. Graphing of phonic words—once a week;
3. Spelling—Four Point Program—twice a week;
4. Dictation—twice a week (on own stories are dictated);
5. Reading whatever Little Stories are available (stories on tag board using combinations of words students can read and spell used to develop skill). Students are not encouraged to guess at words in context. Drill on sight words is done at the end of the time when phonograms have been learned. Books are gradually introduced to read at home. Skills are built gradually. Progress is evaluated on an ongoing basis using a Phonics Proficiency Scale developed by Gillingham to

test mastery. Once phonics and reading are improved oral spelling is worked on through ear training. Practice and the feel of words are key elements of the approach. The teacher, Gillingham (1960) states, must be skilled in the use of the materials and able to judge progress.

Ansara (1982) states that even after fifty years of implementation of the Orton-Gillingham-Stillman Approach, not enough research comparing it with other approaches exists. There are many anecdotal and case reports; however, there are few research reports.

Beth Slingerland (1976) developed a detailed program adapting the Orton-Gillingham-Stillman Approach for use in primary grade classrooms and group screening tests. Slingerland was trained by Gillingham. Slingerland's research used pre and post test intervention, but does not compare the approach with other strategies.

Two research studies, conducted over 40 years apart, that show how Orton's theories can be successfully applied to instruction and the success of the Orton-Gillingham Approach are Marion Monroe's (1932) *Children Who Cannot Read* and Kline and Kline's (1975) "A Follow-up Study of 216 Dyslexic Children."

Monroe (1932) used the diagnostic and instructional strategies developed during work done in the 1920s in Iowa with Orton to measure the results of remedial reading intervention done under varying conditions for varying lengths of time for 235 children and adolescents attending the Chicago schools. Remediation was adjusted according to subtype identified during evaluation such as visual, auditory or motor. Final information on 189 students taught in two experimental groups and one control group was reported. The students in the three groups had similar reading profiles before intervention. Group I received the instructional procedures outlined by Orton and were taught by trained tutors. Group II received instruction at school from classroom teachers trained in the Orton procedures. Group III, the control group received remediation at school with unspecified "ordinary" methods. Pre and post testing was done on all three groups. Group I made an average gain of 1.39 years after 6.8 months of instruction. Group II made a .79 improvement and group III gained only .14. Monroe's (1932) study, Ansara (1982) states, is an early study showing the effective application of Orton's procedures in a school and clinical setting.

Kline and Kline (1975) followed 216 dyslexic students referred over a four year period because of severe learning disabilities. All were given the same psycho-educational tests and the Orton-Gillingham Approach was advised for those diagnosed as having developmental dyslexia. In the follow-up 92 students received Orton-Gillingham Approach tutoring in a clinical setting and 29 students received language experience or whole-word approach intervention in a school setting and a few students did not receive any intervention. Post treatment evaluation indicated that 95.7 percent of the clinic group compared to 44.8 percent of the school group showed overall improvement. Marked improvement with reading achievement at grade level was found for 46.7 percent of the clinic group as compared to 13.8 percent of the school group. Dramatic improvement for reading above grade level over a short period of intervention was found for 17.5 percent of the clinic group compared to 3.4 percent of the school group. Only 4.3 percent of the clinical group failed to show any improvement compared to 49 percent of the school group.

Ansara (1982) states that this study demonstrates the success of the Orton-Gillingham Approach. More research is needed.

Wepman (1960) stated that since auditory discrimination of most sounds is not achieved until the 3rd grade, he questions Gillingham's statement that all students use the kinesthetic auditory strategies used in the Orton-Gillingham Approach because of spelling problems students demonstrate. Strang, McCullough and Traxler (1967) state that if students are able to learn by the whole word approach it should be used. Gates (1947) lists the following problems associated with the Orton-Gillingham Approach:

1. Procedures are rigid;
2. Students are not interested because no real reading is done;
3. There is a delay in using meaningful material;
4. Labored reading with much lip movement develops as a result of the approach. Gates (1947) also states that the students for whom the approach is intended pay too much attention to small details. Frostig (1966) states that students with auditory perception problems should not be taught by the Orton-Gillingham Approach because it accentuates this problem and could be discouraging for these students.

Harris and Sipay (1985) state that for some remedial students who have not made progress with other approaches, rapid progress is made with a systematic phonic method when the instruction is matched to the student's ability to master the skills taught. Gearheart (1973) states that the Orton-Gillingham Approach has had good results and should be used for "those cases where other factors indicate the likelihood of its success."

Orton (1966) states that several teachers who were associated with Orton and Gillingham have developed programs and materials which are adaptations of the Orton-Gillingham Approach applying the ideas Orton developed.

Chall (1967) cites research comparing phonic approaches such as the Orton-Gillingham Approach with other approaches for disabled readers, concluding that phonic approaches, if correctly used, produce good results. "Progress may be slower with a phonic emphasis than with other approaches, but the end results are probably more satisfactory."

Orton (1946) concluded that while his approach is not perfect for all reading problems, it has worked. "I do not claim them to be a panacea for reading troubles of all sorts, but I feel that we understand the blockade which occurs so frequently in children with good minds and which results in the characteristic reading of the strephosymbolic type of children."

Orton (1966) presents a summary of the approach developed by her husband and Gillingham, stating it contains the following elements: the use of "kinesthetic elements to reinforce the visual-auditory language associations and to establish left to right habits of progression ... teaching the phonic unit in isolation but giving special training in blending; introducing the consonants and the short sounds of the vowels first and building three-letter words with them for reading and spelling; programming the material in easy, orderly, cumulative steps."

Annotated Bibliography

Ansara, Alice, "The Orton-Gillingham Approach to Remediation in Developmental Dyslexia." In *Reading Disorders: Varieties and Treatments*. R.N. Malatesha and P.G. Aaron, eds. New York: Academic Press, 1982, pp. 409–433.
  Presents a discussion of Orton's research, diagnoses and remediation procedures and Gillingham's contribution in the form of the Teaching Manual. Provides a detailed discussion of the approach and research about the approach. A comprehensive discussion with references.
Chall, Jeanne S. *Learning to Read: The Great Debate*. New York: Harcourt Brace, 1967, 1984, 1996, pp. 168–170, 176–177.
  A brief discussion of the Orton-Gillingham Approach with research described.
Eisenson, J., Auer, J., and Irwin, J.V. *The Psychology of Communication*. New York: Appleton-Century, 1963.
  Discusses hemispheric dominance stating that the non-dominant hemisphere has a generalized, but important function. States that the left hemisphere is responsible for language no matter what the hand preference and that language and handedness are independent.
Frostig, Marianne. "The Needs of Teachers for Specialized Information on Reading." In *The Teacher of Brain Injured Children*. W.M. Cruickshank, ed. New York: Syracuse University Press, 1966.
  Evaluates the Orton-Gillingham Approach stating that the approach would be discouraging for pupils with auditory perception problems.
Galaburda, A.M. "Developmental Dyslexia: Current Anatomical Research." *Annals of Dyslexia* 33 (1983): 41–53.
  Describes brain research which focuses on the causes for dyslexia.
Galaburda, A.M., ed. *Dyslexia and Development: Neurobiological Aspects of Extra-Ordinary Brains*. Cambridge, MA: Harvard University Press, 1993, pp. 269–298.
  A collection of chapters by researchers examining the premise that dyslexia is a developmental set of brain diseases which causes other problems in behavior and learning. Chapter 14 by Steven C. Schachter discusses Orton's research on handedness and

speech problems. The whole volume is useful for understanding Orton's early research in light of 20th century research methods and technology.
Galaburda, A.M., and Kemper, T.L. "Cytoarchitectonic Abnormalities in Developmental Dyslexia: A Case Study." *Annals of Neurology* 6 (1979): 94-100.
   A case study discussing irregularities in brain development of dyslexics.
Galaburda, A.M., LeMay, M., Kemper, T.L., and Geshwind, N. "Right-Left Asymmetries in the Brain." *Science* 199 (1978): 852-856.
   A discussion of research on hemispheric asymmetries. This is useful for understanding Orton's early speculations.
Gates, Arthur I. *The Improvement of Reading*. New York: Macmillan, 1947, pp. 494-497; 310-313.
   Describes the Orton-Gillingham Approach as based on word sounds. Discusses Orton's research on mixed dominance. Provides limited references.
Gearheart, B.R. *Learning Disabilities: Educational Strategies*. St. Louis, MO: Mosby, 1973, pp. 103-107.
   Provides a detailed discussion of the Gillingham-Stillman Approach with a useful list of references. This textbook is a good starting point on the approach.
Geshwind, N. "Cerebral Lateralization, Biological Mechanism, Associations, and Pathology II; A Hypothesis and a Program for Research." *Archives of Neurology* 42 (1985): 521-552; II 42 (1985): 634-654.
   Continues to discuss lateralization of the brain providing medical evidence for a hypothesis about its cause and a discussion of further research.
Geshwind, N. "Why Orton Was Right." *Annals of Dyslexia* 32 (1982): 13-39.
   Provides a discussion of Orton's research and current research and practice in the field of dyslexia concluding that Orton would approve of the Orton Society's intent to fulfill his mission to diagnose and remediate dyslexia.
Geshwind, N., and Galaburda, Albert, M., eds. *Cerebral Dominance: The Biological Foundations*. Cambridge, MA: Harvard University Press, 1984.
   A collection of articles on brain asymmetry research providing information about this field and its implications for learning. Provides the late 20th century research findings for Orton's early research.
Geshwind, N., and Levitsky, W. "Human Brain: Left-Right: Asymmetries in Temporal Speech Region." *Science* 161 (1968): 186-187.
   Discusses asymmetries in the structure of the brain that provide modern evidence for Orton's early research.
Gillespie-Silver, Patricia. *Teaching Reading to Children with Special Needs: An Ecological Approach*. Columbus, OH: Bell and Howell, 1979, pp. 347-348.
   This textbook presents an overview of the Gillingham-Stillman Approach.
Gillingham, Anna, and Stillman, Bessie W. *The Gillingham Manual: Remedial Training for Students with Specific Disabilities in Reading, Spelling, and Penmanship*. Cambridge, MA: Educators Publishing Service, 1960; 1997.
   This is the complete guide to the Orton-Gillingham-Stillman Approach providing detailed instructions, a bibliography, glossary and a guide to pronunciation symbols. A very comprehensive, detailed work. Provides the history of and rationale for the approach.
Gillingham, Anna, and Stillman, Bessie W. *Remedial Work for Reading, Spelling, and Penmanship*. New York: Hackett and Wilhelms, 1936.
Harris, Albert J., and Sipay, Edward R. *How to Increase Reading Ability: A Guide to Developmental and Remedial Methods*. New York: Longman, **1985**, 1987, 1988, pp. 267-271, 437-438.
   A brief description of the approach in this basic text is a good starting point under "Word Recognition Skills and Problems." Describes the approach as based on sounding and blending. Provides a brief discussion of brain research and reading.
Hinshelwood, James. *Congenital Word Blindness*. London: Lewis, 1917.
Hinshelwood, James. *Letter-, Word- and Mind-Blindness*. London: Lewis, 1900.

These two publications are the earliest works on reading problems stating that the cause of congenital word blindness was a deficiency in the local area of the brain in which visual images are stored. Orton was familiar with Hinshelwood's theory that dyslexia is caused by a developmental anomaly; however, Orton believed that other areas of the brain could assume the function. Orton disputed Hinshelwood's theory that word blindness was the result of a malformation of the angular gyrus—the storage area of the brain. Late 20th century research by Galaburda supports Hinshelwood's hypothesis by stating that irregularities occur in the brains of dyslexics. These are interesting early works worth reading along with the modern research.

Johnson, Peter, and Allington, Richard. "Remediation." In *Handbook of Reading Research Volume II.* Rebecca Barr, Michael L. Kamil, Peter B. Mosenthal, and David Pearson, eds. Mahwah, NJ: Erlbaum, 1996, pp. 987, 998, 999.

Discusses the approach under The Emergence of Remedial and Special Education and Consequences of Remedial Instruction providing brief information in the form of a critique.

Kline, Carl L., and Kline Caroline L. "Follow-Up Study of 216 Dyslexic Children." *Bulletin of the Orton Society* 25 (1975): 127–144.

This follow-up study of 216 dyslexic students referred for severe learning problems over a four year period. All the students were given the same psycho-educational battery of tests and diagnosed with developmental dyslexia. The Orton-Gillingham-Stillman Approach was recommended.

Masland, Richard L. "Foreword." In Samuel Torry Orton, *Reading, Writing and Speech Problems in Children and Selected Papers.* Austin, TX: Pro-Ed, 1989, pp. vii–x.

Provides a discussion of Orton's writings and research with an interesting discussion of brain research done more than fifty years after Orton. Updates the research on dyslexia and states how the new research agrees and parallels Orton's work. This reprint of Orton's work from the 1920s through the 1940s has a biography by Mrs. Orton and a bibliography of Orton's work is a valuable primary source.

Monroe, Marion. *Children Who Cannot Read.* Chicago: University of Chicago Press, 1932.

Reports the success of Orton's diagnostic and remediation procedures with results for 189 students in two experimental groups and one control group. The same diagnostic procedures were used for all three groups. This is an early study demonstrating that Orton's teaching procedures could be used in clinical and school settings. Unfortunately Monroe did not report what strategies were used to teach the control group.

Myers, Patricia I., and Hammill, Donald D. *Methods for Learning Disorder.* New York: John Wiley & Sons, 1969, pp. 199–215.

Describes the work of Orton and Gillingham under the heading of Phonic Systems. Provides a comprehensive discussion of Orton's research and the approach. A good starting point with a bibliography.

Orton, June L. "The Orton-Gillingham Approach." In *The Disabled Reader.* John Money, ed. Baltimore: Johns Hopkins University Press, 1966, pp. 119–145.

Provides a history, conceptual background, diagnostic considerations, the method used by Orton and Gillingham, the Gillingham-Alphabetic Method, and a conclusion describing the value and use of the approach.

Orton, Samuel Torry. *Reading, Writing, and Speech Problems in Children and Selected Papers.* New York: Norton, 1937; Austin, TX: Pro-Ed, 1989.

This primary source contains Orton's works on learning disorders. This primary source provides Orton's pioneering articles.

Orton, Samuel Torry. "The Sight Reading Method of Teaching Reading as a Source of Reading Disability." *Journal of Educational Psychology* 20 (February 1929): 135–143.

This is a critique of the sight word method stating that it causes reading problems for students. This method is not useful for all students and an alternative method is needed.

Orton, Samuel Torry. "Some Disorders in Language Development of Children." *Language in*

Relation to Psycho-Motor Development. Langhorne, PA: Child Research Clinic of the Woods Schools, 1946.

    A report of twenty years of research and practice done by Orton.

Slingerland, Beth H. *A Multi-Sensory Approach to Language Arts for Specific Language Disability Children: A Guide for Primary Teachers.* Cambridge, MA: Educators Publishing Service, 1976.

    This is a detailed manual adapting the Orton-Gillingham Approach for use by primary grade teachers.

Strang, Ruth, McCullough, C., and Traxler, A. *The Improvement of Reading.* New York: McGraw-Hill, 1967.

    States that if students can learn from the whole-word strategy they should not be taught by any other approach.

Wepman, Joseph M. "Auditory Discrimination, Speech, and Reading." *Elementary School Journal* 60 (1960): 245–247.

    This is a critique of the Orton-Gillingham Approach stating that auditory discrimination of most sounds is not mastered until the end of the third grade, and therefore, other methods can be used for remediation.

The Language Experience Approach

The language experience approach connects all of the language arts using the student's life experiences as the foundation for reading material. Harris and Hodges (1995) state that the language experience approach is "an approach to language learning in which students' oral compositions are transcribed and used as materials of instruction for reading, writing, speaking, and listening."

Tierney and Readence (2000) state that teachers provide language-rich experiences and "respect and use children's language as a basis for expanding children's literacies." Teachers have recognized the value of using students' language and experiences as the basis for beginning reading instruction since the early part of the 20th century. Tierney and Readence (2000) state that many researchers such "as E. Huey (1908), R. Gans (1941), L. Lamoreaux and D.M. Lee (1943), J. Sullivan (1986), R. Van Allen (1976), and R. Stauffer (1970) have suggested an experience-based approach to teaching reading."

This method became known as the language experience approach. Research states that children have an innate capacity for acquiring and using language and this ability, Tierney and Readence (2000) state,

> can and should be directed toward the acquisition of reading abilities. To this end, proponents of the language experience approach and of the role of the environmental-print advocated taking advantage of the experiences that children bring to reading. By conveying these experiences through language, children can move back and forth from oral to written expression. From this foundation, children develop quite naturally the ability and interest to read widely, deeply, and fluently.

Roach Van Allen's language experience approach originated from work done with the San Diego, California, Department of Education. This research identified language experiences that are the most valuable for the development of reading abilities. Allen (1976) identified three strands of experience that contribute the most to reading:

1. Experiencing communication in a variety of situations;
2. Studying many types of communication;
3. Relating communication of others to one's self.

Allen lists 20 experiences, under these strands which are part of four types of activities which are a vital part of the language experience of all students: Language Recognition, Language Acquisition, Language Production, and Language Prediction. Activities include: oral sharing of ideas, listening to and reading language of others, recognizing high frequency words. Allen (1976) provides a detailed description of how to use language experience as the basis for reading instruction. The program can be used with students of all ages and provides a complete language arts program for working with students in a variety of ways such as whole class instruction, small group instruction, and individualized instruction.

Allen's (1976) work is based on the belief that students learn to read and write in the same way they learn to speak. Teachers should, Allen and Allen (1976) suggest, acknowledge that language acquisition skills vary among students based on factors such as age, geographic region, socio-economic group, and habit. It is also important to realize that language changes, Tierney and Readence (2000) state, "slowly, continuously, creatively, and personally." Allen (1976) states that "the one big responsibility of a teacher at any level" is to help students to use and adopt as part of their behavior several ideas about themselves and language. Allen and Allen (1966) state that students should learn that:

> What I can think about, I can talk about.
> What I can say, I can write (or someone can write about).
> What I can write, I can read.
> I can read what others write for me to read.

In this framework students learn to discuss experiences, write about experiences, read their own stories, and read material written by others. Students learn to express themselves in a variety of ways, learn new words, practice known words, do research on a topic of interest, and write about experiences. All the language arts are learned and practiced.

Allen's ideas about the approach have grown and changed and in 1976 he restated the 1966 ideas:

> I can think about what I have experienced and imagined.
> I can talk about what I think about.
> What I can talk about I can express in some other form.
> Anything I can record I can tell through speaking or reading.
> I can read what I can write by myself and what other people write for me to read.
> As I talk and write, I use some words over and over and some not so often.
> As I talk and write, I use some words and clusters of words to express my meanings.

As I write to represent the sound I make through speech, I use the same symbols over and over.
Each letter of the alphabet stands for one or more sounds that I make when I talk.
As I read, I must add to what an author has written if I am to get full meaning and inherent pleasure from print.

Many of the activities suggested by Allen are used in the balanced reading program (used in the New York City public schools.) Allen suggests the use of learning centers which help students develop self-expression through creative writing and drama; language study through editing material, practice of skills, and dictation; time for thinking about or reflecting on language through puppets, leisure reading time and listening activities. Allen has suggested an arts and crafts center, a discovery center connected to science, a writing/publishing center where students can write, edit and publish their work. The other activities should include a place to relax and read many kinds of print material, a center with activities for grammar and word study skills.

Allen did not originate the language experience approach, but his work helped its "emergence, popularity and evolution" according to Tierney and Readence (2000). Sampson, Allen and Sampson (1991) continue to examine and refine the approach in light of changing student needs and populations. They discuss the use of computers as part of the approach, describing specific software and the implementation of the approach with children for whom English is not their first language.

The language experience approach based on the work of Roach Van Allen has evolved and adapted to change. It is not *the* perfect approach and should be used a part of a total literacy program; however, it is an approach that works for many children.

Russell G. Stauffer (1970) states that the language experience approach is "The Eclectic Approach to Reading Instruction" because it takes the most effective practices from many sources and uses them in "a functional communication-oriented way." Stauffer (1970) states that the basis of the language experience approach lies in the relationships which exist among language, experience, and thought and the communication skills of reading, writing, listening and speaking. The approach uses the linguistic, intellectual, social, and cultural wealth children bring with them to school. "By focusing on language as a means of communication, the transfer from oral language usage to written language is made functionally. Reading does become talk written down." Stauffer writes that phonics is taught from the children's phonological wealth and used to decode each child's oral language as it is written and then to decode the writing of other authors. Phonics is taught from the very start of instruction. The syntax and semantic skills of each child are used in a communication context. Stauffer also states that the use of word order and word meaning is taught in a practical and useable way to make word recognition and retention easier. Once basic reading skills have been learned, Stauffer says, the critical reading-thinking skills are taught through Directed Reading-Thinking Activities in groups emphasizing intellectual and affective interaction; students self-select books according to interests and tastes and sharing is done in individualized instruction. The library is used for selecting books. Group instruction which encourages interaction of the minds and individualized instruction emphasizes student actions are accomplished. Stauffer writes that the library becomes the center of the reading program and communication of what is read completes the merging of all the language arts.

The program, according to Stauffer, begins with extensive reading in grade one and develops as the central activity because students read a great deal and "convert their interests into tastes as they prepare" reports to share. Students learn many ways to share their work and the importance of preparation. All the activities encourage reading that is positive and a regard for reading as a way to gain knowledge. Creative writing helps to make writing, spelling and creating functional. Children need good handwriting so that others can read their work and spelling is developed for the same reason. The program offers many opportunities to write creative, original responses. Where formal spelling is introduced, the ability developed in creative writing becomes more fine tuned and functional.

Stauffer states that the highest compliment a teacher can have is to be called "an eclectic teacher" because he/she is one who "takes advantage of good practices whenever she/he can ... regardless of their source." The best title for the language experience approach is "The Eclectic Approach to Reading" because the best practices are used regardless of their origin and they are used in a "functional communication-oriented way."

The program Stauffer describes consists of dictated experience stories, the use of word-banks, and creative writing. Children become good users of the classroom and school library as a source of inspiration and information. For Stauffer, the approach "represents an integration of conditions all of which are rightly a part..." of the language arts and reading instruction. The language arts include reading, writing, listening, and speaking and are based on the social-personal reason for communication. The experience part of the approach, according to Stauffer, includes a student's "perceptual and conceptual world ... interests, curiosities, and creativity, culture and ... capacity to adjust, learn and use ... these experiences."

Spache and Spache (1977) state that the language experience approach is "unique among all other approaches in its rejection of ... dichotomizing of language development into separate and unrelated learnings." The approach

The Language Experience Approach 101

affirms that the language arts are interrelated and interdependent. Children learn to read from past and present experiences with language, not only from books. Spache and Spache (1977) state "the language experience method begins where the child is in terms of ... ability to think with words and stimulates simultaneously ... language development in all media of expression and reception, in the hope of leading toward the ultimate goal of ability to read the writing of others."

The language experience approach starts in the early days of school with group dictated chart stories. The children, Stauffer (1970) states, share an experience such as a tour of the school or the examination of a familiar object or a picture. This stimulates discussion among the children and leads to a chart story recorded by the teacher. The children listen to the teacher read the chart they have dictated. Then the children read the chart and learn the words. The students draw pictures. Stauffer (1970) states that after reading the story together and identifying individual words by matching them on cards or pointing to the word the teacher says, stories are then duplicated for each student so that words can be identified individually. Stauffer (1970) suggests that students keep a file of words they have learned from group or individual stories. After writing group chart stories for several weeks the teacher groups students according to social maturity and language ability. Students in groups and the teacher create more dictated stories. Individual students also dictate stories. Spache and Spache (1977) state that a rotating schedule of teacher-student conferences provides opportunities for sharing stories, illustrating stories, gaining practice with word cards to learn new words, and using books to research new ideas and new words.

Stauffer (1970) states that students use word-banks to keep the words they have learned to read by sight. The word-bank contains words from dictated stories. Each known word is written on a card and filed in a box. These words are a resource and a dictionary. Stauffer (1970) states that the words should be used for creating new stories, learning word attack skills, categorizing words and finding these known words in print in other contexts.

Phonics instruction, Spache and Spache (1977) state, develops from a "say-it, see-it" foundation in which students learn to represent by letters the sounds they want to put on paper. Instruction comes from pupil need, not by deductive teaching, Spache and Spache (1977) state. Phonic elements may be taught to individuals or small groups emphasizing the change from sounds said to written form. Phonics and spelling are taught in the same sequence as in a basal reader program, but in small groups with emphases on words students use in their stories. These skills are taught when they are needed by the children as a result of their own work. Spache and Spache (1977) and Stauffer (1970) state that resource materials such as dictionaries, lists of words that have a common phonic or spelling element, and other sources of words are provided. Children's books are provided to encourage recreational reading.

Stauffer (1970) states that creative writing is an important part of the program. The compositions that Stauffer (1970) states "reflect a child's own choice of words, ideas, order, spelling and punctuation" constitute creative writing. Using word-bank words to create sentences and then stories stimulates writing, spelling and word recognition. Students use paper with space for an illustration. Stauffer (1970) states that when students construct sentences using their word-banks every day they meet success and are motivated to write. Students begin to use words that are not in their word-banks. First students ask the teacher for the needed words, but as they gain confidence they try to spell the words themselves. The teacher helps with phonics and spelling instruction as it is needed. Students learn to apply phonics and spelling generalizations correctly. The teacher should also provide straightforward, simple instructions for writing. Stauffer (1970) suggests providing paper with room for a picture and wide lines so that the writing is kept on the lines and is uncluttered. Students should, Stauffer (1970) suggests, write about what they want or the teacher can suggest a topic. Students should do their best writing using their best handwriting and should be told to spell the needed words as best they can. The teacher should be available to help when needed and encourage students by asking questions. Stauffer (1970) cautions that the writing should be "a perfection of pupil expression unhampered by adult standards. Improved standards will follow automatically." When the teacher circulates among the authors offering help and encouragement the writing will be productive.

Stauffer (1970) believes that the students' creative writing is writing for personal or social reasons. Students will write to communicate to themselves and to classmates. Motivation for writing includes current events, invitations and thank you notes, science, social studies and health activities, holidays, trips, cooking, and events at home. Stauffer (1970) provides a list of topics and suggestions for using science activities as the bases for creative writing.

Tierney and Readence (2000) state that Stauffer's language experience approach provides "a comprehensive, well-articulated ... experience-based language arts program for initial reading." They state that the approach can be used with students of all ages and varying abilities. The approach provides many activities for use with reading, writing, listening and speaking and can be used as a supplement or in place of a complete reading program, according to Tierney and Readence (2000).

Research on the language experience approach is extensive. Spache and Spache (1977) state that interest in the language experience approach was so widespread that it was included in six of the First-Grade Reading Studies. The First-Grade Reading Studies consist of twenty-seven studies completed during 1964 and 1965 comparing basal readers with the Initial Teaching Alphabet, the language experience approach, the linguistic approach, and the phonics approach. The studies were commissioned by the U.S. Office of Education Cooperative Research Branch in 1964.

Spache and Spache (1977) examined the one to three year studies of the First-Grade Studies and state that the research supports the following conclusions:

1. The language experience approach must be recognized as an effective, independent method for developing primary grade reading development;
2. The language experience approach may be used in addition to the other methods, but should not only be thought of as such;
3. The language experience approach is just as efficient in developing reading skills for middle-class students as the basal approach;
4. The language experience approach becomes equally effective as the basal approach after two years of instruction for bilingual and students from low-socio-economic backgrounds;
5. The language experience approach appears superior in measures of quality, quantity, and diversity of vocabulary in writing even in the first grade;
6. Students trained in the language experience approach begin to show broader background knowledge in social studies, science and spelling in the second grade than students who were taught by the basal approach;
7. Teachers who were trained to use the language experience approach appear to use a less authoritarian classroom climate and continue to use the approach even when test results are inconclusive and they go back to using basal readers;
8. The language experience approach has been used successfully with children and adults who are developmental or remedial readers, with content area reading, and with those for whom English is a second language.

Specific research studies done by Kendrick and Bennett (1967) analyzed the results to examine low socio-economic and high socio-economic backgrounds and differences between male and female subjects. Stauffer and Hammond (1967) found that the students taught by the language experience approach excelled in nine of ten areas in which significant differences were found. Directed Reading-Thinking activities were used to introduce students to basal readers after they learned 150 vocabulary words. Stauffer and Hammond (1967) state that success was influenced by these activities. Vilscek,

Morgan, and Cleland (1966) report success for their subjects in content area reading and spelling. Harris and Serwer (1966) studied inner city students and found that they did not do as well as expected with the language experience approach, but the experimental group scored higher than other classes in the same grade in the same school. McCanne (1966) found that the bilingual population did not succeed in the approach.

Studies that followed students into the second grade included Kendrick and Bennett (1967) who found that results from the first grade were different in the second grade. In the second grade writing words for boys in the low socio-economic group continued to be a success. Stauffer and Hammond (1967 and 1969) found that girls from the language experience group did better in paragraph meaning, spelling, content area concepts, oral reading rate and accuracy, in the mechanics of writing. Boys from the basal reader group continued to excel in arithmetic computations.

Harris and Morrison (1969) found that after three years there was no significant difference in test scores yet teachers who learned and used the language experience approach exhibited interesting characteristics. Teachers became more creative, less structured in classroom management, and continued to use the approach in addition to the basal approach.

Cramer (1970) found that the language experience approach helped pupils spell regular and irregular words better than pupils who were taught by the basal approach.

The research on pupil writing ability done by Sulzby and Teale (1991) indicates that the language experience approach theory described by Stauffer (1970) and Allen and Allen (1966) can be considered "an important precursor to current research in emergent writing." These early researchers pointed to the importance of children understanding that print was composed by "real people like themselves; and that children themselves could produce such writing speech."

It appears that current research on oral and written language in the emergent stages reinforces what Stauffer and Allen found to be true about the language experience approach during the 1960s and 1970s.

Annotated Bibliography

Allen, R.V. *Language Experiences in Communication.* Boston: Houghton-Mifflin, 1976.
 An in-depth description of the language experience approach providing the rational and strategies for using the approach.
Allen, R.V., and Allen, C. *Language Experience Activities.* Boston: Houghton-Mifflin, 1976.
 This is a classroom activities guide to over 250 activities to use in learning centers.
Allen, R.V., and Allen, C. *Language Experience in Reading, Levels I, II, III.* Chicago: Encyclopedia Britannica, 1966.

This resource provides suggestions for teaching activities and resources for using this approach in the classroom.

Almy, Millie, Chittenden, Edward, and Miller, Paula. *Young Children's Thinking*, New York: Teachers College Press, 1966.

This classic provides an extensive examination of cognitive development in the early childhood years.

Boney, C. Dewitt. "Teaching Children to Read as they Learned to Talk." *Elementary English Review* 16, no. 4 (April 1939): 139–141.

Discusses what we now think of as a whole language approach to teaching reading. Provides a basis for the language experience approach.

Bruner, Jerome S., Oliner, Rose R., and Greenfield, Patricia M. *Studies in Cognitive Growth.* New York: Wiley, 1966.

Provides a comprehensive examination of cognitive development.

Burrows, Alvina T., Jackson, Doris C., and Saunder, Dorothy C. *They All Want to Write.* New York: Holt, Rinehart & Winston, 1964.

An examination of strategies for teaching writing providing the practical interpretation of theory. This is a classic in the field.

Cramer, Ronald L. "An Investigation of First Grade Spelling Achievement." *Elementary English* 47 (February 1970): 230–240.

Reports that students taught to read with the language experience approach were better at spelling regular and irregular words in the first grade than pupils taught to read by the basal approach.

Dewey, John. *Democracy and Education.* New York: Macmillan, 1916.

This is a good foundation for understanding the importance of the language experience approach because Dewey describes many aspects of classroom practice based on using direct experience to facilitate learning. This is a classic and has been used as the basis for many methods in all content areas.

Gans, Roma. *Guiding Children's Reading through Experience.* New York: Teachers College, 1941.

Based on Dewey's philosophy this classic explains the value of using direct experience to teach young children to read.

Hahn, Harry T. "Three Approaches to Beginning Reading Instruction—ITA, Language Experience, and Basal Readers-Extended into Second Grade." *Reading Teacher* 20 (May 1967): 711–715.

Provides an examination of the first-grade studies extended into the second grade. Compares the three approaches and discusses the research results.

Hale, Maryanne. "Linguistically Speaking: Why Language Experience?" *Reading Teacher* 25 (January 1972): 328–331.

Describes seven linguistic reasons why the language experience approach should be used with beginning readers. States that the relationship between oral language and reading is part of the linguistic definition of reading. The language experience approach is also based on this relationship. States that the language experience approach is a linguistic based approach because the connection between oral and written language is the basis for early reading instruction.

Hale, Maryanne. *Teaching Reading as a Language Experience.* Columbus, OH: Merrill, 1970.

This book explains the use of language experience approach strategies in the classroom.

Harris, Albert J., and Morrison, Coleman. "The Craft Project: A Final Report." *Reading Teacher* 22 (January 1969): 335–340.

Reports the research done with the CRAFT Project-Comparing Reading Approaches in First-Grade Teaching with disadvantaged children. Examines the language experience approach and the basal method used with students in grades one, two, and three. Provides six recommendations for working with students.

Harris, Albert J., and Serwer, Blanch L. "Comparing Reading Approaches in First Grade Teaching with Disadvantaged Children." *Reading Teacher* 20 (May 1967): 698–703.

Examines the language experience approach, basal approach, and I.T.A. Reports the research results.

Harris, Theodore L., and Hodges, Richard E., eds. *The Literacy Dictionary: The Vocabulary of Reading and Writing*. Newark, DE: International Reading Association, 1995.

A dictionary providing definitions of terms related to literacy.

Hildrith, Gertrude H. "Experience Related Reading for School Beginners." *Elementary English* 42 (March 1965): 280–284, 289.

Describes the importances of relating early reading instruction to student's real experiences.

Huey, E. *The Psychology and Pedagogy of Reading*. New York: Macmillan, 1908.

An early 20th century examination of the theory and practice of reading instruction. Discusses the relationship between direct experience, oral language, and reading.

Kendrick, William, and Bennett, Clayton L. "A Comparative Study of Two First-Grade Language Arts Programs Extended into Second-Grade." *Reading Teacher* 20 (May 1967): 747–755.

Compared the results of using the language experience approach and the basal approach using the gender and socio-economic status of the pupils.

Lamoreaux, L., and Lee, D.M. *Learning to Read Through Experience*. New York: Appleton-Century-Crofts, 1943.

Describes strategies the classroom teacher can apply for teaching reading using student's oral language and direct experiences.

Lee, D.M., and Allen, R.V. *Learning to Read Through Experience*. New York: Appleton-Century-Crofts, 1963.

This is a lengthy overview of the language experience approach providing some guidance for the implementation of the approach.

McCanne, R. "Approaches to First Grade English Reading Instruction for Children from Spanish-Speaking Homes." *Reading Teacher* 19 (May-June 1966): 670–675.

Discusses problems encountered using the language experience approach with students for whom English is a second language.

Sampson, M., Allen, R.V., and Sampson M. *Pathways to Literacy: A Meaning-Centered Approach*. New York: Holt-Rinehart & Winston, 1991.

A textbook on teaching reading using the language experience approach. Provides theoretical foundation and practice application of the approach.

Spache, George D., and Spache, Evelyn, B. *Reading in the Elementary School*. Boston: Allyn & Bacon, 1977, pp. 122–140.

This textbook presents a discussion of the language experience approach providing research findings, method, and materials. A very good bibliography is included.

Stauffer, R.G. "The Effectiveness of Language Arts and Basic Reader Approaches to First Grade Reading Instruction-Extended into Third Grade." *Reading Research Quarterly* 4 (Summer 1969): 468–499.

This research report describes in detail the investigation of 22 third grade classes in three towns comparing the Basic Reader Approach and the Language Arts Approach. Followed students into the third grade and found that on the Stanford Achievement tests in content areas, and on the Gilmore oral test language experience students achieved significantly higher scores than the basic reading approach students.

Stauffer, R.G. *The Language Experience Approach to Teaching Reading*. New York: Harper and Row, 1970.

This is the guidebook for the language experience approach providing an in-depth discussion of the basis for the approach and how to implement it.

Stauffer, R.G. "Libraries and Reading Instruction." In *Directed Reading Maturity as a Cognitive Process*. New York: Harper and Row, 1969.

Describes the use and importance of libraries in the language experience approach. Tells how to use libraries for reading and writing instruction.

Stauffer, R.G., and Hammond, W.D. "The Effectiveness of Language Arts and Basic Reader

Approaches to First Grade Reading Instruction—Extended into Second Grade." *Reading Teacher* 20 (May 1967): 740–746.

Reports the results of a two year study examining the difference between the effects of two methods of instruction in grades one and two. The language experience approach and the basal reader approach were compared. Concludes that while both approaches are effective, the language experience approach was the most effective based on standardized test results. One exception was male arithmetic achievement. Non standardized test results which examined writing skills also indicated that the language experience approach produced superior achievement.

Stauffer, R.G., and Hammond, W.D. "The Effectiveness of Language Arts and Basic Reader Approaches to First-Grade Reading Instruction—Extended into Third Grade," *Reading Research Quarterly* 4 (Summer 1969): 468–499.

Describes a shift to basal readers from the language experience approach as soon as students have mastered an adequate reading vocabulary. This moves the language experience approach towards the use of basal readers as students become more able readers using their own stories.

Sullivan, J. "The Global Method: Language Experience in Content Areas." *Reading Teacher* 39 (1986): 664–669.

Describes the application of the language experience approach strategies to content area instruction.

Sulzby, Elizabeth, and Teale, William. "Emergent Literacy." In *Handbook of Reading Research, Volume II*. Rebecca Barr, Michael L. Kamil, Peter Mosenthal, and P. David Pearson, eds. Mahwah, NJ: Erlbaum, 1991, pp. 727–757.

Discusses the language experience approach in the section on "Definitions of Writing" providing research references to state that "the language experience approach was an important precursor to current research in emergent writing."

Tierney, Robert J., and Readence, John E. *Reading Strategies and Practices: A Compendium*. Boston: Allyn & Bacon, 2000, pp. 198–226.

Provides a discussion of the language experience approach as developed by Allen and Stauffer. Includes an annotated bibliography.

Vilscek, Elaine C., Cleland, Donald L., and Bilka, Loisanne. "Coordinating and Integrating Language Arts Instruction." *Reading Teacher* 21 (October 1967): 3–10.

A report of a longitudinal study of the effect of basal approach and language experience approach on urban pupils. Concludes that the language experience approach pupils demonstrated superiority in comprehension in the content areas in the second grade.

Vilscek, Elaine, Morgan, Lorraine, and Cleland, Donald. "Coordinating and Integrating Language Arts in the First Grade." *Reading Teacher* 201 (October 1996): 31–37.

Describes the positive use of the language experience approach as part of an integrated language arts curriculum for first grade students.

Young, Virgil M., and Young, Katherine A. "Special Education Children as the Authors of Books." *Reading Teacher* 22 (November 1968): 122–125.

Reports on a 1965 to 1966 program with 12 special education students who wrote two "books" of stories as part of a year long language experience program to motivate, build spelling, reading and verbal skills and to teach the relationship between oral and written language. Concludes that the program was a success because students gained confidence and skill. Also reports that the approach was effective, but not a cure all. Teachers who involve students as active participants in learning receive positive learning results.

The Individualized Reading Approach

The individualized reading approach enables each student to make progress at his or her own pace using self-selected material from trade books based on interest and ability.

According to Harris and Hodges (1995) individualized reading is an approach which encourages students to select their own reading material from trade books and to move at their own pace. The "teacher adjusts instruction to student needs in small-group work and individual conferences." The approach was "developed in the 1950s as an alternative to basal reading programs." Burns, Roe and Ross (1996) state that there are seven characteristics of an individualized reading approach:

1. Self-selection—students select books that they are interested in and the teacher may offer suggestions; however, the final selection is the student's. The motivation is intrinsic because students read what they have selected. Each student is reading a different book which may or may not be about the same topic.
2. Self-pacing—students read at their own pace. No one is required to keep up with a group. Students may take as much or as little time as they need to finish a book.
3. Strategy and skill instruction—skills are developed either individually or in a small group depending on student needs. All word recognition and comprehension strategies are taught when the need arises.
4. Record keeping—the students keep track of the books they have read, new vocabulary words, and new strategies they have learned. The teacher must be familiar with the needs of each student and which books can be read independently, which need help from the teacher, and which are too difficult. The teacher must have read each book in the library of choices and must keep records of students' progress.

The Individualized Reading Approach   109

5. *Student-teacher conferences*—the teacher meets with each student on a regular basis to discuss progress, problems, and the current book.
6. Sharing activities—Bagford (1985) states that the teacher plans weekly time periods in which students share their activities with either a small group or the whole class. These sessions can be called "book auctions" in which students bid for the chance to read the book being discussed next. The student sharing is an "auctioneer" who motivates others to bid on his or her book.
7. Independent work—Bagford (1985) states that students do independent work rather than reading during a specific reading period with a group.

Hacker (1980) states that the exposure to a variety of literary genres helps students build schemata or a knowledge base about each type of literature to assist in dealing with each type of literature, developing better comprehension, and a large vocabulary. Bagford (1985) suggest that the choices help students learn that reading is fun. Students also develop greater fluency because they read at a comfortable level.

Organizing an individualized reading program requires, according to Draper, Schwietert and Lazar (1960) and Burns, Roe and Ross (1996), several procedures such as locating many books and other reading materials for the classroom library, becoming familiar with the needs and strengths of each child in the class, explaining to the students what the individualized approach is and how they will learn to read, and developing procedures for selecting and returning books, reading, record keeping, conferencing, and working independently.

The classroom library needs to be organized for easy selection. Color coding books according to level of difficulty can help students make selections among books they know they can read independently. Various forms can be duplicated to help students keep records of their reading. Burns, Roe and Ross (1996) suggest an interest inventory as a good starting point for book selection. An evaluation sheet can list title, author and evaluation (such as good, ok, bad) for primary grades and author, title, comments for the upper grades. Students also need a place to record new words and their meanings. Folders are suggested as a way of keeping all forms in one place and easy to locate.

Procedures for conferences must also be very specific so that teachers and pupils come prepared. The length of each conference, where it will take place and what will be discussed are important considerations. Conferences, Burns, Roe and Ross (1996) and Draper, Schwietert and Lazar (1960) suggest, should: (1) help the student select a book, (2) check comprehension, oral reading, skill development, and strategy use, (3) provide skill and strategy instruction and (4) help students learn how to share.

Individualized reading is a very big undertaking that requires a great deal of time and energy from the teacher and the students. It is a program that cannot be organized and fully implemented in one school year. A teacher should decide, Burns, Roe and Ross (1996) and Groff (1972) state, whether to implement it with part of the class at a time or as a part-time activity (for example, once a week) to make the procedure easier for all to handle. The children need to learn to work well independently and the teacher needs to learn to work well with individuals.

There are several advantages and disadvantages associated with the individualized reading approach. Draper, Schwietert and Lazar (1960), Burns, Roe and Ross (1996) and Blakely and McKay (1972) state that the advantages are:

1. The approach respects the individual child making provision for each child's individual differences;
2. The approach has built in motivation because the child is an active participant in the learning process which helps the student develop independence;
3. The approach does not compare students in a negative way;
4. The approach has built in increased student-teacher contact helping both to get to know each other and to work as a team;
5. The approach helps students learn the value of reading in a more authentic situations because they select their own material;
6. The approach provides more flexibility for the teacher to develop reading strategies for each student;
7. The approach minimizes the differences among students;
8. The approach lessens classroom management problems because everyone is engaged in meaningful activities;
9. The approach helps students grow personally;
10. The approach allows students and teachers to integrate the curriculum because all of the language arts are used and projects integrate other curriculum areas. Students read nonfiction and fiction. Creatively and critical thinking are developed.

Burns, Roe and Ross (1996) name the following as disadvantages:

1. The increased amount of record keeping for the teacher;
2. The need to have a large multilevel library which the teacher knows in depth;
3. Scheduling conferences and small group lessons may cause problems because class sizes may be large and other curriculum areas must be covered;
4. There is no sequential approach to teaching skills and strategies.

Many aspects of the individualized approach have been incorporated into other approaches providing students and teachers with some of the advantages of the approach without a commitment to the approach as the only way to teach reading.

Austin, Morrison, Morrison, Sipay, Gutmann, Torrant and Woodbury (1963) reported that observation of individualized reading raised questions such as:

1. Can instruction based exclusively on the individualized approach "succeed if used by teachers with only minimal pre-service and in-service education who are possibly unaware of the sequential development of skills constituting reading?"
2. Do teachers have "the knowledge, wisdom, and know-how" to cope with problems that arise during pupil-teacher conferences for which little advanced planning can be done?
3. How much control do teachers have over student book selections so that readiness instruction to meet the needs of each pupil can be done? "Observations made during the field study failed to alleviate this concern."

Spache and Spache (1977) state, "individualization demands a true recognition of individual differences in learning rate, learning modalities, and the child's actual functioning in the act of reading."

Research conducted on the results of the individualized reading approach reported by Spache and Spache (1977) provides objective information about the effects of the approach in classrooms. Vite (1961) examined seven controlled studies comparing the individualized approach with ability grouping. Three of the studies provide decisive test results in favor of ability grouping and four of the studies provided test results in favor of the individualized approach. Spache and Spache (1977) report that "test scores are inadequate in measuring many of the outcomes of a reading method ... most of the results of individualized reading ... cannot be evaluated in this fashion." Safford (1960) used local and national norms to examine the reading progress of pupils in seven classes using the individualized approach. The results indicated that students made less than expected progress and there was no significant advantage for average and superior students in the program. Johnson (1965) conducted a three year study with 28 first, second, and third grade classes comparing the individualized approach to the basal reading approach. Results favored the individualized approach at the end of the first and third grades using several ways to measure reading. Bond and Dykstra (1967) reported that two of the first grade classes in the cooperative reading research studies that used the individualized approach showed very positive feelings about reading as measured by an attitude scale; however, there was no significant difference in reading ability.

Harris and Sipay (1980) report that many research studies focusing on the individualized approach to reading are faulty. Duker (1968) stated that "much of the reported research suffers from poor research design, inadequate sampling, careless measurement and a biased attitude...." Smith (1965) states that "research on individualized instruction is not conclusive. Most studies have evolved from the desire to compare the relative effectiveness of the individualized plan and the group basal reading plan." Smith stated that more well controlled studies are needed to generate more definitive data. Smith found that the research studies presented two general conclusions:

1. Students and teachers using the individualized approach "work with higher interest than do those in groups with which they compared";
2. Students using the individualized approach read more books than students in the control groups.

Sartain (1969) examined research reports on individualized reading instruction and reported seven conclusions:

1. Individualized instruction "can be somewhat successful under certain conditions";
2. Individualized instruction "requires highly competent teachers";
3. Students develop favorable attitudes toward reading and like the personal attention of the pupil-teacher conference;
4. Students often, but not always, read more books;
5. Students with special needs and "less capable pupils" are likely not to be as successful as other pupils using the approach;
6. Teachers doubt the adequacy of skills learning because the individualized approach does not have a sequential skills program or "adequate opportunities for readiness"; and
7. Teachers reported a lack of time to provide individual conferences.

Harris and Sipay (1980) conclude that the individualized approach to reading can "produce excellent results where conditions are favorable." The characteristics of the program are useful for a recreational reading program and will probably ... be an integral part of the total reading programs in more and more schools."

Many of the strategies of the individualized reading approach can be found in the whole-language and integrated language arts approach. The use of literature instead of readers, discussions and response to literature, literature circles, flexible grouping, and the use of literature across the curriculum can be traced to the individualized approach to reading.

Annotated Bibliography

Austin, Mary C., Morrison, Coleman, Morrison, Mildred B., Sipay, Edward R., Gutmann, Ann R., Torrant, Katherine E., and Woodbury, Charles A. *The First R: The Harvard Report on Reading in Elementary Schools*. New York: Macmillan, 1963.

    This is a survey of elementary school reading programs based on a national study of one thousand school systems across the United States sponsored by Harvard University and the Carnegie Corporation. It described methods of teaching reading, professional, teacher development, the role of the administrator, and problems. In the chapter called "Providing for Individual Differences" the individualized reading approach is discussed. The theory and practice of the approach is described under the subheadings: number of volumes available, self-selection, conferences, development of reading skills, teacher's knowledge of book content and record keeping. The observers concluded that there were many advantages seen; however, they questioned whether the use of the approach by teachers with minimal pre-service and in-service training would cause problems. Teachers need knowledge of the sequential development of reading skills, wisdom, and know-how "to cope with the reading problems that arise at the individual conferences for which little, if any advanced planning can be done." The observers also questioned the "extent to which teachers control the reading selections ... to provide readiness instruction appropriate for each pupil..." as each progresses to more difficult materials.

Bagford, Jack. "What Ever Happened to Individualized Reading?" *Reading Teacher* 39 (November 1985): 190–193.

    Discusses research evidence on the value of individualized reading and suggests that teachers "resurrect some of the strengths of individualized reading of the 1960s." Suggests that a program of wide reading which includes individualized reading activities will improve fluency because the goals of reading are best achieved by a balanced program of "direct instruction and immersion in the total reading process." In this well balanced program, Bagford states, all students have scheduled time to select what they want to read and to practice the skills they have learned. "Goals of fluency, vocabulary development, enjoyment, and comprehension are promoted better when reading is experience in a more total form."

Blakely, W. Paul, and McKay, Beverly "Individualized Reading as Part of an Eclectic Reading Program." *Elementary English* 43 (March 1966): 214–219; In *Elementary Reading Today: Selected Articles*. W.H. Miller, ed. New York: Holt, Reinhart and Winston, 1972, pp. 111–120.

    Reports the results of research conducted during the 1962-1963 school year. Two hundred and fifty questionnaires were sent to grade four to six teachers in fifty Iowa school systems. The authors conclude that based on 111 responses "individualized reading procedures may enrich and strengthen an eclectic reading program."

Bond, Guy L., and Dykstra, Robert. "The Comparative Research Program in First Grade Reading Instruction." *Reading Research Quarterly* 2 (Summer 1967): 5–142.

    Discusses the first grade reading studies conducted in 1964–1965, describing the effectiveness of various approaches to early reading instruction including the individualized approach.

Burns, Paul C., Roe, Betty D., and Ross, Elenor P. *Teaching Reading in Today's Elementary Schools*. Boston: Houghton-Mifflin, 1996, pp. 343–353.

    Defines and presents characteristics of the individualized approach. Presents the purpose served by conferences with students and list advantages and disadvantages of the approach. Useful sources cited.

Burns, Paul C., Roe, Betty D., and Smith, Sandy. *Teaching Reading in Today's Elementary Schools*. Boston: Houghton-Mifflin, 2002, pp. 283–288.

    Provides an update on the individualized approach citing research comparing it to the literature-based approach.

Carlton, Lessie, and Moore, Robert H. "Individualized Reading." *NEA Journal* 53 (November 1964): 10–12; In *Elementary Reading Today: Selected Articles*. W.H. Miller, ed. New York: Holt, Reinhart and Winston, 1972, pp. 96–100.

Briefly answers 14 questions about individualized reading such as: what is individualized reading? when is the best time to begin an individualized reading program? and what are some of the outstanding advantages of individualized approach? No references are cited and answers to more questions could have been helpful.

Draper, Marcella K., Schwietert, Louise, and Lazar, May. *A Practical Guide to Individualized Reading for Teachers and Supervisors in the Elementary School*. Publication No. 40. New York: New York City Board of Education, 1960.

This curriculum bulletin was revised in 1963, 1968 and 1972. It was sent to all New York City classroom teachers. The authors clearly describe the ways to implement an individualized reading program, how to develop classroom strategies including group lessons, record keeping and small group lessons. A section on the theory includes the nature of learning, the nature of reading, the principles of skills development, and problems that might occur. There is a section on assessment and a discussion on using the approach with slow readers. An extensive bibliography is included. This is an excellent starting point for background on the individualized reading approach.

Duker, Sam. *Individualized Reading: An Annotated Bibliography*. Metuchen, NJ: Scarecrow Press, 1968.

Presents an extensive list of works on individualized reading at the time of publication. This is useful background information about the approach.

Groff, Patrick. "Helping Teachers Begin Individualized Reading." *National Elementary School Principal* 43 (February 1964): 47–50; In *Elementary Reading Today: Selected Articles*. Wilma H. Miller, ed. New York: Holt Reinhart and Winston, 1972, pp. 101–106.

Groff addresses 12 questions about individualized reading to provide teachers and administrators with help in planning and implementing and individualized program. A brief list of sources is provided for questions four and seven. Provides a list of answers to objections about the approach.

Hacker, Charles J. "From Schema Theory to Classroom Practice." *Language Arts* 57 (November/December 1980): 866–870.

States that students can read their own language patterns more easily than those in basal readers. The language experience approach is consistent with schema theory because it uses students' first-hand experiences and students have adequate schemata to understand the material. Students develop schemata for reading, including the concept that written words have meaning, from the language experience approach.

Harris, Albert J., and Sipay, Edward R. *How to Increase Reading Ability: A Guide to Developmental and Remedial Methods*. New York: Longman, **1980**, 1985, 1987, 1988, pp. 104–109.

Presents an overview of the individualized reading approach citing research about characteristics, strategies, and evaluation procedures. States that "large number of studies involving IDR have appeared, but many are faulty." Discusses the future of individualized instruction. A good introduction to the approach.

Harris, Sandra. "Bringing About Change in Reading Instruction." *Reading Teacher* 49 (May 1996): 612–618.

Discusses the problems teachers have when asked to adapt to a new approach to teaching reading. Discusses whole language and literature-based instruction, but the concepts apply to the individualized approach as well. Presents recommendations about adapting to change and an interesting list of resources.

Harris, Theodore L., and Hodges, Richard E. eds. *The Literacy Dictionary The Vocabulary of Reading and Writing*. Newark, DE. International Reading Association, 1995.

Defines the individualized reading approach and briefly describes it.

Jacobs, Leland. "Individualization Is Not a Thing." in *Individualizing Reading Practices*. Alice Mill, ed. New York: Teachers College, 1958, pp. 1–17; *TC Record* 59 (March 1958): 319–329.

The Individualized Reading Approach

Discusses the characteristics of the individualized approach stressing the need for skill development and time for recreational reading. Provides a clear discussion of the approach.

Jenkins, Marion "Self-Selection in Reading." *Reading Teacher* 11 (December 1957): 84-90.

Describes individualized programs in three schools as reported by principals who concluded that the individualized approach provided favorable results in students and teachers. No data is cited.

Johnson, Rodney H. "Individualized and Basal Primary Reading Programs." *Elementary English* 42 (December 1965): 902-904.

Describes a three year study of 28 first, second and third grade classes in Wisconsin schools using the individualized approach and the basal approach. Concludes that the individualized approach provided better results at the end of first and third grade as seen by scores on the Metropolitan Achievement Test.

Karlin, Robert. "Some Reactions to Individualized Reading." *Reading Teacher* 11 (December 1957): 95-98.

States that since the individualized approach eliminates the basal reader as the foundation of the reading program, a number of problems arise for students. Karlin lists the problems which result when teachers use only the individualized approach.

Lazar, May, "Individualized Reading: A Dynamic Approach." *Reading Teacher* 11 (December 1957): 75-83.

Discusses the benefits of individualized reading for students and the teacher.

Rollins, Kaye. "How Do I Begin an Individualized Reading Program?" *Education* 82 (September 1961): 36-38; In *Elementary Reading Today*. W.H. Miller, ed. New York; Holt, Reinhart and Winston, 1972, pp. 107-110.

Rollins explains how she began implementation of the individualized approach in her classroom. Tells how she presented the plan, how self-selection of books works, how to keep records, how to organize conferences and concludes with the success of the program listing four advantages. This is a first person account from a classroom teacher.

Rouch, Roger, and Birr, Shirley. *The Diagnostic/Language Development Approach to Individualized Reading Instruction*. West Nyack, NY: Parker, 1976.

Describes how to implement a combined reading program using strategies from the individualized approach and informal diagnostic tests. Describes how to teach skills using the language experience approach and individualizing strategies. Lesson plans are included with detailed diagnostic procedures and teacher made games for learning centers. This is a detailed "how to" book.

Safford, Alton L. "Evaluation of an Individualized Reading Program." *Reading Teacher* 13 (April 1960): 266-277.

Describes an evaluation of an individualized reading program in Los Angeles, California, in 1958. Describes the procedure, the rational, the results and the conclusions of the study. States that further studies are needed with a larger population to find out if the results of this study can carry over when the students reach middle school and high school. A longitudinal study is recommended.

Sartain, Harry W. "Advantages and Disadvantages of Individualized Reading." In *Individualized Reading Instruction: A Reader*. L.A. Harris and C.B. Smith, eds. New York: Holt, Reinhart and Winston, 1972, pp. 86-96.

Discusses the strengths and areas in need of improvement in the individualized approach.

Sartain, Harry W. "A Bibliography on Individualized Reading." *Reading Teacher* 13 (April 1960): 262-265, 270.

Discusses the interest in individualized reading and that there is not enough research to help teachers. Presents a review of the literature at the time to help teachers learn more about the approach useful now as a starting point for a review of the literature.

Sartain, Harry W. "The Research Base for Individualized Reading, Instruction." In *Reading and Realism Proceedings of the Thirteenth Annual Convention International Reading Association.* J. Allen Figurel, ed. Newark, DE; International Reading Association, 1969, pp. 523-530.

Describes efforts by educators to improve education. Present qualities of excellence in education and homogeneous grouping as a procedure that failed citing research evidence. Discusses individualized instruction by citing research studies and explaining the problems of implementing the approach. Concludes that the teacher is the key to the program's success, stating "excellence in the teaching of reading now requires and always will require an excellent teacher and a situation, including the best tools which enables that teacher to provide highly individualized instruction." Includes an excellent bibliography.

Sartain, Harry W. "The Roseville Experiment with Individualized Reading." *Reading Teacher* 13 (April 1969): 277-281.

Describes the 1958 study to determine whether 660 second graders in Roseville, Minnesota, would make better progress learning reading skills using the individualized approach or the ability grouping approach using supplementary books and readers. Concludes that "the individualized method does not produce better reading gains than a strong basal approach, there is no reason to forfeit a well planned basic system. Instead the benefits of the individual conferences should be obtained by their addition to the basic reading plan."

Smith, Nila Banton. *American Reading Instruction.* Newark, DE; International Reading Association, 1965, pp. 347-351.

Provides a brief history of the approach with a selected reading list. Discusses the Dalton System and the Winnetka Plan of the 1920s as the basis for the individualized approach of the 1950s and 1960s. States that "Research on individualized instruction is not conclusive.... Additional studies are needed in which various factors are more tightly controlled...." States that the studies that have been conducted have two general conclusions: students are more interested in reading when they are taught by the individualized approach and students read more books than students in control groups.

Spache, George D., and Spache, Evelyn B. *Reading in the Elementary School.* Boston: Allyn and Bacon, 1977.

Describes the individualized approach in detail citing research findings about its effectiveness. A useful bibliography is provided.

Spencer, Doris U. "Individualized Versus a Basal Reader Program in Rural Communities-Grades One and Two." *Reading Teacher* 21 (October 1967): 11-17.

A research study designed to evaluate the effectiveness of individualized reading in first and second grades in the 1964-1965 school year. Spencer compared a basal reading program with the individualized approach and a number of conclusions based on hard data were reached. The study confirms the findings of an earlier study for first graders. Extensive discussion of conclusions and implications for instruction are presented. The current research followed first graders into the second grade. The general concession was that students taught under the individualized reading approach made greater progress than the basal group.

Veatch, Jeannette. "Individualized Reading: The Revolution That Had to Come," *Journal of the Reading Specialist* 2 (March 1963): 34-38.

Discusses the start of the individualized approach as teacher initiated rather than research initiated. Self-selection of material is found to be the reason the approach is a success because it provides for readiness and individual differences.

Vite, Irene W. "Individualized Reading—The Scoreboard on Control Studies." *Education* 81 (January 1961): 286-290.

Presents a discussion of seven control studies comparing the individualized approach with ability grouping, finding that three studies favored ability grouping and four studies favored the individualized approach.

Readability

Readability means the level of difficulty of understanding material read and an estimate of one's ability to understand what is read.

According to Harris and Hodges (1995) there are two definitions for the term readability. One states that readability is the level of difficulty of understanding of material because of the style of writing. Factors such as format, typography, content, literary form and style, vocabulary difficulty, sentence complexity, concept load, and cohesiveness contribute to the readability of material. Also many variables such as the reader's motivation, abilities, background knowledge and interest contribute to readability. "Text and reader variables interact in determining the readability of any piece of reading material for any individual reader."

Readability, Harris and Hodges (1995) further state, is "an objective estimate or prediction of reading comprehension of material usually in terms of reading grade level, based on selected and quantified variables in text, especially some index of vocabulary difficulty and of sentence difficulty."

Harris and Sipay (1985) state the difficulty of reading material can be determined by the use of a readability formula, the use of a cloze or informal reading test, or by considered judgment. Judgment and readability formulas are used to determine "how readable the material will be in general." These methods are less time consuming than administering a cloze or informal reading inventory; however, they are also not as accurate in finding the difficulty of material for a particular student. Tests must be read by the student, but take more time to administer and grade. All three procedures have advantages and disadvantages and Harris and Sipay (1985) and Klare (1984) state that none can be considered perfectly accurate or reliable.

Harris and Hodges (1995) state that readability formulas are "objective methods of estimating or predicting the difficulty level of reading materials by analyzing samples from them, with results usually expressed as a reading grade level...." These formulas are based on the difficulty level of the vocabulary and syntax and several related factors singly or in combination usually "in terms of a multiple-regression equation. Word length or familiarity and average sentence length in words tend to be the most significant or convenient predictors of the reading difficulty of materials.... Estimates of formula validity are usually based on relationships with three types of criteria: (a) reading comprehension scores (b) reading speed or efficiency (c) acceptability determined either by readers' or experts' judgments or by reader perseverance." The widely used formulas in the 20th century were: the Dale-Chall Readability Formula; the Flesch Readability Formula; the Fry Readability Graph; and the Spache Readability Formula according to Klare (1984), Harris and Hodges (1995), and Hiebert (2002). The Dale-Chall Formula developed by Edgar Dale and Jeanne S. Chall, first published in 1948, estimates the difficulty of reading material using a percentage of words not on the "Dale List of 3,000 Familiar Words" and on the average number of words in sample sentences. This formula predicts 50 percent comprehension using a table that gives corrected reading grade levels. The Flesch Formula was developed by Rudolph Flesch to estimate the difficulty level of reading material for adults by using the length of sentences in words, the number of affixes, and the number of personal references in 100 word samples of reading material. The original formula was published in 1943 and revised in 1948 using the number of syllables per 100 words and sentence length in words and was renamed the Reading Ease Formula.

Edward B. Fry developed the Fry Readability Graph or Readability Scale in 1965 by estimating the difficulty of material using the number of syllables and sentences in 100 word samples corresponding to grade-level values on a graph. Modifications have extended the scale for use with preprimary level material and college level material.

In 1953 George D. Spache published a readability formula to estimate the difficulty of reading material at the primary level using average sentence length in words and number of words. The formula has been revised using an updated list of words.

According to Klare (1984) those researchers who developed readability formulas examined more than 250 variables that could predict the difficulty of reading material. Two factors have been of most interest to researchers, semantic difficulty and syntactic difficulty. It has been concluded that semantic difficulty is the better predictor. Britton, et al. (1982) state that material with less frequently used words and difficult syntax requires students to apply more thinking skills, knowledge and judgment to understand the material than is required for material with simpler syntax and more commonly used words. MacGinitie and Tretiak (1971), Harris (1976), Klare (1976), Entin and Klare (1978), Klare (1974–1975), and Guthrie (1972) found that most of the variance in readability measurement was due to syntax and semantic difficulty, which are also the two most valid ways to measure readability. These factors were also found to be sufficient measures of readability except, Klare (1974–1975) states, when exacting research is required. Guthrie (1972) found that these two measures were better evidence of the extent to which students learn something new from reading a passage than linguistic measures.

Schuyler (1982) states that over 50 readability formulas have been designed for various kinds of reading material. There are also several used for specialized material such as FORCAST, according to Sticht (1975), designed for finding the readability of job-related material, and ARI, which Smith and Kincaid (1970) state was developed for readability of technical material.

Some formulas such as the SEER and the Rauding Scale, Singer (1975) and Carver (1975–1976) state, do not require computations. These formulas compare material of unknown difficulty with material of known difficulty and a judgment is made about which known difficulty level the unknown level is most like. Schuyler (1982) cautions that the easy to use formulas also have the least consistent results.

Readability formulas have been criticized for many reasons. Harris and Sipay (1985) state that the main reasons for criticism are "(1) readability formulas do not indicate very well how comprehensible a text is going to be for an individual and (2) the formulas are poor guides for writing comprehensible material." Harris and Sipay (1985) believed that while the criticisms about comprehensibility were correct the critics should have examined the misuse of these formulas.

Klare (1984) states that a readability formula is a device for predicting a quantitative, objective, estimate of the difficulty of reading material. The problems arise because modern formulas are very good at doing what they were designed to do, predict how difficult reading material is compared with a criterion measure. Problems come when researchers do not recognize what the term "prediction" means. Klare (1984) states that there is a difference between *prediction* and *production*. In production the aim is to make reading material that is easier to understand. Prediction research is only required to show a relationship between the reading material and the criterion measure. Production research must show that when variables are engineered and material is rewritten it significantly increases the student's ability to comprehend the material.

Dreyer (1984) states that only matching a readability grade score with a student's grade equivalent test score does not tell how well a particular student will comprehend material. The selection of reading material for a specific student must be selected with variables such as the student's motivation and background knowledge and the vocabulary, structure, and cohesion of the material in mind according to Dreyer (1984).

Selden (1981) states that trying to make a readability formula more accurate by adding measures of syntax makes a formula a better predictor of material for upper grades but has little effect on lower grade material.

Readability formulas, Harris and Sipay (1985) state, have been criticized for the way they were validated. Schuyler (1982), Anderson (1983), and Klare (1984) agree that two formulas may be highly correlated as to the rank order in which reading material is placed but disagree consistently about the level of difficulty of material.

Chall and Conrad (1984) state that readability formulas were not developed to be an indicator of readable writing, but as indicators of how difficult material is to read. Readability formulas were not intended to give specific information about the characteristics that make reading material difficult according to Selden (1981).

Attempts to make material easier to understand has resulted in rewriting and simplifying material. Davison and Kantor (1982) found that simplification of material may make it harder to understand because replacing complex and compound sentences with short simple sentences often makes the link between ideas less clear. Anderson, Armbruster, and Kantor (1980) found that removing details and replacing words which are not as precise as the most difficult words also decreases understanding. Condensing ideas may cause "conceptual overload" for readers. Shorter sentences and easy words reduce the readability formula score, but according to Shuy (1981) this does not make the material clearer or easier to read. Funkhouser and Maccoby (1971) and Shaffer (1977) suggest that when both sentence length and word difficulty are changed comprehension is higher.

Klare (1984) states that the limitations of readability formulas must be understood if they are to be used correctly. Educators should realize that they need to use the formula that will best predict the difficulty of material for the students who will read it. Klare (1984) also suggests that teachers should not rely only on readability formulas, but should learn about the material they wish to use. Klare (1976) examined research about the validity of readability and concluded that:

1. At times, motivation can override the effects of readability on comprehension.
2. Easier readability may increase the likelihood that pupils will continue to read, even when it does not result in better comprehension.
3. It is more important to improve the readability of low-preferred than high-preferred material.
4. The grade-equivalent scores provided by readability formulas are not precise values.
5. Readability formulas may (*a*) underestimate the difficulty of material in which a pupil has limited background information; and (*b*) overestimate the difficulty for highly intelligent and well-informed readers.

Barchers (1998) states that a quick way to use readability is to use a word processing program that has a readability assessment choice. "Simply type or scan in several representative passages from the beginning, middle and end of the text and obtain a score for each section. This will give ... an idea of the complexity of the material according to that formula. However, readability designations can be misleading because readability formulas don't take into account features that can provide 'considerate text.'" Armbruster, Osborn and Davison (1985), Anderson and Davison (1988), and Bruce and Rubin (1988) report that the considerate text features are: author style; idea complexity; page organization; use of headings; visual material such as pictures, charts and graphs; reader's motivation; and the background knowledge the reader brings to the text.

Simonsen and Singer (1992) caution that readability formulas can help educators judge which material students will be able to read without difficulty; however, content area material contains challenging concepts and difficult vocabulary. Publishers may simplify material by shortening sentences and using more commonly used words which often makes the material less comprehensible because less data is contained in the material. To lesson the effects of simplified texts Simonsen and Singer (1992) suggest that teachers select material by evaluating grade levels and examining the characteristics of the material, resources presented for the reader, elaboration on concepts, consistency of material presented, and pre-reading guides. Teachers and students need to set purposes for reading and reflect on what has been read.

Hiebert (2002) discusses methods of judging text difficulty as part of standards and as assessment. In national and state standards Hiebert (2002) states ... "the goal of "proficient reading of grade-appropriate" text is frequently cited." Literature, research standards, and politicians have publicized the need for students to become proficient readers of grade appropriate material by the third grade. Hiebert (2002) found that despite all the publicity there are no definite statements about what these texts are like or what skills are needed to read them. Neither the report of the National Reading Panel, *Teaching Children to Read* (2000), nor the *No Child Left Behind* (2001) report specifies what makes texts appropriate for one grade and other texts appropriate for subsequent grades. State and national standards do not, Hiebert (2002) states, provide specific information on "the nature of texts with which students at different levels need to be proficient. When exemplar texts are identified ... there is substantial variability across them. Neither ... specify the critical competencies that are required to be successful with these texts."

Hiebert (2002) describes several methods of evaluating text difficulty levels. These methods are (1) CWF or Critical Word Factor; (2) readability using Fry graph; (3) lexiles; (4) text developing; and (5) standards.

Critical Word Factor is a method of judging how difficult reading material is by examining the occurrence of less familiar and more challenging words. Hiebert (2002) states that words that are easy to decode should be treated differently from words that are more difficult to decode. Hiebert (2002) states that Critical Word Factor is "an indicator of the task demands for recognizing words in primary level texts. The CWF indicates the number of words that will be difficult in a text when measured against a curriculum. Extended samples from texts are used to establish the number of unique words per 100..." Unique words are examined to find the number of words that are "outside the high frequency curriculum and, among this latter group of words, those with phonic or syllabic patterns that are beyond that level's curriculum." Hiebert (2002) states that it is difficult to find curricular words that are recognizable in the primary grades so an "assumed" curriculum was established consisting of core words. The core words must be recognized for the student to successfully read 90 percent of material, the percentage at which students are reading at their instructional level. After testing 500 textbooks as samples of primary grade material, Hiebert (2002) states that the Carroll, Davies and Richman (1971) word frequency list of 1,000 most frequent words matched the assumed curriculum words. Words related to these 1,000 words because of the inflected endings such as "ed," "ing" and a student's ability to recognize all vowel patterns in single syllable words was used. The CWF data is different from readability formula data.

Text leveling is a method of determining the grade level of a trade book. The term comes from a process used in Reading Recovery described by Peterson (1991) and the guided reading process as described by Fountas and Pinnell (1999). There are 20 Reading Recovery levels and 26 guided reading levels of books selected by "(1) book and print features; (2) content, themes, and ideas; (3) text structure; and (4) language and literary elements" according to Fountas and Pinnell (1999 and 2001). Features such as book length; print size; number of illustrations; subject matter; technical nature of the subject; complexity of ideas in the book; plot; genre; character development; author's point of view; sentence structure; variety and range of vocabulary; phrases and sentences; number of words and number of multi-syllable words; and number of high-frequency words are used to examine a book according to Fountas and Pinnell (1999). Books are assigned a level with an approximate grade level equivalent. For example:

Book Level	Grade Level
A	Kindergarten
B	Grade 1
C	Kindergarten
H	Grade 2
L	Grade 3
P	Grade 4

Hiebert (2002) states that "anchors are not provided that illustrate the range of difficulty on any of these dimensions.... Further, no research studies have reported on the relative weight given to different dimensions ... or whether the dominant factors vary from different types of texts ... print features would expect to weigh in more heavily at the very early levels such as A through E but not at levels V through Z."

The Lexile system claims not to be a readability formula according to Smith, Stenner, Horabin, and Smith (1989). Hiebert (2002) explains that Lexiles are based on "semantic difficulty, as measured by the presence of the texts' words on a word list and syntactic difficulty, as measured by sentence length...." MetaMetrics (2000) states that the Lexile framework consists of six ranges "for the elementary grades: First Grade: 200-370; Second Grade: 340-500; Third Grade: 480-670; Fourth Grade: 620-820; Fifth Grade: 770-910; and Sixth Grade: 870-1000." The authors state that the Lexile system measures texts up to college level with Lexiles that go up to 1600.

Hiebert (2002) presents data on several books evaluated by the Lexile system. "*Harry Potter and the Goblet of Fire* (Rowling, 2000) ... is given a Lexile of 880.... *Charlotte's Web* (White, 1952) has a Lexile of 680 which is the same Lexile rating as John Grisham's (1990) *The Firm*.... This ... illustrates the ambiguity of data presented in a scale from 200 through 1600 which has been disassociated from its semantic and syntactic criteria. For third grade level, for example, the range of 480-670 provides little indication of the corpus of words students need to recognize automatically...." The authors describe sentence length and words from the Carroll, Davies, and Richman (1971) list of commonly used words and the frequency with which they appear as the basis for judging Lexiles. Hiebert (2002) states that the Lexile system does not give an indication of precisely which group of most commonly used words relate to which level.

Hiebert (2002) concludes that researches must describe "the nature of literacy tasks of the digital age and the proficiencies that are required to be successful with these tasks...." to provide help for teachers who select reading material and students who need to gain the necessary level of reading proficiency. One important element that must be considered, Hiebert (2002) states, is describing parts of material that challenge readers. Methods of evaluating reading difficulty include: (1) CWF, which is a new method and still evolving; (2) text leveling, which does not give enough information to help teachers level books well; (3) the Lexiles system, which does not identify the critical processes students lack; and (4) using the quality of literature and the engagingness or the ability to hold student attention as standards, an approach that needs further investigation. Hiebert (2002) suggests that a great deal of research is needed to find out how "different types of texts influence the task for readers. Such models will eventually be complex and, Leu and Kinzer (2000) believe, will include the medium of the text (e.g., electronic or printed form). To ignore the features of text and to assume that the quality of literature is all that matters ... is an inadequate response...." Educators must consider the role texts play in helping students become successful, fluent readers in the digital age.

Determining the readability level of reading material and matching students' ability to material is a complex and important task. There is no simple way to determine readability levels and it appears that there is not only one definitive method for doing this.

Annotated Bibliography

Adams, Marilyn Jager. *Beginning to Read: Thinking and Learning About Print*. Cambridge, MA: MIT Press, 1990.
   Discusses the way to help young children learn to read presenting information about phonics and word recognition skills as part of comprehension.
Alverman, D., and Guthrie, J. *Themes and Directions of the National Reading Research Center (National Reading Research Center Perspectives in Reading Research No. 1)*. Athens: University of Georgia, National Reading Research Center, 1993.
   Discusses selecting reading material using the quality of the literature or a standard of how interesting or attractive the material is to students.
Anderson, Jonathan. "Lix and Rix: Variation on a Little-Known Readability Index." *Journal of Reading* 26 (March 1984): 490–496.
   Describes converting the lix scores to grade levels by counting the number of long words per sentence.
Anderson, Richard C., and Davison, Alice. "Conceptual and Empirical Bases of Readability Formulas." In *Linguistic Complexity and Text Comprehension: Readability Issues Reconsidered*. Alice Davidson and Georgia M. Green, eds. Hillsdale, NJ: Erlbaum, 1988, pp. 23–53.
   Discusses the research foundations of readability formulas listing limitations.
Anderson, Richard C., Hiebert, Elfredia H., Scott, Judith A., and Wilkinson, Ian A.G. *Becoming a Nation of Readers: The Report of the Commission on Reading*. Champaign, IL: The Center for the Study of Reading, 1985.
   A major work which presents research information about the reading process to answer "what is reading?" using five descriptors stating that skilled reading is a constructive, fluent, strategic, and motivated process, and a lifelong search. Anderson et al. state that the purpose of the study was to "summarize the knowledge acquired from research and to draw implications for reading instruction."
Anderson, Thomas H., Armbruster, Bonnie B., and Kantor, Robert. "How Clearly Written Are Children's Textbooks? Or, of Bladderworts and Alfa." *Reading Education Report* No 16. Champaign, IL: Center for the Study of Reading, University of Illinois, August 1980.
   Condensing ideas and delegating details may not clarify meaning, but may increase density and confuse the reader.
Armbruster, Bonnie B., Osborn, Jean H., and Davison, Alice L. "Readability Formulas May Be Dangerous to Your Textbooks." *Educational Leadership* 42.7 (April 1985): 18–20.
   Discusses the disadvantages of readability formulas listing features they do not take into consideration.
Barchers, Suzanne, I. *Teaching Reading: From Process to Practice*. Belmont, CA: Wadsworth, 1998, pp. 348–382.
   A textbook for pre-service educators which presents an overview of readability as part of a discussion about content area reading.
Baumann, J.F.; Hoffman, J.V., Duffy-Hester, A.M., and Ro, J.M. "The First R Yesterday and Today: U.S. Elementary Reading Instruction Practices Reported by Teachers and Administrators." *Reading Research Quarterly* 35 (2000): 338–377.

Reports that publishing companies are still a source of determining textbook difficulty levels.

Bormouth, John R., ed. *Readability in 1968*. Urbana, IL: National Council of Teachers of English, 1968.

Presents a comprehensive discussion of readability and its applications.

Brennan, A., Bridge, C., and Winograd, P. "The Effects of Structural Variation on Children's Recall of Basal Reader Stories." *Reading Research Quarterly* 21 (1986): 91–103.

Examined the relationship between the sentence structure of stories and student comprehension.

Britton, Bruce K., Glynn, Shawn, Meyer, Bonnie J., and Penland, M.J. "The Effects of Text Structure on Use of Cognitive Capacity During Reading." *Journal of Educational Psychology* 74.1 (February 1982): 51–61.

Discusses the problems students face when reading material with words that are not commonly used and difficult sentence structure.

Bruce, Bertram, and Rubin, Andree. "Readability Formulas: Matching Tool and Task." In *Linguistic Complexity and Text Comprehension: Readability Issues Reconsidered*. Alice Davidson and Georgia M. Green, eds. Hillsdale, NJ: Erlbaum, 1988, pp. 5–22.

Discusses the selection and use of readability formula.

Burmeister, Lou E. "A Chart for the New Spache Formula." *Reading Teacher* 29 (January 1976): 384–385.

Provides information for interpreting the Spache Readability Formula.

Carroll, J.B., Davies, P., and Richman, B. *The American Heritage Word Frequency Book*. Boston: Houghton-Mifflin, 1971.

A list of words and the frequency with which they appear.

Carver, Ronald P. "Measuring Prose Difficulty Using the Rauding Scale." *Reading Research Quarterly* 11 (1975–1976): 660–684.

Describes how to use the Rauding Scale, a readability formula that does not require calculations.

Chall, Jeanne S., and Dale, Edgar. *Readability Revisited: The New Dale-Chall Readability Formula*. Cambridge, MA: Brookline, 1995.

Presents a discussion of readability measurement and the application of a revised formula to the process.

Chall, Jeanne S., and Conrad, Sue S. "Resources and Their Use for Reading Instruction." In *Becoming Readers in a Complex Society. 83rd Yearbook of the National Society for the Study of Education, Part I*. A. Purves and O. Niles, eds. Chicago: University of Chicago Press, 1984, pp. 209–232.

Describes the correct use of readability formulas.

Dale, Edgar, and Chall, Jeanne S. "A Formula for Predicting Readability." *Educational Research Bulletin*, Ohio State University 27 (1948): 11–20, 28, 37–54.

A description of the original Dale-Chall readability formula with insight into its development.

Davison, A., and Kantor, R.N. "On the Failure of Readability Formulas to Define Readable Texts: A Case Study from Adaptations." *Reading Research Quarterly* 17 (1982), 187–209.

Reports that simplification makes material harder to understand for the reader because links between words become less clear.

Dreyer, Lois G. "Readability and Responsibility." *Journal of Reading* 28 (January 1984): 334–338.

Describes the importance of matched motivation and other factors, not just grade level, to insure that students can successfully read material.

Entin, Eileen B., and Klare, George R. "Factor Analysis of Three Correlation Matrices of Readability Variables." *Journal of Reading Behavior* 10 (Fall 1978): 279–290.

A detailed examination of factors that affect the readability of material.

Fountas, Irene C., and Pinnell, Gay Su. *Guiding Readers and Writers: Grades 3–6*. Portsmouth, NH: Heinemann, 2001.

Discusses the process of guided reading and leveled books for grades 3–6. This is a teacher resource.

Fountas, Irene C., and Pinnell, Gay Su. *Matching Books to Readers Using Leveled Books in Guided Reading, K–3.* Portsmouth, NH: Heinemann, 1999.

Explains the process of leveling books for the classroom including extensive lists of books that are leveled and ready to use.

Froese, Victor. "Cloze Readability Versus the Dale-Chall Formula." In *Teachers Tangible Techniques: Comprehension of Content in Reading.* B.S. Schulwitz, ed. Newark, DE: International Reading Association, 1975.

Compares the readability of material using cloze procedure and the Dale-Chall formula. Concludes that results are not the same because of the limitations of the cloze procedure.

Fry, Edward. "My Point of View." In *Reading Researchers in Search of Common Ground.* Rona F. Flippo, ed. Newark, DE: International Reading Association, 2001, pp. 35–40.

Fry discusses his perspective on reading instruction. States that readability is an important way to match students to books that they can read. Matching students and materials correctly, Fry states, leads to success because students need practice to perfect reading skills. Material that is at a reasonable level for the student to read will help instruction and student enjoyment. Students will read more and practice skills if the material is at the right level for each student.

Fry, Edward. "A Readability Formula That Saves Time." *Journal of Reading* 11 (April 1968): 513–516.

Describes the use of the Fry Readability graph to assess difficulty level quickly.

Funkhouser, G.R., and Maccoby, N. "Study on Communicating Science Information to a Lay Audience, Phase II." Institute for Communication Research, Stanford University, September 1971.

Discusses studies about the rewriting of difficult material stating that both sentence length and word difficulty must be changed for comprehension to improve.

Guthrie, John T. "Learnability, Versus Readability of Texts." *Journal of Educational Research* 65 (February 1972): 273–280.

States that readability formulas provide better evidence of what students have learned from reading than do linguistic measures of reading levels.

Harris, Albert J. "Some New Developments in Readability." In J.E. Merrett, ed., *New Horizons in Reading.* Newark, DE: International Reading Association, 1976, pp. 331–340.

Describes the variance in readability formulae listing specific reason for validity.

Harris, Albert J., and Jacobson, Milton D. "A Framework for Readability Research: Moving Beyond Herbert Spencer." *Journal of Reading* 22 (February 1979): 390–398.

Discusses the modern use of readability formulas and their evaluation.

Harris, Albert J., and Jacobson, Milton D. "A Comparison of the Fry, Spache, and Harris-Jacobson Readability Formulas for Primary Grades." *Reading Teacher* 33 (May 1980): 920–923.

Describes each readability formula telling how it can be used to determine the readability level of primary grade material.

Harris, Albert J., and Sipay, Edward R. *How to Increase Reading Ability. A Guide to Developmental and Remedial Methods.* New York: Longman, **1985**, 1987, 1988, pp. 597–603.

A discussion of readability formulas describing, use, limitations, and research. A useful start with an excellent bibliography.

Harris, Theodore L., and Hodges, Richard E. *The Literacy Dictionary. The Vocabulary of Reading and Writing.* Newark, DE: International Reading Association, 1995.

Defines readability and describes the Dale-Chall, Flesch, Fry, and Spache readability formulas.

Hiebert, Elfrieda. "Standards, Assessment and Text Difficulty." In *What Research Has to Say About Reading Instruction, 3d edition.* Alan E. Farstriep and S. Jay Samuels, eds. Newark, DE: International Reading Association, 2002, pp. 337–369.

An excellent discussion presenting ways to judge the difficulty of reading material other than readability formulas. Presents information about challenges that national and state standards and assessment initiatives created for educators in trying to match texts to student ability.

Klare, George R. "Assessing Readability." *Reading Research Quarterly* 10.1 (1974–1975): 62–102.

Presents an evaluation of readability as a concept and specific formulas.

Klare, George R. "Readability." In *Handbook of Reading Research*. P. David Pearson, ed. New York: Longman, 1984, pp. 681–744.

Presents an extensive look at readability, its history, research, and application with an excellent bibliography.

Klare, George R. "A Second Look at the Validity of Readability Formulas." *Journal of Reading Behavior* 8 (Summer 1976): 129–152.

Discusses the process by which readability formulas are validated and how this affects accuracy.

Klare, George R. "A Table for Rapid Determination of Dale-Chall Readability Scores." *Educational Research Bulletin* 31 (February 13, 1952): 43–47.

Presents a table to assist teachers in calculating readability using the Dale-Chall formula.

Layton, James R. "A Chart for Computing the Dale-Chall Readability Formula Above Fourth Grade Level." *Journal of Reading* 24 (December 1980): 239–244.

Describes the application of the Dale-Chall Formula to upper grade material.

Leu, D.J., Jr., and Kinzer, C.K. "The Convergence of Literacy Instruction and Networked Technologies for Information and Communication." *Reading Research Quarterly* 35 (2000): 108–127.

Discusses the importance of electronic material in literacy instruction; states that teachers must consider both print and electronic media.

Longo, Judith A. "The Fry Graph: Validation of the College Levels." *Journal of Reading* 26 (December 1982): 229–234.

Discusses the upper levels of the Fry graph and their validity for judging material at the college level.

Lorge, Irving. "Predicting Readability." *Teachers College Record* 45 (March 1944): 404–419.

An original discussion of a pioneering formula.

MacGinitie, Walter H., and Tretiak, Richard. "Sentence Depth Measures as Predictors of Reading Difficulty." *Reading Research Quarterly* 6 (Spring 1971): 364–376.

A research discussion of a means to predict reading problems in students.

MetaMetrics. "The Lexile Framework for Reading." Durham, NC: Metta Metrics, 2000. http://lexile.com\Faq.htm

A description of the Lexile system of determining text difficulty.

National Reading Panel. *Teaching Children to Read: An Evidence-Based Assessment of the Scientific Research Literature on Reading and Its Implications for Instruction*. National Institute of Health (Publication No. 00-4769). Washington, DC: National Institute of Child Health and Human Development, 2000.

A major national report on research on and instructional strategies for reading instruction in American Schools.

Peterson, B. "Selecting Books for Beginning Readers: Children's Literature Suitable for Young Readers." In *Bridges to Literacy: Learning from Reading Recovery*. D.E. DeFord, C.A. Lyons and G.S. Pinnell, eds. Portsmouth, NH: Heinemann, 1991, pp. 119–147.

Describes the 20 levels of books in the Reading Recovery program.

Schuyler, Michael R. "A Readability Formula Program for Use on Micro Computers." *Journal of Reading* 25 (March 1982): 560–591.

Reviews readability formulas and discusses the various kinds of material each was designed for.

Selden, Ramsey. "On the Validation of the Original Readability Formulas." In *Text Readability: Proceedings of the March 1980 Conference. Technical Report No. 213*. Davidson et al., eds.

Champaign: Center for the Study of Reading, University of Illinois, August 1981, pp. 10–26.
    Provides a history of the early readability formulas discussing how they were validated. A good start for background information.
Shaffer, Gary L. "An Investigation of the Relationship of Selected Components of Readability and Comprehension at the Secondary School Level." In *Reading: Theory Research and Practice.* P. David Pearson and J. Hansen, eds. Clemson, SC: National Reading Conference, 1977, pp. 244–252.
    Reports on the important connection between sentence length and word difficulty for comprehension at the secondary level. Discusses simplification of material.
Shuy, Roger W. "Four Misconceptions About Clarity and Simplicity." *Language Arts* 58 (May 1981): 557–561.
    States that simplicity does not mean clarity of writing. Simplifying material might cause it to become more difficult rather than easier to understand.
Simonsen, Stephen, and Singer, Harry. "Improving Reading Comprehension in Content Areas." In *What Research Has to Say About Reading Instruction.* 2d edition. S. Jay Samuels and Alan E. Farstrup, eds. Newark, DE: International Reading Association, 1992, pp. 200–219.
    Describes how to supplement content area instruction to ensure success. Presents a brief discussion of readability in content area material.
Singer, Harry. "The SEER Technique: A Non-Computation Procedure for Quickly Estimating Readability Level." *Journal of Reading Behavior* 7 (Fall 1975): 255–267.
    Describes the SEER technique for judging reading difficulty.
Smith, D., Stenner, A.J., Horabin, I., and Smith, M. "The Lexile Scale in Theory and Practice: Final Report." Washington, DC: Metta Metrics (ERIC Document Reproduction Service No. ED 307577), 1989.
    Describes the Lexile System presenting information about its development and use.
Smith, E.A., and Kincaid, J.P. "Deviation and Validation of Automated Readability Index for Use with Technical Material." *Human Factors* 12 (1970): 457–464.
    Describes specialized readability indexes designed for job related technical material.
Spache, George D. *Good Reading for Poor Readers.* Champaign, IL: Garrard, 1974.
    This is a tool to help teachers match books to the ability of each student, even those having difficulty. A classic.
Spache, George D. "A New Readability Formula for Primary-Grade Reading Materials." *Elementary School Journal* 53 (March 1953): 410–413.
    Describes a formula for judging the difficulty level of lower grade material.
Sticht, Thomas C. ed. *Reading for Working: A Functional Literacy Anthology.* Alexandria, VA: Human Resources Research Organization, 1975.
    Developed a formula for determining the readability of job-related material for adults.
Williams, Robert T. "A Table for the Rapid Determination of Revised Dale-Chall Readability Scores." *Reading Teacher* 26 (November 1972): 158–165.
    Provides a means for quick calculation of reading difficulty using the Dale-Chall formula.

Oral Reading

Oral reading is the practice of reading aloud to communicate. Until the 1920s reading instruction was mostly oral. Researchers found, according to Harris and Sipay (1985), that student reading was slow and laborious and silent reading was imprecise. Opitz (2002) states that by the 1920s it was believed that students should read silently because in real life people read silently most often. It was suggested that silent reading instruction would help students become more accurate faster, more precise readers who were better able to read a wide variety of material for many purposes.

Oral reading practices remained part of instruction especially in the early elementary grades. A common practice had all the students in a group open their books to the same page while one student read aloud as the others followed silently. Students took turns reading aloud several sentences. This, Tierney and Readence (2005) and Opitz (2002) identify as "circle reading" or "round-robin reading." This became a much criticized technique because frequently only the child reading aloud was paying attention to the text. The other group members were looking ahead to where they might be called upon, giving more attention to illustrations, reading another selection, or causing difficulties with other students. Research by Anderson, Mason and Shirey (1984) and Wilkinson and Anderson (1995) as well as reviews of research by Allington (1984) and Brulnsman (1981) indicate that round-robin reading was not the best strategy to develop accurate reading comprehension skills.

Oral reading is a communication skill which effectively presents information or entertains listeners, according to Tierney and Readence (2005), Harris and Sipay (1985), and Opitz (2002). If oral reading is used for a specific purpose and the student's presentation is assessed in terms of how well communication was achieved, oral reading is of value. The National Reading Panel (2000) reviewed research that provided evidence showing that repeated oral reading activities contribute to positive achievement in word recognition skills, fluency and comprehension skills across a wide range of grade levels.

Opitz (2002) and Harris and Sipay (1985) state that oral reading contributes to the development of reading success in several ways. Harris and Sipay (1985) identify positive aspects, stating that oral reading:

1. Gives the teacher a quick way to assess progress in word recognition, phrasing, and specific instructional needs;
2. Provides practice in oral communication skills for the reader and listening skills for the audience;
3. Provides the development of more effective speech patterns;
4. Provides opportunities for dramatization of stories where memorization is not practical;
5. Provides a way to help shy students improve social adjustment.

Opitz (2002) identifies 5 purposes for oral reading:

1. To develop comprehension skills;
2. To learn that oral reading is useful for communication to an audience in a performance;
3. To help struggling readings;
4. To assess reading progress; and
5. To involve parents in student skill practice. Oral reading, Opitz (2002) believes, can assist students to develop a positive attitude, comprehension strategies such as predicting; summarizing; making inferences; listening comprehension; listening vocabulary; visualization; questioning; monitoring one's reading; use of language cues; reading with expression; fluency; phrasing and skimming. Oral reading is useful for a specific purpose.

Taubenheim and Christensen (1978) suggest that purposes for oral reading include:

1. Learning to take turns in a small group when peers are the audience and do not have copies of the text;
2. Observation by the teacher to assess individual problems and habits;
3. Audience listening;
4. Finding and reading answers to questions orally after reading a selection silently;
5. Learning choral reading;
6. Presenting parts in a script or play; and
7. Reading with varied intonations.

Since oral reading is a means of communication, specific activities that provide oral practice are helpful. Activities such as oral reports and demonstrations, interviewing, debates, storytelling and story reading, choral reading, and mini performances are very useful.

Oral reports and demonstrations occur in the intermediate grades. These activities require accurate, well organized content and good oral communication skills.

Oral reports and demonstrations are given after students have done research on a topic and written a report. It is a way for students to share findings with the rest of the class. An oral report must have a clearly stated topic, logically developed ideas and a well thought out conclusion. Roe and Ross (2006) state that students take notes from the report and create a web or outline before presenting the report to the class. Practice is an important part of a well presented report. Students should speak clearly and make eye contact with the audience. Students should be able to describe the sources they used to get the information and where they were located. Book reports that are presented orally should summarize part of the plot without telling the end of the story. Pictures and role playing may also help create an effective book report.

Demonstrations must be researched and planned. Students need materials to show the listeners how to do something. Science experiments are very good for demonstrations as well as directions for making something or building something. Sequence of events is an important comprehension skill required for a demonstration. Students need to plan, organize and practice a demonstration before presenting it to an audience, Roe and Ross (2006) advise. Skills such as articulation, wording, gestures, fluency and eye contact are an important part of the demonstration.

Interviewing is a skill used to obtain information from a person for a specific purpose. Students need to learn how to develop open-ended questions that lead the interviewee to tell more about the subject. Students need to use listening and speaking skills as well as reading skills to conduct an interview. Students need to decide on the reason for the interview, plan open-ended questions after researching and reading about the interviewee's job or expertise, list the questions on index cards, and learn to take notes from an oral presentation. After the interview review the notes and answers to the questions to write an article, develop an oral presentation or present a report.

Panel discussions use the inquiry teaching strategy which encourages students to decide on topics to study and direct discussions. This involves content area activities and Strickland and Feeley (2003) believe panel discussions enhance language skills. Students prepare to speak on a topic or issue they have researched. A moderator prepares an introduction and asks members of the panel to speak while the rest of the class act as the audience. Research, content area information, speaking skills and listening skills are involved. Students present information using notes from research.

Debates consist of two teams who present opposing sides of an issue. After the positive and opposition teams present their reasons for supporting or opposing an issue based on research a summary is provided and the audience establish criteria for judging the results of the debate. Everyone must read, research, and write. The audience and participants practice listening skills.

Story reading and storytelling involves Readers Theater and play reading. Readers Theater involves students in reading a script to an audience as does play reading. A narrator reads a description and readers take the part of characters. The audience listens to the presentation. Green (1979) states that radio or play reading helps students communicate accurately from oral reading, summarize and restating orally read information, and comprehending oral information. The participants read their parts with expression and characterization.

Storytelling moves away from reading a story to learning the material and telling the story to the audience. Props can be used in both telling and reading stories. Sequence of events, retelling, summarizing and listening skills are used.

Choral reading is the oral interpretation of literature by two or more voices spoken as one according to Roe and Ross (2006). Tierney and Readence (2005) state that choral reading provides students with practice reading with expression, confidence by providing an opportunity to be part of a group and learn to appreciate oral expression. Norton, Norton, and McClure (2003) list 5 forms of choral speaking:

1. Refrain—one person presents a large part of the poem or story and the class repeats the chorus together;
2. Line a child or line a group—one person or the group begin the first line, another person or the group recite the next line;
3. Antiphonal or dialogue—alternative parts are spoken by different groups such as high and low voices or boys and girls;
4. Cumulative—one group speaks the first verse and the next group joins in with the second verse. Each verse adds a group everyone speaks;
5. Unison—everyone speaks or reads the selection together.

Poetry and stories are used. Students actively interpret the mood of the selection emphasizing the humor, mystery or sadness of the selection through use of voice and gestures.

The National Reading Panel (2000) states that repeated oral reading with guidances and help leads to "meaningful improvements in reading expertise." Speaking and listening skills are involved. Students participate in a meaningful experience that helps provide positive attitudes toward group participation and develops imagination.

Mini performances, a program developed by Morado, Koenig, and Wilson (1999) for at-risk students, helps develop language skills using literature, drama, music, and movement. A script is used as in readers theater and play presentation along with props. Students reenact a story for an audience using comprehension skills while the audience uses listening skills. Participants listen to each other to present a complete play.

Students are able to practice the material used in these strategies before presentation so that problem words and ideas are polished, expression is developed, and material becomes interesting to the audience. Oral reading does not need to be mechanical and unfocused. A specific purpose for oral reading provides all students with meaningful practice of reading skills.

Annotated Bibliography

Allington, R.L. "Oral Reading." In *Handbook of Reading Research*. P.D. Pearson, R. Barr, M.L. Kamie and P. Mosenthal, eds. New York: Longman 1984.
   Reports research on oral reading strategies. A good review of research.
Alvermann, D.E., Dillon, D.R., and O'Brien, D.G. *Using Discussion to Promote Reading Comprehension*. Newark, DE: International Reading Association, 1987.
   Describes strategies to improve reading comprehension skills through discussion activities.
Anderson, R.C., Mason, J., and Shirey, L. "The Reading Group: An Experimental Investigation of a Labyrinth." *Reading Research Quarterly* 20 (1984): 6–39.
   Discusses alternatives to oral reading practices.
Brulnsman, R. "A Critique of Round-Robin Oral Reading in the Elementary Classroom." *Reading-Canada-Lecture* 1 (1981): 78–81.
   Describes research on the problems of using the round-robin oral reading strategy.
Evans, K.S. "Fifth-Grade Student's Perceptions of How They Experience Literature Discussion Groups." *Reading Research Quarterly* 37 (2002): 46–69.
   Reports student comments about the literature discussion experience. Provides insight from the perspective of students.
Green, F.P. "Radio Reading." In C. Pennock, ed., *Reading Comprehension at Four Linguistic Levels*. Newark, DE: International Reading Association, 1979, pp. 104–107.
   Describes Radio Reading and explains how it is used.
Harris, Albert J., and Sipay, Edward R. *How to Increase Reading Ability: A Guide to Developmental and Remedial Methods*. New York: Longman, 1985.
   A classic text providing an excellent overview of oral reading its purposes and strategies.
Manna, Anthony L. "Making Language Come Alive Through Reading Plays." *Reading Teacher* 37 (April 1984): 712–717.
   Presents the use of play reading as a useful oral reading strategy.
Meier. T. "Why Can't She Remember That? The Importance of Storybook Reading in Multilingual Multicultural Classrooms." *Reading Teacher* 57 (2003): 242–252.
   Describes the story reading strategies useful for multilingual students and explains reasons for its use.
Morado, C., Koenig, R., and Wilson, A. "Mini Performances, Many Stars! Playing with Stories." *Reading Teacher* 53 (1999): 116–123.
   Describes the mini performances strategy as an oral reading process.
National Reading Panel. *Teaching Children to Read: An Evidence-Based Assessment of the Scientific Research Literature on Reading and Its Implications for Reading Instruction*. Wash-

ington, DC: National Institute of Child Health and Human Development, 2000 (NIH Publication No. 00–4754).
  Advocates guided oral reading as a useful strategy for success in fluency, word recognition and comprehension across grade levels.

Norton, D.E., Norton, S.E., and McClure, A. *Through the Eyes of a Child.* Upper Saddle River, NJ: Merrill/Prentice Hall, 2003.
  Presents a discussion of using literature in the classroom with specific strategies that work well.

Opitz, Michael, and Rasinski, Timothy. *Good-Bye Round Robin: 25 Effective Oral Reading Strategies.* Portsmouth, NH: Hanemann, 1998.
  Provides specific purposes and strategies for engaging in meaningful oral reading.

Opitz, Michael. "Oral Reading." In *Literacy in America: An Encyclopedia of History, Theory and Practice.* Barbara J. Guzzetti, ed. Santa Barbara, CA: ABC-CLIO, 2002.
  A summary of oral reading purposes and practices.

Roe, Betty D., and Ross, Elinor P. *Language Arts Through Literature and Thematic Units.* Boston: Pearson, 2006. Chapter 6.
  Providing a useful text chapter on oral language strategies.

Shane, Harold G. "The Expanding Role of Oral Reading in School and Life Activities." In *Oral Aspects of Reading.* H.M. Robinson, ed. Supplementary Educational Monographs No. 82, Chicago: University of Chicago Press, 1955.
  An early recommendation for the use of oral reading strategies.

Strickland, D.C., and Feeley, J.T. "Development in the Elementary Years." In *Handbook of Research on Teaching the English Language Arts.* J. Flood, D. Lapp, J.R. Squire, and J.M. Jensen, eds. Mahwah, NJ: Erlbaum. 2003, pp. 339–356.
  Describes various reading strategies that lead to reading success.

Taubenheim, Barbara, and Christensen, Judith. "'Let's shoot' Cock Robin! Alternatives to Round-Robin Reading." *Language Arts* 55 (1978): 975–977.
  Offers different strategies for oral reading.

Tierney, Robert J., and Readence, John E. *Reading Strategies and Practices: A Compendium.* Boston: Pearson, 2005.
  Chapter six discusses several oral reading strategies with good bibliographies.

Wilkinson, I.A.A., and Anderson, Ro. "Sociocognitive Processes in Guided Silent Reading: A Microanalysis of Small Group Lessons." *Reading Research Quarterly* 30 (1995): 710–740.
  Reports on a research study of small group oral reading citing best practices.

Miscue Analysis

Miscue analysis is a method of using a student's errors or misuses as an indication of his or her strengths and weaknesses in reading.

According to Harris and Hodges (1995) miscue analysis is "a formal examination of the use of miscues as the basis for determining the strengths and weaknesses in the background experiences and language skills of students as they read." Miscue, Harris and Hodges (1995) state, is a term used by Kenneth S. Goodman to describe "a deviation from text during oral reading or a shift in comprehension of a passage.... The assumption is that miscues are not random errors, but are attempts by the reader to make sense of the text. They, therefore, provide a rich source of information for analyzing language and reading development."

Goodman (1995) states that "just as young children learning to speak show their growing control over the grammar of their language by their "errors" ... readers use the same process by producing their errors as they do for their accurate reading. By comparing their observed oral responses to the text with the expected responses that would appear accurate to a listener I had a continuous window on their reading. I could see the process of reading at work.... The errors ... showed they were using their knowledge of language to make sense of the printed text...." Goodman (1995) states that the term miscue replaced the term error because it was a more precise description of what the reader did. "If language provides cues that readers use, then why not call these unexpected responses 'miscues.' It was a term ... in use in the theater. And it had the advantage that it implied cue use rather than random error."

Goodman (1969) states that the research goal was to development "a better understanding of the reading process, a more complete theory of reading and a taxonomy of miscue analysis appropriate to all readers." Nettles (2006) states that miscue analysis is a tool to help assess "how well the reader can recognize and understand vocabulary, as well as understanding the explicit and implicit message of the text."

Goodman (1995) states that research required an instrument to make it possible to use miscue analysis easily in a variety of settings. In 1972 Yetta

Goodman and Carolyn Burke developed the "Reading Miscue Inventory" and in 1987 Dorothy Watson assisted in the revision. A series of questions is used to identify types of miscues and their possible significance. The Inventory provided an easier way for teachers and clinicians to collect and analyze data. Roe, Smith, and Burns (2005) state that "The Reading Miscue Inventory considers both the quantity and quality of miscues or unexpected responses. Instead of simply considering the number of errors and giving equal weight to each, the teacher analyzes the R.M.I. for the significance of each miscue. Knowing the type of miscue and what might have caused it provides more information about reading difficulties than knowing only the number of miscues." Y. Goodman (1995) states that miscue analysis provides insight into the reading process and assists the analysis of oral reading. Roe, Smith, and Burns (2005) state that analyzing the kinds of miscues a student makes provides assistance in discovering why the student is having trouble reading. "To some extent, miscues are the result of the thought and language the student brings to the reading situation.... Analyzing miscues in terms of the student's background or schemata enables the teacher to understand why some miscues were given and to provide appropriate instructional strategies that build on the student's strengths."

The procedures used in miscue analysis, Goodman (1973), Harris and Sipay (1985), and Wixson (1979) state, are:

1. A reading passage providing a continuity of meaning is selected for the reader. The selection must be somewhat difficult and long enough to generate a minimum of 25 miscues.
2. The selection is retyped and each line is numbered to correspond with the appropriate page and line from the original text, to be used as a code sheet for recording miscues.
3. The reader is informed that the reading will be unaided and that she/he will be asked to retell the story after she/he has finished reading. The code sheet is marked as the reader reads the selection. The reading and retelling are tape recorded for future reference.
4. The reader is permitted to retell the story without interruption. Following the unaided retelling, the reader is asked probing questions designed to explore areas omitted in the retelling.
5. The miscues are coded.
6. Miscue patterns are studied, interpreted, and translated into instruction.

Harris and Sipay (1985) state that the selection the student reads orally must be: (1) new to the student; (2) complete with a beginning, middle and end; (3) one grade level above the reading material the student usually reads;

and (4) long enough and difficult enough to generate at least 25 miscues. The examiner does not help the student with word recognition; however, the examiner asks the student to guess what the word is after a 30 second hesitation. If the student cannot provide the word the examiner tells the student to continue reading even if she/he skips the word or phrase. "Following the oral reading, the child retells the story, with some general guiding questions posed by the examiner if necessary. Comprehension is scored subjectively by the examiner.... The procedure does not yield a reading-level score, rather, it provides insight into the reading strategies employed by the reader."

The miscues are coded using a set of nine questions used with the "Reading Miscue Inventory." According to Goodman and Burke (1972) the questions the examiner asks about each miscue are:

1. Dialect. Is a dialect variation involved in the miscue?
2. Graphic Similarity. How much does the miscue look like what was expected?
3. Sound Similarity. How much does the misuse sound like what was expected?
4. Intonation. Is a shift in intonation involved?
5. Grammatical Function. Is the grammatical function of the miscue the same as the grammatical function of the word in the text?
6. Correction. Is the miscue corrected?
7. Grammatical Acceptability. Does the miscue occur in a structure which is grammatically acceptable?
8. Semantic Acceptability. Does the miscue occur in a structure which is semantically acceptable?
9. Meaning Change. Does the miscue result in a change of meaning?

Burke (1976) states that the information from these questions provides a profile of a student's strengths and weaknesses. "The complete profile yields a variety of information including: the degree to which the reader's miscues disrupted comprehension; the degree to which the miscues were graphophonically, syntactically, and semantically similar to the original text; and the relationship between each miscue, the text, and the other miscues produced."

Wixson (1979) states that since there are no normative data to use in the interpretation of a reader's miscue patterns, available research must be used for this purpose. There are, however, problems with the research studies. Wixson (1979) found that the research studies on miscue analysis lacked essential information such as: (1) specific details about the sample population; (2) the methods and conditions of the study; and (3) the statistical results of the analysis. Hood (1975–1976) states that there are questions about the comparability of the results of procedures used by different researchers.

Wixson (1979) notes the problems related to miscue analysis studies but states that there are patterns of miscues that point to several trends. Research done by Allen (1969), Biemiller (1970), Burke and Goodman (1970), Clay (1966), Kolers (1970), Weber (1970), Goodman (1976), Coomber (1972), Menosky (1971), Goodman and Goodman (1977), Green (1974), Au (1977), Jensen (1972), and Goodman (1965) was analyzed and Wixson (1979) concluded that the following patterns appeared as trends:

1. Most readers, regardless of age and/or proficiency, produce a greater number of contextually (i.e., syntactically and semantically) acceptable miscues than graphophonically similar miscues.
    a. The majority of most readers' miscues are syntactically acceptable.
    b. Most readers produce a large percentage of syntactically acceptable miscues than they do semantically acceptable miscues.
2. Young beginning readers' miscues tend to include a large number of read word substitutions and "no response" omissions.
3. As readers mature the percentage of graphophonically similar miscues tends to increase initially.
    a. The percentage of "no response" omissions tends to decrease with age.
    b. Older readers tend to substitute non-word and/or real words they have never before seen in print.
4. Less proficient readers tend to produce a relatively large percentage of graphophonically similar miscues than more proficient readers.
    a. Less proficient readers make fewer attempts to correct their miscues than more proficient readers.
    b. Less proficient readers tend to correct acceptable and unacceptable miscues at almost an equal rate.
5. As readers become more proficient the percentage of graphophonically similar miscues tends to stabilize.
    a. The proportion of syntactically and semantically acceptable miscues increases with proficiency.
    b. Proficient readers tend to omit known words that are not essential for understanding.
    c. Proficient readers tend to correct more of their miscues than less proficient readers.
    d. Proficient readers tend to correct unacceptable miscues at a higher rate than acceptable miscues.

Hood (1978) states that miscue analysis takes a great deal of time and reports the following limitations:

1. Some miscue scores have questionable reliability because the classification of miscues varies among examiners.
2. Classification of some miscues as "good" or "bad" seems to differ with the reader's age and reading ability.
3. The relationship between passage content and the reader's background seems to influence test results (the same is true for most tests).

4. Miscues made by a given reader are related to the overall accuracy level at which they were made. For example, when word-recognition accuracy was 90 percent or less and the passage was less related to the reader's experience, there were proportionally more nonsense-word responses or no responses and fewer serious errors were self-corrected. At and above the 95 percent level of accuracy, proportionally more minor errs occurred.
5. Examiner's opinions regarding the contextual appropriateness of miscues vary tremendously.

Cohen and D'Alessandra (1978) and Leibert (1982) state that if an analysis of word-recognition miscues is to be done present the words on which the student made the miscue after the test. If the student can pronounce the word correctly most of the time the miscue should not be counted. When a student is given a second chance to pronounce a word it is frequently corrected. Carefully analyze the student's miscues to find out: (1) how semantic, syntactic, and graphic cues are used; (2) which word-recognition and decoding strategies were used and how well they were used; (3) what kinds of words, word parts, or particular words are causing problems; and (4) what effects do word recognition errors have on comprehension.

Christie and Alonso (1980) advise caution in analyzing miscues that are found across a series of graded paragraphs because the difficulty of the material can significantly affect the kinds of errors made. Students make fewer semantically acceptable miscues and self-corrections at their frustration level. They, however, make more graphically similar and grammatically acceptable miscues at the frustration level. Christie (1981) reports that a student's reading ability may have an impact on the use of graphophonemic cues. As proficient readers mature they rely less on such cues while poorer readers continue to rely on graphic cues.

Pflaum (1980) reports that disabled readers made more errors that change meaning and resulted in lower comprehension scores. When these students used more phonic cues their comprehension scores went up. Beebe (1979–1980) reports that substitution miscues usually lowered understanding and recall of what was read: "only uncorrected unacceptable substitutions had a negative impact on comprehension and recall. Self-corrections and acceptable substitutions were associated with higher comprehension and retelling scores."

Wixson (1979) presents a detailed investigation of miscue analysis and concludes that miscue analysis "succeeded in bringing about an awareness of reading as a language process, and in sensitizing people to the necessity of a method of evaluation which will accurately reflect this process in operation...." The exact framework of the relationship between oral reading errors as analyzed by miscue analysis and the reading process is not clear. "Further, it is unknown whether miscue analysis succeeds in identifying the critical features of the reader's oral reading performance which reveal their relative proficiency with the reading process.... There appears to be a critical need for additional research in the area of miscue analysis...." Wixson (1979) concludes by stating that miscue analysis procedures will be potentially useful for research and assessment because the analysis is conducted in conditions similar to classroom reading instruction. It is a method for evaluation which observes the whole reading process; however, changes in the analysis will make the method more useful.

Annotated Bibliography

Allen, P. David. "A Psycholinguistic Analysis of the Substitution Miscues of Selected Oral Readers in Grades Two, Four, and Six and the Relationship of These Miscues to the Reading Process: A Descriptive Study." Ph.D. dissertation, Wayne State University, 1969.
    Describes the miscues of readers at three grade levels, finding more miscues that fit the original context of the material than graphically similar to the original.
Allen, P. David. "Some General Implications Concerning Specific Taxonomy Categories." In *Findings of Research in Miscue Analysis: Classroom Implication*. P.D. Allen and D.J. Watson, eds. Urbana, IL: ERIC Clearinghouse on Reading and Communication Skills, National Council of Teachers of English, 1976, pp. 70–75.
    Discusses the relationship between categories of miscues with emphasis on correction, graphic and phonemic proximity, intonation, and semantic word relationships.
Antastasiow, Nicholas. "Reading Miscue Inventory." In *Eighth Mental Measurements Yearbook, Vol. II*. O.K. Buros, ed. Highland Park, NJ: Gryphon Press, 1978, pp. 1318–1319.
    Presents a review of the "Reading Miscue Inventory" discussing its strengths and limitations. Stating that the manual provides only a limited number of instructional suggestions and does not provide data telling if remediation of miscues improves reading ability. Concludes that the Inventory will help a skilled teacher using other measures to make instructional decisions about comprehension instruction after oral reading.
Au, K.H. "Analyzing Oral Reading Errors to Improve Instruction." *The Reading Teacher* 31 (1977): 46–49.
    Examines oral reading errors and presents strategies for using the analysis.
Beebe, Mona Jane. "The Effect of Different Types of Substitution Miscues on Reading." *Reading Research Quarterly* 15.3 (1979–1980): 324–336.
    In a study of the miscue substitutions made by 46 fourth grade boys. Beebe found that not all the miscues caused lower comprehension levels. Not all the substitution miscues made by the students had the same effect on comprehension of the material.
Biemiller, A.J. "The Development of the Use of Graphic and Contextual Information as Children Learn to Read." *Reading Research Quarterly* 6 (1970): 75–85.
    Analyzes the oral miscues of first grade students and describes the kinds of miscues made most frequently.
Brown, Joel, Goodman, Kenneth S., and Marek, Ann M. *Studies in Miscue Analysis: An Annotated Bibliography*. Newark DE: International Reading Association, 1996.
    This is a chronological list of books, articles, and dissertations from 1898 to 1995. The authors provide very brief annotations. This is a valuable resource for locating material about miscue analysis. Goodman provides an introduction discussing his research.
Burke, Caroline L. "Reading Miscue Research: A Theoretical Position." In P.D. Allen and D. Watson (eds.), *Finding Research in Miscue Analysis: Classroom Implications*. Urbana, IL: National Council of Teachers of English, 1976, pp. 10–23.
    Describes the taxonomy questions and gives examples of how miscue analysis explains the reading process.

Burke, Caroline L., and Goodman, Kenneth S. "When a Child Reads: A Psycholinguistic Analysis." *Elementary English* 47:1 (January 1970): 121-129.
Presents an analysis of the oral reading miscues of a 4th grade student, describing that the analysis shows how the reading process works.
Burlie, C.L., and Goodman, K.S. "When a Child Reads: A Psycholinguistic Analysis." *Elementary English* 47 (1970): 121-129.
Studied a fourth grade student's patterns of miscues stating that 85 percent of the miscues were acceptable syntactically to the original material.
Burns, Paul, Roe, Betty D., and Ross, Elinor. *Teaching Reading in Today's Elementary Schools*. Boston: Houghton-Mufflin, 1988, pp. 507-509.
Describes the procedures for miscue analysis presenting the administration and interpretation procedures of the Reading Miscue Inventory.
Christie, James F. "The Effects of Grade Level Reading Ability on Children's Miscue Patterns." *Journal of Educational Research* 74 (July/August 1981): 419-423.
Reports that acceptable miscues in context increase by grade level and student ability in the 2nd, 4th and 6th grades for students reading above and below grade level.
Christie, James F., and Alonso, Patricia A. "Effects of Passage Difficulty in Primary-Grade Children's Oral Reading Error Patterns." *Reading Research Quarterly* 51.1 (March 1980): 40-49.
Studied the effects of the difficulty of reading material on the number of oral reading errors made by first and third grade pupils.
Clay, M.M. "A Syntactic Analysis of Reading Errors." *Journal of Verbal Learning and Verbal Behavior* 7 (1968): 434-438.
A study of 100 five year olds found that the majority of their miscues were semantically and syntactically acceptable.
Clay, Marie M. "Emergent Reading Behavior." Unpublished doctoral dissertation, University of Auckland, Auckland, New Zealand, 1966.
Presents an analysis of the errors of a five-year-old reader, describing acceptability and strategies for correcting the errors.
Cohen, Marvin, and D'Alessandro, Cynthia. "When Is a Decoding Error Not a Decoding Error?" *Reading Teacher* 32 (December 1978): 341-344.
States that students self correct errors when given a second chance to read the material. When a word has been pronounced correctly most of the time it should not be considered a miscue if mispronounced on a test of words.
Coomber, J.E. "A Psycholinguistic Analysis of Oral Reading Errors Made by Good, Average and Poor Readers." Ph.D. dissertation, University of Wisconsin, 1972.
Presents a comparison of the types of oral reading errors made by students at three ability levels. Concludes that all students make errors that are syntactically acceptable.
Goldsmith, Josephine S., Nicolich, Mark J., and Haupt, Edward J. "A System for the Analysis of Word and Context-Based Factors in Reading." In *New Inquiries in Reading Research and Instruction*. J.A. Niles and L.A. Harris, eds. Rochester, NY: National Reading Conference, 1982, pp. 185-190.
Describes changes to "The Reading Miscue Inventory" which will provide more information about how students use the graphophonic cue system. Also suggests changes to provide a more standard statistical system of analysis of miscues.
Goodman, Kenneth S. "Analysis of Oral Reading Miscues: Applied Psycholinguistics." *Reading Research Quarterly* 5 (Fall 1969): 9-30.
Presents an analysis of oral reading and argues that reading must be considered a psycholinguistic process. Includes theoretical evidence.
Goodman, Kenneth S. "A Linguistic Study of Cues and Miscues in Reading." *Elementary English* 42:6 (October 1965): 639-643.
This is an early study examining words read in and out of context. Concludes that even first graders are able to read words in context that they cannot recognize in isolation.
Goodman, Kenneth S. "Miscues: Windows on the Reading Process." In *Miscue Analysis: Applications to Reading Instruction*. Kenneth S. Goodman, ed. Urbana, IL: ERIC Clear-

inghouse on Reading and Communication Skills, National Council of Teachers of English, 1973, pp. 3-14.

    Discusses the role of miscue research in understanding the reading process.

Goodman, Kenneth S. "What We Know About Reading." In *Findings of Research in Miscue Analysis: Classroom Implication*. P. David Allen and Dorothy J. Watson, eds. Urbana, IL: ERIC Clearinghouse on Reading and Communication Skills, National Council for Teachers of English, 1976, pp. 57-70.

    Discusses the reading process explaining how students read. Tells how fluent and less fluent readers differ in their miscues and how miscue research can help to make inferences about the reader's control of the reading process. States that research on miscues can be used for instructional purposes to help students improve control.

Goodman, Kenneth S., and Goodman, Yetta M. "Learning About Psycholinguistic Processes by Analyzing Oral Reading." *Harvard Educational Review* 47 (1977): 317-333.

    States that an examination of children's oral reading provides insight into the psycholinguistic process of reading.

Goodman, Yetta. "Miscue Analysis for Classroom Teachers: Some History and Some Procedures." *Primary Voices K-6* 3.4 (November 1995): 2-9.

    Discusses the history of miscue analysis research and presents specific procedures.

Goodman, Yetta, and Burke, Caroline. *Reading Miscue Inventory*. New York: Owen, 1972.

    Procedures for analyzing miscues and how to code the results. Presents nine questions to help the teacher code student miscues and develop a profile of the student's strengths and problems.

Goodman, Yetta, Watson, Dorothy J., and Burke, Caroline L. *Reading Miscue Inventory: Alternative Procedures*. New York: Owen, 1987.

    Presents methods for teachers; an explanation of miscue analysis; coding information; and alternative procedures. This is a practical guide for classroom teachers.

Green, B.H.L. "A Psycholinguistic Analysis of the Multiple Attempts Produced in Oral Reading by Selected Readers Upon the Single Appearance of an Item Within a Text and Upon Recurring Throughout a Text." Ph.D. dissertation, Wayne State University, 1974.

    Examined and compared students' oral reading errors and their several attempts to read a word which appears once and more than once in a selection.

Harris, Albert J., and Sipay, Edward, R. *How to Increase Reading Ability: A Guide to Developmental and Remedial Methods*, New York: Longman, **1985**, 1987, 1988, pp. 214-220.

    A concise discussion of the research about miscue analysis presenting both sides of the issue.

Harris, Theodore L., and Hodges, Richard E. eds. *The Literacy Dictionary. The Vocabulary of Reading and Writing*, Newark, DE: International Reading Association, 1995.

    Defines miscue and miscue analysis.

Hood, Joyce. "Is Miscue Analysis Practical for Teachers?" *The Reading Teacher* 32.3 (December 1978): 260-266.

    Discusses a modified version of miscue analysis.

Hood, Joyce. "Qualitative Analysis of Oral Reading Errors: The Inter-Judge Reliability of Scores." *Reading Research Quarterly* 11 (1975-1976): 577-598.

    Investigated the comparability of scores produced by different researchers. Questions the score reliability in miscue analysis studies.

Jensen, L.J. "A Psycholinguistic Analysis of Oral Reading Behavior of Selected Proficient, Average, and Weak Readers Reading the Same Material." Ph.D. dissertation, Michigan State University, 1972.

    Analyzed the oral reading errors of students at three levels reading the same material and compared the types of errors made.

Kolers, P.A. "Three Stages of Reading." In *Basic Studies on Reading*. H. Levin and J.P. Williams, eds. New York: Basic Books, 1970.

    Discusses the miscues of students at various stages of development.

Leibert, Robert E. "A Study of Word Errors by Second, Third, and Fourth Grade Pupils Reading the Dolch Word List." In *New Insights in Reading Research and Instruction*. J. Niles and L.A. Harris, eds. Rochester, NY: National Reading Conference, 1982, pp. 166-169.

Analyzes student miscues and states that words pronounced correctly the majority of the time should not be called errors when mispronounced on a test.

Menosky, D.M. "A Psycholinguistic Description of Oral Reading Miscues Generated During the Reading of Various Portions of Text by Selected Readers from Grades Two, Four, Six, and Eight." Ph.D. dissertation, Wayne State University, 1971.

Compares the oral reading miscues of students at four grade levels.

Nettles, Deane Hood. *Comprehensive Literacy Instruction in Today's Classrooms: The Whole, the Parts, and the Heart*, Boston: Allyn and Bacon, 2006.

Presents a brief discussion of the use of miscue analysis as an assessment tool.

Pflaum, Susanna W. "The Predictability of Oral Reading Behavior on Comprehension in Learning Disabled and Normal Readers." *Journal of Reading Behavior* 12 (Fall 1980): 231-236.

This study found that disabled readers had higher rates of errors that changed meaning and lowered the comprehension accuracy.

Pikulski, John J., and Shanahan, Timothy. "Informal Reading Inventories: A Critical Analysis." In *Approaches to the Informal Evaluation of Reading*. J.J. Pikulski and T. Shanahan, eds. Newark, DE: International Reading Association, 1982, pp. 94-116.

Found that errors increase when the difficulty of the reading material increases. Students also change their strategies when the material becomes more difficult. Students are less likely to correct miscues that change the meaning of what is read. States that these findings dispute Goodman's recommendation to only use difficult material for miscue analysis and suggests that miscue analysis should assess both the instructional and frustration levels of students.

Roe, Betty D., Smith, Sandy H., and Burns, Paul C. *Teaching Reading in Today's Elementary Schools*. Boston: Houghton-Mifflin, 2005, pp. 480-482.

A brief discussion of miscue analysis presenting procedures for use.

Sims, Riedine. "Miscue Analysis: Emphasis on Comprehension." In. *Applied Linguistics and Reading*. R.E. Shafer, ed. Newark, DE: International Reading Association, 1979, pp. 101-111.

Presents a simplified set of questions to ask about each miscue to provide better information about comprehension levels.

Singer, Harry. "Reading Miscue Inventory." In *8th Mental Measurements Yearbook, Volume II*. O.K. Buros ed. Highland Park, NJ: Gryphon, 1978, pp. 1319-1322.

States that the Reading Miscue Inventory "lacks standardized directions and selections, explicit rational and stipulated criteria for determining cutting points for diagnostic patterns, norms for interpreting scores, reliability and validity data for diagnosis and for prescribed reading strategies." Suggests procedures for improving the test.

Weber, Rose-Marie. "First Graders' Use of Grammatical Context in Reading." In *Basic Studies on Reading*. H. Levin and J.P. Williams, eds. New York: Basic Books, 1970.

Examines the miscues made by first grade students.

Weber, Rose-Marie. "A Linguistic Analysis of First Grade Reading Errors." *Reading Research Quarterly* 5 (1970): 427-451.

A detailed discussion of the errors first grade students make during oral reading.

Weber, Rose-Marie. "Review of Findings of Research in Miscue Analysis: Classroom Implications." *Journal of Reading Behavior* 9 (Winter 1977): 416-419.

States that there is cohesiveness among all the chapters which presents a unified point of view. "Conflicting findings of different interpretations..." are not presented. The material does not address related findings obtained by other methods.

Wixson, Karen L. "Miscue Analysis: A Critical Review." *Journal of Reading Behavior* 11 (Summer 1979): 163-175.

Presents a detailed discussion of miscue analysis citing relevant research. States that "the information reported ... suggests that both the assumptions underlying miscue analysis and the procedures used to analyze miscues requires additional rigorous empirical explication and validation." Excellent overview of the procedure.

Initial Teaching Alphabet—ITA

Initial teaching alphabet is based on the belief that a phonemically regular alphabet would make learning to read easier. The irregularities of the English language are the reason why students have problems learning to read.

According to Harris and Sipay (1985), a belief that the irregularities in the sound-symbol system of the English language has caused problems for those learning to read has led to the design of a phonemically regular alphabet. Harris and Hodges (1995) state that augmented alphabets designed to "make spelling and reading easier by adding letters to the existing alphabet so that each letter or grapheme represents a different phoneme of the spoken language" have been proposed since John Hart developed the Orthographie in 1568.

Harris and Sipay (1985), Harris and Hodges (1995), Chall (1996), and Gillespie-Silver (1979) describe the initial teaching alphabet (ITA) as an augmented alphabet developed in England by Sir James Pitman in the 1950s consisting of 44 characters instead of 26. ITA is not an approach to teaching reading. The 44 characters include 24 of the 26 letters of the English alphabet and 20 new letters that stand for sounds that have no one letter of their own. ITA presents capital letters in the same shape as lower case letters, but larger in size. Separate symbols stand for each of the 44 consonant and vowel sounds. The system regularizes spelling so that, as Downing (1967 and 1969b) states, one and done become wun and dun to match the spelling pattern for fun, run, and sun. Transition to traditional orthography occurs at the end of the first grade. ITA is only to be used for beginning reading instruction, Chall (1996) states, and after students become fluent ITA readers transfer to traditional orthography takes place. Chall (1996) states that this procedure is not unknown because she describes the Ecole Francaise method of teaching children to read or decode in French first and then in the second grade students learn to read English. French spelling is, like ITA, more regular than English. Chall (1996) notes that the students at the Ecole Francaise do not need much instruction in English reading and errors in oral reading consisted of pronunciation of English words with a French accent.

The originators of ITA, Chall (1996), Gillespie-Silver (1979), Harris and

Sipay (1985) state, did not suggest changing the way reading is taught, only the print of the medium. Basal readers similar to such series in use when ITA was introduced in 1961 in England and 1963 in America were used, Block (1972) states. The American *Easy-to-Read: i/t/a program* by Mazurkiewicz and Tanyzer used principles of the basal-readers in print at the time.

Chall (1996) reports that the research done in England with ITA by Downing (1964a and 1964b, 1966a, 1965) which used a small population and reported (1) ITA may be easier to learn than traditional orthography; (2) better comprehension, accuracy, speed and oral word recognition; (3) after 18 months one half of the ITA group transferred to traditional orthography and tested better on silent reading comprehension than the control group.

In the First Grade Reading studies, Stauffer (1967) compared the results of twenty-seven research studies during the 1964-1965 school year. ITA was compared with basal readers, the linguistic approach, phonics plus the basal approach, and the language experience approach. Stauffer (1967) reports that there were twenty experimental and twenty control classes with 1000 students in each study. Results indicate that (1) ITA produced significantly superior ability in word recognition and spelling as measured by three different tests; (2) no significant difference in comprehension, rate or accuracy of oral reading, usage and English mechanics.

The ITA did help develop better word recognition skill, but not necessarily better phonics skills or comprehension skills. Spache and Spache (1977) question whether a letter-sound approach which is often more effective with bright students and less effective with below average students can help students become fluent readers. Spache and Spache (1977) state that perhaps an approach such as ITA could become supplementary for specific students rather than an approach for all pupils.

Annotated Bibliography

Block. J.R. "Newsreport Interview." *Reading Newsreport* 6 (1972): 4–8, 47.
    Discusses the American use of ITA and the work done in Pennsylvania by Albert Mazurkiewicz and in New Jersey by Anita Metzer.
Chall, Jeanne S. *Learning to Read: The Great Debate*. New York: Harcourt Brace, 1996, 3d edition.
    Chall provides a comprehensive description of the ITA approach with research evidence about use and effectiveness. Includes a lengthy bibliography. This is the most useful view of the approach.
Cutts, Warren G. "The Value of ITA: It's Too Soon to Know Definitely." *NEA Journal* (September 1964): 20–22.
    A reply to the Downing and Rose article stating that while Cutts is not opposed to the approach he believes that more research is needed and lists five factors which make him question the available research results.

Downing, John A. "The I.T.A. (Initial Teaching Alphabet) Reading Experiments." *Reading Teacher* 18 (1964): 105–109.

Describes the research done in England for the American reader.

Downing, John A. "Current Misconceptions About I.T.A." *Elementary English* 42 (1965): 492–501.

Discusses the ITA approach and the wrong information supposed about its use.

Downing, John A. "E.S.A. School Teachers Assess I.T.A." *Special Education* 56 (1967): 12–16.

Describes the use of ITA in special education settings and the teachers' evaluation of its effectiveness.

Downing, John A. "How Effective Is I.T.A.?" In *Current Issues in Reading*. Vol. 13, part 2. Nila Banton Smith, ed. Newark, DE: International Reading Association, 1969, pp. 338–344.

Defends the use of ITA by describing its benefits and the research he did with a Ford Foundation grant. Tells how ITA works in the classroom by listing its contributions to instruction. Downing ends with a lengthy bibliography to substantiate his conclusions.

Downing, John A. "*The I.T.A. Reading Experiments; Three Lectures on the Research in Infant Schools with Sir James Pitman's Initial Teaching Alphabet*. London: Institute of Education, University of London, 1964.

A detailed report of the British research and use of ITA with young children.

Downing, John A. "Progress Report on I.T.A." In *Readings on Reading*. A. Benter, J. Dalbel, and L. Kise, eds. Scranton, PA.: International Textbook, 1969, pp. 469–476.

Defends the use of ITA by telling about the progress of the approach citing research.

Downing, John A., and Rose, Ivan, "The Value of ITA: We're Enthusiastic." *NEA Journal* (September 1964): 20–22.

Describes ITA and defends the use of the approach because test results indicate that children make the transfer easily to traditional orthography and after eighteen months with the approach students should superior test scores.

Gillespie-Silver, Patricia. *Teaching Reading to Children with Special Needs: An Ecological Approach*. Columbus, OH: Merrell, 1979.

A textbook in special education which describes the ITA approach discussing the British and American research briefly. Tells how the approach can be used with special needs students.

Harris, Albert J., and Sipay, Edward. *How to Increase Reading Ability: A Guide to Developmental and Remedial Methods*. New York: Longman, 1985, 1987, 1988.

This classic text describes the ITA approach and briefly refers to the research.

Harris, Theodore L., and Hodges, Richard E., eds. *The Literacy Dictionary: The Vocabulary of Reading and Writing*. Newark, DE: International Reading Association, 1995.

Provides a definition of the ITA approach. A good starting point for research.

Smith, Nila Banton. *American Reading Instruction*. Special Edition. Newark, DE: International Reading Association, 2002, pp. 363–367.

Smith provides an in-depth discussion of ITA reviewing the *Downing Readers* used in England and the Mazurkiewicz and Tanyzer *I/T/A Easy to Read Series*. Provides an excellent bibliography. This is an update of the original 1965 edition.

Spache, George D., and Spache, Evelyn B. *Reading in the Elementary School*, 4th edition. Boston: Allyn and Bacon, 1977.

Discusses the comparison of the ITA approach, the basal approach, the linguistic approach, and the language experience approach in the First Grade Reading Studies. This text provides a good bibliography.

Stauffer, Russell G., ed. *The First Grade Reading Studies: Findings of Individual Investigations*. Newark, DE: International Reading Association, 1967.

This is the complete report of the results of the 1964–1965 twenty-seven studies comparing several approaches to find which is the best for early reading instruction. Reports on the effectiveness of ITA as compared to the basal, linguistic, and language experience approaches.

Words in Color

Words in Color is a word identification program developed by Caleb Gattegno which presents each phoneme in a distinct color. It is a method of presenting written language in a phonetic way. According to Gattegno (1962) the program consists of 39 phonemes presented on large wall charts with black backgrounds. It is a phonics program. Letters and words are written on the chalkboard in colored chalk which corresponds with the phoneme color on the chart. Books used are printed in black and white.

Zintz (1970) states that Words in Color "is a system of writing the language in a phonetic manner by having a distinct color for each phoneme." The program, which Chall (1996) calls a phonics program, was developed by Caleb Gattegno (1962), who states that the program consists of 39 phonemes shown on large wall charts. Each phoneme is shown in a distinct shade of color. The wall charts have black backgrounds. When letters and words are written on the chalkboard, colored chalk is used which is coded with the same phoneme color on the chart. The books used are printed in black and white.

Myers and Hammill (1969) state that "Words in Color" uses two elements of the linguistic method: "a strong emphasis on phonics and the avoidance of pronouncing the consonants in isolation." Each sound is represented by a color. For example Myers and Hammill (1969) state that "the sound 'a' as in spade will always be represented in the blue-green color regardless of whether it is spelled 'a,' 'ei,' 'ea' or any other way."

Students learn the short vowel sounds first and then build letter combinations using an approach that Gattegno (1962, 1968) calls visual dictation in which the teacher and students point to successions of sounds from written sequences on the chalkboard. Students "learn in this way to associate a spatial sequence of letters with a temporal sequence of sounds." A transfer from color to black and white regular print is based on the assumption that once students have learned the sound of the letters they will not need the color to help. Visual dictation, Gattegno (1968) explains, is an activity using a pointer. The teacher taps, for example, the letter "a." The rhythm can vary from slow to fast. The pupils orally say what is tapped: aaa (a word) a aa aaa (several words in a sentence). The letters are grouped with spaces to indicate word and sentence patterns. Gattegno (1968) states that "this gives practice in seeing that the amount of distance between signs indicates the time pattern for utterances" and students began to understand that written words are separated from each other by more space than the space between the letters in one word and that reading moves from left to right. All of the short vowels are taught this way.

Once the vowels are learned as representing five distinctive sounds, consonants are introduced. The consonants are not, Gattegno (1968) states, sounded in isolation, but syllables are formed and sounded. Students do not, Gattegno (1968) states, say "this is the vowel a, they say white says a." The next letter, p, dark brown, is introduced and is only sounded with one vowel. The teacher writes

        a   u   i   e   o
        p

on the chalkboard and taps with the pointer

        ap   up   ip   ep   op

and asks "what is this?" The students reply ap (as in apple). The next step is reversal of syllables such as:

        pa   pu   pi   pe   po

Gattegno (1968) states that the pointer should be moved quickly to link the two signs. If students do not say pa (as in pad) the teacher says "This is pa. What do you say for pu pe pi po?" Gattegno (1968) states that "it is important that pupils who have already learned to reverse au into ua see these new syllables as the reverses of those met earlier." The teacher can also go a step further and use the color by saying "what is the reverse of pink, brown?"

Once the consonants are learned more syllables can be created such as:

        tap it   top it
        tip it   pop it
        tip it up pat

Gattegno (1968) states that memory is not loaded because the student is "not required to retain anything, there is a reason which directs him to say what he says." Students are not praised, Gattegno (1968) states, or rewarded because "the recognition of the fact that ability to function leads to better functioning."

Students move through all 21 charts and they are helped to "understand the connection between the temporal aspect of spoken speech and the spatial arrangements of print," Gattegno (1968) states. Students come to reading with spoken language and Gattegno (1968) believes that "to read is to restore the voice to the printed page" and reading is "a by product of the extension of intellectual and linguistic powers," not an independent activity. Students do not know reading by itself; students know how to read as they know how to walk and talk. Gattegno (1968) states that reading, like driving a car, requires practice because through practice, not instructions, one learns how to drive. When one receives a driver's license his/her skill level is lower than that of more experienced drivers. Gattegno (1968) continues to state that beginning readers have enough skill to obtain "a license to read ... it is only after this that through practice the learner advances further and further into reading meeting greater demands and some hazards." Gattegno (1968) explains that the early activities in "Words in Color" are limited to those areas of language that allow the student to show some but not all of the linguistic behaviors associated with the whole of the language. Skill will develop through the use of selected limited activities. As students practice performance improves. Gattegno (1968) states, "practice develops a skill and as performance of the skill increases, more highly developed practice increases it still further."

Gattegno (1968) provides a list of aspects of language students must cope with to "bridge the gap between spoken and written speech" and states how to use these to develop a plan for learning based on the reality of the process. Gattegno (1968) states that:

1. The problem is not the correspondence between spoken and written speech, but "the relationship of teacher to learner and the techniques of teaching." The teacher needs to be aware of what the student must master to make the correspondence between spoken and written speech and know strategies to help the student achieve this so that learning is quick and smooth. Problems occur when the teacher forgets that the aim is to communicate meaning "through finding speech in print in a natural way or ... ignores the fact that learning requires concentration without distraction" then problems occur.

2. Since the conventions of the written code of language are arbitrary without rational justification, introduce an arbitrary "aspect of a game played without any relationship to the meaning or spelling of spoken language." In this way the left to right convention, the horizontal alignment of letters and words, and "certain designs or sets of designs that are associated with certain sounds" are met.

3. Vowels can be sounded by themselves, but consonants can only be sounded where linked to vowels to form syllables. When multiple consonants are found in written words, there are strategies that help students sound them "blended—as they come naturally in speech—rather than by isolation."

4. A pointer is used as a link between signs that make words or between words that make sentences to maintain time. The move-

ment of the pointer "reveals the temporal sequence that needs to be followed in order to" begin the instructions the student needs to figure out for him/herself the spoken word or sentence.

5. When words are said "only the complete statement with proper intonation and rhythm can convey full meaning.... Reading-as-talking is of fundamental importance from the beginning."
6. Students need to study words as designs in order to achieve correct spelling. They need to "photograph" words, not just scan them. Special activities are needed to "induce learners to look at, take in, and evoke words as designs. Color can help to convey a phonetic clue to words like a relief map does to the spatial arrangement of an area, easing the task of the eye functioning panoramically as a camera. Color is used in the designs of letters and words in order to reduce the chances of overlooking correct spelling."
7. Students need to become aware of words as aspects of reality and become interested in words to develop new endless observations about the structure, the relationship of sounds, forms and meaning of words. Reversing the order of words can help students learn to analyze sentences. When students can analyze word order they can "move from the purely technical considerations onto a linguistic study and later pass ... to a literary level" when decoding no longer takes all the student's energy. Students need to study words, their individual characteristics, and "the order of their component signs." The game of transformations helps students become aware of the phonetic structure of words.
8. Words in Color educates the linguistic powers of students through direct and vicarious experiences and sharing one's own inner experience with others. Gattegno (1968) states that Words in Color is a successful program where students "understand that the successive certificates of reading acquired through the program are merely stepping stones toward independent and critical reading and creative writing, and toward the use of a vocabulary which is continually expanding and increasingly sensitive and adequate to the meaning the writer intends to communicate."

Sister M. Raphael (1966) provides background about the Words in Color approach, stating that Caleb Gattegno was a British educator who developed the approach after observing children in Switzerland learn music with color. Gattegno developed a color coded arithmetic approach and in 1957 working in Ethiopia on a UNESCO project taught the Amharic language using color. Raphael (1966) states that Gattegno reduced the time needed to learn to read and write the 251 signs in Amharic from five months to ten hours. Gattegno experimented with Spanish and Hindi, which are phonetic, and began working on English, which is not phonetic. In 1964 Gattegno presented Words in Color to the Washington, D.C., schools.

Raphael (1966) states that the irregularity of English has caused problems for beginning readers and is the reason used by opponents of the phonics approach to encourage alternate approaches. Many students continue to have problems when they encounter letters that are pronounced differently in several words. Raphael (1966) cites the "oo" sound in to, too, two, crew, through, flu, true, fruit, shoe and you as causing problems. In Words in Color all the letter combinations that are pronounced "oo" are green and the color is the clue to pronouncing the word.

Raphael (1966) states that Gattegno identified 270 different sounds in English using twenty-six letters. Gattegno reduced these 270 sounds to 47 main sounds. The colors represent the 20 vowel and diphthong sounds and the 27 consonant sounds. Materials necessary for instruction include 47 colors of chalk. The color for a sound remains the same no matter how a word is spelled. Raphael (1966) cites the n in no, the ne in phone, the kn in know, the pn in pneumonia, the gn in gnat as all being represented by the color lavender as the n sound. The student, Raphael (1966) states, "initially views our nonphonetic language as a phonetic language without changing the traditional spelling." The books that are part of the approach are black and white and white chalk is used on the chalkboard for all writing; only the teacher uses colored chalk.

The Words in Color approach consists of materials for the teacher, materials for the whole class, and materials for individual students. A teacher's guide provides detailed suggestions for the sequence and scope of each lesson. The class uses 21 color charts which contain 600 words, eight phonic code charts in color and word cards for more than 1,200 words printed in black on colored cardboard. Each student is given a word-building book, three reading books containing a vocabulary of 1,200 words, a story book, and worksheets.

Raphael (1966) states that the 21 charts gradually introduce the sounds beginning with the most regular spellings and progressing through almost all regular and irregular signs of English. The eight phonic code charts are systematically organized to show the signs (spellings) found in English. Four of these charts present the vowels and their various spellings and four charts present the consonants with their various spellings. Raphael (1966) explains that the word cards present words for different parts of speech. Each part of speech is printed in a special color. "By printing the words together in sentences, learners discover the structural elements of complete sentences. If a word can be used as more than one part of speech, it is printed on more than one color card." This is done so that the students learn inductively that every complete sentence always has a structural element and only sometimes includes other structural elements.

Raphael (1966) states that materials used for individual students are printed in black on white paper or card. As soon as the first sound is presented, students can recognize the words in a word-building book, learn words made of the sound in the first of three reading books, and use words on the first worksheet. According to Raphael (1966), since the students work simultaneously with words printed in color and words printed in black, progress does not depend on remembering colors. The use of materials is flexible depending on student needs and level of readiness. One color and its sound is presented at a time and a new color and sound are not presented until the last one has been mastered. Raphael (1966) states that some letters are represented by very close colors so that students learn immediately that they need to use the shape to identify the letter such as b and d.

According to Raphael (1966) Words in Color was used by 15,000 students in 1965 across the United States. The program was also tested with adults and teenagers unable to read in the Cleveland, Ohio, Community Antipoverty Programs.

Zintz (1970) states that Words in Color is very complicated and may not help students learn reading as a thinking process. Bernstein (1967) states that Words in Color may be too complex and the transition from color to black and white print may unnecessarily complicate the reading process. Spache (1970) stated that the lack of supporting data led him to conclude that Words in Color did not provide any advantage for the learner. Spache (1970) stated that when a student is presented with several clues the student selects one clue for retention and adding color or a different type face or different symbols may complicate the task and "these additional clues may be discarded in the transition to normal reading" and are not helpful.

Jones (1965), however, reports that color was an important factor in visual perception in beginning reading. In a study with adult illiterates Hinds (1966) found that the group that was taught by the Words in Color approach scored significantly better in both mean reading vocabulary and reading comprehension compared to the group taught by another approach. Dodds (1966) compared word recognition, spelling, and comprehension scores at the end of the first grade and during the second grade for students taught by basal readers and Words in Color. The Words in Color group scored better in all areas at the end of the first grade and scored significantly higher in comprehension during the second grade. Hill (1967) and Kaufman (1972) found no significant difference between groups taught by Words in Color and basal readers. Dean (1966) found that the discrimination of color may be difficult for some students and students may become very good at word-calling without comprehension. Myers and Hammill (1969) state that Dean's finding could be applied to any strongly phonic reading approach because young students have limited experience and may not understand the words which they can "read."

Annotated Bibliography

Bernstein, M.C. "Reading Methods and Materials Based on Linguistic Principles for Basic and Remedial Instruction." *Academic Therapy Quarterly* 2 (1967): 149–154.
    Discusses several reading approaches and their use with general education and remedial students. Presents a critique of Words in Color as too complicated.
Chall, Jeanne S. *Learning to Read: The Great Debate*. New York: Harcourt Brace, 1996.
    Presents only a brief description of Words in Color calling it a phonics program.
Dean, J. "Words in Color." In *The First International Reading Symposium*. J. Downing, ed. New York: Day, 1966.
    Presents the advantages and disadvantages of the approach stating that students will have comprehension problems because color discrimination will create word-callers who do not understand what they decode.
Dodds, W.A. "A Longitudinal Study of Two Beginning Reading Programs—Words in Color and Traditional Basal Readers." Ph.D. dissertation, Case Western Reserve University, 1966.
    Reports the results of a comparison of Words in Color and basal readers in grades one and two.
Gattegno, Caleb. *Teaching Reading with Words in Color: A Scientific Study of the Problems of Reading*. New York: Educational Solutions, 1968.
    This is a detailed guide to the approach providing reproductions of all charts and the justification for the methods of the approach.
Gattegno, Caleb. *Words in Color: Teacher's Guide*. Chicago: Learning Materials, 1962.
    The first American guide to the approach outlining its application in the classroom.
Gillespie-Silver, Patricia. *Teaching Reading to Children with Special Needs: An Ecological Approach*. Columbus, OH: Merrill, 1979.
    This text on reading methods for special education students presents a brief discussion of Words in Color with research references. A good starting point for information about the approach.
Hill, Frank G. "A Comparison of the Effectiveness of Words in Color with the Basic Reading Program Used in the Washington Elementary School District." Ph.D. dissertation, Arizona State University, 1967.
    Reports on the first use of Words in Color in American schools showing no significant difference in reading progress where compared to the basic approach in Washington, D.C., schools.
Hindes, L.R. "An Evaluation of Words in Color or Morophologico-Algebraic Approach to Teaching Reading to Functionally Illiterate Adults." Ph.D. dissertation, Case Western Reserve University, 1966.
    Reports on the success of Words in Color with adults.
Jones, K. "Color as an Aid to Visual Perception in Early Reading." *British Journal of Educational Psychology* 35 (February 1965): 21–27.
    Reports that color is a highly significant factor in visual perception in beginning reading instruction and is helpful to young students.
Kaufman, M. *Words in Color for Intensive Remedial Instruction*. Boston: Northwestern University, 1972.
    Compared Words in Color in remedial programs to basal readers and reported no significant difference between the two approaches.

Lockmiller, P., and DiNello, M.C. "Words in Color Versus a Basal Reader Program with Retarded Readers in Grade 2." *Journal of Educational Research* 63 (1970): 330–334.

Reports no significant difference between Words in Color and basal readers with borderline retarded students.

Myers, Patricia I., and Hammill, Donald D. *Methods for Learning Disorders*. New York: John Wiley & Sons, 1969.

A text which presents methods of assessment and teaching for students with learning disorders. Presents an overview of Words in Color.

Raphael, Sister M. "Color: A New Dimension in Teaching Reading." *Catholic School Journal* LXVI (October 1966): 56–57.

Presents a detailed description of Words in Color method and materials in clear language. Useful to read before and with Gattegno's guide.

Spache, George D. *Good Reading for Poor Readers*. Champaign, IL: Garrard, 1970.

This is an evaluation of many different types of materials and publications which are useful for use with students who have reading problems.

Zintz, W.V. *The Reading Process: The Teacher and the Learner*. Dubuque, IA: Wm C. Brown, 1970.

This is a text on reading instruction which describes various methods and materials.

The Linguistic Approach

The linguistic approach teaches regularly spelled words with an emphasis on sound letter correspondence without teaching rules about sound-letter correspondence.

Chall (1996) states that "linguistics is the scientific study of the nature of language." This field of study had an important effect on beginning reading instruction especially in the late 1960s and 1970s. Smith (1965) states that many journal articles and convention presentations in the 1960s focused on linguistics and reading. The discussion of linguistics and reading, however, began in the 1940s with Leonard Bloomfield's articles questioning the emphasis on meaning in teaching reading. Bloomfield (1942) suggested a shift to teaching the code or the alphabetic habit first. Chall (1996) states that Bloomfield believed that children came to school able to use oral language very well and reading instruction should first teach the corresponding printed vocabulary. Teach regularly spelled words first, Bloomfield (1942) stated, even though English spelling is irregular. Burns, Roe, and Ross (1988) state that "there is no one linguistic approach to teaching reading; however, a number of approaches have been built around linguistic principles." Harris and Sipay (1985) state that Bloomfield recommended strategies that included: (1) start with teaching the names of the letters not the sounds, (2) start with words that have three letters with a consonant-vowel-consonant pattern that only has short vowel sounds, (3) use lots of words that vary by only one letter such as Dan, Man, Fan, Pan, (4) do not teach rules about sound-letter correspondence because students will develop their own generalizations when sound and spelling correspond in a regular ways, and (5) use words in sentences.

Spache and Spache (1977) and Seymour (1969) add that phonologists advise (1) pictures should not be used because they provide context clues, (2) do not use phonics because it teaches sounds of words and students already know the sound of their language; phonics teaches that each letter has a sound, but letters stand for sounds; that letters can be silent, which is impossible, and that letters make sounds, which is not true because people make sounds; we recognize words by successive decoding of graphemes, not by word form, length, configuration or context clues as Bloomfield and Bloomfield (1961), Bougere

(1969) and Fries (1963) state, and Lefevre (1961), Fries (1963) and Bloomfield (1961) state those who advocate the whole word method confuse reading and understanding because a student can learn to read without being able to understand what is read; Fries (1963) states that sound-symbol recognition is more important than interpreting the meaning of words; Spache and Spache (1977) state that the phonologists believe that speech is the most important language function, not reading and writing, and therefore children who have normal speech are ready to read.

According to Chall (1996) Bloomfield and Fries did not agree with the definition of reading accepted by the rest of the educational community. Fries (1962) believed that the reading process is divided into three stages: "The first is the transfer or beginning stage in which ... the process of learning to read in one's native language is the process of transfer from auditory signs for language signals, which the child has already learned, to the new visual signs for the same signals. The second is the productive stage, in which the responses to the visual patterns become unconscious. The third is the imaginative stage ... when the reading process itself is so automatic that the reading is used equally with or even more than live language in the acquiring and developing of experience—when reading stimulates the vivid imaginative realization of vicarious experience."

Bloomfield and Bloomfield (1961) and Fries (1963) both were against sounding and blending and suggested that during the transfer stage students practice with words grouped according to contrasting spelling patterns such as can, cane, and rat, rate. This strategy encouraged students to discover the relationship between sounds and letters.

Lefevre (1964) suggests a linguistic program that Chall (1996) states was "closer to the older sentence and experience methods (as well as the current conventional basal-reader approach) than to the linguistic approaches.... Lefevre is concerned more with syntactical aspects of language (sentence structure and grammar) and less with the relationship between sounds and letters."

Spache and Spache (1977) state that Lefevre (1968) believes that the sentence, not word perception, is the unit of meaning. He suggests teaching students to listen to stories and pay attention to sentence order, word order, and intonation of sentences. Students begin by reading whole sentences.

The reading materials that claimed to be based on linguistic principles, Spache and Spache (1977) and Chall (1996) identify as *Let's Read* by Bloomfield and Barnhart; the *Merrill Linguistic Readers* by Fries, Wilson and Rudolph; *The Linguistic Readers* by Smith, Stratemeyer et al.; *The Basic Reading Series* by Goldberg and Rasmussen; *Sounds and Letters Series* by Halls; *The Miami Linguistic Readers*; the *Structural Reading Series* by Stern; and *The Royal Road Readers* by Daniels and Diack.

Spache and Spache (1977) question the differences found among these materials and state "if all these readers are supposed to be based on the same fundamental principles of linguistics, the contradictory practices are puzzling...." Spache and Spache (1977) list the differences among these readers as:

Fries: No pictures; words in sentences; regularly spelled words; nonsense words and sentences

Bloomfield and Barnhart: Pictures; lists of words, nonsense words in sentences

Goldberg and Rasmussen: Pictures; regular and irregular words

Smith and Stratemeyer: Pictures; stories and poetry

Daniels and Diack: Pictures; uses story to introduce new words; does not control sentence patterns; words and sounds are introduced as needed.

Chall (1996) states that there were very few studies of linguistic approaches before 1965. DeLawter (1975) compared second graders taught by the Miami and Merrill linguistic readers and second graders taught by basal readers. It was found that after two years of instruction the students taught by linguistic approaches made non-word miscues in oral reading. The basal reader group made oral miscues for real words. It was concluded that pupils using a linguistic approach make a higher percent of mistakes for non-words and this shows that the errors orally were similar to printed words but semantically wrong. These students corrected words based on letter sounds not context of semantic clues. DeLawter (1975) found that these students were responding to graphophonemic clues which are the least significant clues for printed words to obtain meaning.

Schneyer (1969) compared Fries' readers to basal readers and reported that the basal group performed better in spelling, paragraph meaning and phonic skills. The group using basal readers performed at superior levels for reading rate and accuracy in oral reading. Average ability students did superior work in comprehension and high ability students performed superior work on phonic skills. In a third grade follow-up study, Schneyer (1969) found that the only significant difference between the groups was that phonics skills were better for the basal reader group. The linguistic group used more running words in writing and performed superior work in oral reading rate, but not in accuracy.

Chall (1996) reports only two studies using Bloomfield's linguistic system and three studies that provide indirect information on the validity of Bloomfield's theories. Sister Mary Fidelia (1959) compared an experimental grade one group that received a separate period of word-attack practice based on Bloomfield's theory and a control grade one group that received a separate period of analytic phonics. There was no significant difference between these two groups on standardized silent reading tests after six months. The experimental group, Sister Mary Fidelia (1959) reports, also used basal readers in addition to the Bloomfield materials, and Chall (1996) questions the conclusions about the Bloomfield approach. Sister Mary Edward (1964) described a study of an experimental modified linguistic group using the Bloomfield system and a control group using basal readers and phonics. At the beginning of the 4th grade the experimental group tested significantly higher than the control group on standardized silent reading tests for vocabulary, rate and comprehension. Chall (1996) questions the results because the modified linguistic approach taught consonant sounds and Chall stated that Bloomfield advised against the direct teaching of letter-sound correspondence. Chall (1996) reports on several other studies such as an unpublished experiment by Bishop (1962) in which adults were taught eight Arabic words by letter-sound correspondence because letters correspond exactly with their sounds in the Arabic language. One group learned by letter sound correspondence and one group learned by words or the look-say approach. The results, Chall (1996) reports, indicated that the group who learned by letter-sound correspondence or direct phonics instruction were better able to transfer what they learned to figure out new words. The study, Chall (1996) states, "indicates that some people are able to induce correspondence for themselves even though not directly taught to do so..." and that direct teaching of sound-letter correspondence helps improve word learning. Not every pupil may need such teaching, but it helps those who cannot "discover the correspondence for themselves." Chall (1996) states that children will succeed less frequently yet the Bloomfield and Fries approaches "expect children to do this and only this at the beginning."

Chall (1996) states that the work of Fries and Bloomfield has a theoretical effect on thinking about reading instruction, but there is little evidence on the effect that the approaches have in the classroom. These approaches need further experimental testing. To conclude that the linguistic approach will be better than phonics instruction, is uncertain, but they may not be better approaches for teaching irregularly spelled words.

Wardhaugh (1969) reported that although the linguistic approach helps students recognize words better, oral reading rate and accuracy were poor. Linguists oppose sound-symbol teaching, but their approaches do not produce better comprehension results. McCullough (1968) states that after more research it is hoped that linguists will help in teaching "the relativity of language—the vaunts in sounds because of adjoining letters and the influence of context upon words and sentence meanings.... We hope that the linguists will cease trying to superimpose adult logic upon children's learning ... we don't sound the whole sentence before we utilize clues to structure, sense some possible clues to meaning and relationship, formulate hunches about the total meaning and see possible applications of this meaning to past and future ideas."

Heilman (1968) states that "while every linguist is entitled to hypothesize as to how reading should be taught, there is nothing in the body of linguistic science which relates to the issue of how children learn to read." Martin (1965) stated that linguists appeared to be trapped by an emphasis on individual words and leads no further than phonics programs. There may, however, be a "...potential contribution of structural linguistics to children's reading material once someone finds a way to translate linguistic insights into wholesome language patterns." Sentences such as "Nat is a fat cat" have been found in readers since readers were first developed, but Martin (1965) states "the fact that they are now paraded under the label of linguistics does not camouflage their weakness."

Annotated Bibliography

Anderson, Paul S. *Linguistics in the Elementary School Classroom*. New York: Macmillan, 1971.
    A collection of articles from professional journals divided into six parts: What is Linguistics?; Linguistics and the Child's Language and Thought; Linguistics and Reading; Linguistics and Spelling; Linguistics and Usage; and Linguistics and Grammar. Anderson provides a preface, a Professional Bibliography, and a Classroom Bibliography. Each part has a brief introduction.

Betts Emmett A. "Reading and Linguistics." *Education* 83 (1963): 515-526.
    States that linguists are not teachers or reading specialists and tend to overemphasize the use of linguistics in reading instruction. Betts states that linguists do not consider how linguistic principles apply to children in a regular classroom. Concludes that while linguistics is neither educationally nor psychologically acceptable it can contribute to more effective reading instruction. The major problem is the way linguistics is applied to reading.

Bishop, Carol. "Transfer of Word and Letter Training in Reading." M.A. thesis, Cornell University, 1962.
    A research study with adults which looked at the effect of previous training in letter-sound correspondence on the success in learning eight Arabic words. The study found that some individuals can induce correspondence by themselves without direct instruction.

Bloomfield, Leonard. "Linguistics and Reading." *Elementary English* 19 (1942): 125-130a, 183-186b.
    Bloomfield questioned the emphasis on meaning in teaching reading, suggesting that early reading instruction emphasize the alphabet habit or the "code." Children, Bloomfield stated, came to school fluent in spoken language, and reading should provide them with "the printed equivalents" of oral language. He suggested starting with regularly spelled words.

Bloomfield, Leonard, and Barnhart, Clarence. *Let's Read: A Linguistic Approach*. Detroit: Wayne State University Press, 1961.
    Describes Bloomfield's system of teaching and includes 245 lessons for instruction.

Bougere, Marguerite Bondy. "Selected Factors in Oral Language Related to First Grade Reading Achievement." *Reading Research Quarterly* 5 (Fall 1969): 31–58.

Discusses the relationship between oral language development and success in learning to read in the first grade.

Burns, Paul C., Roe, Betty D., and Ross, Elinor. *Teaching Reading in Today's Elementary Schools*. Boston: Houghton-Mifflin, 1988, pp. 336–338.

This text on reading instruction provides an overview of the linguistic approach. A useful bibliography is provided. This is a good starting point for an investigation of the approach.

Chall, Jeanne S. *Learning to Read: The Great Debate*, 3d edition. New York: Harcourt Brace College, 1996.

This classic provides an excellent discussion of the history of reading instruction providing a description of the linguistic approach and research evidence. The book is a report of a three year Carnegie Corporation research study undertaken to discover the most effective approaches to teaching young students to read. Chall provides a comprehensive work with an extensive bibliography.

Creswell, T.J., and McDavid, Virginia. "Linguistics and the Teaching of Reading," *Elementary English* 40 (1963): 93–96.

Discusses the application of linguistics to reading instruction providing specific suggestions.

DeLawter, Jayne A. "The Relationship of Beginning Reading Instruction and Miscue Patterns." In *Help for the Reading Teacher: New Directions in Research*. William D. Page, ed. Urbana, IL: National Conference for Research in English, 1975, pp. 42–51.

Report of a two year study comparing word miscues in oral reading between second graders taught by the linguistic approach and the basal approach. Concludes that the linguistic group made miscue errors for non-words because the graphophonemic cue is the least important for getting meaning from printed words.

Devine, T.G. "Linguistic Research and the Teaching of Reading," *Journal of Reading* 9 (March 1966): 272–277.

A critique of the application of linguistic principles to teaching reading. States that studies that use linguistic structure as a strategy for improving reading comprehension are failures. Offers suggestions for overcoming this problem stating what should be done.

Edward, Sister Mary. "A Modified Linguistic Versus a Composite Basal Reading Program." *Reading Teacher* 17 (1964): 511–515.

Reports on a study using a modified Bloomfield linguistic approach which taught consonant sounds. This is not in compliance with Bloomfield's theory of linguistics. The study does not state whether the performance of the experimental group was affected by direct teaching of letter-sound correspondence.

Fidelia, Sister Mary. "The Relative Effectiveness of Bloomfield's Linguistic Approach to Word-Attack as Compared with *Phonics We Use*." Ph.D. dissertation, School of Psychology and Education, University of Ottawa, Ottawa, Canada, 1959.

A study of two groups of first graders. The experimental group was given a separate period of word-attack practice based on Bloomfield's theory and the control group received a period of modified analytic phonics instruction. Concluded that there was no significant difference between the groups after six months of instruction.

Fries, Charles C. *Linguistics and Reading*. New York: Holt, Rinehart, and Winston, 1963.

Discusses the application of linguistic principles to the teaching of reading. Analyzes the reading process in terms of language meaning, discusses linguistic theory. Fries states the book is concerned with teaching reading in terms of the "knowledge concerning human language which linguistic sciences has achieved." Provides information about linguistic sciences from the 19th century to the 1960s; the nature of the reading process; phonics; spelling; and materials and methods of a linguistic approach to reading.

Goldberg, Lynn, and Rasmussen, Donald. "Linguistics in Reading." In *Explorations in Reading*. Albert J. Mazurkiewicz, ed. Bethlehem, PA: Lehigh University Conference Proceedings, 2 (June 1962): 22–27.

   Discusses the application of linguistic principles to reading instruction. States that nonsense words, even when they fit the pattern of regularity of word sounds, do not help students learn to read. These nonsense words have no meaning and cannot be learned even though they are phonemically consistent.

Goodman, Kenneth S. "A Linguistic Study of Cues and Miscues in Reading." *Elementary English* 42 (October 1965): 639–643.

   Analyzes oral reading errors and the relationship between translating letters to sounds and interpreting the meaning of printed words.

Harris, Albert J., and Sipay, Edward R. *How to Increase Reading Ability: A Guide to Developmental and Remedial Methods*. New York: Longman, 1985, 1987, 1988.

   A classic textbook on reading instruction. Provides an overview of the linguistic approach citing research findings. A good bibliography is included.

Heilman, Arthur W. "Research Findings Concerning Phonics in Beginning Reading." In *A Decade of Innovations: Approaches to Beginning Reading*. Elaine Vilscek, ed. Newark, DE: Proceedings International Reading Association, 12, part 3, 1968, pp. 100–106.

   Discusses the application of linguistic principles to reading instruction. States that while linguists "hypothesize about how reading should be taught, there is nothing in the body of linguistic science which relates to the issue of how children learn to read."

Howes, Virgie M., and Darrow, Helen F. *Reading and the Elementary School Child: Selected Readings on Programs and Practices*. New York: Macmillan, 1968.

   A collection of readings on approaches to teaching reading. Includes a discussion of the linguistic approach.

Lefevre, Carl A. "Language Patterns and Their Graphic Counter Parts: A Linguistic View of Reading." In *Changing Concepts of Reading Instruction*. New York: Proceedings International Reading Association, 6 (1961): 245–251.

   Explains the relationship between oral and written language from the linguistic perspective. Presents the application of linguistic theory to reading instruction.

Lefevre, Carl A. *Linguistics and the Teaching of Reading*. New York: McGraw Hill, 1964.

   Presents an explanation of the contributions of linguistics to "teaching the skills of literacy-reading and writing.... The method proposed ... is a whole-sentence method that applies a scientific description of American English utterances to the problem of teaching reading. No one can get meaning from the printed page without taking in whole language patterns at the sentence level because these are the minimal meaning-bearing structures of most written communications." Outlines how to apply structural linguistics to reading instruction.

Lefevre, Carl A. Reading Instruction Related to Primary Language Learning: A Linguistic View." *Journal of Developmental Reading* 4 (Spring 1961): 147–158.

   Discusses the relationship between early oral language learning and reading instruction. Stresses that larger speech patterns such as statements, requests, structural elements such as parts of speech, functional words and grammatical inflections are the core teaching material for reading instruction.

Lefevre, Carl A. "The Simplistic Standard Word Perception Theory of Reading." *Elementary English* 45 (March 1968): 349–353, 355.

   Presents a discussion of his theory of linguistics stating that the sentence not word perception is the unit of meaning. Suggests that reading be taught by having students listen to stories and pay attention to sentence order and most important intonation of sentences.

Martin, Bill, Jr. "Literature, Linguistics, and Reading." *Florida Reading Quarterly* 1 (March 1965): 9–22.

   Presents a critique of linguistic teaching material stating that the sentence structure is weak and will have potential once translated into "wholesome language patterns."

McCullough, Constance M. "Applying Structural Linguistics in Beginning Reading: Vital Principles in Need of Application." In *A Decade of Innovations: Approaches to Beginning Reading*. Elaine C. Vilscek ed. Bethlehem, PA: Proceedings, International Reading Association, 12 part 3 (1968): 180–191.

    States that linguistics may be able to help teach the relativity of language or the variation in sounds due to adjoining letters and the affect of context on word and sentence meaning. Provides an analysis of linguistic theory suggesting that linguists need to rethink their application of adult logic on children's learning so that their theory will help provide better reading instruction.

Pikulski, John J. "Linguistics Applied to Reading Instruction." *Language Arts* 53 (April 1976): 373–377.

    Discusses the use of linguistic principles in reading instruction, stating that they have been applied in contradicting claims causing problems for those who attempt to use the strategies. There is no one clear strategy.

Ruddell, Robert B. "Reading Instruction in First Grade with Varying Emphasis on the Regularity of Grapheme-Phoneme Correspondences and the Relation of Language Structure to Meaning." *Reading Teacher* 19 (May 1966): 653–660.

    Discusses the First Grade studies done by the U.S. Office of Education, reporting the results of the comparison between the linguistic and basal approaches.

Ruddell, Robert B. "Reading Instruction in First Grade with Varying Emphasis on the Regularity of Grapheme-Phoneme Correspondence and the Relation of Language Structure to Meaning-Extended Into Second Grade." *Reading Teacher* 20 (May 1967): 730–739.

    A follow-up study comparing linguistic and basal approaches found that the results were different at the end of grade one and grade two, but there was very little difference between the approaches. The linguistic group did show improvement in language structure training and better skill in word recognition.

Schneyer, J. Wesley. "Reading Achievement of First Grade Children Taught by a Linguistic Approach and a Basal Reading Approach." *Reading Teacher* 8 (May 1966): 647–652.

    Compares the results of teaching using the linguistic and basal approaches reports on oral reading, phonics skills and writing, finding that the basal group performed better in spelling, paragraph meaning and phonic skills. Average pupils in the basal group performed very well in comprehension and high ability students performed very well in phonic skills.

Schneyer, J. Wesley. "Reading Achievement of First Grade Children Taught by a Linguistic Approach and a Basal Approach Extended Into Third Grade." *Reading Teacher* 22 (January 1969): 315–319.

    In this follow-up study of the 1966 study Schneyer found that third graders taught by the basal approach demonstrated significantly better phonic skills than the linguistic group, but the group taught by the linguistic approach demonstrated superior skill in writing using more running words and were superior in reading rate, but not in accuracy in oral reading.

Seymour, Dorothy Z. "The Difference Between Linguistics and Phonics." *Reading Teacher* 23 (November 1969): 99–102, 111.

    Describes the differences between phonics and linguistics, stating that phonics teaches how to pronounce words rather than how to read them. States that phonics should be eliminated in its current form because phonics teaches errors in language. Lists the errors to which phonics instruction leads.

Sheldon, William D., Nichols, Nancy J., and Lashinger, Donald R. "Effect of First Grade Instruction Using Basal Readers, Modified Linguistic Materials and Linguistic Readers-Extended Into Second Grade." *Reading Teacher* 20 (May 1967): 720–725.

    Reports that at the end of the first grade the basal group demonstrated superior rate and accuracy in oral reading. In the second grade the linguistic groups demonstrated better ability in spelling, word meaning, and oral comprehension.

Sheldon, William D., Stinson, Frange, and Peebles, James D. "Comparison of Three Methods of Reading: A Continuation Study in the Third Grade." *Reading Teacher* 22 (March 1969): 539–546.

In this follow-up study Sheldon et al. did not find any differences in reading skills at the end of third grade. Concluded that no matter what reading approach was used some of the students in each group were still disabled readers.

Smith, Frank, and Goodman, Kenneth. "On the Psycholinguistic Method of Teaching Reading." *Elementary School Journal* 71 (January 1971): 177–181.

States that there are no real linguistic reading programs, only reading programs written by linguists. Questions the effectiveness of linguistic reading programs.

Smith, Henry L. "A Review of *Let's Read: A Linguistic Approach*." *Language* 5 (1963): 67–78.

A critique of Bloomfield's book stating that educators and linguists should work together to plan reading programs.

Smith, Nila Banton. *American Reading Instruction*. Newark, DE: International Reading Association, 1965, 2002.

Presents a history of the linguistic approach describing the programs developed by Bloomfield and Fries.

Spache, George D., and Spache, Evelen. *Reading in the Elementary School*. Boston: Allyn and Bacon, 1977.

A textbook on teaching reading. Provides detailed discussion of the linguistic approach with relevant research reports and a bibliography. Provides a very good introduction and starting point for information about the linguistic approach

Strickland, Ruth. "Linguistics and the Teaching of Reading." *Education Digest* 29 (April 1964): 47–50.

Provides a detailed distinction between the linguist's idea of reading and the reading teacher's idea of reading.

Wardhaugh, Ronald. "Is the Linguistic Approach an Improvement in Reading Instruction?" In *Current Issues in Reading*. Nila Banton Smith, ed. Newark, DE: Proceedings International Reading Association, 13, part 2 (1969): 254–267.

The aim of this paper, Wardhaugh states, is to demonstrate the type of linguistic knowledge used in reading methods and materials. States that this knowledge is "neither ... current linguistic knowledge nor is it always sound knowledge, linguistically or pedagogically." Evaluates research evidence and materials concluding that a linguistic method of teaching does not exist. Provides a good discussion of claims by linguists; research on phoneme-grapheme correspondences; modified alphabets; syntax studies; the missing dimension—current linguistics. Provides a good bibliography.

Wilson, R.G., and Lindsay, H. "Applying Linguistics to Remedial Reading." *Reading Teacher* 16 (1965): 452–455.

Describes the use of linguistic theory with students who are reading below grade placement. Provides another view of linguistic principles.

Emergent Literacy

Emergent literacy is the earliest stage in the development of reading ability. It is the stage at which children begin to associate printed words with their meaning. Children begin to realize that letters have sounds, words are made up of letters, and words have meaning.

According to Harris and Hodges (1995), emergent literacy is "development of the association of print with meaning that begins early in a child's life and continues until the child reaches the stage of conventional reading and writing." Sulzby and Teale (1991) state that emergent literacy is "the reading and writing concepts and behaviors of young children that precede and develop into conventional literacy."

Teale (1995) states that the term emergent literacy was the result of a new theoretical perspective on how young children learn to read and write. During the 1970s and 1980s, researchers began searching for a clear term to describe early language development. "Reading readiness" (the readiness to benefit from beginning reading instruction) was no longer a viable term. Teale believes that emergent literacy describes "reading and writing development from the child's point of view. Emergent literacy examines changes over time in how the child thinks about literacy and in the strategies the child uses in attempts to comprehend or produce written language." Young children's concepts about reading are different from those of the fluent reader.

Instruction, Sulzby and Teale (1991) state, must address the special needs of the emergent reader. Concepts develop as children observe and interact with literate members of their learning community. This idea descends directly from Froebel's (1862) advice to teachers, "Come let us learn with our children," and Dewey's (1896; 1899; 1916) concept that children learn best when they are directly involved in and part of their own learning. The underlying principles of emergent literacy, according to Sulzby and Teale (1991), are:

1. Involve children in reading and writing activities starting on the first day of school;
2. Create a print-rich environment which has a wide variety of print to explore;

3. Make written language an important and functional part of the environment;
4. Make sure lessons and activities include written language to achieve many goals.

Owocki (2001) lists four principles necessary for understanding and facilitating literacy:

1. Literacy developments as a social and cultural practice. Like Dewey (1916), Gee (1996) believes that reading and writing take place within groups of people who interact socially;
2. Literacy develops through hypothesis testing. Children continually generate new hypotheses and test them based on what they already know about language. Hypotheses are challenged and changed by social and print understanding;
3. Literacy develops idiosyncratically. Each child develops differently, and literacy develops in a personalized, unique way;
4. Literacy concepts develop simultaneously. Children develop more than one concept at a time.

To ensure that young children develop the concepts needed to learn to become fluent readers and writers, teachers need to use instructional strategies that encourage emergent literacy. Teale (1995) suggests:

1. Teachers should read to the whole group, small groups, and individuals and discuss the story. Discussion among children and the teacher helps understanding development. Make literature a vital part of the daily activities;
2. Children should "read" books. Children need the opportunity to handle books on a daily basis in a library or reading corner;
3. Written language should be everywhere, embedded in all activities, including the calendar, charts, and lists of activities as part of the daily routine;
4. Children should respond to books in a variety of ways such as art, music, discussion, and dramatic reenactment;
5. Writing should be an everyday activity. The teacher should write a daily message, stories, notes, and invitations so that the children can observe and learn to write using pictures, scribbles, letters, and words;
6. Children should hear the consistent sounds of the language through poetry, nursery rhymes, games, and language play to develop an awareness of the sounds of language;
7. Letter-sound association activities must be part of the daily activities.

Emergent literacy is more than readiness to learn to read. It is concept and skill development and immersion in language.

Annotated Bibliography

Campbell, Robin, ed. *Facilitating Preschool Literacy*. Newark, DE: International Reading Association, 1998.
  A book of readings by various authors. Part one contains chapters about children constructing literacy, part two contains chapters about literacy in the home and part three contains chapters about literacy learning in preschool settings.
Dewey, John. *Democracy and Education*. New York: Macmillan, 1916.
  Applies the ideas of democratic society to the problems of education. This classic describes the democratic concept in education, education as growth, education as a social function and interest and discipline.
Dewey, John. "Interest as Related to [the Training of the] Will." *National Herbert Society Year Book for 1895*. Bloomington, IL: National Herbert Society, 1896, pp. 209–255.
  A classic discussion of the importance of student interest in activities.
Dewey, John. *The School and Society*. Chicago: University of Chicago Press, 1899.
  Discusses the relation between life in the classroom and life in society. Three lectures present the philosophy of Dewey's "new" idea of education as experimental, child-centered, and directed toward the reformation of society.
Froebel, Friedrich. *Padagogik Des Kindergarten*. Berlin: W. Lang, 1862; *The Pedagogics of the Kindergarten*. Trans. Josephine Jarvis. New York: D. Appleton & Co., 1895.
  Discusses the theory of unity, interrelatedness of all educational experiences, the conditions of child development, and the kindergarten program. Describes in detail the use of the Gifts and the importance of songs, games, and movements.
Gee, James Paul. *Social Linguistics and Literacies: Ideology in Discourses*. Bristol, PA: Faemer Press, 1996.
  Discusses the importance of the social aspect of learning to read and write. States that reading and writing takes place within groups of people who interact socially as a learning community.
Harris, Theodore L., and Hodges, Richard E. (eds.). *The Literacy Dictionary: The Vocabulary of Reading and Writing*. Newark, DE: International Reading Association, 1995.
  Presents a clear definition of emergent literacy. This is a good starting point for understanding the concept.
Newman, Susan B., and Roskos, Kathleen A., eds. *Children Achieving: Best Practices in Early Literacy*. Newark, DE: International Reading Association, 1998.
  A book of 13 chapters written by experts addressing important issues in the field of early literacy. Provides insight into how children acquire literacy, reading and writing practices, culturally responsive instruction, instruction for children with learning disabilities and how do teachers grow and learn as professionals.
Owocki, Gretchen. *Literacy Through Play*. Portsmouth, NH: Heinemann, 1999.
  This is a resource book to assist preschool and primary grade teachers organize and implement strategies for teaching reading, writing and spelling in developmentally appropriate ways. Owocki explains how to organize the classroom and observe students as they construct knowledge about the world and language through play.
Owocki, Gretchen. *Make Way for Literacy: Teaching the Way Young Children Learn*. Washington, DC: National Association for the Education of Young Children, 2001.
  Explains how literacy develops in young children and presents research-based strategies for helping children develop reading, writing, speaking, and spelling skills. Owocki presents four principles that help teachers understand and encourage the development of literacy skills in practical, developmentally appropriate ways.

Strickland, Dorothy, and Morrow, Lesley Mandel, eds. *Emerging Literacy: Young Children Learn to Read and Write*. Newark, DE: International Reading Association, 2000.

A series of twelve articles by experts in the field of emergent literacy addressing topics such as oral language, emergent writing, skills in kindergarten, and designing the classroom. A practical research-based book which will provide the foundations and practical application of methods for emergent literacy.

Sulzby, Elizabeth, and Teale, William H. "Emergent Literacy." In *Handbook of Reading Research Volume II*. Rebecca Barr, Michael L. Kamil, Peter Mosenthal, and P David Pearson, eds. Mahwah, NJ: Erlbaum, 1991, pp. 727–758.

Presents a discussion of emergent literacy research providing definitions; questions; methodological and theoretical perspectives; storybook reading; patterns of change in storybook-reading instruction; writing instruction; home learning; phonemic awareness and an extensive bibliography.

Teale, William H. "Young Children and Reading; Trends Across the 20th Century." *Journal of Education* 177 (1995): 95–125.

Presents a good discussion of emergent literacy and its development.

Teale, William H., and Sulzby, Elizabeth, eds. *Emergent Literacy: Writing and Reading*. Norwood, NJ: Ablex Publishing, 1986.

A group of eight chapters by experts on various aspects of emergent reading and writing strategies such as how children become writers and readers, oral and written language; learning to read from books; home background and literacy development. Provides useful bibliographies for each chapter.

Story Grammar

Story grammar is a way to analyze a story so that students gain a better understanding of the story elements which leads to better reading comprehension.

According to Harris and Sipay (1985) and Tierney and Readence (2000), Arthur I. Gates (1947) stated that the importance of a sense of story was a valuable contribution to the comprehension of narrative. Research on story grammar almost forty years later described and empirically tested the importance of this concept on student comprehensions. Harris and Hodges (1995) state that story grammar is "a device or grammar used for specifying relations among episodes in a story and to formulate rules for generating other stories." Tierney and Readence (2000) state that this is a method of analyzing stories, helping students develop a sense of story, and ensuring that the guidance that teachers give is true to the story line. Sadow (1982) states that a story is a series of events related to one another in specific ways. Tierney and Readence (2000) state that stories have a predictable grammar that students can identify and use to comprehend stories.

Harris and Sipay (1985) identify five elements that well organized stories have in common: (1) setting; (2) problem is identified; (3) character's reaction to the problem and his/her goal; (4) attempts to achieve the goal; and (5) resolution of the problem. Cunningham and Foster (1978) list setting, theme, plot, and resolution as the structure of a story grammar. Tierney and Readence (2000) state that the story grammar helps students develop and use a sense of story and directs the questions the teacher uses to help comprehension during a guided reading.

When students listen to and read stories they develop a story schema which Rand (1984) calls "an internal representation" or framework of the story that includes an ordering of the story elements in which the parts of the story are causally or temporally related. Applebee (1978) and Whaley (1981) state that as students mature their concept of story becomes more sophisticated and better developed. After age eight students remember stories more completely. Younger students know a great deal about stories, but cannot remember all the details, according to Pellegrini and Galda (1982). The story schema helps students comprehend a story by organizing expectations for content which happens in a specific order. McConaughy (1982) states that story schemata help students select which information is most important for comprehending the story so that they can attend to those elements. Calfee and Spector (1981) state that when a story does not fit a student's story schema, comprehension of the story decreases and may become very poor. Stein and Trabasso (1981) state that the comprehension level of young students depends on how well the story is formed and how well the students understand the interactions and social situations in the story.

Burns, Roe, and Ross (1988) state that teachers use a variety of activities to help students develop a knowledge of story grammar. Discussing story structure in terms of folktales and fairy tales which have parts that are easy to identify and are familiar to students is a good activity as is retelling stories. Predicting what will happen next in a story after reading or hearing a story followed by a discussion of the predicted parts helps comprehension. Using stories with sections missing, asking students to fill in the blank spaces, and discussing the answers also helps students gain a sense of story structure. Whaley (1981) suggests giving the students sentence strips with the story sentences written on them to arrange the sentences that fit. The sentences are mixed up and students are instructed to rearrange these parts to make a good story. Spiegel and Fitzgerald (1986) suggest that each student write a story setting then pass the paper to a buddy who will add a beginning and pass it to another buddy. This process continues until all the parts are added such as "reactions, attempts, outcomes, and endings." When the story is finished it is read aloud. Fowler (1982) advocates the use of story frames or a sequence of blanks linked by transition words that show a line of thought: "Our story is about _____. _____ is an important character in our story. _____ tried to _____. The story ends when _____." Fowler (1982) states that story frames are useful as the start of a discussion of a story already read because frames are open-ended. The discussion will draw varied ideas from students. It should be stressed that ideas for filling in the blanks should relate reasonably to the material that came before it. Students can work alone after they have learned and practiced the technique with the rest of the class. Fowler (1982) reports that story frames are very useful with primary grade and remedial students.

Fitzgerald (1989), Gordon and Pearson (1983), Davis and McPherson (1989) agree that teaching story structure helps students' comprehension skills improve because the mental representation of story structure can help comprehension. A story map, Davis and McPherson (1989) state, is "a graphic representation of all or part of the elements of a story and the relationship between them." A story map shows plot, setting, characters, and themes visually but also can emphasize the author's pattern in a predictable book. Some story maps are based on story grammar or the plot structure, but others show structured overviews. Davis and McPherson (1989) suggest constructing a story map by putting the theme in the center in a circle and arranging the main events or settings in sequential order in a second level of circles. More circles with characters, events and actions can be connected to the second-level circles and each may have more circles attached to them in a clockwise order. Children learn to fill in story structure during reading. Primary grade students can construct simplified story maps only of the characters using pictures with short phrases. Story maps help students understand how stories are organized, develop schemata for a story that will be read, and organize a discussion after reading. Students who use the story map to develop schemata try to predict the story from the map and then read the story to confirm or change predictions. Story maps also help students keep ideas organized during reading. After reading students can reconstruct the map or discuss its relation to story events. Reutzel (1985) states that maps improve comprehension for narrative and expository material.

Tierney and Readence (2000) state that a story map is useful for generating questions for guided reading using explicit and implicit events and links between events. Beck and McKeown (1981) state that the story map ensures that questions match the progress of the story ideas and events. Beck and McKeown (1981) suggest using the story's progression of events and ideas before requesting that students discuss ideas out of order or extend interpretation of the story. The extension of ideas from the story helps comprehension after a story map has been drawn.

Harris and Sipay (1985) and Tierney and Readence (2000) present similar research findings related to story grammar and story maps. Using story grammars as a strategy to help students better understand stories and the use of story maps to generate questions to guide selected sections of a story are attempts to apply research to practice. The question raised is whether these strategies consider all factors.

Cunningham and Foster (1978) found that students who were the least able readers enjoyed using story grammar and reported that the technique improved comprehension. Marshall (1983), Tierney and Cunningham (1984) also report that students who had problems with comprehension benefited from using story grammar. Dreher and Singer (1980) studied fourth graders and criticized the study done by Cunningham and Foster (1978) stating that students had a well developed sense of story and did not require story grammar instruction.

Fitzgerald and Spiegel (1983) studied 20 fourth graders who were selected because they did not have a good sense of story. These students' comprehension improved after instruction in story grammar, leading Fitzgerald and Spiegel (1983) to conclude that since they were able to identify students in need of help and the students showed improved comprehension after instruction, the use of story grammar with selected students is justified.

Research about story maps done by Beck and McKeown (1981) found that integrated and sequential questions lead to better comprehension of a story than random questions or a combination of provocative questions, opportunities for interpretative responses and story line questions. Tierney and Readence (2000) state that there are no research results to substantiate the Beck and McKeown (1981) results. It would appear that a well organized set of questions would be better than random questions, but less reasonable is the idea that "provocative questions and interpretative probes may detract from story understanding. Often such probes may be what engages the reader; indeed, they may fuel the reader's interest to read more thoughtfully and diligently."

Several issues are common to story maps and grammars. Brewer and Lichtenstein (1982) found that what characterizes a story are more aesthetic aspects of a reader's response, such as suspense. Therefore, a story grammar structure does not make a story a story. It is suggested that students' emotional responses to a story could be used in combination with identification of story elements. Perhaps students should be encouraged to enjoy a story instead of taking the story apart and examining the parts. Tierney and Readence (2000) state that there is not enough data to state conclusively what is the best procedure. Teachers need to answer these questions subjectively.

Annotated Bibliography

Applebee, Arthur N. *Children's Concept of Story: Ages 2-17*. Chicago: University of Chicago Press, 1978.
    Describes the development of story knowledge and reading comprehension.
Beck, I., McCaslin, E.S., and Burge, A.M. *Instructional Dimensions That May Affect Comprehension*. Pittsburg, PA: University of Pittsburgh Learning Research and Development Center, 1979.
    Describes the story map and compares it with the guided reading of a basal reader story.
Beck, I., and McKeown, M.G. "Developing Questions That Promote Comprehension: The Story Map." *Language Arts* 58 (1981): 913-918.
    Describes the story map and tells why it should be used to improve comprehension skills.
Brewer, W.F., and Lichtenstein, E.H. *Stories Are to Entertain: A Structural-Affect Theory of Stories* (Tech. Rep. No. 265). Urbana-Champaign: University of Illinois, 1982.
    States that suspense is more valuable in story comprehension than story grammars. This presents negative comments about story grammars.
Burns, P.C., Roe, B.D., and Ross, E.P. *Teaching Reading in Today's Elementary Schools*. Boston: Houghton-Mifflin, 1988, pp. 223-229.
    This is a good overview of story grammar, story maps, and schema. A useful text for developing background and direction for further reading.

Calfee, Robert, and Spector, Janet E. "Separable Processes in Reading." In *Neuropsychological and Cognitive Processes in Reading*. F. Pirozollo and M. Wittrock, eds. New York: Academic Press, 1981, pp. 3-29.
   Describes schema theory and reading comprehension levels.
Cudd, E.T., and Robert, L.L. "Using Story Frame to Develop Comprehension in a First Grade Classroom." *Reading Teacher* 41 (1987): 74-81.
   Presents writing activities to help students respond to story frames.
Cunningham, J., and Foster, E.O. "The Ivory Tower Connection: A Case Study." *Reading Teacher* 31 (1978): 365-367.
   A case study of the use of story grammars with sixth graders.
Davis, Z.T., and McPherson, M.D. "Story Map Instruction: A Road Map for Reading Comprehension." *Reading Teacher* 43 (1989): 232-240.
   Presents practical suggestions for using story maps.
Dreher, M.J., and Singer, H. "Story Grammar Instruction Unnecessary for Intermediate Grade Students." *Reading Teacher* 34 (December 1980): 261-268.
   A study using the suggestions of Cunningham's and Foster's 1978 story grammars with 6th graders. This study does not agree with Cunningham and Foster and questions the necessity of story grammar activities with upper grade students.
Emery, D.W. "Helping Readers Comprehend Stories from the Character's Perspective." *Reading Teacher* 49 (1996): 534-541.
   Tells how to add character's perspective to story maps to help students comprehend stories better.
Fitzgerald, J. "Enhancing Two Related Thought Processes: Revision in Writing and Critical Reading." *Reading Teacher* 37 (December 1989): 42-48.
   Discusses the relationship between the revision of writing and critical reading as the same process for students.
Fitzgerald, J., and Spiegel, D.L. "Enhancing Children's Reading Comprehension Through Instruction in Narrative Structure." *Journal of Reading Behavior* 15 (1983): 1-17.
   Research with twenty 4th graders who had problems understanding story structure. Reports how instruction in story structure helped the students.
Fowler, Gerald, "Developing Comprehension Skills in Primary Students Through Use of Story Frames." *Reading Teacher* 36 (November 1982): 176-179.
   Presents details for using story frames with primary grade students.
Gates, Arthur I. *The Improvement of Reading*. New York: Macmillan, 1947.
   A classic text that discusses the development of a sense of story as important for reading comprehension.
Gordon, Christie, and Braun, Carl. "Using Story Schema as an Aid to Reading and Writing." *Reading Teacher* 37 (November 1983): 116-121.
   Provides suggestions for developing story schemata to improve comprehension and writing skills.
Gordon, Christie, and Pearson, D.P. *Effects of Instruction and Inferencing for Students' Comprehension Abilities* (Tech. Rep. No. 269). Urbana-Champaign: University of Illinois Center for the Study of Reading, 1983.
   Describes the relation between story structure and comprehension skills. A very useful source.
Gurney, D., Gersten, R., Dimino, J., and Carnine, D. "Story Grammar: Effective Literature Instruction for High School Students with Learning Disabilities." *Journal of Learning Disabilities* 23 (1990): 335-342.
   A research report of the effective use of story grammar with learning disabled students at the secondary level.
Harris, Albert J., and Sipay, Edward R. *How to Increase Reading Ability: A Guide to Developmental and Remedial Methods*. New York: Longman, **1985**, 1987, 1988, pp. 488-489.
   This classic text provides an excellent overview with references on schemata and story grammar. This is a good starting point for the topic.

Harris, Theodore L., and Hodges, Richard E., eds. *The Literacy Dictionary: The Vocabulary of Reading and Writing.* Newark, DE: International Reading Association, 1995.
   Provides a definition of story grammar, story maps, and schemata.
Mandler, J.M., and Johnson, N.S. "Remembrance of Things Passed: Story Structure and Recall." *Cognitive Psychology* 9 (1977): 111–151.
   This provides justification for the employment of the story grammar strategy.
Marshall, Nancy. "Using Story Grammar to Assess Reading Comprehension." *Reading Teacher* 36 (1983): 616–620.
   Suggests ways to use story grammar as a means of assessing students' comprehension skills.
McConaughy, S.H. "Developmental Changes in Story Comprehension and Levels of Questioning." *Language Arts* 59 (September 1982): 580–589.
   Describes the importance of focusing attention on story schemata as a foundation for better comprehension.
Olsen, Mary. "A Dash of Story Grammar and...Presto! A Book Report." *Reading Teacher* 39 (February 1984): 458–461.
   Describes the use of story grammar as a guide to effective book report writing.
Pearson, P.D. *Asking Questions About Stories.* Boston: Ginn, 1982.
   Describes how to use story maps with basal reader stories. A good start for material on story maps.
Pellegrini, A., and Galda, L. "The Effects of Thematic-Fantasy Play Training in the Development of Children's Story Comprehension." *American Educational Research Journal* 19 (Fall 1982): 443–452.
   Describes the role of play in story comprehension and story recall at various ages.
Rand, Muriel K. "Story Schema: Theory, Research, and Practice." *Reading Teacher* 37 (January 1984): 377–382.
   Presents the theory and application of story schemata in the classroom.
Reutzel, D. Ray. "Reconciling Schema Theory and the Basal Reading Lesson." *Reading Teacher* 39 (November 1985): 194–197.
   Describes how to use schema theory effectively with a basal lesson.
Reutzel, D. Ray. "Story Maps Improve Comprehension." *Reading Teacher* 38 (January 1985): 400–404.
   Describes the use of story maps as a way to ensure that students better understand what they read.
Rubin, Andee." Making Stories Making Sense." *Language Arts* 57 (March 1980): 285–293, 298, 334.
   Describes the creation of stories and story grammar.
Rumelhart, D.E. "Notes on Schema for Stories." In *Representation and Understanding: Studies in Cognitive Science.* D.G. Bobrow and A.M. Collins, eds. New York: Academic Press, 1975.
   This is a solid theoretical discussion of story grammar. It is one of the foundation works on the subject.
Sadow, Marilyn W. "The Use of Story Grammar in the Design of Questions." *Reading Teacher* 35 (February 1982): 518–522.
   Discusses story grammar and tells how to generate questions using story grammar.
Smith, M., and Bean T. "Four Strategies That Develop Children's Story Comprehension and Writing." *Reading Teacher* 37 (December 1983): 295–301.
   Provides four specific strategies to help students develop story schemata to better understand what they read.
Spiegel, D.L., and Fitzgerald, J. "Improving Reading Comprehension Through Instruction About Story Parts." *Reading Teacher* 39 (1986): 676–685.
   Describes how to improve students' comprehension by teaching story parts. A practical article.

Stein, N.L., and Glenn, C.G. "An Analysis of Story Comprehension in Elementary School Children," In *New Directions in Discourse Processing.* R.O. Freedle, ed. Norwood, NJ: Ablex, 1979.
   Describes research on schemata and comprehension. Investigated the effect of age and time on story comprehension.
Stein, Nancy L., and Trabasso, Tom. *What's in a Story: An Approach to Comprehension and Instruction* (Tech. Rep. No. 200). Champaign: Center for the Study of Reading, University of Illinois, April 1981.
   Describes the interpretation of story through the social situations and interaction in the story based on schemata.
Thorndyke, P.W. "Cognitive Structures in Comprehension and Memory of Narrative Discourse." *Cognitive Psychology* 9 (1977): 77–110.
   A theory and research discussion of comprehension and recall of story related to story grammar instruction.
Tierney, R., and Cunningham, J. "Research on Teaching Reading Comprehension." In *Handbook of Reading Research.* P.D. Pearson, ed. New York: Longman, 1984, pp. 609–655.
   Presents an in-depth discussion of research on reading comprehension with an extensive bibliography.
Tierney, Robert J., and Readence, John E. *Reading Strategies and Practices: A Compendium.* Boston: Allyn and Bacon, 2000, pp. 422–428.
   Provides a good introduction and reference to research on story grammar and story maps.
Whaley, Jill F. "Story Grammar and Reading Instruction." *Reading Teacher* 34 (April 1981): 762–771.
   Discusses the use of story grammar as a component of comprehension and describes the changes in story concept with maturation.

Reading Recovery Program

The Reading Recovery Program is an intensive early intervention program for at-risk students. According to Harris and Hodges (1995) the Reading Recovery Program is "a registered trademark for an early intervention program..." created by Marie Clay for first graders at-risk in reading. "The program requires a highly trained specialist who can accelerate children's rate of learning so they succeed when returned to the regular classroom."

Tierney and Readence (2000) state that the Reading Recovery Program is "a one-to-one intervention program for the poorest readers in the first grade and an intensive training program for teachers." This is an intensive program that provides each student at-risk with an additional 30 minutes a day of individualized reading instruction with a specially trained teacher using specific lessons for 12–15 weeks. Pinnell, Fried and Estice (1990) describe the specific procedures and lessons intended to help at-risk students develop the strategies necessary to improve their own reading ability by reading two to three familiar stories, reading a story from a previous day while the teacher keeps a running record, working on word analysis, writing a message, and discussing and reading a new book. At the end of the lesson students select material to read at home.

Marie Clay developed the program in New Zealand in the 1970s based on her findings about the differences between "high and low progress readers." Clay (1988) states that low progress readers only use a limited range of strategies and often rely on what they retrieve from memory paying little attention to the visual details of the text. High progress readers use a variety of strategies and are able to shift strategies when needed. These successful readers "operate on print in an integrated way in search for meaning, which results in high accuracy and high self-correction rates...." These readers self monitor and integrate prior knowledge about the rules of printed language which helps reading become automatic.

Clay developed Reading Recovery Program for teachers who asked for help with a program for young children with reading problems. Clay (1982) observed children and teachers for two years and then field tested procedures with at-risk children for a year. The Reading Recovery Program was put into use in 1979 in New Zealand and in 1984 in Australia and the United States.

The Reading Recovery Program is based on Marie Clay's (1988) beliefs about the reading process:

1. Reading is a process based on strategies that take place in the mind of the reader. The program aims at helping students learn to use strategies in a flexible way to develop a "meaning orientation to print";
2. Reading and writing work together to strengthen a basic knowledge of both processes. The program helps students use reading and writing in a flexible way to develop connections between them;
3. Students learn to read by reading and in order to become skilled students must read actively;
4. "Children need to develop fruitful concepts of what reading is" by experiencing activities that integrate reader-based and text-based processes;
5. It is important to help students who have problems as soon as possible;
6. Students who have problems can and do make progress when the teacher and student work together to accelerate growth and develop independent learning strategies.

Admission to the program is based on a diagnostic procedure which includes the kindergarten teacher's observations, the first grade teacher's observations, and student responses to six measures of reading tasks:

1. Letter identification;
2. Word test of high frequency words;
3. Concepts about print—what the student knows about print and how the student handles books;
4. The words the student knows and his/her ability to write high frequency words;
5. A dictation test—the student's ability to hear and record sounds in words;
6. A running record of the student's error and highest level at which 90 percent accuracy in reading is achieved.

Clay (1993) believes that observation of the child provides a picture of what the child can do and has problems doing. The summary of the observation survey provides:

1. Justification for including the child in the Reading Recovery Program;

2. Data about functioning and evidence of growth;
3. Information about how and where to start the work.

Clay (1993) describes the first ten days of the program as a period of exploration or "roaming around the known." This period helps the teacher and the student with: opportunities to develop trust; opportunities to observe what the student is and is not able to do in a non-testing situation; opportunities for observation in a systematic way; opportunities for the student to feel that he/she is engaged in real reading and writing activities; opportunities for building a basis for subsequent learning on which the teacher can develop the individualized program.

The Reading Recovery Program is based on an intensive 30 minute lesson that allows the individual student and teacher to work on a number of reading and writing activities. Pinnell, Fried and Estice (1990) state that these activities include: reading a familiar book out loud while the teacher keeps a running record of the reading and teaches important points right away; working with letters to construct words; writing a message or a story; and reading a new book.

The program will be individualized to meet the needs of each student. The teacher is trained to use many procedures which may be used for each pupil's particular needs and to develop each pupil's abilities. The lesson framework is a guide within which each student's skills and problems will be addressed. Different materials and strategies will be used for each student. The aim of the program is to help each student improve by providing strategies to monitor, look for clues, find new things for themselves, check cues, strengthen by reviewing, self correct and solve new problems as each develops smoothly, faster reading with longer, less predictable selection in which the language is not as familiar to the student.

The program lasts from 12 to 15 weeks with no set time for the pupil to complete the program. The pupil completes the program when he/she can read as well as the average level for his/her grade without extra help. The Reading Recovery teacher is trained intensively for one year in the procedures of the program and undergoes annual follow-up training.

Research by Clay (1985) and Juel (1988) indicates that children having problems with reading at the end of first grade will continue to have problems by the end of the fourth grade. O'Connor (2000), Scanlon and Vellutino (1996), and Torgesen (2000) report that the number of children with reading difficulties can be significantly reduced if comprehensive, systematic, intensive intervention is provided. Slavin, Karweit, and Wasik (1994) report that early intervention that focuses on prevention is more beneficial than remediation.

Shanahan and Barr (1995) did an evaluation of Reading Recovery and reported that first graders who received Reading Recovery instruction made large growth in reading during the first year. The growth in reading for these students compared well to the growth of students who were high achievers in the first grade and received only instruction in the classroom or classroom instruction and compensatory help. The Reading Recovery Program provides not only early intervention in a one-to-one tutoring environment, but as Wasik and Slavin (1993) state, a more comprehensive instructional design which includes a broader focus on the parts of the reading process. Mantzicopoulous, Morrison, Stone and Setrakian (1992) found that programs such as Reading Recovery that included more of the reading process—reading for fluency, comprehension strategies, and better sound and word-level instruction in phonemic awareness, alphabet, phonics, and spelling—were more effective. Programs with certified trained teachers, Wasik and Slavin (1993) found, were more effective. Reading Recovery teachers are provided with a year long training program and must be certified teachers.

Invernizzi (2002) reports that research on the effectiveness of one-to-one programs such as Reading Recovery has examined: "(1) the structure and content of the lesson plan; (2) the consistency, frequency, and duration of lessons; and (3) the guidance knowledge and skill of the tutors...." The National Reading Panel Report (2000) states that early intervention programs should include a balance of oral reading, phonemic awareness and phonics, and comprehension. The Reading Recovery Program uses a repeat reading of a story read the day before as part of the routine for all students. Samuels (1979) states that this practice encourages fluency and automatic word recognition. Dowhower (1987) states that this develops better comprehension and reading expression.

Iverson and Tunmer (1993) have incorporated more direct phonics instruction and spelling patterns into Reading Recovery. These additions have been made in response to reports that Reading Recovery uses a student-centered, less systematic phonics approach which waits for the teachable moment to give a phonics mini lesson according to Invernizzi (2002). Vocabulary is taught indirectly through tutor directed new books. Invernizzi (2002) states that the book introduction also includes review of new words in context on several pages. The best way to help students understand what they read is through planned interaction between the student and the material. Writing is also an important motivational strategy which promotes comprehension. Clay (1988) states that reading and writing work together to strengthen knowledge of both processes.

Invernizzi (2002) reports that successful early intervention should include daily practice such as the Reading Recovery routine of reading familiar books = guided oral reading, working with letters = alphabetics, writing a sentence = comprehension strategies, and learning a new book = a balanced lesson.

Invernizzi (2002) states that the frequency and duration of tutoring is an important part of an early intervention program. Clay (1988) states that Reading Recovery lessons last 30 minutes every day for 12-15 weeks with no set date for termination of services. Students who read at a level that matches the middle group in their class no longer need Reading Recovery services.

Hiebert (1994) reports that there is a question about the stability of success over time in Reading Recovery. There is a decline by the end of grade three. Vellutino et al. (1996) state that no matter what early intervention program is used some students need to have ongoing help to ensure success.

Tierney and Readence (2000) report that the Reading Recovery Program has been well researched and concerns such as cost, teacher training methods, and emphasis on phonics rather than more whole language strategies have been discussed. Tierney and Readence (2000) conclude that the success of the Reading Recovery has been well documented by Marie Clay and many other researchers and provides a commitment to "account ability in terms of expectations for students, training teachers, training teacher leaders and above all, research that scrutinizes these enterprises and their impact."

Annotated Bibliography

Allington, Richard. "How to Get Information on Several Proven Programs for Accelerating the Progress of Low-Achieving Children." *Reading Teacher* 46.3 (November 1992): 246-247.
    Discusses the North American Reading Recovery Program, Success for All program, and Accelerated Schools program to help students develop reading skills.
Ballash, Karen M. "Remedial High School Readers Can Recover Too." *Journal of Reading* 37.8 (1994): 686-687.
    Describes how a teacher paired the Reading Recovery Program techniques with authentic, high interest reading techniques to help older students acquire improved literacy skills.
Barnes, Bonnie L. "But Teacher You Went Right On: A Perspective on Reading Recovery." *Reading Teacher* 50.4 (December 1996-January 1997): 284-292.
    Discusses the Reading Recovery Program stating she does not feel comfortable with the way the program responds or does not respond to students.
Barnes, Bonnie L. "Response to Browne; Fitts; McLaughlin; McNamara; and Williams." *Reading Teacher* 50.4 (December 1996-January 1997): 302-303.
    States that perhaps first graders having reading problems do not need early intervention in the Reading Recovery Program, but more time in a whole-language, print rich classroom before they are ready to focus on the conventions of print.
Browne, Ann, Fitts, Maryellen, McLaughlin, Bennetta, McNamara, Mary Jane, and Williams, Judy. "Teaching and Learning in Reading Recovery: Response to 'But Teacher You Went Right On'" *Reading Teacher* 50.4 (December 1996-January 1997): 294-300.
    Five Reading Recovery teachers discuss the Program in response to Bonnie Barnes' critique of the program. The teachers address specific strategies and features of the Reading Recovery Program. Responds to concerns Barnes expresses about the weaknesses of the program.
Center, Yola, Wheedall, Kevin, Freeman, Louella, Outhred, Lynne, McNaught, Margaret. "An

Evaluation of Reading Recovery." *Reading Research Quarterly* 30.2 (April, May, June 1995): 240–263.

An evaluation of the Reading Recovery Program in ten New South Wales primary schools. Students were randomly assigned to Reading Recovery or a control group in which they got only the support given to at-risk readers. Low achieving students from five matched schools where Reading Recovery was not offered were a comparison group. Reports that after 15 weeks the Reading Recovery group was performing at a level superior to the control group on all measures of reading achievement except two of three tests measuring metalinguistic ability. After 30 weeks there was no difference between the control group and the Reading Recovery group. One year after the intervention ended 35 percent of the Reading Recovery group had improved with the program, 35 percent of the students had not "recovered," and 30 percent would have improved without intervention because the same percentage of the control group and the comparison group learned to read at the average level at this stage.

Clay, Marie. *The Early Detection of Reading Difficulties*, 3rd ed. Auckland, New Zealand: Heinemann, 1985.

This is a discussion of the Reading Recovery Program from its originator. Provides detailed discussions of all procedures used in the program and the rationale for each.

Clay, Marie. *Observing Young Readers: Selected Papers*. Portsmouth, NH: Heinemann, 1982.

Provides research reports about how young readers make progress over time.

Clay, Marie. *Reading Recovery: A Guidebook for Teachers in Training*. Portsmouth, NH: Heinemann, 1993.

This is a detailed, comprehensive discussion of ways to observe children's progress in reading. It is a comprehensive guide to implementing the Reading Recovery Program.

Dowhower, S.L. "The Effects of Repeated Reading on Second Grade Transitional Reader's Fluency and Comprehension." *Reading Research Quarterly* 22 (1987): 389–406.

Reports on repeat reading of a selection and the development of better comprehension and expression by second grade students.

Dudley-Marling, Curt, and Murphy, Sharon. "A Political Critique of Remedial Reading Programs: The Example of Reading Recovery." *Reading Teacher* 50.6 (February 1997): 460–468.

Presents suggestions for changing the Reading Recovery Program. Examines the job of remedial reading programs and states how Reading Recovery is a good case for viewing how these programs maintain the status quo by protecting the structure of schooling and society in schools. Presents social criticism of remedial reading programs.

Harris, Theodore L., and Hodges, Richard E. eds. *The Literacy Dictionary: The Vocabulary of Reading and Writing*. Newark, DE: International Reading Association, 1995.

Defines the Reading Recovery Program.

Hedrick, Wanda B., and Pearish, Alice. "Good Reading Instruction Is More Important Than Who Provides the Instruction or Where It Takes Place." *Reading Teacher* 52.7 (March 1999): 716–726.

Discusses several "pull-out" reading programs providing support for Reading Recovery. States that Reading Recovery helps first graders become independent readers who learn to be more successful in their homeroom class.

Hicks, Cynthia P., and Villaume, Susan Kidd. "Finding Our Way: Critical Reflections on Literacy Development in Two Reading Recovery Children." *Reading Teacher* 54.4 (December 2000): 460–468.

Discusses why the Reading Recovery Program was more successful for one first grade student and not another.

Hiebert E. "Reading Recovery in the United States: What Difference Does It Make to an Age Cohort?" *Educational Researcher* 23.9 (1994): 15–25.

Discusses the progress made by Reading Recovery students over time after the intervention.

Hill, Lola Bouley, and Hall, Mary Groenwould. "Reading Recovery: Questions Classroom Teachers Ask." *Reading Teacher* 44.7 (March 1991): 480–483.

Two Reading Recovery teachers provide information to answer questions teachers ask about the program.

Invernizzi, Marcia A. "The Complex World of One-on-One Tutoring." In *Handbook of Early Literacy Research*. Susan B. Newman and David K. Dickinson, eds. New York: Gullford, 2002, pp. 459–470.

A discussion of early intervention one-on-one programs providing information about Reading Recovery, Success of All, Book Buddies and the Howard Street Program. Compares the programs and uses a case study to tell how tutoring can be integrated into the wider school program.

Iverson, A.J., and Tunmer, W.E. "Phonological Processing Skills and the Reading Recovery Program." *Journal of Educational Psychology* 85 (1993): 112–126.

Reports on direct instruction in phonics and spelling patterns in the Reading Recovery Program. States that this enhances the program.

Juel, C. "Learning to Read and Write; A Longitudinal Study of Fifty-Four Children from First through Fourth Grade." *Journal of Educational Research* 80 (1988): 437–447.

Research that states that children who have problems reading in the first grade will continue to have the same problems in the fourth grade.

MacKenzie, Karla A. "Using Literacy Booster Groups to Maintain and Extend Reading Recovery Success in the Primary Grades." *Reading Teacher* 55.3 (November 2001): 222–234.

Describes literacy boosters which is part of a primary grade comprehensive literacy program. Reading Recovery students got extra help to maintain and expand the progress they made after they exit the program.

Mantzicopoulous, P.; Morrison, D.; Stone, E.; and Setrakian, W. "The Use of the SEARCH /TEACH Tutoring Approach with Middle-Class Students at Risk for Reading Failure." *Elementary School Journal* 92:5 (1992): 573–586.

Describes the SEARCH/TEACH tutoring approach, stating that students need more than just one-to-one tutoring. Students require help with fluency, phonics, comprehension, and spelling.

O'Connor, R. "Increasing the Intensity of Intervention in Kindergarten and First Grade." *Learning Disabilities Research and Practice* 15.1 (2000): 43–54.

Describes the importance of comprehensive, systematic early intervention programs in the primary grades.

Pinnell, Gay Su, Fried, Mary D., and Estice, Rose Mary. "Reading Recovery: Learning How to Make a Difference." *Reading Teacher* 43.4 (December 1990): 282–295.

Discusses the United States research findings and the structure of the Reading Recovery Program in detail through the experiences of a teacher in the program;

Pinnell, Gay Su, Lyons, Carol A., DeFord, Diane E., Bryk, Anthony S., Seltzer, Michael. "Comparing Instructional Models for the Literacy Education of High-Risk First Graders." *Reading Research Quarterly* 29.1 (January-February-March 1994): 8–39.

Describes a study that compared the effectiveness of the Reading Recovery Program to three other programs with 324 poorly achieving first graders in ten school districts. Students were randomly assigned to each program. Reports that the Reading Recovery students scores were significantly better than the other students on dictation text reading level, the Gates-MacGinitie test and the Woodcock. A macro-analysis of video taped lessons indicated that the components of the program that led to success were one-to-one lessons, lesson framework, and teacher staff development.

Rasinski, Timothy V. "Commentary: On the Effect of Reading Recovery: A Response to Pinnell; Lyons; Deford; Bryk and Seltzer." *Reading Research Quarterly* 30.2 (April-May-June 1995): 264–270.

Questions the effects of the Reading Recovery Program and other corrective programs. States that the difference between Reading Recovery and other programs in teacher training, experience, and use of time for instruction may account for the differential effects of Reading Recovery instead of any other characteristics of Reading

Recovery. Challenges the reported cost of the Reading Recovery Program as opposed to group intervention programs and the effects of group programs.

Report of the National Reading Panel. *Teaching Children to Read: An Evidence-Based Assessment of the Scientific Literature and Its Implications for Reading Instruction.* Washington, DC: National Institute of Child Health and Human Development, 2000.

This is a detailed review of the literature on American reading instruction.

Samuels, J.S. "The Method of Repeated Reading." *The Reading Teacher* 32 (1979): 403–408.

Reports that repeated readings of a text help students increase fluency, word recognition and comprehension.

Scanlon, D.M., and Vellutino, F.R. "Prerequisite Skills, Early Instruction and Success in First Grade Reading: Selected Results from a Longitudinal Study." *Mental Retardation and Developmental Disabilities* 2 (1996): 54–63.

Discusses the importance of early intervention in reducing reading difficulties.

Shanahan, Timothy, and Barr, Rebecca. "Reading Recovery: An Independent Evaluation of the Effects of an Early Instructional Intervention for At-Risk Learners." *Reading Research Quarterly* 30.4 (October-November-December 1995): 958–996.

Provides an in-depth examination of the gains made in Reading Recovery and a critique of the program. States that students make larger than expected growth. States that the Reading Recovery Program is less effective and costs more than it claims and does not cause changes in classroom instruction. Reports that the Reading Recovery Program should be supported with recommendations to make it a better program.

Slavin, R.E., Karweit, N.L., and Wasik, B.A. *Preventing Early School Failure: Research, Policy, and Practice: The First Comprehensive, Direct Comparison of Programs Designed to Prevent Failure in the Early Grades.* Boston: Allyn and Bacon, 1994.

A very useful discussion of programs for early intervention with research supporting their advantages over remediation in later grades.

Spiegel, Dixie Lee. "A Comparison of Traditional Remedial Programs and Reading Recovery: Guidelines for Successful Programs." *Reading Teacher* 49.2 (October 1995): 86–96.

A discussion of remedial programs such as Chapter I as compared to Reading Recovery. States that the strategies used in Reading Recovery may have more success.

Tierney, Robert J., and Readence, John E. *Reading Strategies and Practices: A Compendium,* Boston: Allyn and Bacon, 2000, pp. 127–135.

Describes the Reading Recovery Program in detail.

Torgesen, J.K. "Individual Differences in Response to Early Intervention in Reading: The Lingering Problem of Treatment Resisters." *Learning Disabilities Research and Practice* 15.1 (2000): 55–64.

Discusses the problems associated with early intervention programs and suggests how success can be achieved.

Vellutino, F.F., Scanlon, D.M., Sipay, E.R.; Small, S.G.; Pratt, A.; Chen, R.; and Denckla, M.B. "Cognitive Profiles of Difficult-to-Remediate and Readily Remediated Poor Readers: Early Intervention as a Vehicle for Distinguishing Between Cognitive and Experiential Deficits as Basic Causes of Specific Reading Disability." *Journal of Educational Psychology* 88 (1996): 601–638.

Reports that there are students who need ongoing help to achieve success no matter how intense the early intervention program.

Wasik, Barbara A., and Slavin, Robert E. "Preventing Early Reading Failure with One-to-One Tutoring: A Review of Five Programs." *Reading Research Quarterly* 28.2 (April-May-June 1993): 178–200.

Discusses research on five early intervention one-to-one tutoring programs intended to help at-risk first grade students. Examines the Reading Recovery Program, Success for All Prevention of Learning Disabilities, The Wallach Tutoring and Programmed Tutoring Reading through 16 studies that evaluated each program. Reports that each program provided success as compared to more traditional remedial programs and proved more lasting success over time. Reports on the cost effectiveness of the programs.

Phonemic Awareness

Phonemic awareness is the ability to tell the differences and similarities among the sounds of spoken language.
Strickland (2002) states that phonemic awareness "involves knowledge of the individual sounds in spoken language." Research by Stahl and Murray (1994) and Stanovich (1994) indicates that "a child's ability to distinguish between phonemes is one of the best predictors of reading success." Williams (1995) states that phonemes are abstract and when a word is pronounced the phonemes are blended and not pronounced individually. Elkonin (1963) believed that developing phonemic awareness would be a useful foundation for beginning reading instruction. Subsequent research proved Elkonin's hypothesis was correct.
Phonemic awareness is measured, Williams (1995) states, in a variety of ways, such as asking if two words rhyme, matching sounds to words, blending, isolating phonemes, and dividing words into phonemes. According to Moustafa (1997) and Strickland (2002), phonemic awareness should not be taught in isolation, but with many literacy experiences. Williams (1995) suggests that using games that encourage students to practice segmenting spoken words helps develop phonemic awareness. "This is not simply phonics instruction, but rather training that enhances concurrent or subsequent phonics instruction or reading instruction.... In addition, teachers can make sure that children are given literature that focuses on playing with sounds through rhyme (and) alliteration...."
Ferreiro (1986) and Schickendanz (1999) state that children discover that a relationship exists between letter patterns and sound patterns. "In turn they transition from visual to sound-based hypothesis. As part of the transition it is common for children to explore a symbolic hypothesis—the notion that letters correspond with spoken syllables...."
Richgels, Poremba, and McGee (1996) found that when children pay attention to speech sounds and use what they have discovered about letter sound relationships they use written language in more functional and meaningful ways. In order to help children, Griffith and Olson (1992) suggest using songs and games that highlight the sounds of the language, and Pearson

(1993) suggests using literature that plays with the sounds of the language to develop phonemic awareness. Richgels, Poremba and McGee (1996) also suggest that shared reading experiences can develop phonemic awareness in context rather than in isolation. Selecting a story, copying the story on a chart to highlight word features to be emphasized, using activities that encourage students to show what they already know about letters in words, and applying what is known and new to the story develops skills necessary to understand that "speech consists of a series of small sound units," according to Adams (1990), Pearson (1993), Yopp (1992) and Stanovich (1993/1994).

Ehri and Nunes (2002) conclude that phonemic awareness helps students at all grade levels learn to read. They state that "segmenting and blending are especially effective.... Teaching children to manipulate phonemes using letters is more effective than teaching ... in the oral mode without letters." Since children's abilities differ Ehri and Nunes recommend pretesting to assess the kind of phonemic awareness instruction that is needed by each student. "Phonemic awareness is not an end but rather a means to enhancing children's learning of the alphabetic system for use in their reading and writing" according to Ehri and Nunes. Phonemic awareness is not a reading program by itself, but rather an important component of reading instruction.

Share, Jorm, Maclean, and Matthews (1984) report that phonemic awareness is one of the best ways to predict how well children entering school will succeed in kindergarten and first grade reading. Research by Bus and VanIjzendoorn (1999) and Ehri et al. (2001) using controlled experiments concluded that teaching phonemic awareness significantly increases the reading success rate for beginning readers. The only group for which long-term success was not high was older learning disabled students because, according to Byrne and Fielding-Barnsley (1993, 1995), this group did not have phonemic awareness instruction early enough.

Research findings indicate that teaching phonemic awareness skills along with spelling and comprehension skills in the beginning reading period leads to long term reading success.

Annotated Bibliography

Adams, Marilyn Jager. *Beginning to Read: Thinking and Learning About Print.* Cambridge, MA: MIT Press, 1990.
   Uses research to discuss the development of reading ability. States that phonics can be taught in a whole language program. There is an afterword by Dorothy Strickland and Bernice Cullenan.
Ayres, Linda R. "Phonological Awareness Training of Kindergarten Children: Three Treatments and Their Effect." In *Reconsidering a Balanced Approach to Reading.* Constance Weaver, ed. Urbana, IL: National Council of Teachers of English, 1998, pp. 209–255.

Phonemic Awareness 185

Examines the effectiveness of three instructional techniques to teach phonemic awareness to kindergarten students and the effects of these techniques on students' reading achievement at the end of the first grade.

Blachman, Benita A. "Phonological Awareness." In *Handbook of Reading Research III*. M.L. Kamil, P.B. Mosenthal, P.D. Pearson and R. Barr, eds. Mahwah, NJ: Erlbaum, 2000, pp. 483–502.

Provides an in-depth discussion of phonological awareness citing extensive research. An in-depth bibliography is provided.

Burns, Paul C., Roe, Betty D., and Smith, Sandy H. *Teaching Reading in Today's Elementary Schools*. Boston: Houghton-Mifflin, 2002, pp. 38–43.

A text on reading instruction with a good chapter on "Emergent Literacy." This is a starting point for an overview of phonemic awareness.

Bus, A., and VanIjzendoorn, M. "Phonological Awareness in Early Reading: A Meta-Analysis of Experimental Training Studies." *Journal of Educational Psychology* 9 (1999): 403–414.

Describe the results of controlled experiments stating that teaching phonemic awareness skills significantly increases reading success for beginning readers.

Byrne, B., and Fielding-Barnsley, R. "Evaluation of a Program to Teach Phonemic Awareness to Young Children: A One Year Follow-up." *Journal of Educational Psychology*, 85 (1993) 104–111.

Byrne, B., and Fielding-Barnsley, R. "Evaluation of a Program to Teach Phonemic Awareness to Young Children: A Two and Three Year Follow-up and a New Preschool Trial." *Journal of Educational Psychology* 87 (1995): 488–503.

Reports that older learning disabled students did not have long term success after phonemic awareness instruction because the instruction was not provided early enough in this group's school career.

Ehri, L.C., and Nunes, S.R. "The Role of Phonemic Awareness in Learning to Read." In *What Research Has to Say About Reading Instruction*. Alan E. Farstrup and S. Jay Samuels, eds. Newark, DE: International Reading Association, 2002, pp. 110–139.

Provides an in-depth examination of phonemic awareness research with a valuable bibliography and discussion questions. Cautions that phonemic awareness is a means to enhance students' learning rather than an end in itself. Other skills must be taught to ensure reading and writing success.

Ehri, L.C., Nunes, S.R., Willows, D.M., Schuster, B.V., Yaghoub-Zadeh, Z., and Shanahan, T. "Phonemic Awareness Instruction Helps Children Learn to Read: Evidence from the National Reading Panel's Meta-Analysis." *Reading Research Quarterly* 36 (2001): 250–287.

Reports the meta-analysis results of the National Reading Panel. States that less than 20 hours per school year is devoted to phonemic awareness instruction, but this instruction significantly increases the reading success rate for beginning readers.

Elkonin, D.B. "The Psychology of Mastering the Elements of Reading." In *Educational Psychology in the U.S.S.R.* B. Simon and J. Simon, eds. New York: Routledge, 1963, pp. 165–179.

States that phonemic awareness instruction should be a foundation for beginning reading instruction. An early discussion of the value of phonemic awareness instruction.

Ferreiro, E. "The Interplay Between Information and Assimilation in Beginning Literacy." In *Emergent Literacy: Writing and Reading*. W.H. Teale and E. Sulzby, eds. Norwood, NJ: Ablex, 1986, pp. 15–49.

Discusses the relationship between letter patterns and sound patterns that children discover and in so doing make a transition from a visual to a sound based hypothesis about language.

Goswami, Usha. "Early Phonological Development and the Acquisition of Literacy." In *Handbook of Early Literacy Research*. Susan B. Newman and David K. Dickenson, eds. New York: Guilford Press, 2003, pp. 111–125.

Presents research on phonological development describing a discussion of various factors that contribute to this development and the ability to read. Extensive bibliography and a suggestion that learning about phonological awareness in different languages would be a useful tool for a better understanding of factors that affect the acquisition of this skill.

Griffith, Priscilla L., Kleslus, Janell P., and Kromrey, Jeffery D. "The Effect of Phonemic Awareness on the Literacy Development of First Grade Children in a Traditional or Whole Language Classroom." *Journal of Research in Childhood Education* 6 (Spring/Summer 1992): 85–92.

Examines the connection between the reading approach used and the development of decoding, spelling, and writing skill in students who enter the first grade with different levels of phonemic awareness. Students in two first grade classes in rural Florida schools were studies. Compared data on achievement for students taught by whole language approach and students in a basal reading approach students who did not receive direct phonemic instruction did as well as students who received direct instruction.

Griffith, Priscilla L., and Olson, Mary W. "Phonemic Awareness Helps Beginning Readers Break the Code." *Reading Teacher* 45.7 (March 1992): 516–523.

Defines phonemic awareness, and states that phonemic awareness is important as a prerequisite for understanding the relationship between letter sounds and spoken words. Cites research, describes games and activities to use as part of a kindergarten and grade one activities in the language arts curriculum to ensure that children succeed in beginning reading. Provides a list of trade books to use for activities.

Moustafa, Margaret. "Reconceptualizing Phonics Instruction." In *Reconsidering a Balanced Approach to Reading*. Constance Weaver, ed. Urbana, IL: National Council of Teachers of English, 1997, pp. 135–157.

Reports on phonics instruction research which focuses on letter-sound correspondence. Discusses the factors that produce skilled readers. States that effective reading instruction builds on students' knowledge of language experiences. The ability to recognize words is more useful in decoding new words than letter-sound knowledge.

Pearson, P. David. "Focus on Research: Teaching and Learning Reading: A Research Perspective." *Language Arts* 70 (October 1993): 501–511.

Presents a review of research and suggestions for reading instruction.

Richgels, Donald J., Poremba, Karla J., and McGee, Lea M. "Kindergarteners Talk About Print: Phonemic Awareness in Meaningful Texts." *Reading Teacher* 49.8 (May 1996): 632–642.

Describe a game activity that uses phonemic awareness in contextualized reading and writing in kindergartens. Concludes that students need a functional, meaningful way to learn about language and its sounds from books that are relevant to ongoing activities to demonstrate what they know rather than specifically to read. A good application of theory to practice.

Schickendanz, Judith A. *Much More Than the ABCs: The Early Stages of Reading and Writing*. Washington, DC: National Association for the Education of Young Children, 1999.

Provides suggestions for helping young children develop the skills needed to achieve success in beginning literacy. Uses research as the basis for classroom and home activities. Provides references and suggests children's books for each chapter.

Share, D., Jorm, A., Maclean, R., and Matthews, R. "Sources of Individual Differences in Reading Acquisition." *Journal of Educational Psychology* 76 (1984): 1309–1324.

Discusses ways to predict success in early reading stating that phonemic awareness is one of the best predictors of success in kindergarten.

Stahl, S., and Murray, B. "Defining Phonological Awareness and Its Relationship to Early Reading." *Journal of Educational Psychology* 86 (1994): 221–234.

Discusses phonological awareness as a way to predict reading success. Defines phonological awareness.

Stanovich, Keith E. "Romance and Reality." *Reading Teacher* 47.4 (December 1993/January 1994): 280–291.

This is a review of his research about reading. States that research must be used to answer all questions about reading. Extensive references.

Strickland, Dorothy. "The Importances of Early Intervention." In *What Research Has to Say About Reading Instruction*. Alan E. Farstrup and S. Jay Samuels, eds. Newark, DE: International Reading Association, 2002, pp. 69–86.

Provides a discussion of early intervention with suggestions for early reading instruction. A very good bibliography is included.

Torgesen, Joseph K., Morgan, Sharon T., and Davis, Charlotte. "Effects of Two Types of Phonemic Awareness Training on Word Learning in Kindergarten Children." *Journal of Educational Psychology* 84 (September 1992): 364–370.

Examines the results of two types of oral language learning programs on the development of phonological awareness skills and word learning ability in kindergarten students. Describes both programs and concludes that only students who were trained to use blending and segmenting skills demonstrated positive effects on reading and word learning.

Williams, Joanna. "Phonemic Awareness." In *The Literacy Dictionary: The Vocabulary of Reading and Writing*. Theodore L. Harris and Richard E. Hodges, eds. Newark, DE: International Reading Association, 1995, pp. 185–186.

This is an overview of phonemic awareness that provides a good starting point for understanding the topic.

Williams, Joanna. "Teaching Decoding with an Emphasis on Phonemic Analysis and Phonemic Blending." *Journal of Educational Psychology* 27 (1980): 1–15.

Provides specific suggestions for teaching the segmentation of spoken words. The program was evaluated with two samples of learning disabled students and a control group. The results indicate that phonemic awareness training is valuable.

Yopp, Hallie Kay. "Developing Phonemic Awareness in Young Children." *Reading Teacher* 45.9 (May 1992): 696–703.

Presents suggested activities to help students as young as preschool age develop phonemic awareness. Discusses the research base for the importance of developing phonemic awareness as the foundation for reading instruction. Cautions that the activities discussed should not replace interactions with language and print, but should supplement these experiences.

The Whole Language Approach

The whole language classroom is child centered and collaborative because everyone is part of a community of learners. The contributions of each child are important because everyone in the room learns to read and write together. Language is vital to learning. The materials of instruction are not prepared textbooks, but materials used every day in the real world such as literature, menus and magazines. Learning is viewed as a personal commitment for which students take responsibility and engage in self-evaluation.

Burns, Roe, and Smith (2002) state that whole language is a belief system which connects the student to the curriculum. Strickland (1995) states that whole language is "both a professional movement and a theoretical perspective. It embodies a set of applied beliefs governing learning and teaching, language development, curriculum, and the social community." It can be described as part of the progressive view of education that is concerned with and dissatisfied with existing methods. Strickland believes that while whole language has been influenced by many theories and philosophies about language development, reading and writing development it is "a unique and evolving framework, rare among educational movements in that the great majority of its proponents" are classroom teachers. Pearson (2002) states that "the insights from linguistics, psycholinguistics, cognitive psychology, sociolinguistics, and literacy theory" are the key principles on which whole language is based.

Burns, Roe, and Smith (2002) state that the teacher in the whole language classroom is an observer of students and a facilitator of activities tailored to the needs of each student. Whole language practice is based on the belief that children learn to read as they learn to talk in a natural way and at different rates. The teacher needs to observe students closely to develop activities based on the many needs and abilities of each student. The individual child is the most important element in the whole language classroom.

Strickland (1995) states that assessment is the demonstration of each child's ongoing activities rather than standardized test results.

Goodman (1992) Watson (1994) Cullinan (1992) and Church (1994) state that learning in the whole language classroom is satisfying to the individual who enjoys the self-selected activities and experiences. Oldfather (1994) believes that student participation in selecting materials and activities and sharing oral and written work with peers leads to intrinsic motivation.

Skills are not taught in isolation, but as part of reading and writing activities as the need to use the skill arises, according to Yatvin (1991) Spiegel (1992), Newman and Church (1990). Skills are not an end in themselves, but are necessary to make language learning successful.

In order to implement whole language, teachers must have what Church (1994) calls a thorough understanding of language development, children's literature, and methods of teaching reading and writing across content areas. There is, however, not only one model to follow to create a whole language classroom according to Newman and Church (1990). Implementation of many techniques used in whole language classrooms is acceptable.

Pearson (2002) states that there has never been one interpretation of whole language. Differences among researchers and teachers about how to develop skills and strategies resulted in many different interpretations of the whole language philosophy. In some classrooms, Pearson states, teachers were told to "be patient, skills will emerge from meaningful communication activities; others spurred things by taking advantage of spontaneous opportunities from mini lessons; still others were willing to spur spontaneity." Whole language was, even with this wide range of interpretations, Pearson states, "the conventional wisdom in rhetoric, if not in reality" by 1995.

Strickland (1995) states that while whole language is appropriate for all children it may not suit every teacher. Grade level and philosophical differences as well as commitment to continuous ongoing staff development may account for the reluctance to fully implement whole language. Whole language has been recommended as appropriate for all grade levels; however, Strickland states that early childhood teachers implement it most frequently. This is not amazing since early childhood teachers use their knowledge of child development and "the principles and practices associated with whole language come more 'naturally' to them." In the upper grades Strickland states the emphasis is more on content and the whole language theory with its blend of process and product may "seem too indirect and inefficient." Teachers in upper grades need to use procedures that are easier to teach and evaluate.

One of the major concerns with maintaining whole language theory is the investment of time needed for ongoing staff development. Change takes time and effort and is not fast. Strickland (1995) believes that the strengths of whole language are "profound and enduring (and) the impact and future of whole language will rest on the educational community's commitment to look beyond labels to examine thoughtfully the theory and practice whole language represents."

Pearson (2002) presents reasons why pure whole language practice has fallen out of favor in the 21st century:

1. Not teaching the use of informational texts as a skill caused students in middle school and high school to be unable to gain information from informational material;
2. There was not enough direct teaching because students were to "discover" the need for skills;
3. There was no teaching and modeling of strategies for locating ideas and information;
4. Many schools used the name, but not the principles;
5. There was the lack of a systematic plan for professional staff development;
6. There was a growing dissatisfaction with extreme positions;
7. Changes in research emphases toward a more experimental position;
8. A renewed emphasis on code in beginning reading instruction with a return to phonics and skill based practice;
9. The making of reading research a political issue;
10. The emphasis on showing measurable results by public policy makers;
11. A shift toward professional development based on scientific research results rather than reflection and teacher judgment so that every student is learning the same thing at the same grade level in every school and
12. A strong emphasis on school and district wide policy.

Many of the practices used in the whole language classroom were part of the early childhood classroom. The use of literature; big books so that the whole class can read together; sharing one's work; working in groups; teaching through thematic units which use all content areas; and assessing student products as evidence of growth rather than a test school are all valid and useful practices. Pearson (2002) believes in an ecologically balanced approach which respects the whole range of research in education, respects the insight of practice, and respects the history of education. We do not need a standoff between one theory and another with educators taking the middle road, Pearson states, we need a "symbiotic relationship among elements within a coordinated system." In this system authentic activity and direct instruction can coexist. Perhaps, Pearson suggests, we will create a hybrid in which there are few frequent dramatic shifts of position to different and "new" approaches.

Annotated Bibliography

Altwerger, Bess, Edelsky, C., and Flores B. "Whole Language: What's New?" *Reading Teacher* 27 (November 1987): 144–154.

The authors describe whole language procedures making distinctions between whole language and other approaches. The article is specific and detailed. States that "whole language is not practice. It is a set of beliefs, a perspective." Materials do not create a whole language classroom; the "beliefs and interactions" of the teacher create the whole language classroom. Lists important premises about language on which the whole language perspective is based.

Burns, Paul C., Roe, Betty D., and Smith, Sandy H. *Teaching Reading in Today's Elementary Schools.* Boston: Houghton-Mifflin, 2002, pp. 19–21.

States that whole language is a philosophy or a belief system. Briefly describes how whole language is implemented.

Chall, Jeanne S. *The Academic Achievement Challenge: What Really Works in the Classroom?* New York: Guilford Press, 2000, pp. 58–68.

Chall discusses whole language under the heading "Trends in Reading Instruction in the Last 100 Years." Notes "the tendency of its proponents to claim newness for its good practices where history tells us they have been in wide use for a long time." Proceeds to explain components such as authentic literature and the combination of reading, writing language and speaking. Discusses the phonics/whole language problem using research back to the 1910s work of Thorndike and 1920s approaches. Concludes that the child centered, romantic view of whole language which focuses on children's choices and interests is the reason teachers were attracted to the approach. "It is a romantic view of learning. It is imbued with love and hope. But sadly, it has proven to be less effective for reading achievement than a more traditional, teacher-centered view, particularly for those who are at risk while learning to read." An extensive bibliography is included.

Church, Susan M. "Is Whole Language Warm and Fuzzy?" *Reading Teacher* 47 (February 1994): 362–370.

Challenges the comment made by a teacher that "whole language is warm and fuzzy" and therefore does not challenge students and does not have expectations. Church focuses on writing, the teacher's role in the whole language approach, the question of practicing skills, and the kinds of teacher training workshops designed to describe whole language procedures. Concludes that staff development must focus on whole language principles and help teachers collaborate on learning communities for success.

Church, Susan M. "Rethinking Whole Language: The Politics of Educational Change." In *Becoming Political: Reading and Writings in the Politics of Literacy Education.* Patrick Shannon, ed. Portsmouth, NH: Heinemann, 1992, pp. 238–249.

Church describes her efforts to ask questions about educational change in her school district in Dartmouth, Nova Scotia. Discusses the personal changes questioning policy caused and the process of implementing whole language or student centered learning in secondary schools. Presents a clear view of the change process through an examination of the whole language philosophy. Addresses the issue of teacher empowerment.

Crafton, Linda G. *Whole Language: Getting Started...Moving Forward.* Katonah, NY: Richard C. Owen, 1991.

Crafton explains how to develop and manage a whole language classroom from the teacher's point of view. Connects the theory and practice in a practical way. Describes how teachers and students can learn reading, writing, listening and speaking in an environment of mutual learning. Seven Chicago area teachers tell what they do in their classrooms. Students, parents and teachers have contributed to this book.

Cullinan, Bernice E. "Whole Language and Children's Literature." *Language Arts* 69 (October 1992): 426–430.

Discusses the basal readers that contain selections of quality literature providing students with a fulfilling and enjoyable learning to read experience. Describes the role of literature in the whole language approach.

Dixon-Krauss, Lisbeth. "Whole Language: Bridging the Gap from Spontaneous to Scientific Concepts." *Journal of Reading* 18 (Fall, 1992): 16–26.

Reports on the use of whole language literature instruction and traditional textbook instruction with 19 third graders over a six week period. In Phase I textbooks, brainstorming and worksheets were used to teach an American history unit. In Phase II whole language literature-based instruction using trade books and mini lessons were used. Assessment was done using an objective social studies test that accompanied the class textbook. After six weeks it was concluded that as a result of the Phase II whole language instruction, all students placed significantly better than during Phase I traditional instruction. Both social studies and reading scores were higher for all 19 students.

Edelsky, C., Altwerger, B., and Flores, B. *Whole Language—What's the Difference?* Portsmouth, NH: Heinemann, 1991.

The authors present a description of the theory on which whole language is based and the history of the approach.

Goodman, Kenneth S. "Whole Language Research: Foundations and Development." *Elementary School Journal* 90 (1989): 205–219; In *What Research Has to Say About Reading Instruction*. S. Jay Samuels and Alan E. Farstrup, eds. Newark, DE: International Reading Association, 1992, pp. 46–69.

States that whole language practice is built on the research work of Peaglt, Vygotsky, Dewly, Halleday and others who have investigated the reading and writing processes. Argues that whole language is built on a solid research foundation. States that because whole language classrooms are innovative the research that takes place is also innovative. The research used to assess whole language must evaluate it from its perspective and principles. Concludes with a challenge for researchers and a message to teachers stating that "There is a solid research base to whole language.... What (teachers) are attempting is different and much more ambitious than the objectives of traditional classrooms.... Whole language offers a challenge to researchers.... It involves bold new innovative programs.... The professionals in this grassroots movement are eager to have research support." Researches must do useful pertinent research. The teachers will move forward with or without research support.

Goodman, Kenneth S. "Why Whole Language Is Today's Agenda in Education." *Language Arts* 69 (1992): 354–363.

Goodman presents a discussion of the whole language approach from the constructivist point of view. Describes the curriculum, the teacher's role, and the classroom organization.

Goodman, Yetta M. *Notes from a Kidwatcher: Selected Writings of Yetta M. Goodman.* Sandra Wilde, ed. Portsmouth, NH: Heinemann, 1996, pp. 286–298.

Discusses the relationship between Vygotsky's psychological theory of language and the whole language approach. Discusses the work of John Dewey, Paolo Freire and Frank Smith and other researchers in the context of language development and how this work relates to whole language practice and philosophy. Discusses the role of the teacher, collaboration in the learning community, and the importance of error in language development. States how the research supports the whole language practice.

Goodman, Yetta M. "The Roots of the Whole Language Movement." *Elementary School Journal* 90 (1989): 113–127; In *Notes from a Kidwatcher: Selected Writing of Yetta M. Goodman*, ed. Sandra Wild. Portsmouth, NH: Heinemann, 1996, pp. 264–285.

Goodman traces the history of the whole language movement by discussing the contributions of Comenius, Dewey, Vygotsky, Rosenblatt, Ashton Warner, Huck, Granes, Clay, Jacobs, Taba, Kilpatrick and all the writers of the whole language movement in the 1970s. Examines the influences from reading, early childhood education, integrated curriculum and composition. Goodman explains her own life history in the movement and what she has learned. Concludes that "whole language is embedded in the traditions of science and humanism." The term whole language must not remain static, but must grow and change to reflect the dynamics of the field.

Goodman, Yetta M., and Goodman, Kenneth S. "Vygotsky in a Whole Language Perspective." In *Vygotsky and Education: Instructional Implications and Applications of Sociohistorical Psychology*. Louis C. Moll, ed. New York: Cambridge University Press, 1990, pp. 223–250. Describes Vygotsky's theories as part of whole language.

Goodman, Yetta M., Hood, Wendy J., and Goodman, Kenneth S., eds. *Organizing for Whole Language*. Portsmouth, NH: Heinemann, 1991.

The editors provide practical advice for implementing whole language teaching focusing on classroom organizational techniques.

McWhirter, Anna M. "Whole Language in the Middle School." *Reading Teacher* 43 (April 1990): 562–565.

McWhirter tells how she used dialogue journals and reading workshops to motivate middle school students. This is a first person account of whole language techniques used with middle school students.

Milligan, Jerry L., and Berg, Herbert. "The Effect of Whole Language on the Comprehension Ability of First Grade Children." *Reading Improvement* 29 (Fall 1992): 146–154.

Describes a study of eight first grade classes in a suburban school district. Four classes used the whole language approach and the control group of four classes used the adopted basal series. At the end of the school year the Cloze Deletion Test to assess comprehension was administered to all eight classes. The 2 groups were compared by levels of ability, sex "of the 2 comparisons 6 produced significant differences." Concludes that students at all 3 levels in the whole language group scored higher than the mean score on the Cloze test than did the students in the basal group.

Moorman, Gary B., Blanton, William, and McLaughlin, Thomas. "The Rhetoric of Whole Language." *Reading Research Quarterly* 29 (1994): 309–329.

Presents a critical evaluation of the figurative language used by the supporters of whole language.

Newman, Judith M., and Church, Susan M. "Myths of Whole Language." *Reading Teacher* 44 (September 1990): 20–26.

Lists 19 myths about whole language under the headings: skills, instruction, evaluation, learning and other myths. After each myth the reality is discussed. The authors conclude by dispelling the myths in a discussion of whole language citing their experiences, research, and advise about how to create progress towards change in instruction and dispelling myths.

Oldfather, Penny. "What Students Say About Motivating Experiences in a Whole Language Classroom." *Reading Teacher* 46 (May 1993): 672–681.

Discusses students' motivation to read from interviews and observation of students. Provides information in the students' own words. Discusses the translation of student ideas into practice and the importance of the teacher's responsiveness to students. States that the challenge "is to achieve a comfortable balance between choice and structure that takes into account" (1) student needs and interest; (2) curriculum and administrative mandates; (3) teaching styles and (4) teacher's ability to develop a balance between sharing control and the teacher's responsibility to students.

Pearson, P. David. "American Reading Instruction Since 1967." In *American Reading Instruction*, special edition. Nila Banton Smith. Newark, DE: International Reading Association, 2002, pp. 419–486

Presents a discussion of the trends in reading instruction with an extensive discussion of whole language and the reasons for its demise. Provides an extensive list of sources in the Endnotes.

Pearson, P. David. "RT Remembrance: The Second 20 Years." *Reading Teacher* 45 (January 1992): 378-385.

Discusses the directions *The Reading Teacher* has taken over a 20 year period from 1968 to 1991. Provides a chart listing 22 categories into which the articles can be placed. Pearson questions whether the journal led, followed, shaped or has been shaped by the field of reading. Concludes that the journal is of great value because of the blind review process in selecting articles. Pearson believes that the journal "is influenced directly by what is going on in the field, but does not come anywhere close to representing the full range of activity." However, it is an important part of professional development. Documents the interest in whole language.

Raines, Shirley C., ed. *Whole Language Across the Curriculum Grades 1, 2, 3*. New York: Teachers College Press, 1995.

Raines and four colleagues provide whole language activates for grades 1, 2 and 3. Part I discusses how teachers are using whole language; Part II tells how to integrate the curriculum and use portfolio assessment. The epilogue presents challenges for teachers. Activities are clearly presented. Whole language techniques in writing, math, play, the arts, social studies and language arts are presented with help to assess the results. The bibliographies for each chapter are helpful.

Reutzel, D.R., and Cooter, R.B. "Whole Language: Comparative, Effects on First Grade Reading Achievement." *Journal of Educational Research* 83 (1990): 252-257.

Presents evidence showing that students taught by the whole language approach score as well as or better than first grade students taught by a basal reader approach on standardized achievement tests at the end of the first grade.

Shannon, Patrick. *The Struggle to Continue*. Portsmouth, NH: Heinemann, 1990.

States that whole language and critical literacy are not new, but have developed from the same progressive educational ideas. States that teachers must continue to be aware of the heritage of the progressive tradition to use what exists in education. Shannon states that this is a call to use what we have rather than "reinventing the theory or inspiration" to continue the struggle for quality education. Describes the split into child-centered and social reconstructionist movements in the field of education.

Spiegel, Dixie Lee. "Blending Whole Language and Systematic Direct Instruction." *Reading Teacher* 46 (September 1992): 38-44.

Explains how to integrate systematic direct instruction in the whole language classroom. States that direct instruction is needed in the whole language classroom to strengthen literacy education and better meet the needs of all the students. Describes the benefits of direct instruction and how to "build bridges between whole language and more traditional approached." An extensive bibliography is provided.

Strickland, Dorothy. "Whole Language." In *The Literacy Dictionary: The Vocabulary of Reading and Writing*. Theodore L. Harris and Richard E. Hodges, eds. Newark, DE: International Reading Association, 1995, pp. 279-281.

Defines and describes the whole language approach. Discusses concerns and controversies and the future of whole language. A bibliography at the end of the dictionary provides further reading for a more in-depth view of the approach.

Turbill, J., and Cambourne, B. *Coping with Chaos*. Portsmouth, NH: Heinemann, 1987.

Provides a detailed description of how to implement whole language theory in classrooms. This is an attempt to help teachers deal with the variety of activities occurring at the same time in a whole language classroom by telling them what to expect.

Turner, Juliane C. "The Influence of Classroom. Contexts on Young Childrens' Motivation for Literacy." *Reading Research Quarterly* 30 (1995): 410-441.

Describes the differences in the motivation for reading in first grade classrooms using the whole language approach and a basal reader program.

Watson, Dorothy J. "Whole Language: Why Bother?" *Reading Teacher* 47 (May 1994): 600-607.

Describes the teacher's vital role in whole language instruction. Watson discusses the root of the whole language philosophy and her own commitment to the approach. Describes whole language tenets, the value of practice, and the whole language community. A brief list of sources is included. Tells why she bothers with the approach.

Weaver, Constance. *Understanding Whole Language from Principles to Practice*. Portsmouth, NH: Heinemann, 1990.

Weaver clearly describes the theory and practice of the whole language approach for teachers, parents and administrators. Useful references provided. Helps translate theory into practice.

Wilde, Sandra, ed. *Notes from a Kidwatcher: Selected Writings of Yetta M. Goodman*. Portsmouth, NH: Heinemann, 1996.

An excellent selection of Goodman's writings from a variety of sources. Articles are reprinted with a brief introduction to each section. Concludes with a curriculum vitae of Goodman. The bibliographies are most helpful (see Goodman's articles above).

Willinsky, John. "Theory and Meaning in Whole Language: Engaging Moorman, Blanton, and McLaughlin." *Reading Research Quarterly* 29 (1994): 334–339.

Discusses the Moorman, Blanton, and McLaughlin critique of whole language rhetoric in the same issue on pages 309–329 (see Moorman et al. above) using examples from whole language theory. Both articles make interesting reading when compared side by side.

Yatvin, J. *Developing a Whole Language Program*. Richmond, VA: Virginia State Reading Association, 1991.

Intended for classroom teachers. Provides a detailed description of how to start and maintain a whole language program. A valuable resource.

Literature Circles

Literature circles is an approach which encourages students to discuss what they read in small groups and decide how to share their reading. Students respond to what they read in a variety of ways providing more opportunities for student involvement in their own learning.

According to Harris and Hodges (1995) literature circles "are the part of a literature-based reading program in which students meet to discuss books they are reading independently." Egawa (1990) and Heald-Taylor (1996) state that in literature circles teachers select several books, provide multiple copies, introduce one book, allow students to select the book they wish to read, and participate by having group discussions about the book they are reading, respond in journals or logs, and help decide how to share their reading. Tierney and Readence (2000) state the literature circles technique provides students of all ages the opportunity to participate in student-led discussions of student selected books. This is a "way of making classroom interactions around reading richer, more dynamic, more real, and more collaborative."

Literature circles developed as teachers looked for more ways to involve students in discussions about literature and as ideas about the nature of comprehension, the role of discussion, the nature of response, collaboration, and the importance of self-monitoring and student involvement changed, according to Tierney and Readence (2000). It may not be possible to find all the pieces that make up literature circles because teachers have developed, modified, adapted, borrowed, reorganized, and extended practices as they saw the possibilities including its use in collaboration with other techniques. Tierney and Readence (2000) state that literature circles have elements from techniques such as cooperative learning, learner-centered assessment, author cycle, and comprehension. Literature circles is closely related to a combination of independent reading and collaboration.

Short and Kauffman (1996) were the first to use the term literature circles as a result of their observations of a teacher and the structure and function of small group literature discussions, according to Tierney and Readence (2000). Daniels (1994) describes the specific details of literature circles and the history and advantages of the technique. Daniels' book, Tierney and Readence (2000) believe, is the first reference for the technique. Although teachers invented the technique they were influenced by changes and ideas about reading over the past twenty years. Daniels (1994; 2002) lists several ideas as the essential elements of literature circles: (1) constructivist ideas about reading comprehension which focus on the strategic nature of meaning before, during, and after reading; (2) reader response theory based on a belief in the important role of personal responses and the importance of different responses to each student's developing interpretations of the material being read; (3) the importance of independent reading as a contribution to better reading ability; (4) the importance of the underlying structure from teachers and peers as support for readers in the form of predictability, playfulness, an emphasis on meaning, role reversal and modeling and creating a language for talking about books; (5) the importance of successful collaboration, the features of group dynamics, clear expectation, mutually developed norms, shared leadership, and responsibility, open lines of communication, diverse friendship patterns and methods of resolving conflict; and (6) the importance of using a balanced method of instruction.

Spiegel (1996) states that participation in a community of readers helps students explore half-formed ideas from a variety of perspectives. Students need to back up their responses and should be receptive to the various interpretations presented by group members, but also should feel comfortable enough to disagree. These flexible, small, temporary discussion groups meet for about 20 minutes to discuss a story, book, article or poem. Each member participates and takes a specific responsibility. Regular meetings take place and discussion jobs rotate. When a selection is finished the group decides how to share the important parts of the material with the rest of the class. Groups then switch members and start a new selection. Formal discussion jobs can be discontinued when everyone can conduct their own self-sustaining discussions, Daniels (1994) states. Burns, Roe and Smith (2002), Roe and Ross (2006), and Daniels (1994; 2002) describe the important components of literature circles as: fun is important; evaluation is informal consisting of observation, portfolios and self evaluation; groups share their ideas with the whole class when a selection is finished; students play rotating roles such as introducing ideas and discussion questions; the teacher is the facilitator and monitor, not a participant; students lead the discussions which should be open, allow disagreement, have personal connections and present open-ended question; readers are encouraged to use notes or study guides from different perspectives; regular meeting time is scheduled; each group reads a different book; small temporary groups form based on the books students select; and students select their own reading materials.

When teachers begin literature circles the kind of orientation students need to the process, Daniels (1994; 2002) states, depends on the sophistication and experience of the students with cooperative learning activities. Students who have worked with peers in group activities will need less background, can select books and set up groups on their own. When groups are formed, Daniels (1994; 2002) suggests the teacher provide a discussion of the roles the students might play as they read and discuss their books. Teachers can provide duplicated material to guide the students according to the role they are assigned such as discussion director; passage master; connector; and illustrator; researcher; summarizer; character captain; vocabulary enricher; scene setter. Role sheets contain questions, a description of the role the student is assigned, the pages read, and the names of the group members. Group discussion lasts about 20 minutes with the aim to have a "natural conversation" about the book.

Students who have less experience with group activities will need, Daniels (1994; 2002) states, a more gradual introduction starting with one story and one role for the whole class. A discussion of the process of literature circles is a good idea after small group discussions. In future sessions assign other roles on practice and gradually increase the length of material and multiple roles so that several groups are working at one time.

Daniels (1994; 2002) suggests that the sharing of group projects helps students become acquainted with students in other groups. The planning of a sharing project offers the teacher opportunities to review and discuss solutions to problems with each group. Burns, Roe, and Smith (2002) state that literature circles groups meet two to five times a week for two to three weeks. At group meetings students decide how far to read at each meeting to complete the book and have discussion topics for each meeting. A leader conducts each meeting which usually includes silent reading, writing, and sharing literature logs, asking open-ended questions, discussion, and extension activities. Spiegel (1996) states that participation in a community of learners helps students look at ideas from different perspectives, substantiate their contributions, become more accepting of the contributions of all group members, and learn to disagree.

Teachers become observers and facilitators who work with students to complete assessment activities. Daniels (1994; 2002) suggests portfolio projects and artifacts which require teacher-student conferences about achievements, goals and areas for improvement. Daniels (1994; 2002) does not believe grades should be given, but suggests elements such as productivity, growth, and the quality of reading could be considered. Productivity includes participation in conferences, preparation for conferences, and the quantity read by students. Growth includes improvement, reading a variety of books, and applying new learning. Quality includes considering the extent and difficulty of what is read and the mature nature of projects. Daniels (1994; 2002) stresses that the evaluation is based on the teacher's observations, the materials included in the portfolios, and conferences.

Literature logs are an important part of literature circles. Several researchers such as Jewell and Pratt (1999), Spiegel (1998), Hancock (1992), Handloff and Golden (1995), Berger (1996), Fuhler (1994), and Popp (1997) discuss the use and importance of literature logs and response journals, stressing that students should be encouraged to use personal experience, feelings, and go beyond the printed page to make these logs meaningful. Teachers learn about literacy processes from logs. Spiegel (1998) states that effective literature circles depend on teacher discussions about the teacher's involvement in the groups, how much and when teacher directed instruction should take place, how material is selected, how groups are to be formed and organized, and how to assist students to respond in the best way to what they read. Personal response to what is read should be used in place of correct answers to questions about what is read. Students should read many genres by many authors and compare, initiate, connect to literature in their groups and in their lives.

Tierney and Readence (2000), Roe and Ross (2006), and Burns, Roe, and Smith (2002) agree that there are many benefits to be gained from literature circles. Teachers are encouraged to adapt, expand, reflect and perfect practices to suit the needs of students. The suggestions about practices are proposals rather than hard and fast rules about how to conduct literature circles. Daniels (1994; 2002) in fact states that every session he has observed shows changes and differences from the definition of literature circles in some way.

Tierney and Readence (2000) state that "while there appears to be little direct evidence of improvement in overall reading achievement (as a result of literature circles) there is indirect evidence based upon careful study of classrooms that engage in cooperative discussions...." There is, they argue, evidence of the value of student-led discussion groups, and Daniels (1994; 2002), Roe and Ross (2006), and Burns, Roe, and Smith (2002) state that literature circles can result in significant changes in student interest, involvement in and sharing in reading. Literature circles may also motivate more in-depth consideration of ideas in what is read. Tierney and Readence (2000) believe that teachers need (1) more guidelines for observation and support of students; (2) more guidance in ways to help students to examine reading in more depth, examine their arguments, adopt the roles that are needed, and deal with long-term goals for literature circles; (3) more discussion and study of the connections to practices such as writing or drama might help; (4) a more dynamic use of roles might be described when readers are encouraged to take on more than one role; (5) to be alert to the possible confusion a role can cause, when, for example, students focus too much on their role in the discussion and the reading of the book suffers; (6) ways to focus on roles that emerge from the reading rather than imposing roles; (7) more consideration of linguistic diversity; (8) further exploration of differences in student expectations of the norms for participation.

Literature circles have the potential for many positive results at all grade levels. More research and guidance for teachers are needed.

Annotated Bibliography

Berger, Linda R. "Reader Response Journals: You Make the Meaning ... and How." *Journal of Adolescent and Adult Literacy* 39 (February 1996): 380–385.
    Suggests specific questions to encourage students to provide more in-depth responses in response journals.

Brabham, Edna Green, and Villaume, Susan Kidd. "Continuing Conversations About Literature Circles." *Reading Teacher* 54 (November 2000): 278–280.
    Offers specific suggestions for ways to respond to literature through literature circles.

Burns, Paul, Roe, Betty, and Smith, Sandy. *Teaching Reading in Today's Elementary Schools*. Boston: Houghton-Mifflin, 2002, pp. 268–273.
    Presents a solid discussion of literature circles. This is a good starting point.

Daniels, Harvey. *Literature Circles: Voice and Choice in the Student-Centered Classroom*. New York: Stenhouse, 1994; *Voices and Choices in Book Clubs and Reading Groups*. Portland, ME: Stenhouse, 2002.
    A classic which provides information on the history, theory and use of literature circles. The 2002 update provides more strategies and examples from classrooms.

Eeds, M.A., and Peterson, R. "Teaching as Curation: Learning to Talk About Literature." *Reading Teacher* 45.2 (1991): 118–126.
    Discusses the teacher's changing role in literature circles as a facilitator not as the evaluator.

Egawa, Kathy. "Harnessing the Power of Language: First Graders' Literature Engagement with *Owl Moon*." *Language Arts* 67 (October 1990): 582–588.
    Discusses using literature as the center of the curriculum. States student questions are the result of repeated reading of the story and thinking about the story.

Fuhler, Carol J. "Response Journals: Just One More Time with Feeling." *Journal of Reading* 37 (February 1994): 400–415.
    Discusses the importance of including specific ideas and personal feelings in literature logs.

Hancock, Margorie R. "Literature Response Journals: Insights Beyond the Printed Page." *Language Arts* 69 (January 1992): 36–42.
    Discusses how awareness of response patterns in literature journals can assist teachers in encouraging students' to extend responses to include personal experiences related to the material read.

Handloff, Elaine, and Golden, Joanne. "Writing as a Way of 'Getting to' What You Think and Feel About a Story." In *Book Talk and Beyond*. Nancy Rosser and Miriam Martinez, eds. Newark, DE: International Reading Association, 1995.
    Discusses literature logs and response journals and how teachers can learn about the literacy processes of each student through log entries.

Harris, Theodore L., and Hodges, Richard E. *Literacy Dictionary: The Vocabulary of Reading and Writing*. Newark, DE: International Reading Association, 1995.
    Provides a definition of literature circles.

Harste, J.C., Short, K.G., and Burke, C. *Creating Classrooms for Authors and Inquirers: The Reading Writing Connection*. Portsmouth, NH: Heinemann, 1996.
    Describes how to involve students as readers telling how to establish and encourage literature circles. A useful guide.

Heald-Taylor, B. Gail. "Three Paradigms for Literature Instruction in Grades 3–6." *Reading Teacher* 49 (March 1996): 456–466.

Describes three models for literature instruction providing specific information for practice.

Jewell, Terry A., and Pratt, Donna. "Literature Discussions in the Primary Grades: Children's Thoughtful Discourse About Books and What Teachers Can Do to Make It Happen." *Reading Teacher* 52 (May 1999): 842–850.

Describes specific strategies for encouraging second and third graders to think out loud about material they have read. Provides suggestions for ways teachers can provide feedback that helps students feel free to respond.

Labbo, L.D. "Beyond Story Time: A Socio-psychological Perspective on Young Children's Opportunities for Literacy Development During Story Extension Time." *Journal of Literacy Research* 28 (1996): 405–428.

This is a study of the different roles students assume during story time.

Nole, E. "Social Issues and Literature Circles with Adolescents." *Journal of Reading* 38 (1994): 88–93.

Describes how adolescents can work in literature circles to investigate social issues.

Popp, Marcia. *Learning Journals in the K–8 Classroom.* Mahwah, NJ: Erlbaum, 1997.

A discussion of literature logs and the types of entries to include at various grade levels. Provides specific guidelines.

Raphall, Taffy, et al. "Research Directions: Literature Discussion in the Reading Program." *Language Arts* 69 (January 1992): 54–61.

Describes directions for further research in using literature discussions. Presents directions for where more work is needed.

Roe, Betty D., and Ross, Elinor. *Integrating Language Arts Through Literature and Thematic Units.* Boston: Ally & Bacon, 2006, pp. 274–277.

Provides a good overview of literature circles. This is a good starting point.

Rosser, Nancy, and Martinez, Meriam, eds. *Book Talk and Beyond: Children's Response to Literature.* Newark, DE: International Reading Association, 1995.

This is a classic guide to literature response techniques. A most useful resource.

Short, K.G., and Kauffman, G. "So What Do I Do? The Role of the Teacher in Literature Circles." In *Book Talk and Beyond: Children and Teachers Response to Literature.* N.L. Rosser and M.G. Martinez, eds. Newark, DE: International Reading Association, 1996.

Provides a detailed discussion of the teacher's role in literature circles.

Spiegel, Dixie Lee. "The Role of Trust in Reader Response Groups." *Language Arts* 73 (September 1996): 332–339.

Discusses participation in literature circles and the importance of feeling comfortable enough to disagree with peers in a discussion.

Spiegel, Dixie Lee. "Silver Bullets, Babes and Bath Water: Literature Response Groups in a Balanced Literacy Program." *Reading Teacher* 52 (October 1998): 114–124.

Discusses how books are selected and how to assist students to respond to their selections effectively.

Tierney, Robert J., and Readence, John E. *Reading Strategies and Practices: A Compendium.* Boston: Allyn and Bacon, 2000, pp. 293–301.

Provides a description, rational, and cautions about literature circles. This is good background for more reading.

Literature-Based Reading Approaches

The use of fiction and nonfiction selections to motivate students and help them use personal experiences to better understand what they read is one aim of literature-based approaches.

According to Barone, Eeds, and Mason (1995) the aims of a literature-based approach to reading are to connect stories to the reader's personal background knowledge, to analyze stories and whole selections for specific story elements, and to monitor the pupil's understanding of the story. Literature also provides readers with "opportunities to engage in life experiences that they would otherwise miss." This shift from basal readers to trade books as the basis for reading was begun in the 1980s as a result of more quality children's literature being available, widespread use of whole language theory, and the spread of reader-response theory according to Cullinan (1989), Goodman (1989), Fisher and Hiebert (1990), Rosenblatt (1978), McGee (1992), Iser (1980), Bleich (1978), and Barr (1992).

Roe, Smith, and Burns (2005) state that the literature-based program uses trade books or books that are not textbooks written for instructional purposes. These are fiction and nonfiction books usually found in a classroom library, read aloud to a class, and suggested for recreational reading. Teachers have used trade books to supplement basal readers and for content area instruction in social studies or science. One aim of the literature-based program is to motivate students to read by choice. For techniques to motivate Shiflett (1998) suggests methods often used in advertising such as book talks based on marketing techniques and finding books that interest students. Teachers need to "sell" the book to motivate interest in reading.

McGee and Tompkins (1995) state that the successful implementation of the literature-based program depends on a thorough understanding of "the theoretical perspectives on literature and reading and ... the reasons for using a particular book and a particular instructional approach." Teachers must develop well organized, precise instructional goals, precise expectations for student activities, and a well organized precise teaching plan for implementation. Teachers must know the students' developmental level to select books that meet the ability of each student.

Roe, Smith, and Burns (2005) state that the necessary skills and strategies can be taught "within the context of material the children are actively involved in reading." A well organized instructional plan which includes teaching comprehension strategies using literature helps students understand and enjoy reading more, according to Baumann, Hooten and White (1999). Ruddell (1992) states that during the reading of literature, strategies should be monitored by both the student and the teacher who take equal responsibility for the student's learning and using comprehension strategies. Fuhler (1990) states that after-reading activities should include retelling the stories with or without a flannel board, rewritten reactions, and discussions about the book with peers and the teacher. Students can also, Fuhler (1990) states, use an author's style as a model for their own writing. Lunsford (1997) states that mini-lessons using literature improved writing workshop activities.

Roe, Smith, and Burns (2005) identify four approaches that are most frequently used as part of a literature-based program: whole-class core book reading, literature circles with multiple copies of selected books, thematic literature units, and individualized reading. According to Routman (1988) and Lehman, Freeman, and Allen (1994) the materials that constitute the literature-based program "include picture books, big books, predictable books, folktales, fables, myths, fantasy, science fiction, poetry, contemporary realistic fiction, historical fiction, nonfiction informational books and biographies." Harris and Hodges (1995), Huck (1977) and Scharer (1992) state that the best quality literary trade books are the best materials to help students achieve reading success in a literature-based program. Galda, Cullinan, and Strickland (1993) state that the necessities of a literature-based program are: (1) a teacher who has knowledge of literature and serves as an enthusiastic guide; (2) a setting that encourages students to interact socially and discuss books or engage in activities with others in reaction to books; (3) classroom organization that provides opportunities for students to choose what they will do with books; and (4) time and materials necessary to read and respond to books. Students gain reading skills in a book-rich environment. Cullinan (1989), Galda, Cullinan, and Strickland (1993), and Tompkins and McGee (1993) agree that the literature-based program is based on the following features: (1) literature is either the only material or the primary material used for reading instruction; (2) students have opportunities to independently read books of their choice; (3) extended periods of time are provided for independent and joint reading and writing activities; (4) activities involving discussion and joint writing projects are encouraged; (5) daily read-aloud or shared reading of literature is an important part of the program.

Literature-based programs can be implemented in many ways with the inclusion of a combination of the four approaches Roe, Smith, and Burns (2005) identified. The first approach is whole-class reading of a core book. Usually a class-set of the same trade book is made available so that each student has a personal copy. Books are selected, Roe, Smith, and Burns (2005) state, because they either fit into the curriculum for a particular subject such as social studies or science, are judged to be of excellent literary quality, or the teacher likes the book and thinks that it can be used to motivate students or teach a specific skill or attitude. The reading is divided into pre-reading activities, activities during the reading, and follow-up or post-reading activities.

Yopp and Yopp (2006) cite research from many sources to show that using a literature-based approach facilitates growth in literacy skills. Galda and Cullinan (2003), Chomsky (1972), Morrow (1992), Nagy, Herman and Anderson (1985), Cohen (1968), DeFord (1981), Feitelson, Kita and Goldstein (1986), Morrow, O'Connor and Smith (1990) are listed because their work shows that literature helps language development, increases comprehension and helps students learn to read better. Eldredge and Butterfield (1986), Hagerty, Hiebert and Owens (1989), Larrik (1987) and Tunnell and Jacobs (1989) demonstrated that attitudes toward reading were positive influences; better written expression was found by DeFord (1981, 1984), Eckhoff (1983), and Lancia (1997). Students developed better knowledge of linguistics and written language was found by Purcell-Gates, McIntyre, and Freppon (1995). Students also developed a better understanding of content area material when literature was used, according to Bean (2000) and Morrow and Gambrell (2000).

The pre-reading activities begin with sharing experiences that relate to the content of the book, its topic or theme or its characters. Teachers, Roe, Smith, and Burns (2005) state, set a purpose or purposes for reading. Atwell (1987, 1992) suggests a mini-lesson on a literary element such as characterization. Predictions can be made about the story from the title or the cover or from experience with other books by the same author. Questions to answer during reading are posed. Establishing background from a KWL activity will help students use prior information and experiences to better understand the story. For example—"Have you ever lost a pet? How did you feel?" Teachers may read aloud from a part of the book to help motivate and activate prior knowledge.

During reading Roe, Smith, and Burns (2005) suggest oral discussion either in small groups or as a whole class; teacher generated questions to guide the reading of the next section of the book; literature logs as part of a written dialogue with the teacher or a peer to help students think critically and creatively about what they are reading. Wollman-Bonilla (1989) and Fuhler (1994) suggest teachers write non-judgmental comments in literature

Literature-Based Reading Approaches 205

logs as a way to help students respond to stories and link personal experiences with what they are reading. Flitterman-King (1988) and McWhirter (1990) suggest that students make note in literature logs of expressions and vocabulary that is new or interesting or that raise questions or cause problems. Literature logs provide students with opportunities to communicate with the teacher and receive a written response.

Follow-up activities after a book has been completed offer opportunities for extending understanding, and broadening ideas gained from reading. Retelling the story can be done in a variety of ways using art, flannel boards, puppet drama, story maps, or as Swindall and Cantrell (1999) suggest, students become the character in the story and other students develop questions to interview the character about. This activity should involve writing another episode or another story for the character. Illustrating the sequence of the story or a favorite part, Roe, Smith, and Burns (2005) suggest, helps teachers assess student comprehension. Students should be encourage to use what they learned in a new context or to read material that is related to the story such as a nonfiction selection about a part of the story read or another book by the same author.

Activities to help students and teachers during and after reading include Shaw's (1988) use of narrative journal entries after each chapter was read to summarize and reflect on the chapter. As Fuhler (1994) states, this procedure helps students to be more actively involved in the reading and gives teachers a view of students' personal transactions with what they are reading. Wertheim (1988) suggests teaching guides for books which list vocabulary, discussion questions, and follow-up activities. Roe, Smith, and Burns (2005) state that this may be too structured for some teachers who want freer expression.

Literature circles provides several books in multiple copies from which students select a book to read. Roe, Smith, and Burns (2005) state that teachers introduce each book to the whole class and students select the one they want. Groups of four to six students are formed and meet two to five times a week. Groups last for two to three weeks. During meetings students discuss the book they are reading, decide how much to read at one time, and decide on activities such as logs, questions for discussion, topics that relate to the story. Brabham and Villaume (2000) state student group leaders facilitate activities and help students direct the discussion rather than answering teacher prepared questions. Spiegel (1996) states that students are required to participate and substantiate their contribution to the group. These communities of readers help students give personal responses rather than the right responses to questions about their reading.

Journals and logs provide opportunities for reactions during reading, Popp (1997) states, not just at the end as with a book report. Handloff and

Golden (1995) state that journal entries help teachers judge student insight and methods of reacting to books. Hancock (1992), Raphael et al. (1992) and Fuhler (1994) state that students who need help in making journal entries specific or need support can gain help from teacher comments in journals.

Jewell and Pratt (1999) suggest that a good way to introduce literature circles is to encourage students to "think out loud about literature selections and then put their thoughts on paper ... offer explicit feedback that validates their thoughts and ideas..." and encourage risk talking in response to a book. During whole class discussion the teacher should model how to respond and talk about this with students. Students become leaders and the teacher becomes a group member. After several weeks of whole class discussion Jewell and Pratt (1999) suggest two groups should be formed to practice smaller group discussion and eventually the small groups of literature circles will form.

Thematic literature units, Roe, Smith, and Burns (2005) state, are based on themes, topics, groups of people, genres, an author, or a specific book. Shanahan, Robinson and Schneider (1995) and Barton and Smith (2000) suggest avoiding narrowing topics too much or including content only because several mention similar subjects. Be specific and clear. Lipson, Valencia, Wixson and Peters (1993) and Bergeron (1996) state that thematic units provide an in-depth study of ideas and help students see the connections between ideas and provide a focus for an integrated study of a topic. Students get a depth and breath of learning and are able to see the reason for activities. A variety of materials and activities allow many things to be accomplished such as "positive attitudes towards reading and writing" time to study a topic and a connection between subjects.

Roberts and Kellough (2004) state that meaningful learning is "learning that results when the learner makes connections between a new experience, prior knowledge, and experiences that were stored in his or her long term memory." Learning that is most meaningful and lasts the longest involves high order thinking skills called conceptual knowledge. "Research results indicate using: (1) a curriculum in which disciplines are integrated; and (2) instructional techniques that involve the learners in social interactive learning such as problem-based and project-centered learning, cooperative learning, peer tutoring, and cross teaching...." Teachers use thematic units to help students develop "an awareness and appreciation for the topic and then ... (become) involved in various activities that connect ... what was being learned with their own lives." The integrated thematic unit is the antithesis of subject-matter-oriented teaching. The integration of subjects in a unit is done in such a way that it matches the developmental needs of students and helps students connect prior learning and new learning in a meaningful way, according to Roberts and Kellough (2004). Thematic units help students pursue their interests individually; help students learn to become independent problem solvers; help students become more involved in direct, purposeful, meaningful learning activities; help students learn what they need and help students maintain high levels of motivation; help students learn that learning is interrelated and knowledge occurs across all curriculum areas; and help teachers present curriculum in "a comprehensive manner and not teach separate subject..." according to Roberts and Kellough (2004).

Norton (1993) presents procedures for thematic units: (1) "identify a theme that can be enriched with literature; (2) ... construct a web with subtopics that become the subjects of study for groups of student; (3) ... students locate books and other resources that will help them investigate their subject; (4) then they share their finding creatively with the rest of the class." Teachers can use a KWL chart, Ogle (1989) suggests, to start a unit with the questions What do I know, What do I want to know and complete the unit with What did I learn. Lauritzen, Jaeger and Davenport (1996) state that one book can be used for a unit focus and teachers should create a cross curricular web for the unit. The focus is the book, and all curriculum areas relate to the characters, setting, plot and theme of the book. "Webbing is a technique that connects a central topic or ... a book to related ideas. A web is a framework that can cut across curricular areas," according to Roe, Smith, and Burns (2005), and no two webs will be the same. Huck, Hepler and Hickman (1997) suggest that a web be used as a plan to study literature and that the web be developed from students' interests and the strengths of the book being used. When students and a teacher create a web they begin to see the many possible directions in which the book can lead them. Students should contribute ideas so that the unit becomes student centered.

Roe, Smith, and Burns (2005) state that units may be based on books that have similar characteristics. These books are by the same author, have the same theme or topic or genre or have other things in common. These are called text-sets and stimulate discussion. Heine (1991) states that text-sets encourage several interpretations. For example, a class may read four or six books by Eve Bunting, and Roser, Hoffman, Labbo and Farest (1992) suggest small-group discussions to compare and contrast the books on a comparison or language chart to help students connect the stories and react to the literature. Books can be compared in response journals by individual students. Books in text-sets can be read together because of the theme, mood or setting. Gallagher (1995) suggests pairing a classic with a contemporary book of the same theme to motivate adolescent students. Connect books that lead to the reading of a classic.

Tompkins and McGee (1993) state that any genre can be used as the focus of a unit such as folktales, fantasy, biography, historical fiction or even poetry. Video tapes or audio tapes can also be used to present books to the whole class after the teacher starts the unit by reading aloud from a book. Discussion should follow and literature log entries and follow-up activities should be used. There should be whole class, small group, and independent activities planned as an integral part of each unit. The culminating activities at the end of the unit should, Marzano (1990) states, include comparing and contrasting some elements of the books, timelines, creative dramatics, and writing based on the theme.

Roberts and Kellough (2004) state that the steps in developing a unit should include: "(1) select a theme; (2) write an overview; (3) identify instructional resources; (4) organize the subject matter; (5) arrange the classroom environment; (6) plan ... culminating activity, or finale; and (7) assess."

The last approach is individualized reading. (See separate chapter in this volume for a detailed discussion of this approach. A brief discussion will be presented here.)

According to Roe, Smith, and Burns (2005), Harris and Sipay (1985) and Bagford (1985) individualized reading allows students to move at their own pace using self-selected books rather than reading in a group keeping pace with other group members. Students get help when necessary and support at all times. The characteristics of the individualized approach are:

1. Self-selection—students choose books that interest them. There is built-in motivation because students read material they have selected;

2. Self-pacing—students read at their own pace. Slower students are not rushed and quicker students are not held back. Students complete books and stories as quickly or as slowly as they find necessary;

3. Strategy and skill instruction—students get needed help in a group or as individuals to build comprehension and word recognition strategies and skills;

4. Record keeping—the teacher helps records of each student's progress noting the independent level, instructional, and frustration level. Lists of strengths and weaknesses are noted along with strategies that will assist the student to make progress. Students record the books read, new words found, and new strategies they have used;

5. Student-teacher conferences—once or twice a week the teacher schedules a conference with each student for different purposes such as observing and assessing progress, demonstrating strategies or reading with a student. Conferences may be very brief such as five minutes or last as long as 15 minutes;

6. Sharing activities—weekly time for students to share the books they have read with the entire class or a small group should be planned

for. Bagford (1985) describes an activity called a book auction in which after students hear from peers they bid for the opportunity to be the next person to read the book; conferences include helping students select a book, checking comprehension of a book being read, checking word recognition strategies and oral reading skills, helping students use skills and strategies and helping students plan how to share; and

7. Independent work—students spend most of their time reading independently rather than in an assigned group.

Teachers, according to Roe, Smith, and Burns (2005), state that the individualized approach helps students build background, exposes students to a variety of literature of different genres, helps students learn from different kinds of material, improves comprehension and expands vocabulary. Teachers need many books on a variety of levels of difficulty, a file of comprehension questions for each book, a file of skill and strategy building activities, and a period of training for students to learn the routines and habits needed to become successful in an individualized program. Roe, Smith, and Burns (2005) state that the individualized approach can be an important part of the literature-based program because:

1. Students have built-in motivation to read the books they have selected themselves;
2. Students are not compared to each other because everyone is reading a different trade book without a grade level;
3. Every student learns at his or her own rate;
4. Conferences provide contact between the student and the teacher on an individual basis;
5. Students develop fluency because they are reading at a level that is comfortable; and
6. Students learn that reading is a pleasant enjoyable activity.

Critics of the approach, Roe, Smith, and Burns (2005) state, list negative aspects of the approach: large numbers of books are necessary and they must be continually replaced, conference scheduling is time consuming and can create problems, too much record keeping is required, and this program does not have a sequential approach to skill development.

Yopp and Yopp (2006) state that the aims of the literature-based approach are to help students learn with text and learn to think more broadly, deeply and critically about ideas they read about; to develop personal responses to what is read; to motivate reading; and to create life-long learners who use literature to become wise participants in society and use literature for personal needs and interests. Raphael (1997) states that literature motivates the imagination, stimulates enjoyment, and helps understanding of oneself and others.

Yopp and Yopp (2006) provide advice about the activities suggested for a literature-based program:

1. Know students and decide what activities to use based on needs and interests;
2. Students will not be able to engage in a "grand conversation" in the beginning stages of the program. They need time to learn how and to unlearn the habit of stating "only one right answer";
3. The activities are not worksheets to be done and graded, but are intended for interactive work among students and the teacher;
4. Do not overuse activities for each aspect of reading. One does not need to use ALL activities at one time; and
5. The most important part of a literature-based program is the opportunity to read and listen to literature many times each day.

Research on literature-based instruction in classrooms, according to Morrow and Gambrell (2000), includes many studies comparing literature-based instruction with other methods; however, there are studies that evaluate using literature as an approach. Studies investigated: literature-based instruction and pupil attitude towards reading; literature-based instruction and special needs students; comparisons of literature-based and skill-based instruction, the effects of literature-based programs on achievement; response to literature through discussion groups; and using literature-based instruction in content areas of math, science and social studies.

The research on literature-based reading has focused on: comparison of literature-based and skills-based classrooms; evaluation of the effects of literature-based programs on literacy achievement; literature discussion groups; literature-based instruction with special populations; and literature-based instruction and attitude toward reading. Morrow and Gambrell (2000) offer discussions of each of these areas including selected studies. The following discussion provides a view of what research says about literature-based instruction.

Reutzel, Oda, and Moore (1989) studied kindergarten students and found that students in a literature-based and skills-based programs differed in print awareness, readiness for reading, and word reading ability. The students in the literature-based program demonstrated better print awareness, were more ready for reading skills, and demonstrated higher word reading ability than students taught by other approaches. Purcell-Gates, McIntyre, and Freppon (1995) compared skill-based and whole language classrooms and found that students in the literature-based program developed a better knowledge of written language than students in skills-based programs. Reutzel and Cooter (1990) studied first graders and found that students in the literature-based whole language program developed better vocabulary and comprehension knowledge than students in other programs. Richek and McTague (1988) used the "Curious George" strategy. Providing books about Curious George with students who had reading problems, they found that this literature-based strategy helped students understand what they were reading better than students who did not use this strategy.

Dahl and Freppon (1995) studied inner city students in the early elementary grades in skills-based and literature-based whole language programs and found that the students in the literature-based programs were able to use more strategies for reading and writing than students in skills-based programs. Freppon (1991) studied students' understanding of the nature and purpose of reading in various instructional programs and found that students in the literature-based programs had a much better understanding of the purpose of reading and used more strategies in reading than students in other programs.

Gambrell and Palmer (1992) found that students developed higher levels of meta-cognitive awareness and thought of reading more as a meaning-making process than students in skills-based programs did.

Several studies investigated the use of basal readers and literature as a supplement to the basal program. Morrow (1992) studied second graders who were randomly assigned to one of three groups: (1) a literature-based reading and writing program with literacy centers and teacher-directed activities with time for independent reading and writing in addition to the basal reading program; (2) a group identical to group #1 with parental involvement with home activities; and (3) a control group only using basal readers. The study lasted for the whole school year and used the entire class involved as the unit of analysis, and the class mean was used for all measures. Even though students in each class were randomly assigned to one of the three groups within the classrooms, students were not randomly assigned to treatment. Morrow (1992) found that students working in the literature groups achieved statistically better progress than the control group in original story writing, retelling stories and story rewriting. The literature-based part of the study was designed as a complement to the basal reading program and the same length of instructional time was spent on reading instruction for all three groups; however, the literature-based part of the study received more time than the basal part of the study.

Morrow, Pressley, Smith, and Smith (1997) investigated the effects of a literature-based approach in addition to a basal approach and science instruction in third grade classes. The aim of the study was to investigate the impact of literature on reading and science achievement. Students were assigned to one of three groups: (1) literature-based reading and literature-based science as a supplement to the basal reading program; (2) literature-based reading and textbook-based science in additional to the basal program; and (3) basal reading and textbook-based science instruction only. The study lasted for the whole school year and used the entire class as a unit of analysis using the class mean for all measures. The results were similar to Morrow's (1992) study, showing superior ability for retelling stories, rewriting stories, and writing original stories. The students in the 1997 study in group one, the most literature intensive group using trade books for reading and science, performed better than the other two groups on the California Test of Basic Skills on reading and total language measures. Group one also performed better than the other two groups on two tests of science content. The results, Morrow, Pressley, Smith, and Smith (1997) believe, indicate that using literature increases content area learning.

Both the 1992 and 1997 studies suggest that adding literature to the basal approach provides better results and learning than using only the basal approach.

Block (1993) studied the effects of the literature-based approach on student thinking strategies. Second and third grade students were randomly assigned by classroom to the experimental or control groups. The literature-based group experienced lessons twice a week for 32 weeks. Each lesson comprised two parts: (1) the teacher explained and modeled a thinking and comprehension strategy such as predicting using written strategy guides; and (2) students selected literature and used the strategy modeled by the teacher. The control group received instruction without the strategy component.

Block (1993) reported that the students in the strategy/literature-based group scored better than the control group on the reading comprehension, vocabulary and total battery sections of the Iowa Test of Basic Skills. These students also, Block (1993) reported, were better able to transfer cognitive strategies to school activities and apply them in tests of creative thinking, critical thinking, and self-esteem than the control group.

In a year long qualitative case study Baumann and Ivey (1997) studied what second grade students learned about reading, writing, and literature in a literature-based strategy instructional program. Baumann was the full-time classroom teacher and Ivey served as participant observer. Personal journals kept by Baumann and Ivey (1997), data from interviews of students and parent interviews, video tapes of classroom activities, samples of students' reading and writing, assessment of students' progress and the teacher's plan book were used as data. Baumann and Ivey (1997) used a content analysis and found that students demonstrated growth in overall reading and learned to view reading as a natural part of school. Students showed growth in written composition, word identification skills and fluency and comprehension skills. Students also became more involved in books as a result of the program. Baumann and Ivey (1997) report that the study "provides support for the efficacy of teaching ... reading and language arts strategies" within a literature-based program. Baumann and Ivey (1997) concluded that literature creates a mutually reinforcing relationship between the strategies being taught and a literature rich environment. Immersion in literature and the skills strategies taught in that context create a program in that each component contributed to and assisted each other. "In other words, the literature enhanced students' reading and writing fluency and their developing literacy abilities promoted their literacy knowledge and appreciation."

According to McGee (1992) research shows that reading and discussing literature provides opportunities to look at many interpretations of literature and to respond at higher levels of abstract and critical thinking. Literature discussion groups provide higher thinking levels according to Almasi (1995, 1996), Baker (1979), Schallert and Kleinman (1979). These researchers state that their findings agree with Vygotsky (1978) who stated that social interaction is essential for the development of language and thought. Students learn with the help of more knowledgeable members of the community and higher level thinking skills and language skills are developed as a result of discussion.

Research done by Almasi (1995), Gambrell (1987), Goatly and Raphael (1992) indicates that students need to participate in discussions of literature with peers to develop more detailed responses. Almasi (1995), Eeds and Wells (1989), and Goatly (1996) state that after students take part in literature discussion groups their behavior indicates better comprehension and evaluation of what is read and better personal responses. Students were better able to remember information, draw inferences, support their inferences and read critically without direct questions from the teacher. Eeds and Wells (1989), Gerla (1996), and Goatly (1996) found that when students participated in discussions they learned quickly to respond more personally to their reading. The collaboration found in discussion groups helps students to construct meaning and clarify confused ideas. Students were observed to direct turn-taking, negotiate leadership, and to use many sources to clarify or agree with the interpretation of a book.

After examining numerous studies of the use of literature-based instruction in various content areas, Morrow and Gambrell (2000) conclude that additional research is needed to find differences in the way students understand concepts learned from textbooks and from literature-based experiences. This research will confirm the expectation that literature-based experiences help students make more meaningful connections with concepts and related ideas. It was concluded by Morrow and Gambrell (2000) that the integration of literature-based instruction into content area instruction should be carefully analyzed because other studies indicate that this procedure motivates students' interest in learning. Studies should focus on student enthusiasm over time to see if it remains high or diminishes. Such studies, Morrow and Gambrell (2000) state, could make "the relevance and importance of both content learning and literature-based instruction more obvious to the learner. If so, literature-based instruction integrated into content areas could be a key ingredient in creating more motivating educational environments."

Morrow and Gambrell (2000) examined studies done by Oberlin and Shugarman (1989), Stewart, Paradis, Ross, and Lewis (1996), Worthy and Invernizzi (1995), Jimenez and Gamez (1996), Goatly (1996), Goatly et al. (1995), Goatly and Raphael (1992) regarding the use of literature-based instruction with special populations and concluded that the research had a limited scope, but "there are promising results with respect to promoting positive attitudes toward reading" and better proficiency in reading. The case studies and interviews used as research tools indicate that special populations can learn better with literature-based instruction; however, more research with these populations is needed.

Morrow and Gambrell (2000) report several studies were done to find out the role of student attitude toward reading. Attitude toward reading affects students' ability to read since it influences the time spent reading and involvement with reading. Attitude toward reading also causes students to decide not to read, but to select another activity because they do not like to read. Research on the effects on student motivation, Morrow and Gambrell (2000) report, provided inconclusive results because the studies presented both positive and negative results. It is concluded that more research is needed to study the effects of literature-based reading and content area instruction on student attitudes towards reading and motivation to learn. McKenna, Kear, and Ellsworth (1995) state that "clearly, the question of the effect of instructional materials and approaches in attitudes towards reading is an important and complex one that calls for broad, program-level comparison studies that closely attend to program fidelity."

Annotated Bibliography

Almasi, J.F. "The Nature of Fourth Graders Socio-Cognitive Conflicts in Peer-Led and Teacher-Led Discussions of Literature." *Reading Research Quarterly* 30.3 (1995): 314–351.
   This extensive research investigation concluded that peer-led discussions provided significantly more verbalization, and student ideas about what they read were enhanced by more talk about reading. Peer-led discussions encouraged students to talk and promote conceptual change.
Almasi, J.F. "A New View of Discussion." In *Lively Discussions: Fostering Engaged Reading*.

L.B. Gambrelli and J.F. Almasi, eds. Newark, DE: International Reading Association, 1996, pp. 2-24.
   Presents techniques to promote dialogue about literature. States that understanding occurs better after discussion about what is read.
Atwell, Nancie. *In The Middle: Writing, Reading and Learning with Adolescents.* Upper Montclare, NJ: Boyton/Cook, 1987, revised 1992.
   A most practical discussion of Atwell's work with adolescent students, describing the strategies she uses to encourage reading and writing.
Bagford, Jack. "What Ever Happened to Individualized Reading?" *Reading Teacher* 39 (November 1985): 190-193.
   Discusses the individualized reading approach, stating a return to using this approach will help students enjoy reading. Suggests strategies for using this technique.
Baker, L. "Comprehension Monitoring: Identifying and Coping with Text Confusion." *Journal of Reading Behavior* 11.4 (1979): 366-374.
   How to assist students in comprehension of material when problems arise.
Barone, Tom, Eeds, Mary Ann, and Mason, Kathleen. "Literature, the Disciplines and the Lives of Elementary School Students." *Language Arts* 72 (January 1995): 30-38.
   Discusses the role of literature in areas of the curriculum. Provides samples of narratives written by students to show the relationship between literature and the other content areas.
Barr, R. "Teachers, Materials, and Group Composition in Literacy Instruction." In *Elementary School Literacy: Critical Issues.* M.J. Dreher and W.H. Slater, eds. Norwood, MA: Christopher-Gordon, 1992, pp. 21-51.
   Discusses the issues that affect reading instruction with emphasis on grouping.
Barton, Keith C., and Smith, Lynne A. "Themes or Motifs? Aiming for Coherence Through Interdisciplinary Outlines." *Reading Teacher* 54 (September 2000): 54-63.
   States that thematic units must be carefully planned interdisciplinary outlines that include important content, change with student interests and needs, and contain authentic tasks. Suggests using children's literature and avoiding prepackaged material that lacks content.
Baumann, James F., Hooten, Helene, and White, Patricia. "Teaching Comprehension through Literature: A Teacher-Research Project to Develop Fifth Graders' Reading Strategies and Motivation." *Reading Teacher* 53 (September 1999): 38-51.
   Describes a research project that taught comprehension strategies through literature to provide 5th grade students with better comprehension and enjoyment of reading. The aim was to teach comprehension strategies in a meaningful context to ensure the application of skills in new situations.
Baumann, James F., and Ivey, Gay. "Delicate Balances: Striving for Curricular and Instructional Equilibrium in a Second Grade Literature-Strategy Based Classroom." *Reading Research Quarterly* 32.3 (1997): 244-275.
   Reports that there is a close relationship between literature-based and strategy-based reading programs and there is no formula for quantifying success. Success results where many delicate balances occur.
Bean, Thomas W. "Reading in Content Areas: Social Constructivists Dimension." In *Handbook of Reading Research, Volume III.* M.L. Kamil, P.B. Mosenthal, P.D. Pearson and R. Barr, eds. Mahwah, NJ: Erlbaum, 2000, pp. 629-644.
   Provides a discussion of the history, theory, practice, and policy of content area reading. Starts with a definition and concludes with a discussion of implications for future research directions. Provides an excellent bibliography.
Bergeron, Betty S. "Speaking Authenticity: What Is 'Real' About Thematic Literacy Instruction?" *Reading Teacher* 49 (April 1996): 544-551.
   States thematic units provide an in-depth method of connecting content to help students understand the reason for activities.
Bleich, D. *Subjective Criticism.* Baltimore: Johns Hopkins University Press, 1978.

An intensive theoretical discussion of the nature of literary criticism.
Block, Cathy C. "Strategy Instruction in a Literature-Based Reading Program." *Elementary School Journal* 94.2 (1993): 139–151.

Describes a literature-based reading program designed to help students improve cognitive strategy use, reading ability, self-esteem, and critical thinking. Describes the two part lesson and research with 178 experimental students.

Brabham, Edna Greene, and Villaume, Susan Kidd. "Continuing Conversations About Literature Circles." *Reading Teacher* 54 (November 2000): 278–280.

Discusses literature circles, telling specific ways to organize and use literature circles including the number of students to include, books to be used and how to prepare students for participation.

Chomsky, C. "Stages in Language Development and Reading Exposure." *Harvard Educational Review* 42.1 (1972): 33.

Reports that the use of literature causes better language development in students.

Cohen, D. "The Effect of Literature on Vocabulary Development and Reading Achievement." *Elementary English* 45 (1968): 209–213, 217.

A literature-program helps students succeed in reading comprehension and develop a better vocabulary.

Cullinan, B.E. "Latching on to Literature: Reading Initiatives Take Hold." *School Library Journal* 35 (1989): 27–31.

A survey of literature-based programs across America provides a history and the 1989 status of the initiative.

Dahl, K.L., and Freppon, P.A. "A Comparison of Inner-City Children's Interpretations of Reading and Writing Instruction in the Early Grades in Skills-Based and Whole Language Classrooms." *Reading Research Quarterly* 30.1 (1995): 50–74.

Compares skills-based and whole language reading instruction and finds that students in literature-based or whole language programs use more strategies than students in skills-based programs.

DeFord, D. "Classroom Contexts for Literacy." In *The Context of School-Based Literacy*. T. Raphall, ed. New York: Random House, 1984, pp. 163–180.

Describes the ways in which literature influences reading and writing skills.

DeFord, D. "Literacy: Reading, Writing and Other Essentials." *Language Arts* 58 (1981): 652–658.

The use of literature provides students with better success in writing and reading skills. Many other language skills are also positively influenced by the use of literature.

Dugan, JoAnn. "Transactional Literature Discussions: Engaging Students in the Appreciation and Understanding of Literature." *Reading Teacher* 51 (October 1997): 86–96.

Describes transactional literature discussions, an activity that encourages reading, writing, and talking about a whole book. Presents the specifics of the activity and tells why it is important. Presents the theoretical foundations and practical use of the activity.

Eckhoff, B. "How Reading Affects Children's Writing." *Language Arts* 60 (1983): 607–616.

Describes the positive effects of literature on students' writing skills.

Eeds, M., and Wells, D. "Grand Conversations: An Exploration of Meaning Construction in Literature Study Groups." *Research in the Teaching of English* 23.1 (1989): 4–29.

Discusses the effects of peer-led discussion groups on reading comprehension skills with 5th and 6th graders.

Egawa, Kathy. "Harnessing the Power of Language: First Graders' Literature Engagement with *Owl Moon*." *Language Arts* 67.6 (October 1990): 582–588.

Describes a study using *Owl Moon* with 1st grade students. Tells how to use literature as the center of the curriculum to provide students with time to listen, learn, think, and ask questions of authors. The questions generated by the students were the results of repeated reading and thinking about a story.

Eldredge, J., and Butterfield, D. "Alternatives to Traditional Reading Instruction." *Reading Teacher* 40 (1986): 32–37.

Explains the positive effects of the use of literature-based reading on student attitudes toward reading and reading success.
Feitelson, D., Kita, B., and Goldstein, Z. "The Effects of Listening to Series Stories on First Graders' Comprehension and Use of Language." *Research in the Teaching of English* 20 (1986): 339-355.
    Describes the relationship between the experience of listening to stories and first graders' skill in comprehension and use of language.
Fisher, Charles W., and Hiebert, Elfrieda H. "Characteristics of Tasks in Two Approaches to Literacy Instruction." *Elementary School Journal* 91.1 (1990): 3-18.
    Compares 2nd and 6th graders in either a literature-based or skills-based reading program observed over 40 days. Uses a task perspective to analyze the classroom process. The task characteristics showed that in the two approaches students gained different knowledge and attitudes toward reading and learning.
Flitterman-King, Sharon. "The Role of the Response Journal in Active Reading." *The Quarterly of the National Writing Project and Center for the Study of Writing* 10.3 (1988): 4-11.
    Describes the importance of the response journal as a tool for student involvement as an active reader.
Freppon, P.A. "Children's Concepts of the Nature and Purpose of Reading in Different Instructional Settings." *Journal of Reading Behavior* 23.2 (1991): 139-163.
    Concluded that students in a literature-based program thought of reading as a meaning-making process and demonstrated higher level metacognition skills than students in skills-based programs.
Fuhler, Carol J. "Let's Move Towards Literature-Based Reading Instruction." *Reading Teacher* 43 (January 1990): 312-315.
    Discusses the use of a literature-based program using trade books. Describes alternatives to basal readers listing the advantages of a literature-based program. Many examples of books are provided.
Fuhler, Carol J. "Response Journals: Just One More Time with Feeling!" *Journal of Reading* 37 (February 1994): 400-405.
    Discusses the importance of including feelings and personal experiences in response journal entries.
Galda, L., and Cullinan, B.E. "Literature for Literacy: What Research Says About the Benefits of Using Trade Books in the Classroom." In *Handbook of Research on Teaching the English Language Arts*. J. Flood, D. Lap, J.R. Squire and J.M. Jensen, eds. Mahwah, NJ: Erlbaum, 2003, pp. 640-648.
    Tells why trade books should be an important part of the reading program presenting research on the effectiveness of the practice. Concludes with directions for research.
Galda, L., Cullinan, B.E., and Strickland, D.S. *Language Literacy and the Child*. New York: Harcourt Brace, 1993.
    This is a useful work on the value of literature in literacy development.
Gallagher, Janice Mori. "Pairing Adolescent Fiction with Books from the Canon." *Journal of Adolescent and Adult Literacy* 39 (September 1995): 8-14.
    Suggests teachers use classic and contemporary books on the same theme to motivate further reading. Presents excellent suggestions that are practical.
Gambrell, L.B. "Children's Oral Language During Teacher-Directed Reading Instruction." In *Research in Literacy: Merging Perspectives*. J.E. Readence and R.S. Baldwin, eds. Rochester, NY: National Reading Conference, 1987, pp. 195-200.
    Describes students' discussion following teacher-directed reading.
Gambrell, L.B., and Palmer, B. "Children's Metacognitive Knowledge About Reading and Writing in Literature-Based and Conventional Classrooms." In *Literacy Research, Theory, and Practice: Views from Many Perspectives*. C.K. Kinzer and D.J. Leu, eds. Chicago: National Reading Conference, 1992, pp. 215-224.

Describes the difference between metacognitive knowledge and view of the reading process in skills-based and literature-based reading programs.
Gerla, J.P. "Response-Based Instruction: At-Risk Students Engaging in Literature." *Reading and Writing Quarterly: Overcoming Learning Difficulties* 12.2 (1996): 149–169.
Describes the use of response to literature to help at-risk students succeed.
Goatly, V.J. "The Participation of a Student Identified as Learning Disabled in a Regular Education Book Club: The Case of Stark." *Reading and Writing Quarterly: Overcoming Learning Difficulties* 12.2 (1996): 195–214.
Reports the contribution made and the learning success of a learning disabled student who participated in a regular education book club.
Goatly, V.J., Brock, C.H., and Raphael, T.E. "Diverse Learners Participating in Regular Education Book Clubs." *Reading Research Quarterly* 30.3 (1995): 352–380.
A study of students with diverse educational and linguistic needs who were included in regular education book clubs. It was concluded that the diversity of the students demonstrated how individual differences contribute in positive ways for all members of the group. The students used their backgrounds and experiences to bring greater understanding to what they read. Diverse learners can enrich the mainstream classroom given the opportunity to do so.
Goatly, V.J., and Raphael, T.E. *Non-Traditional Learners Written and Dialogic Responses to Literature: Fortieth Yearbook of the National Reading Conference.* Chicago: National Reading Conference, 1992, pp. 313–332.
Reports on the success of nontraditional students' response to literature orally and in writing. Found that literature programs afforded more opportunity for better quality responses.
Goodman, Yetta M. "Roots of the Whole Language Movement." *Elementary School Journal* 90 (1989): 113–127.
The history of the whole language movement describing the major influences from psychology, linguistics, philosophy, and education. Describes the contributions from England and New Zealand. Concludes that science and humanism continue to influence holistic perspectives in education. Very interesting and useful background for understanding whole language and the programs which grew out of the philosophy.
Hagerty, P., Hiebert, E., and Owns, M. "Students' Comprehension, Writing and Perceptions in Two Approaches to Literacy Instruction." In *Cognitive and Social Perspectives for Literacy Research and Instruction.* S. McCormeck and J. Zutel, eds. Chicago: National Reading Conference, 1989, pp. 453–459.
Discusses the effects of two approaches to reading on the success of students.
Hancock, Marjorie R. "Character Journals: Initiating Involvement and Identification through Literature." *Journal of Reading* 37 (September 1993): 42–50.
Describes the benefits and uses of character journals as a means of involving students in literature.
Hancock, Marjorie R. "Literature Response Journals: Insights Beyond the Printed Page." *Language Arts* 69.1 (January 1992): 36–42.
Explains how one 6th grader's response journal gave insight into the journals of the entire class. States the response journals are a treasure chest filled with spontaneous thoughts and ideas that might otherwise be forgotten. It is an alternative for collecting ideas about a whole book. A most useful technique for elementary level students.
Handloff, Elaine, and Golden, Joanne. "Writing as a Way of Getting to What You Think and Feel About a Story." In Nancy Roser and Miriam Martinez (eds.), *Book Talk and Beyond.* Newark, DE: International Reading Association, 1995.
States that journal entries help teachers better understand students' responses to what they read.
Harris Albert J. and Sipay, Edward R. *How to Increase Reading Ability: A Guide to Developmental and Remedial Methods.* New York: Longman, 1985, 1987, 1988.

This is a classic text which presents practical suggestions for classroom activities and cites research to support these suggestions.

Harris, Theodore L., and Hodges, Richard E. *The Literacy Dictionary: The Vocabulary of Reading and Writing*. Newark, DE: International Reading Association, 1995.

Provides a definition of terms. This is a good starting point.

Heald-Taylor, B. Gail. "Three Paradigms for Literature Instruction in Grades 3-6." *Reading Teacher* 49 (March 1996): 456-466.

Investigated curriculum as activity, as inquiry and as fact. Discusses the importance of a shift away from fact to activity and inquiry. Tells how to use literature instruction to make changes in the teaching-learning relationship, relationships with students, and how authorship is viewed. Research is cited and methods for implementing change are presented.

Heine, Patricia. "The Power of Related Books." *Reading Teacher* 45 (September 1991): 75-77.

States that compare and contrast is an excellent strategy for an author study.

Henke, Linda. "Beyond Basal Reading: A District's Commitment to Change." *New Advocate* 1.1 (1988): 42-51.

Describes a decision by a school district to move toward a literature-based reading program.

Hiebert, Elfrieda H., and Colt, Jacalyn. "Patterns of Literature-Based Reading Instruction." *Reading Teacher* 43 (October 1989): 14-20.

Describes a comprehensive literature-based program providing information on two dimensions of literacy programs, three patterns of literature-based instruction, and illustrations of total reading programs with the three patterns. Concludes that a total reading program should have combinations of several approaches to teacher-student interaction and selection of material.

Holdaway, D. *The Foundations of Literacy*. Sydney: Ashton-Scholastic, 1979.

Discusses a model for literacy instruction in which students have the opportunity to ask adults questions in story reading and other literacy situations to regulate their own learning.

Huck, Charlotte S. "Literature as the Content for Reading." *Theory Into Practice* 16.5 (1977): 363-371.

Describes the use of children's literature as the basis for a reading program. Emphasizes the importance of reading aloud to students.

Huck, Charlotte S., Hepler, Susan, and Hickman, Janet. *Children's Literature in the Elementary School*. Fort Worth, TX: Harcourt, 1997.

This is a classic resource in children's literature. Suggests using a web to plan a literature study that will use student interests and strengths.

Iser, W. "The Reading Process: A Phenomenological Approach." In *Reader Response Criticism: From Formalism to Post Structuralism*. J.P. Tompkins, ed. Baltimore: Johns Hopkins University Press, 1980, pp. 50-69.

Discusses response theory as an important factor in the move toward including literature in the reading program.

Jewell, Terry A., and Pratt, Donna. "Literature Discussions in the Primary Grades: Children's Thoughtful Discourse About Books and What Teachers Can Do to Make It Happen." *Reading Teacher* 52 (May 1999): 842-850.

Describes changes in a primary grade reading program to increase student engagement in reading material and to use more literature discussion.

Jimenez, R.T., and Gamez, A. "Literature-Based Cognitive Strategy Instruction for Middle School Latina/o Students." *Journal of Adolescent and Adult Literacy* 40.2 (1996): 84-91.

A case study of three seventh grade students for whom English was a second language describing how their reading improved with a literature-based program and how they became more strategic readers.

Koeller, S.A. "The Children's Voice: Literature Connections." *Children's Literature in Education* 19.1 (1988): 3-16.

Discusses the use of basal readers and the importance of using literature to assist students to find personal connections to what they read.

Lancia, P.J. "Literacy Borrowing: The Effects of Literature for Children's Writing." *Reading Teacher* 50 (1997): 470–475.

States that using literature influences students' writing. Students use elements and ideas from stories for their own writing.

Langer, J.A. *A Response-Based Approach to Reading Literature.* Report Series 6.7. Albany, NY: National Research Center on Literature Teaching and Learning, 1994.

Describes methods of developing student response to literature.

Larrik, N. "Illiteracy Starts Too Soon." *Phi Delta Kappa* 69 (1987): 184–189.

Discusses the importance of literature to student attitudes and perceptions of reading.

Lauritzen, Carol, Jaeger, Michael, and Davenport, M. Ruth. "Integrating Curriculum: Contexts for Integrating Curriculum." *Reading Teacher* 49 (February 1996): 404–406.

Suggests teachers use one book for a unit focus from which all content area material can be developed using a web to connect all content areas.

Lehman, B.A., Freeman, E.V., and Allen, V.G. "Children's Literature and Literacy Instruction: 'Literature-Based' Elementary Teachers' Belief and Practices." *Reading Horizons* 35.1 (1994): 3–29.

Report of a survey of 192 teachers attending a conference on literature-based reading instruction. Provides information about teachers' ideas about literature-based instruction. 94 percent believed that literature-based instruction was important, but only 45 percent reported using the program exclusively. There was a reported difference between belief and implementation.

Lipson, Marjorie, Valencia, Sheila W., Wixson, Karen K., and Peters, Charles W. "Integration and Thematic Teaching: Integration to Improve Teaching and Learning." *Language Arts* 70.4 (April 1993): 252–263.

Presents a brief history of curriculum integration and lists four attributes of an integrated curriculum. Answers several questions with very useful information: Why Themes?; What Themes?; Themes as presented in professional material; themes in basal programs; supplementary material. This is a practical and very useful article.

Lunsford, Susan H. "And They Wrote Happily Ever After: Literature-Based Mini-Lessons in Writing." *Language Arts* 74 (January 1997): 42–48.

Describes how the author designed mini-lessons that fit the needs of her students. States that the mini-lessons provided opportunities to share knowledge about writing using examples from the authors of children's literature.

Marzano, Lorraine. "Connecting Literature with Cooperative Writing." *Reading Teacher* 43 (February 1990): 429–430.

Presents culminating activities for thematic units to help students successfully complete a unit.

McGee, Lea M. "Exploring the Literature-Based Reading Revolution (Focus on Research)." *Language Arts* 69.7 (November 1992): 529–537.

Agrees with Rosenblatt's reader's response theory and tells how to motivate students; describes student response, performance and what teachers understand about literature-based instruction.

McGee, Lea M., and Tompkins, Gail E. "Literature-Based Reading Instruction: Who's Guiding the Instruction?" *Language Arts* 72.6 (October 1995): 405–414.

States that instruction varies widely based on the types of teachers. Concludes that becoming a literature-based teacher means becoming aware of differences and similarities of competing theoretical perspectives. To become thoughtful guides teachers must move toward knowledge of many theories for guiding thinking about, responding to, and interpreting literature.

McGee, Lea M., and Tompkins, Gail E. "The Videotape Answer to Independent Reading Comprehension Activities." *Reading Teacher* 34 (January 1981): 427–433.

Discusses use of technology to promote independent reading.

McKenna, Michael C., Kear, Dennis J., and Ellsworth, Randolph A. "Children's Attitudes Toward Reading: A National Survey." *Reading Research Quarterly* 30.4 (1995): 934–955.

Researched the reading attitudes of 18,185 American students in grades 1–6 using two attitude scales. Five results related to attitude were reported. Data on age, gender, and reading ability were reported. Concludes that sensitive methods are needed to examine the factors involved.

McWhirter, Anne M. "Whole Language in the Middle School." *Reading Teacher* 43 (April 1990): 562–565.

Describes how the author developed a program for 8th graders using whole language philosophy and the reading workshop. Suggests that time to read and opportunities to respond to self-selected literature in dialogue journals helps middle school students enjoy learning from reading and writing. Describes how the author changed her teaching to benefit students.

Morrow, Lesley Mandel. "Home and School Correlates of Early Interest in Literature." *Journal of Educational Research* 76 (1983): 221–230.

Reports on the connection between home and school influences on interest in literature.

Morrow, Lesley Mandel. "The Impact of a Literature-Based Program on Literacy Achievement, Use of Literature, and Attitudes of Children from Minority Backgrounds." *Reading Research Quarterly* 27.3 (1992): 251–275.

A study of 166 second grade minority students in a school-based or home-based literature-based program. Reported no differences were found in the performance of either group.

Morrow, Lesley Mandel, and Gambrell, Linda B. "Literature-Based Reading Instruction." In *Handbook of Reading Research, Volume III*. Michael L. Kamil, Peter B. Mosenthal, P. David Pearson, and Rebecca Barr, eds. Mahwah, NJ: Erlbaum, 2000, pp. 563–586.

A discussion of literature-based reading programs, practices, and research. Includes an excellent bibliography.

Morrow, Lesley Mandel, O'Connor, E., and Smith, J. "Effects of a Story Reading Program on the Literacy Development of At-Risk Kindergarten Children." *Journal of Reading Behavior* 22 (1990): 225–275.

Story reading helped at risk kindergarten students better comprehend stories. This research looked at the effects of literature on the skills of kindergarten students who were identified as at-risk for future problems.

Morrow, Lesley Mandel, Pressley, M., Smith, J.K., and Smith J. "The Effect of a Literature-Based Program Integrated Into Literacy and Science Instruction with Children from Diverse Backgrounds." *Reading Research Quarterly* 32.1 (1997): 54–76.

Examined 128 third grade students for attitudes toward reading and science. The two groups used were a literature science program and a literature only program.

Nagy, W., Herman, P.A., and Anderson, R.C. "Learning Works from Context." *Reading Research Quarterly* 20 (1985): 233–253.

A study of 57 8th grade students who read 1,000 word narratives and completed two vocabulary assessments. It was hypothesized that students learn a number of new words incidentally from reading. It was found that a small but significant gain in vocabulary knowledge comes from context.

Norton, Donna E. "Webbing and Historical Fiction." *Reading Teacher* 46 (Feb. 1993): 432–436.

Describes the use of webbing as a visual display of the relationship between ideas and concepts to help students use higher order thinking, better oral interaction, and new ideas. Presents webs for vocabulary, library and units with examples. This is very useful for unit development.

Oberlin, K.J., and Shugarman, S.L. "Implementing the Reading Workshop with Middle School L.D. Readers." *Journal of Reading* 328 (1989): 682–687.

Describes the use of the Reading Workshop with learning disabled middle school students to provide proficiency and a more positive attitude toward reading.

Ogle, Donna M. "The Know, Want to Know, Learn Strategy." In K. Denise Muth (ed.), *Children's Comprehension of Text: Research into Practice*. Newark, DE: International Reading Association, 1989.

Suggests using KWL as a thematic unit strategy for improving comprehension.

Popp, Marcia. *Learning Journals in the K–8 Classroom*. Mahwah, NJ: Erlbaum, 1997.

A useful guide to implementing learning journals in literature-based programs.

Purcell-Gates, V., McIntyre, E., and Freppon, P.A. "Learning Written Storybook Language in School: A Comparison of Low S.E.S. Children in Skills-Based and Whole Language Classrooms." *American Educational Research Journal* 32.3 (1995): 659–685.

Compares the use of storybook language in two types of programs. Concluding that the whole language literature-based program produced better results.

Raphael, Taffy E. *Literature-Based Instruction: Reshaping the Curriculum*. Norwood, MA: Christopher-Gordon, 1997.

Discusses the use of literature-based reading instruction as an effective tool.

Raphael, Taffy, McMahon, Susan, Goatly, Virginia, Bently, Jessica, Boyd, Fenice, Pardo, Laura, and Woodman, Debora. "Research Directions: Literature and Discussion in the Reading Program." *Language Arts* 69 (January 1992): 54–61.

Describes how intermediate grade book clubs help students respond in literature in their own voice. Both the author's shared interpretation and the students' interpretation were encouraged. Tells how to encourage critical literacy as students share their own interpretations of literature.

Reutzel, D.R., and Cooter, R.B. "Whole Language: Comparative Effects on First Grade Reading Achievement." *Journal of Educational Research* 83.5 (1990): 252–257.

Study of the reading success of first grade students in a whole language program.

Reutzel, D.R., Oda, L.K., and Moore, B.H. "Developing Print Awareness: The Effects of Three Instructional Approaches on Kindergarten Students' Print Awareness, Reading Readiness, and Word Reading." *Journal of Reading Behavior* 21.3 (1989): 197–217.

Describes the effects of three approaches on kindergarten children's readiness to read. Concludes that a literature-based program is best suited to the development of many abilities.

Richek, M.A., and McTague, B.K. "The "Curious George" Strategy for Students with Reading Problems." *Reading Teacher* 42 (1988): 220–226.

The evaluation of a remedial strategy using a series of *Curious George* books to motivate students. Concludes that: the material was motivating; carefully planned activities provided increasing independence for students; group interaction helped involvement and created peer teaching opportunities; the reading and writing activities carefully supported techniques; and many chances to read provided success.

Roberts, Patricia, and Kellough, Richard D. *Guide for Developing Interdisciplinary Thematic Units*. Upper Saddle River, NJ: Pearson-Merrill-Prentice-Hall, 2004.

A practice oriented guide for developing and using thematic units. This is a very practical book with many examples of lessons and activities.

Roe, Betty D., Smith, Sandy H., and Burns, Paul C. *Teaching Reading in Today's Elementary Schools*. Boston: Houghton-Mifflin, 2005, pp. 277–299.

A textbook with a good overview of the literature-based approach with useful references.

Rosenblatt, L.M. *The Reader, the Text, the Poem: The Transactional Theory of the Literary Work*. Carbondale: Southern Illinois University Press, 1978.

States that students at all grade levels need to learn to adopt so that they can shift according to the purpose for reading. Students' whole school career should contain a continuous attempt to learn to use reading across the language arts curriculum. Students should adopt early to the purpose and situation to read aesthetically and for skills. They need to be versatile readers.

Roser, Nancy L., Hoffman, James, Labbo, Linda D.; and Farest, Cindy. "Language Charts: A Record of Story Time Talk." *Language Arts* 69 (January 1992): 44-52.

Small group discussion helps students compare and contrast books using a chart to connect the stories and list student reactions. Provides excellent suggestions.

Routman, Regie. *Transitions: From Literature to Literacy.* Chicago: Regby, 1988.

Describes an integrated language arts curriculum and the literacy experiences at home and in school.

Ruddell, Robert B. "Whole Language and Literature Perspective: Creating a Meaning Making Instructional Environment." *Language Arts* 69.8 (December 1992): 612-620.

States that in order to motivate students, teachers need to be meaning-making facilitators using children's literature to help students use cognitive and affective skills.

Schallert, D.L., and Kleinman, G.M. *Some Reasons Why Teachers Are Easier to Understand Than Textbooks* (Reading Education Report No. 9). Champaign: University of Illinois at Urbana-Champaign, Center for the Study of Reading, 1979.

Discusses teachers as interpreters of information and ideas.

Scharer, Patricia L. "Teachers in Transition: An Exploration of Changes in Teachers and Classrooms During Implementation of Literature-Based Instruction." *Research in the Teaching of English* 26.4 (1992): 408-445.

Presents a window into the evolution of attitude and practice that occurs when a literature-based program is adopted.

Scharer, Patricia L., and Detwiler, Deana B. "Changing as Teachers: Perils and Possibilities of Literature-Based Language Arts Instruction." *Language Arts* 69.3 (March 1992): 186-192.

Describes the joys and problems associated with implementing literature-based instruction in a 6th grade class. This is a case study with very good references about theory and practice. Concludes that the teacher faces many perils, but the possibilities are endless.

Shanahan, Timothy; Robinson, Bonita; and Schneider, Mary. "Integrating Curriculum: Avoiding Some of the Pitfalls of Thematic Units." *Reading Teacher* 48 (May 1995): 718-719.

Discusses possible problems teachers can have when developing thematic units and presents ways to avoid common problems.

Shaw, Evelyn. "A Novel Journal." *Reading Teacher* 41 (January 1988): 489.

A brief description of how 5th graders practiced retelling and summarizing in a narrative journal as they read the whole class novel *Call It Courage*.

Shiflett, Anne Chalfield. "Marketing Literature: Variations on the Book Talk Theme." *Journal of Adolescent & Adult Literacy* 41 (April 1998): 568-570.

Describes different ways to encourage students to select books in the same way other products are marketed.

Spiegel, Dixie Lee. "The Role of Teacher Trust in Response Groups." *Language Arts* 73 (December 1996): 332-339.

Discusses student participation in literature response groups, stating that students need to participate and listen to each other's responses.

Spiegel, Dixie Lee. "Silver Bullets, Babies and Bath Water: Literature Response Groups in a Balanced Literacy Program." *Reading Teacher* 52 (October 1998): 114-124.

Warns that there is no one activity or approach that ensures that all students will learn to read and write. Advises using a research based balanced approach using the contributions of many perspectives and approaches to literacy. Provides practical instructional advice based on sound research. Excellent references.

Stewart, Roger A., Paradis, Edward E., Ross, Bonita D., and Lewis, Mary Jane. "Student Voices: What Works on Literature-Based Developmental Reading." *Journal of Adolescent and Adult Literacy* 39 (March 1996): 468-478.

Describes 7th and 8th grade remedial students' discussions about self image as readers after participating in a literature-based reading program. Test results indicated students were more successful than students in other remedial programs.

Strickland, Dorothy S., Dillon, Rose M., Funkhouser, Leslie, Glick, Mary, and Rogers, Corrine. "Research Currents: Classroom Dialogue During Literature Response Groups." *Language Arts* 66 (February 1989): 192–205.

    Four classroom teachers in Fairfax, Virginia, worked with Strickland to rely more on literature and daily response groups than textbooks. The teachers met to discuss the students' talk and changes in the classrooms. Response groups were observed and students were listened to. A shift in control putting students, not teachers, in charge of the groups was found. Students made discussions about learning and everyone became more empowered.

Swindall, Vickie, and Cantrell, F. Jeffery. "Character Interviews Help Bring Literature to Life." *Reading Teacher* 53 (September 1999): 23–25.

    Describes character interviews as a reader response activity in which students interview book characters. Tells how students learn to conduct interviews as a strategy to motivate and help students engage in reading stories. Presents sample interviews and uses research findings to support the use of the activity.

Tompkins, Gail E., and McGee, Lea M. *Teaching Reading with Literature: Case Studies to Action Plans.* New York: Merrill, 1993.

    Presents practical suggestions for using thematic units with a variety of media. Very useful follow-up activities after reading are provided.

Tunnell, M., and Jacobs, J. "Using "Real" Books: Research Findings on Literature-Based Reading Instruction." *Reading Teacher* 42 (1989): 470–477.

    Describes the use of literature-based instruction with a variety of students referring to several studies using this approach. Concludes that students who are part of a literature-based program not only learn how to read, but develop a desire to read. The whole language program provides meaning and pleasure which makes skills instruction meaningful.

Vygotsky, L.S. *Mind in Society: The Development of Psychological Processes.* Cambridge: MA: Harvard University Press, 1978.

    A discussion of cognitive development different from Piaget's theory. A classic work.

Wertheim, Judy. "Teaching Guides for Novels." *Reading Teacher* 42 (December 1988): 262.

    Explains the importance of providing guides for teaching class novels.

Wollman-Bonilla, Julie F. "Reading Journals: Interactions to Participate in Literature." *Reading Teacher* 43 (November 1989): 112–120.

    Describes three students who used reading journals to help them grow in reading and writing at their own pace. Backs up the practice information with research references. A very useful article.

Worthy, J., and Invernizzi, M.A. "Linking Reading and Meaning: A Case Study of a Hyperlexic Reader." *Journal of Reading Behavior* 27.4 (1995): 585–603.

    Provides a case study of a student with problems in comprehension who was able to use literature to focus on meaning and improve comprehension skills.

Yopp, Hallie Kay, and Yopp, Ruth Helen. *Literature-Based Reading Activities.* Boston: Pearson, Allyn & Bacon, 2006.

    A practical resource for classroom teachers which provides a brief introduction to using literature in the classroom and activities for each part of the approach. A good list of references for each chapter is provided.

Zarillo, James. "Teacher's Interpretations of Literature-Based Reading." *Reading Teacher* 43 (October 1989): 22–28.

    Describes the ways in which teachers interpret literature-based reading. Classrooms in Southern California were observed and descriptions of activities are presented. Uses research to describe the observation of five teachers selected for in-depth case studies for an entire school year.

Readers' Theater

Readers' theater is an oral reading of a story by one or more persons. It is not a performance, but an interpretive reading. Harris and Hodges (1995) state that readers' theater is "a performance of literature, as a story, play, poetry ... read aloud expressively by one or more persons rather than acted." Black and Stave (2007) state that "readers' theatre is a strategy that showcases the power of language. It is an interpretive reading activity in which readers bring characters, story, and even content area or text book material to life through their voices, actions, and words." Trousdale and Harris (1993) report that "allowing for interpretation through multiple modes, readers' theatre is often described as a stylized form of dramatization."

Black and Stave (2007), Tierney and Readence (2000), Norton (1997), and Burns, Roe and Smith (2002) describe readers' theater as an oral reading procedure for two or more readers that integrates the language arts through a focus on the interpretation of literature. Readers' theater stimulates motivation to read and improves oral reading, interpretation, listening, speaking, and comprehension skills.

Black and Stave (2007) state that readers' theater encourages the oral interpretation of literature making it an integrated language event. Students select, adapt, and present a story, poem, part of a play, a song, excerpts from a textbook, a newspaper article, part of an historical document or excerpts from a biography. Students use the material as a script and their performance is a reading of the script. Black and Stave (2007) emphasize that the performers use expressive reading, posture, a few selected actions, and carefully chosen elements of production to suggest and enhance the meaning of the material read. The audience becomes part of the production because they visualize meaning from what is being read. It is a combination of the material, the performer, and the audience that makes the material come alive. Herrell and Jordan (2002) state that readers' theater provides an opportunity to interpret material in a non-threatening prepared setting where students become part of the process of rehearsal and repeated readings.

The teacher should be, Black and Stave (2007) suggest, the director and in the early stages serve as the producer and script writer. As students become more familiar with the technique they become more independent and assume the roles of director and script writer. The teacher's involvement depends on the needs and abilities of the group.

According to Tierney and Readence (2000), Norton (1997), and Black and Stave (2007) the performance usually takes place in a classroom although a variety of settings including museums, libraries, art galleries, theaters, and community centers can be used. Black and Stave (2007) suggest that the use of technology such as audio and video broadcasts, websites and the publication of scripts can move the performance outside of the classroom.

Tierney and Readence (2000) and Black and Stave (2007) state that the intended audience for readers' theater is one's fellow students, but it also may include parents and school personnel. Students may move between the roles of performers and audience. Students read aloud with purpose to an audience. Students are reading from material that is familiar because they have read it several times in rehearsal. Students, Trousdale and Harris (1993) state, interpret what is read by experiencing the characters, setting, mood, and action of the story. Coger and White (1982) state that the reading becomes theater because the reading comes alive through the voices of the readers. The audience is involved and both groups share in what is going on. The readers bring a dramatic performance and the audience brings its imagination. Norton (1997) states that both performers and the audience benefit from readers' theater because the performers are motivated to read, think, express themselves orally, and enjoy the stories they present. Team work is encouraged as performers work together to adapt the story using writing skills. Performers develop pride in their work and performance. The audience improves their listening skills and is motivated to read the original story. The performers and the audience are presented with language models.

Material can be chosen from many sources. Sloyer (1982) presents the following criteria for selecting material to dramatize: a well constructed tight plot with suspense and a clear ending; interesting characters presented in a series of events involving a problem; lively dialogue; enough dialogue or material that can become dialogue; brief narrative lines that introduce characters or setting and enhance the plot; repetitive words that encourage audience participation.

Sloyer (1982) outlines steps which will help teachers and students present readers' theater. After material has been chosen discuss a movie or theater with open ended questions that aim to find out how a book is adopted to become a movie. Next students need to see an example of a script and the original book. Time is needed to read both and compare to find out what changes were made to create the script. Students use the sample script as a model for adopting their selection. Much reading, rereading, and discussion needs to occur so that story elements, plot, setting, characters, and theme can be identified to be highlighted for dramatization. Using the chalk-board or poster-board students adapt the story by identifying character roles; the events and how they need to be included; dialogue and narration. Write the dialogue in bold letters in the margin of the poster and assign characters. Encourage students to tell how to use language to make the dialogue more interesting. Reproduce the script. Students need to prepare for the dramatization by learning stage craft elements such as position and actions of performers in the performance space, use of props and body movements. Warm up exercises help performers get ready by experimenting with gestures and dialogue. Rehearse the performers until they are comfortable. After the performance the audience and the cast should discuss characters, staging, and production aspects to provide feedback to performers and highlight possible revisions for the next presentation of the script. Groups within the class can become reviewers, performers, or directors or develop different scripts for other stories. Everyone should become involved.

Tanner (1979) suggests that students analyze selections before presentation looking at:

What do the unfamiliar words mean?
Who is speaking?
Who is listening?
Where and when is the action taking place?
What actions occur?
When does the climax take place?
What is the mood of the story?
What is the theme?
How does the story keep the performers and audience in touch with present day life?

Tanner (1979) emphasizes that there is no one right way to dramatize a story and students need to experiment with different ways to present literature. Teachers need to use basic guidelines, but also let the literature shape the method of performance. Students need help learning to breathe life into the material by stimulating the audience emotionally and intellectually. When students understand the material and become excited about it they make it come alive for themselves and those who listen to the presentation.

Henning (1974) advises three steps to a performance: (1) read the material silently; (2) do a second reading orally allowing students to select parts. This helps development of compromise skills when students accept parts that may not be their first choice. Students become better listeners during the oral reading; (3) the third reading is an oral reading with actions and suggestions for improving problem areas; the performance has an introduction, title and cast of characters presented along with a short musical introduction and simple scenery. Often students are motivated to write original scripts or adapt a favorite story after a performance. Some students developed a radio-type play from favorite literary selections. Research studies comparing readers' theater, storytelling techniques, and silent reading were done.

Mayberry (1975) compared the ways in which readers' theater and solo performance with silent reading affect comprehension. It was concluded that readers' theater and solo performance were more effective than silent reading. Readers' theater was found to be the most effective strategy.

Page (1983) compared the effects of story dramatization and storytelling on the reading of primary grade students. It was concluded that 1st graders understand more after drama. Drama is better for understanding main idea, character motivation, and identification. Storytelling is better for learning inferences. Dramatization helps students empathize with characters, bring their personal experiences to the story, and take "a moment in time and living it at life rate...." Storytelling helps students internalize a story schema, better reflect and evaluate the theme of a story, and become more familiar with literary forms.

Bacon (1972), Coger and White (1973), Moffett and Wagner (1983), Post (1974), and Weingarden (1980) advocate the value of readers' theater as a method of teaching comprehension skills.

Young and Vardell (1993) state that readers' theater offers opportunities to investigate content area material through nonfiction material. The technique is participatory, child centered, and goal directed. Tierney and Readence (2000) state that teachers should not adopt goals that are beyond student abilities to fulfill. Readers' theater formalizes procedures that occur spontaneously. Tierney and Readence (2000) state that the "formality of the procedure extends the use of dramatization of a story to the development of more precise reading, writing, and oral interpretation abilities. At the same time the formality of the procedure may detract from the frequency with which teachers encourage students to project themselves, dramatize story segments, and explore different voices as they read different stories on a more frequent and incidental basis."

Annotated Bibliography

Bacon, W. *The Art of Interpretation*. New York: Holt, Rinehart & Winston, 1972.
    Discusses readers' theater as a valuable technique for interpreting literature.
Black, Alison, and Stave, Anna M. *A Comprehensive Guide to Readers' Theatre: Enhancing Fluency and Comprehension in Middle School and Beyond*. Newark, DE: International Reading Association, 2007.
    Discusses how to use readers' theater to meet literacy standards; how to start using

the technique; how to explore genres; how to use supplementary activities; cross curricular connections; and how to use the technique at various grade levels.

Burns, Paul C., Roe, Betty D., and Smith, Sandy H. *Teaching Reading in Today's Elementary Schools.* Boston: Houghton-Mifflin, 2002.
   This is a brief discussion of readers' theater. A good starting point.

Busching, B.A. "Readers' Theatre: An Education for Language and Life." *Language Arts* 58 (1981): 330–338.
   Describes the reasons for using readers' theater and makes suggestions for using the technique in the elementary school.

Coger, L.T., and White, M.R. *Readers' Theatre: A Dramatic Approach to Literature.* Glenview, IL: Scott Foresman, 1982.
   Presents the history and theoretical principles of readers' theater. Provides scripts and summaries of productions. This is a most valuable resource.

Donmoyer, J., and Donmeyer, R. "Readers' Theatre: 'Give Some for Instances.'" *Literacy Matters* 3 (1991): 4–9.
   Describes how to begin using readers' theater. The entire issue of this journal has articles about readers' theater.

Harris, Theodore L., and Hodges, Richard E. *The Literacy Dictionary: The Vocabulary of Reading and Writing.* Newark, DE: International Reading Association, 1995.
   Provides a definition of reader's theater.

Henning, Kathleen, "Drama Reading, an On-Going Classroom Activity at the Elementary School Level." *Elementary English,* 51 (January 1974): 48–51.
   Describes readers' theater telling how to begin and use the technique.

Herrell, A., and Jordan, M. *Fifty Active Learning Strategies for Improving Reading Comprehension.* Englewood Cliffs, NJ: Prentice Hall, 2002.
   Among the fifty strategies there are several specific to using Readers' Theater to provide success for all students.

Hoyt, L. "Many Ways of Knowing: Using Drama, Oral Interpretation, and the Visual Arts to Enhance Reading Comprehension." *Reading Teacher* 54 (1992): 580–584.
   Describes readers' theater as an effective way to improve skill in reading comprehension.

Maclay, J.H. *Reader's Theatre: Toward a Grammar of Practice.* New York: Random House, 1971.
   Describes the benefits of readers' theater and suggests ways to select material, how to cast, direct, and stage presentation. This is an early and very useful resource.

Mayberry, D.R. *A Comparison of Three Techniques of Teaching Literature: Silent Reading, Solo Performance, and Reader's Theatre.* Ph.D. dissertation, North Texas State University, 1975.
   Reports research on a comparison of techniques for teaching literature.

Millin, S.K., and Rinehart, S.D. "Some of the Benefits of Readers' Theatre Production for Second Grade Title I Students." *Reading Research and Instruction* 39 (1999): 71–88.
   Reports research done with second grade students who had remedial problems and how readers' theater helped them better understand what they read.

Moffett, J., and Wagner, B.J. *Student-Centered Language Arts and Reading K-13: A Handbook for Teachers.* Boston: Houghton-Mifflin, 1983.
   Describes readers' theater and its benefits for a variety of grade levels. This is a useful resource.

Norton, Donna E. *The Effective Teaching of Language Arts.* Upper Saddle River, NJ: Prentice Hall, 1997, pp. 227–235.
   Presents a good overview of reader's theater.

O'Neill, C. "Dialogue and Drama: The Transformation of Events, Ideas, and Teachers." *Language Arts* 66 (1989): 528–540.
   Describes how dramatization effects the teaching of literature for the better.

Page, A. *Children's Story Comprehension as a Result of Storytelling and Story Dramatization: A Study of the Child as Spectator and as Participant.* Ph.D. dissertation, University of Massachusetts, 1983.

Research comparing growth in comprehension skills as a result of drama and storytelling.
Post, R.M. "Readers' Theatre as a Method of Teaching Literature." *English Journal* 64 (1974): 69–72.
   Describes how to adopt readers' theater for use in high school English classes.
Purnes, A.C., Papa, L., and Jordan, S., eds. *Encyclopedia of English Studies and Language Arts*. New York: National Council of Teachers of English, 1994.
   A variety of interesting discussions about readers' theater and related topics.
Shepard, A. "From Script to Stage: Tips for Reader's Theatre." *Reading Teacher* 48 (1994): 184–188.
   This is a detailed discussion of reader's theater. A very useful resource for implementation of the technique.
Sloyer, Shirlee. *Reader's Theatre: Story Dramatization in the Classroom*. Urbana, IL: National Council of Teachers of English, 1982.
   An excellent resource for locating script material. Presents an in-depth discussion with suggestions for planning and presenting material.
Tanner, Fran Averett. *Creative Communication, Projects in Acting, Speaking and Oral Reading*. Pocatello, ID: Clark, 1979.
   Presents a discussion of how to present readers' theater with practical suggestions.
Tierney, Robert J., and Readence, John E. *Reading Strategies and Practices: A Compendium*. Boston: Allyn and Bacon, 2000, pp. 250–255.
   This is a good discussion of readers' theater with a useful bibliography.
Trousdale, A.M., and Harris, V.J. "Missing Links in Literary Response: Group Interpretation of Literature." *Children's Literature in Education* 24 (1993): 195–207.
   Describes readers' theater as an important technique in response to literature.
Tyler, B., and Charad, D.J. "Using Readers' Theatre to Foster Fluency in Struggling Readers: A Twist on the Repeated Reading Strategy." *Reading and Writing Quarterly: Overcoming Learning Difficulties* 16 (2000): 163–168.
   Reports the use of readers' theater as a technique to enhance fluency for students with reading problems.
Weingarden, A.D. "The Value of Reader's Theater: Claims, Programs, and Research." *Research in Education*, ERIC Document Reproduction Service No. ED 182 793, 1980.
   Presents research on the benefits of reader's theater.
Wertheimer, A. "Story Dramatization in the Reading Center." *English Journal* 64 (1974): 85–87.
   Tells how to use readers' theater with reluctant readers.
Wolf, S.A. "What's in a Name? Labels and Literacy in Reader's Theatre." *Reading Teacher* 46 (1993): 540–545.
   Presents a discussion of a one year study of remedial students participating in reader's theater.
Young, Terrell A., and Vardell, Sylvia. "Weaving Readers' Theatre and Nonfiction into the Curriculum." *Reading Teacher* 46 (February 1993): 396–406.
   Presents suggestions for using readers' theater with nonfiction to make students more active nonfiction readers and to make nonfiction more fun for students and teachers.

The Four Blocks Framework

The Four Blocks Framework is a method of structuring instruction to meet the needs of all students. It divides instruction into four parts or blocks in the early grades which avoids ability grouping. Students work in guided reading, self-selected reading, working with words, and writing within a theme to connect all aspects of language.

According to Tierney and Readence (2000) the Four Blocks Framework was designed to "meet the needs of students reading at multiple reading levels...." The Framework is intended to be used for beginning reading instruction and incorporates several major instructional approaches to teach reading daily. Cunningham, Hall, and Sigmon (1999) state that "all children do not learn in the same way...." Teachers also know that children have different literacy levels and multilevel instruction is necessary. Some children are quick and need to be challenged and some children have difficulties and need extra support. Cunningham, Hall, and Defee (1991) state that children begin the first grade with different experience backgrounds and different literacy backgrounds. Teachers need to meet the diverse needs and abilities presented by a heterogeneous first grade class without resorting to ability groups.

Hiebert (1983) and Shannon (1988) report that one of the most widely used practices found in first grade classrooms was ability grouping. During the second month of the first grade students were usually placed in three groups for reading instruction based on ability. Hiebert (1983) and Shannon (1988) state that students usually remained in the same level group for all of their first grade experience and frequently for the rest of elementary school. Students placed in the bottom group, Allington (1983) reports, did not develop adequate reading skills and often received instruction that was less effective than that provided for the other groups. Teachers, according to Cunningham, Hall, and Defee (1991), knew that ability grouping created problems and that students who made progress should be moved into another group, but the range in ability between the bottom group and the next level group was often found to be very wide. Students who were moved would have problems.

Cunningham, Hall, and Defee (1991) attempted to create a model for first grade instruction that would provide for individual differences without ability groups and utilize a variety of instructional approaches. They identified four major approaches to beginning reading because there is no single best approach that fits all students—there is no "one size fits all" for reading instruction because all students do not learn in the same way at the same rate. During the 20th century four major approaches to beginning reading have been identified: (1) basal approach, emphasizing gradually increasing levels of difficulty and teacher-guided reading of material; (2) phonics approach, teaching letter-sound relationships; (3) literature approach in which students choose to read what they want from a variety of books with teacher assistance when needed; and (4) writing approach in which students read their own and classmates' writing as their first reading material.

Cunningham, Hall, and Defee (1991) state that an evaluation of the four approaches revealed important strengths for each. Basal readers provide multiple copies of books with gradually increasing levels of difficulty. The teacher uses the readers to carefully direct comprehension and strategy instruction to facilitate growth and achievement. Phonics instruction, Adams (1990) states, is an important part of beginning reading because the students' first accomplishment must be to figure out how our alphabetic language works. In order to understand what reading is and why it is a necessity for everyone, students should read real books. The ultimate aim of reading instruction is reading real books. Clark (1988) states that writing helps students become fluent readers. Writing is another real activity.

Adams (1990) and Bond and Dykstra (1967 and 1997) conclude that students who are beginning readers achieve better when taught by a combination of approaches to reading, not just by one approach. Cunningham, Hall, and Defee (1991) decided that they would divide their instructional approach into blocks that used the four major approaches to reading. The Four Blocks Framework became: (1) Guided Reading; (2) Self-Selected Reading; (3) Working with Words; and (4) Writing. Tierney and Readence (2000) state that teachers integrate the four blocks to connect them for students by using a thematic approach. Students read, write, and learn words connected to a thematic unit such as Baby Animals; Native Americans; Fall; or City Life.

Cunningham and Hall (1996) state that in order to provide students with many opportunities to become literate, the Four Blocks Framework divides instructional time evenly. The 2¼ to 2½ hours of Language Arts instruction is divided into 30 to 40 minute sections for each of the Four Blocks.

Cunningham, Hall, and Defee (1998), Tierney and Readence (2000), and Cunningham, Hall, and Sigmon (1999) provide detailed descriptions of each of the Four Blocks. *Guided Reading*, originally called the basal block, was expanded to include adapted basal readers, previously used basal readers, trade books in multiple copy sets, and big books. These materials can also be used in a variety of combinations. Cunningham, Hall, and Defee (1998) and Cunningham, Hall, and Sigmon (1999) state that the purposes of this block are "to expose children to a wide range of literature, teach comprehension strategies, and teach children how to read in materials that become increasingly more difficult." Students develop skill in oral reading, vocabulary meaning, and background knowledge. Practice in reading instructional level material is given and students who are having difficulties are assisted in maintaining their level of self-confidence and motivation for reading. In the first stages Guided Reading time is spent in the shared reading of predictable books (books that use repetition, rhythmic language patterns, and familiar concepts), read as a whole class. As the year progresses other books are used and the emphasis moves from reading as a class to reading with a partner or alone. The early stage choral reading (the whole group reading aloud together) and role playing of characters is used. Students read little books that are the same as the big book done as a whole group. The little books are read in small groups or with partners. Later in the year Cunningham, Hall, and Defee (1998) and Cunningham, Hall, and Sigmon (1999) state that there is a change in emphasis from whole class reading to independent reading and reading to a partner. Shared Reading continues, but instead of reading the whole big book to the class the teacher goes through the book leading the students to name what they see in the pictures, making predictions, and identifying a few important and possibly difficult vocabulary words. This procedure is called a "picture walk" and helps set the stage for independent, small flexible group or partner reading of the book. After the students read the book everyone reconvenes as a whole class and chorally reads the book as a whole group. Comprehension strategies are taught and practice is provided. The group checks the predictions they made before reading and story maps are completed. Students reread the same book either with partners or in a small group with the teacher. This rereading can also become an acting out of the story in play form or in a storytelling format. Many activities can be done following the reading. Some teachers have called this format "rug-seat-rug" because students meet together as a whole group, then separate, and then reconvene as a whole to discuss and share.

Cunningham, Hall, and Defee (1998) state that Guided Reading time is not spent on grade-level material all week. Two reading selections are used to meet the needs of all the students. One book will be on grade level and the second book will be on an easier level. Since each book or story is read more than once for different purposes, each student is part of the activity no matter on what level he/she is functioning. All the students become fluent by the time the last reading takes place. Readers who have problems are given help in many ways such as in a teacher led small group activity or with a partner. The small groups change every day and include students functioning at various levels, not just those having problems.

Self-Selected Reading, which Veatch (1959) called individualized reading and Routman (1995) calls Readers' Workshop, allows students to choose what they want to read and can read. Cunningham, Hall, and Defee (1998), Cunningham, Hall, and Sigmon (1999), Tierney and Readence (2000), and Roe, Smith, and Burns (2005) state that students read books on their independent level and select parts of the book to which they want to respond in a variety of ways. This block provides for students reading on many levels because books are arranged according to genre, themes being studied, and easy and difficult reading levels. Old favorites and new books are included in the available choices. Children can read independently or with a partner. During this block the teacher holds conferences and develops anecdotal records of the reading progress of several children every day. The "Reader's Chair" encourages one or two students to share their books with the whole group at the end of the block every day. Books are, Cunningham, Hall, and Defee (1998) suggest, kept in dishpans or buckets according to subject, level of difficulty, and genre. Students who have difficulties can read easier books with a partner or to students in lower grades. In the beginning of the first grade students are told that there are several ways to read a book: (1) *pretend* to read by telling a familiar story; (2) *picture read* from a book and talk about what is in the pictures; and (3) *read the words* of a book. Cunningham, Hall, and Defee (1998) state that students will be motivated to select a book during this block once they know there are three ways to read a book with success.

Writing follows the Writers' Workshop model suggested by Graves (1995), Routman (1995), and Calkins (1994). The block starts with a ten minute mini lesson in which the teacher models one aspect of the writing process. The teacher demonstrates how the word wall is used for spelling difficult words and makes deliberate mistakes. The next day students help the teacher edit the writing.

Each student works independently on a piece of writing. This block encourages students at different achievement levels to succeed. Cunningham, Hall, and Defee (1998), Cunningham, Hall, and Sigmon (1999), and Tierney and Readence (2000) state that teachers encourage students to select a topic and accept the level of the first draft. This allows students to work at their own pace, use as many days as they need to complete the writing, and to find success. Students who have choices select what interests them and what they know about. In this way students can truly function at their own level and everyone's needs are met. A student's ability or problems are not obvious to others when everyone is working independently on different topics. Everyone is not expected to complete a piece of writing every day. Work is ongoing. According to Calkins (1994), Graves (1995) and Routman (1995) Writer's Workshop provides opportunities that encourage the multilevel of the Writing Process. One opportunity is mini-lessons in which the teacher models the writing-thinking process aloud demonstrating various parts of the writing process, one at a time. The teacher models planning, writing, revising, and editing while writing about different topics in different ways. When, Cunningham, Hall, and Defee (1998) and Cunningham, Hall, and Sigmon (1999) suggest, the teacher writes a long piece requiring more than one mini-lesson, rereading what was written the day before should be modeled to establish the continuity of the writing.

Mini-lessons, according to Cunningham, Hall, and Defee (1998) and Cunningham, Hall, and Sigmon (1999), make the writing process multilevel because the students will work on different aspects of the writing process, and the modeling of different topics, forms, and parts of the process helps to differentiate the process. A second opportunity for meeting the needs of students at many levels is the Publishing Conference. Teachers act as "editor-in-chief" and hold a final conference after students have engaged in peer revising and editing. The final conference, Cunningham, Hall, and Defee (1998) state, is an excellent opportunity to individualize instruction because the one-to-one conference presents "teachable moments." Student writing provides clues to needs for further instruction, progress that has been made, and ways to assist students to move to the next developmental level.

Cunningham, Hall, and Defee (1998) and Cunningham, Hall, and Sigmon (1999) state that writing is a very important part of learning to read. For some students who are having problems reading, writing provides the opportunity to use their own experiences expressed in their own language. These struggling readers can (even if no one else is able) read their piece of writing to share and are able to read all of their own written work. "When children are writing, some children are really working on becoming better writers; others are engaging in the same activity, but for them, writing helps them figure out reading," according to Cunningham, Hall, and Defee (1998).

Working with Words is the fourth block. In this block students learn to read and spell high-frequency or the most commonly used words. Students learn the patterns that help them decode and spell many words. The first ten minutes of the block are spent reviewing words displayed on the word wall. This is a display of most used words printed on colored paper with thick black marker arranged in alphabetical order by the first letter of the word. Five words a week are added until there are 110 to 120 words displayed. Students practice reading new and old words by looking at them, saying them, clapping the letters, writing the words, and self correcting the words with the teacher. The next 15 to 25 minutes are spent working on three activities to help students learn to decode and spell better.

The next activity is "Rounding Up Rhymes." The teacher reads a book to the whole class and then encourages them to locate words that rhyme. These words are written on index cards for the pocket chart. The spelling pattern of the words is underlined and then the students write other words with the same pattern so that they all rhyme. Cunningham, Hall, and Defee (1998) state that students read and spell words "based on their new understanding of rhymes and spelling patterns."

The next activity is called "making words." Cunningham and Cunningham (1992) and Cunningham and Hall (1996) state that this is a hands-on activity in which students look for patterns in words and learn that changing one letter or letter order can change the whole word. Students use six to eight paper letters that will form the final word. Tierney and Readence (2000) state that students make words and sort and read them according to several patterns such as: rhyming words, beginning sounds, or ending sounds. Students use the same procedure used in rounding up rhymes for rhyming words finding "main slain, an, man" and transfer words to make "stain, span." Cunningham and Cunningham (1992) and Cunningham and Hall (1996) state that word making addresses the needs of students on all levels because the activity starts with making short words and moves to longer, more challenging words until the final challenge when all the letters must be used to make the secret word. All students can make words and learn to read and spell words at their ability level. Students learn to use visual patterns of known words to read and spell new words.

"Guess the covered word" helps students, Cunningham, Hall, and Defee (1998) state, practice cross-checking meaning with letter sound information. Four or five sentences are written on the chalkboard, each with a word covered by two sticky notes. In this whole class activity students read the sentences and offer several guesses for the covered word. There are many possible correct answers for a word to fit each context and the teacher reminds students of these possibilities. After these first guesses are made, the teacher uncovers the word up to the vowel. Guesses that did not include the letters uncovered are erased and new guesses based on meaning and starting with the revealed beginning letters are encouraged. When the new guesses are recorded the entire word is uncovered and discussed. Teachers cut the sticky notes to fit the size of the word to encourage students to become aware of word length as a clue. This activity is a good review of beginning letter sounds for those students who still need more practice in this skill. More advanced students combine the clues of length, beginning letters, and meaning to identify the word.

These four games provide practice and reinforcement for those who need help with phonemic awareness, spelling patterns, letter substitution, making new words from known words, decoding new words, and using the word wall to help decode new words.

Connecting the Four Blocks using thematic units, Cunningham, Hall, and Defee (1998) state, encourages the use of theme related books for guided reading, theme related topics for writing lessons, theme related books for self-selected reading, and the use of a Theme Board. The Theme Board is used in addition to the Word Wall and contains words that change with each theme. Theme words are necessary for student use during the unit. The word games "rounding up rhymes," "making words," and "guess the covered word" also include theme related words.

Tierney and Readence (2000) comment on the data Cunningham, Hall, and Defee (1998) provide to support their discussion of the success of the Four Blocks Framework, stating that data is based on longitudinal studies to show the success of the Framework. Tierney and Readence (2000) speculate that "perhaps the success of Four Blocks can be attributed to the fact that each teacher who tries it will find at least some part of it to be familiar; since it is not a totally novel approach, it allows teachers an anchor as they implement the Framework." The data was collected at suburban and rural schools with diverse populations. Tierney and Readence (2000) state that Cunningham, Hall, and Defee (1998) insist that teachers use the Framework by giving each of the Blocks the allotted time of 30 to 40 minutes daily, but "beyond that, they believe teachers should have wide latitude in doing instruction in ways they and the students find most effective and satisfying."

Tierney and Readence (2000) state that Cunningham, Hall, and Defee (1998) do not provide a discussion of the problems they have encountered and fail to tell how student achievement correlated with "becoming more strategic and self-motivated literacy learners.... Left undeveloped ... are problems of classroom management that necessarily come with the implementation of a multifaceted approach...." Tierney and Readence (2000) also state that Cunningham, Hall, and Defee (1998) "spend little time discussing issues tied to carefully selecting appropriate material that best meets the students' advancing reading development needs."

Duffy-Hester (1999) presents a review of six reading programs and describes instructional principles derived from these programs to help teachers. One of the programs discussed is the Four Blocks Approach. The programs described were selected because: they address the needs of students who have difficulty or are struggling to learn to read; they were used in public schools with diverse populations; they were based on research on reading and classroom practice; and a detailed description of the progress made by students who were struggling to learn was provided using qualitative and/or quantitative measures of the success of these students. After describing each program Duffy-Hester (1999) lists ten guiding principles for designing or implementing programs that help struggling readers succeed. Within the discussion of the ten principles examples from each program reviewed are presented. Duffy-Hester (1999) states that the Four Blocks Approach is unique because: (1) it combines "several ways of teaching reading into one program.

Realizing that children learn to read in different ways, teachers using this program attempt to teach all children to read by combining several methods of teaching reading into a cohesive yet diverse framework for reading instruction"; and (2) the program "strives to provide instruction that is multileveled, specifically within each of the instructional blocks, activities are included for readers on varying levels of proficiency. Perhaps one of the greatest strengths of this program is that it provides a concrete instructional model for elementary school teachers to use when implementing their reading instructional programs." Cunningham and Hall (1996) stated that the program provides a way to put into practice a balanced reading program and "more nearly" meet the needs of children with a wide range of abilities "who do not all learn in the same way."

Duffy-Hester (1999) lists the ten guiding principles and provides information on the Four Blocks Approach as follows:

1. A reading program should be balanced, drawing on multiple theoretical perspectives—The Four Blocks Approach is according to Cunningham, Hall, and Defee (1998) and Tierney and Readence (2000) a balanced reading program. Stahl (1997) states that a balanced or eclectic program should not suggest that it lacks a solid theoretical foundation. Good teachers have always used "principled eclecticism." Duffy (1997) states that this philosophy is described as using many techniques and "draw thoughtfully from various sources, play many roles, and use many techniques and materials ... to support the reading and overall literacy growth of all the children we teach, particularly children who struggle with reading." Cunningham, Hall, and Defee (1991; 1998) state that there is no one best way to teach reading to all children because children are individuals and do not learn in the same way. Approaches with specific emphasis will help some students and not others.

2. There should be a practical and theoretical justification for every component and element in the reading program—Cunningham and Hall (1996), Cunningham, Hall, and Defee (1998) state that a program is not balanced unless every part of "it has a unique justification that is supported by teacher experience and research." Duffy-Hester (1999) states that the Four Blocks Approach manages instructional time very efficiently because instruction is arranged in four blocks. The program engages all students in activities that have "theoretical and instructional merit" the needs of more students are better supported.

3. The explicit teaching of word identification, comprehension, and vocabulary strategies may take place in conjunction with authentic

reading and writing tasks—"The Four Blocks Approach utilizes this principle often, particularly in the working with words block ... the teacher choosing a 'big word' from a text the students will read, proceeds to students making words from this 'big word' and sorting those words, continues with the students reading from the text from which the 'big word' came, and ends with the students using the word patterns employed in the making words lesson in their future reading and writing...." When skills and strategies are taught explicitly and in conjunction with authentic reading and writing, struggling readers learn more successfully and use the skills in their own reading and writing.

4. On a daily basis, teachers should read aloud to students from a variety of genres and create opportunities for students to read instructional and independent level texts—The Four Blocks Approach contains the Guided Reading and Self-selected Reading blocks and provides the opportunity to read many kinds of texts in many ways daily.

5. Reading instruction should be informed by and based on meaningful reading assessment—The Four Blocks Approach uses portfolios, informal reading inventories, and anecdotal records to inform instruction. Instruction, Duffy-Hester (1999) states, is based on meaningful assessment to meet the needs of students. The Four Blocks Approach bases instruction on student needs and provides materials and activities on a variety of levels with many opportunities to read and write with direct teacher help.

6. Teachers should be decision makers, using their practical, personal, and theoretical knowledge to inform their reading instruction— "Teachers adapted the established reading program to meet their own needs and preferences as well as the reading needs of their students," Duffy-Hester (1999) states. Cunningham, Hall, and Defee (1991; 1998) found that "the teacher was more important than the method...." Teaching style and instructional time were also important parts of the program. Teachers reflect on what they are doing and materials they are using within the program and make decisions about students' instructional needs.

7. Staff development for pre-service and practicing teachers of reading may include providing opportunities for teachers to reflect on their practice—Teachers need to try the blocks and modify their procedures to meet the needs of students and their own teaching. The Four Blocks Approach appears to provide for this important link between research and practice.

8. Reading programs maybe based on multiple goals for student success—The Four Blocks Approach sets and achieves with degrees of success different goals for students on various levels of achievement. Students become engaged, motivated and gain skill because the approach provides for individual differences.
9. Reading programs may provide multiple contexts for student learning—Hiebert and Fisher (1991) state that what students do and what occurs between teacher and students and among students are structures that go beyond the approaches and focus on the opportunity for students to talk about and work on literacy tasks. Students in the Four Blocks Approach participate in diverse tasks and talk. Hiebert and Fisher (1991) state that in reading and writing workshops students engage in different reading tasks and have many chances to talk about the tasks. This is more important than arguing about the one best approach to teaching.
10. Reading program should be designed to support reading growth for all children both the struggling and non-struggling—The Four Blocks Approach helps students on all levels find success according to Duffy-Hester (1999). Spear-Swerling and Sternberg (1996) state that teachers must use programs that are diverse and flexible enough to support the success of all students. Duffy-Hester (1999) states that "reading instructional programs for struggling readers may be based on the same principles as programs for non-struggling readers. It is within these programs and principles that instruction must be individualized to meet the specific reading needs of each child."

McGill-Franzen and Allington (1991) state that for teachers to provide for the needs of all students they must have the "will and the skill" to help all students succeed. Duffy-Hester (1999) concludes that "the teacher is more important and has a greater impact than any single ... program, method or approach...." The belief that all students can succeed and that the teacher rather than the approach is the key to that success can be found in the philosophical foundation of the Four Blocks Framework. Cunningham, Hall, and Defee (1991 and 1998) state that their aim was to "figure out how to provide reading instruction to children with a wide range of entering levels without putting them in fixed ability groups" and provide "multilevel, multi-method instruction that did not use ability grouping, but did meet the diverse needs of a heterogeneous class.... All children do not learn in the same way...." Using the *First Grade Studies* to search for "the best way to teach," Cunningham, Hall, and Defee (1991 and 1998) found that Bond and Dykstra (1967 and 1997) were correct in their conclusions that "the teacher was more important than the method, but that in general, combination approaches work better than any single approach."

The Four Blocks Framework fits the conclusions reached by Duffy-Hester (1999) and Erikson (1991) who stated that "in human literacy learning and teaching there are many differing ladders, many ways to climb, many kinds of power in climbing, and an amazing capacity in human learners of all ages to climb on more than one ladder at once. How to organize schools genuinely for diversity in literacy, treating its multi-dimensionality as a resource rather than a liability and providing various ways to climb high, is a challenge we continue to face...."

Cunningham, Hall, and Defee (1998) reported that they learned a great deal about teachers and students after eight years of research. The Four Blocks Framework was implemented in "hundreds of classrooms in diverse settings with varied populations of children...." The conclusions from these studies are:

1. Teachers who were reluctant to try anything new "will change when the innovation has lots of familiar elements, is doable within the timeframe and materials they currently have, and results in observably better readers and writers";
2. Teachers are individuals and like some blocks better than others, but teach each block every day because "they see children for whom each block is critical and are convinced that if they left any block out, some children would not learn to read well";
3. Teachers can use their own individual teaching style within each block because "there is wide latitude for teachers to carry out the instruction in ways they and the children find most satisfying and effective..." while giving each block its allotted time every day and make each block as multilevel as possible;
4. "Some children seem equally engaged and successful in each block, but others have clearly observable preferences...." Observation reveals that one block may match a certain student's learning personality better than another;
5. Many grouping formats are used for instruction within the blocks and students do not feel that they belong to the top, middle or bottom reading group. "First graders who come with little print experience, but much eagerness to learn maintain that eagerness ... (they) become grade-level or better readers and writers ... when inexperienced but fast learners have multiple opportunities to read and write and don't become discouraged by low-group placement, they make up for lost time....";

6. The most surprising finding from the research was that students who entered the first grade already able to read benefited from the Four Blocks Approach because ability grouping only allowed these readers to read in the second grade books at the end of the first grade, but in the Four Blocks "children spend half their time in the self-selected and writing blocks in which there is no limit to the level at which they can read and write. When there is no limit on how fast they can learn, our best readers will astonish us."

The final conclusion after research, Cunningham, Hall, and Defee (1998) state, is that ability grouping is "limiting for those in the top half of the top group as it is for those in the bottom half of the bottom group."

The Four Blocks Framework appears to be similar to the idea of the one room schoolhouse and the Montessori Method as discussed by Dorothy Canfield Fisher in *Understood Betsy*. Students in both of these methods were allowed to function in a multilevel way within each curriculum area so that one student could work with the 4th grade in reading, with the 3rd grade in spelling, and with the 5th grade in writing. No one was concerned or felt labeled, but accepted the individual differences between and within students. The Four Block Framework is based on research and the 38 years of teaching experience of Cunningham, Hall, and Defee. The researchers started in first grade classes and expanded to other grade levels, schools and locations to find that the original assumptions about how to provide multilevel, multimethod instruction was correct.

Annotated Bibliography

Adams, Marilyn Jager. *Beginning to Read. Thinking and Learning About Print.* Cambridge, MA: M.I.T. Press, 1990.
    Provides a discussion of word identification, phonics instruction, research, and issues about beginning reading instruction and how children learn to read.
Allington, Richard L. "Children Who Find Learning to Read Difficult: School Responses to Diversity." In *Literacy for a Diverse Society: Perspectives, Practices, and Social Policies.* E. H. Hiebert, ed. New York: Teachers College Press, 1991, pp. 237-252.
    Discusses the problems struggling students have and how schools attempt to remediate the problems.
Allington, Richard L. "The Reading Instruction Provided Readers of Differing Reading Abilities." *Elementary School Journal* 83 (1983): 549-559.
    Reports on a study of students having problems learning to read. Concludes that students who do not read well are not given the necessary opportunities to become fluent readers.
Allington, Richard L., and Walmsley, Sean A., eds. *No Quick Fix Rethinking Literacy Programs in America's Elementary Schools.* New York: Teachers College Press, 1995.
    Contributors discuss effective programs, assessment, traditional approaches to reading which are not effective and ways to improve literacy instruction to meet the needs of all students. Allington's introduction discusses the history of literacy instruc-

tion. Walmsley and Allington present an "Afterword" "asking where do we go from here?" There are 12 chapters by experts in the field.

Bond, Guy L., and Dykstra, Robert. "The Cooperative Research Program in First Grade Reading Instruction." *Reading Research Quarterly* 2 (1967): 5–142; 32 (1997): 345–427.

Reports of research comparing various approaches to first grade reading instruction. A classic, valuable work which concludes that a combination of methods is the best way to teach since there is no one best way to teach all children to read.

Calkins, Lucy McCormick. *The Art of Teaching Writing.* Portsmouth, NH: Heinemann, 1994.

Describes the writing workshop and its place in the language arts program.

Clark, L.K. "Invented Versus Traditional Spelling in First Graders' Writing: Effects on Learning to Spell and Read." *Research in the Teaching of English* 22 (1988): 281–309.

Reports on the effects of two methods on the reading and writing achievement of first grade students.

Cunningham, P.M., and Hall, D.P. *The Four Blocks: A Framework for Reading and Writing in Classrooms That Work.* Australia: Windward Productions, 1996.

Describes the Four Blocks in detail.

Cunningham, Patricia M., and Allington, Richard. *Classrooms That Work: They Can All Read and Write.* Boston: Allyn and Bacon, 2003.

Presents strategies for working with students of varying abilities to provide success in reading and writing skills.

Cunningham, Patricia M., and Cunningham, James M. "Making Words; Enhancing the Invented Spelling-Decoding Connection." *Reading Teacher* 46.2 (October 1992): 106–115.

Describes a strategy called making words to help students improve phonetic skills to help make reading easier.

Cunningham, Patricia M., Hall, Dorothy P., and Defee, Margaret. "Non-Ability Grouped, Multilevel Instruction: A Year in a First-Grade Classroom." *Reading Teacher* 44.8 (April 1991): 566–571.

This is the original research and description of the Four Blocks Approach. Presents the reasons, the research, and the data from the first project.

Cunningham, Patricia M., Hall, Dorothy P., and Defee, Margaret. "Non-Ability Grouped, Multilevel Instruction: Eight Years Later." *Reading Teacher* 5.8 (May 1998): 652–664.

This is a follow-up of the 1991 research which includes more research data about the use of the Four Blocks Approach in more classrooms. A detailed discussion of the Approach over time is provided.

Cunningham, Patricia M., Hall, Dorothy P., and Sigmon, Cheryl M. *The Teacher's Guide to The Four Blocks: A Multimethod, Multilevel Framework for Grades 1–3.* Greensboro, NC: Carson-Dellorsa, 1999.

A detailed handbook for classroom teachers describing how to use the Four Blocks Approach.

Duffy, Gerald G. "Powerful Models or Powerful Teachers? An Argument for Teacher-as-Entrepreneur. In *Instructional Models in Reading.* S.A. Stahl and D.A. Hayes, eds. Mahwah, NJ: Erlbaum, 1997, pp. 351–365.

Discusses the importance of teachers as decision makers. Argues that teachers need to be in charge of the instructional models they wish to use. Concludes that the best instruction is done by independent, enterprising teachers "who view instructional models as ideas to be adapted rather than tenets to be followed."

Duffy-Hester, Ann M. "Teaching Struggling Readers in Elementary School Classrooms: A Review of Classroom Reading Programs and Principles of Instruction." *Reading Teacher* 52.5 (February 1999): 480–495.

Presents a description of six reading programs including the Four Blocks Approach that are helpful for students having problems learning to read. Presents principles from the programs and other research that can be used by classroom teachers. This is a good analysis of the Four Blocks Approach.

Erikson, F. "Foreword." In. *Literacy for a Diverse Society: Perspectives, Practices, and Social Policies.* E.H. Hiebert, ed. New York: Teachers College Press, 1991, pp. vii–x.

    Discusses diversity in students and the importance of a multidimensional approach to teaching reading so that all students will learn. States that diversity among students and finding the approaches that will help students is a continuing challenge.

Fielding, Linda, and Roller, Cathy. "Making Difficult Books Accessible and Easy Books Acceptable." *Reading Teacher* 45.9 (May 1992): 678–685.

    Presents activities to help students who are having problems reading become more successful reading the books they want to read and learn to select books that they are able to read. The activities are intended to make independent reading time productive and enjoyable for all students.

Fisher, Dorothy Canfield. *Understood Betsey.* New York: Henry Holt, 1917; reissued 1999.

    Describes the changes in a child's school life when she moves from an urban school to a one-room rural school. This is a children's novel by an advocate of the Montessori Method.

Graves, Donald H. *A Fresh Look at Writing.* Portsmouth, NH: Heinemann, 1995.

    A reexamination of the Writing Process by its originator.

Hall, Dorothy P., and Cunningham, Patricia M. "Becoming Literate in First and Second Grades: Six Years of Multi-Method, Multilevel Instruction." In *Literacies for the 21st Century Research and Practice, Forty-Fifth Yearbook of the National Reading Conference.* Donald J. Leu, Charles K. Kinzer, and Kathleen A. Hinchman, eds. Chicago: National Reading Conference, 1996, pp. 195–204.

    Describes five years of research using the Four Blocks Approach including data on the schools participating. Concludes that using an instructional framework that provides a variety of different approaches to meet the needs of students working on many levels is effective.

Hall, Dorothy P., Prevatte, Connie, and Cunningham, Patricia M. "Eliminating Ability Grouping and Reading Failure in the Primary Grades." In *No Quick Fix: Rethinking Literacy Programs in American Elementary Schools.* Richard L. Allington and Sean Walmesley, eds. New York: Teachers College Press, 1995, pp. 137–158.

    Describes the problems students have when they are grouped by ability for reading instruction and a three year, two school research project designed to help students with diverse needs learn to read. This is a discussion of the early testing of the Four Blocks Approach.

Hiebert, E.H. "An Examination of Ability Grouping for Reading Instruction." *Reading Teacher* 18 (1983): 231–255.

    Presents a discussion of the effect of ability grouping on students' reading.

Hiebert, E.H., and Fisher, C.W. "Task and Talk Strategies That Foster Literacy." In *Literacy for a Diverse Society: Perspectives, Practices, and Policies.* E.H. Hiebert, ed. New York: Teacher's College Press, 1991, pp. 141–156.

    Discusses the importances of student-teacher discussions and student-student discussions during reading and writing activities. State that productive talk about activities helps students learn to read and write more successfully.

McGill-Franzen, Anne, and Allington, Richard L. "The Gridlock of Low Reading Achievement: Perspectives on Practices and Policies." *Remedial and Special Education* 12 (1991): 20–30.

    Examines the problems of students who continue to perform below grade level in reading.

Roe, Betty D., Smith, Sandy H., and Burns, Paul C. *Teaching Reading in Today's Elementary Schools.* Boston: Houghton-Mifflin, 2005, pp. 501–502.

    This text provides a brief description of the components of the Four Blocks Approach.

Routman, Regie. *Transitions.* Postmouth, NH: Heinemann, 1995.

    Describes how teachers can change to an integrated, literature-based language arts program. Provides clear specific guidelines for teachers.

Shannon, Patrick. "Reading Instruction and Social Class." *Language Arts* 62 (1988): 604–613.
   Discusses the effects of ability grouping for reading on students, stating that students at the lower socio-economic levels seldom receive the level of instruction they need.
Sigmon, Cheryl M. *Implementing the Four Blocks Literacy Model*. Greensboro, NC: Carson-Dellosa, 1997.
   A detailed guide to help teachers use the Four Blocks Approach.
Spear-Swerling, L., and Sternberg, R.J. *Off Track: When Poor Readers Become "Learning Disabled."* Boulder, CO: Westview Press, 1996.
   Describes how reading problems can be relabeled as more serious problems because the reading program was not flexible enough to meet the needs of those students.
Stahl, Steven A. "Instructional Models in Reading: An Introduction." In *Instructional Models in Reading*. Steven A. Stahl and David A. Hayes, eds. Mahwah, NJ: Erlbaum, 1997, pp. 1–29.
   Describes approaches to reading and concludes that "principled eclecticism" is what good teachers have always done as a way to adjust to the needs of students by using a variety of approaches. Teachers need to be able to find many ways to help all of their students learn to read.
Tierney, Robert J., and Readence, John E. *Reading Strategies and Practices: A Compendium*. Boston: Allyn and Bacon, 2000, pp. 7–12.
   An overview of the Four Blocks Approach discussing rationale, intended audience, description of procedures, cautions, and comments. A good starting point.
Veatch, Jeannette. *Individualizing Your Reading Program*. New York: Putnam, 1959.
   A classic discussion of the method and materials necessary for meeting the needs of diverse learners.

Cloze Procedure

The cloze procedure is an approach that presents a paragraph or story with about every 5th word deleted. The reader must supply the missing words to make sense of the selection. According to Harris and Sipay (1985) the cloze procedure asks the reader to supply words that have been deleted from a selection. The technique was invented in 1897 by Ebbinghaus but did not become widely used until W.L. Taylor described the cloze procedure as a way to measure readability in 1953. The procedure also was adapted to measure reading comprehension. Harris and Sipay (1985) state that the cloze procedure can be used as a way to measure reading ability and as a strategy for improving comprehension skills.

Tierney and Readence (2000) state that the cloze procedure has been suggested for students at all levels for various reasons such as assessment of the use of context clues, the readability level of texts, and for instructional placement. Taylor (1953) stated that cloze procedure was a strategy to help a reader or listener intercept a message from a writer or speaker "mutilating its language pattern by deleting parts, and so administer it to "receivers" (readers and listeners) that their attempts to make the pattern whole again potentially yield a considerable number of cloze units."

Tierney and Readence (2000) tell that the cloze procedure is based on the "psychological notion of closure ... and the concept of redundancy within language." A cloze passage is developed, according to Harris and Sipay (1985) and Tierney and Readence (2000), by selecting a 300 word passage leaving the first sentence complete and after the fifth word in the second sentence deleting every fifth word until there are fifty deleted words. The removed words are replaced by underlined blanks that are fifteen spaces long.

The passage is a random selection from material that represents the difficulty of the text. "The cloze procedure is given as a test to students similar to those for whom the material is intended." The passage score—the percentage of correct answers—is closest to the average score is used as a test according to Harris and Sipay (1985).

Bormuth (1975) states that fifty deletions gives a reliability coefficient of about .85. Fifty deletions are necessary for high reliability. Passages longer than

250 words are needed if the deletions come less often. The first and last sentences are left complete. Random deletions yield a better measure of reading ability than deletions of specific types of words, according to Robinson (1981).

Harris and Sipay (1985) state that students should be given guided practice so that they know how to do the task before the test is given. Students read the entire passage silently and think of words that best fit the blanks. Then students reread the passage silently and write in the deleted words. Harris and Sipay (1985) and Tierney and Readence (2000) state that most authors suggest that only the exact word that has been deleted be scored as a correct answer. Some examiners accept synonyms because the student's ability to use synonyms indicates comprehension. Some examiners accept the exact word and also acceptable synonyms. When synonyms are used there is no standard for determining the functional reading level. The score is determined by the number of correct answers divided by the number of deleted words given as a percentage.

Bormuth (1968) states that the cloze scores indicate that the instructional level is a score of between 44 percent and 57 percent. The frustration level is a score below 44 percent. The independent level is a score above 57 percent. Studies done by Rankin (1971), Peterson, Paradis and Peters (1973) indicate results similar to Bormuth's scores. These studies only accepted the exact word as correct. Harris and Sipay (1985) and Tierney and Readence (2000) state that there is no complete agreement among researchers about the scoring criteria. Bormuth (1975) suggests scoring criteria vary with grade level and the type of material. Pikulski and Tobin (1982) state that 30 percent–50 percent indicates the instructional level, below 30 percent is the frustration level, and above 50 percent is the instructional level. The majority of scoring criteria are useful for all students regardless of their ability. Peterson and Carroll (1974) state that scores of between 38 percent and 44 percent were the instructional level scores for disabled readers.

Tierney and Readence (2000) and Harris and Sipay (1985) state that a modification of the cloze procedure is called the maze test. In the maze test each deleted word is followed by three choices. Guthrie, Burnham, Caplan, and Seifert (1974) state that the maze can be used to assess the level of difficulty of material and comprehension. The maze test asks the student to select from three possible choices: (a) the exact word, (b) a word that is the same part of speech, or (c) a word that is a different part of speech. When students read three or more passages with a 90 percent score they are reading independently. Scores between 60 percent and 69 percent indicate the instructional level and scores below 60 percent indicate the frustration level.

Harris and Sipay (1985) report that the matching cloze test is another modification. The matching cloze puts the deleted words in a cluster next to the selection. There are no established standards for scoring this test.

The cloze procedure is also used as an instructional strategy to improve comprehension skills. Harris and Sipay (1985) state that filling in the blanks requires students to "process the information surrounding the deletion" and add that "doing so requires very similar cognitive processes to those used in reading un-mutilated text." It is believed that the skill students learn from completing the cloze activity will transfer to reading non cloze material.

Several researchers have listed procedures to follow when using the cloze procedure as a teaching strategy. In order to select material for this strategy Schell (1972), Gove (1975), Bortnick and Lopardo (1973), and Bloomer (1962) state that material should be on the student's independent reading level in the beginning of the strategy. Stories and poems can be selected from content area texts, readers or language experience stories. Teachers can develop their own material, and the researchers state that this is the most effective material. Material should be shorter than that used for a cloze procedure test. For first graders single sentences should be used at first, later moving to selections with 10 to 15 deletions. Designing a cloze exercise should follow a logical progression starting with: (1) one word deleted followed a two-word multiple choice; (2) two-word multiple choice with a few choices graphically similar to the correct word; (3) two choices that are the same part of speech; (4) three choices with one word the same part of speech, and a word that is a different part of speech. Teachers can move on to less studied items including (1) a single graphophonic clue in which only one word will fit; (2) a single graphophonic clue in which several choices are possible, and (3) several passages where there are no graphophonic clues. Schell (1972) suggests that the first exercises delete nouns and verbs and later adjectives and adverbs can be deleted.

Tierney and Readence (2000) state that instruction in the early childhood classroom might include oral cloze activities. The teacher tells the students that he/she will say several sentences but will leave out the last word of each sentence. The teacher then asks the students what words will fit and make sense at the end of each sentence. A discussion should follow and students should state why they selected their answers. This oral activity is the natural introduction to written cloze activities. Tierney and Readence (2000) state that the written activities should follow a specific sequence:

1. A whole class activity using a written cloze passage presented on an overhead slide. The teacher instructs the group to read the whole passage before deciding what words fit the blanks. Ask a student to read the passage to the class and fill in the missing words.
2. Ask students with different responses to tell why their answers fit. Discussion should center on Gove's (1975) suggestions: (a) why did you select this word? (b) what word or group of words helped you decide that your word fit the blank? (c) How does the word you put

in the blank contribute to the meaning of the passage? (d) When you fill in the word you selected what does the sentence or passage mean? (e) How does the word you filled in help the meaning in a different way? And (f) when you fill in the word you selected does the sentence or paragraph have a different meaning? Students should add to the discussion with suggestions for other words.
3. Next students should work on individual worksheets followed by small group discussion in which the teacher asks for reasons why a word was selected. Whole class discussion follows with more interesting word choices and reasons for their selection.
4. Upper grade students should progress to worksheets with blanks that offer a variety of possible choices of words and the discussion that follows the completion of the exercise is the key to the successful use of the cloze procedure. Jongsma (1980) states that the cloze activity without the follow-up discussion will not help students learn to comprehend material better. The discussion leads to better comprehension.

Research studies provide lists of advantages and limitations for the cloze procedure as an assessment tool and as a teaching strategy.

Harris and Sipay (1985) state that there is no complete agreement among researchers as to the scoring criteria for cloze tests. Bormuth (1975), Pikulski and Tobin (1982) and Peterson and Carroll (1974) present different scoring criteria for disabled readers. Grundin et al. (1978) state that even when students do well on a cloze test the score does not guarantee that the students can identify the main idea of a passage or that they have an overall understanding of the material they read. Smith (1978) states that success on a cloze test is influenced by two important variables: (1) the student's ability to use language that consists of language development and reading ability; and (2) the student's acquaintance with the content of the passage being read.

Kibby (1980), Shanahan, Kamil, and Tobin (1982), Shanahan and Kamil (1983), and Leys et al. (1983) state that the cloze test is not a valid measure of reading comprehension because it does not measure the unity of information across sentences. Warwick (1978), Rankin (1978) and Cziko (1983) disagree. Johnston (1983) believes that the literary style and a student's familiarity with the topic may influence the score because it will be easier for the student to predict what words are likely to be part of the passage. Sauer (1969), Hodges (1972), Entin and Klare (1978), Smith and Beck (1980), and Shanahan and Kamil (1982) have found that cloze test results do not compare closely with the student's functional reading level as scored on other tests. Cloze scores only correlate .63 with a student's free recall.

Tierney and Readence (2000) caution that the cloze procedure is not closely connected to comprehension. Completing a cloze activity does not directly improve comprehension skill. Comprehension is dependent on (1) the reader's purpose; (2) follow-up activities; and (3) the demands of the text.

Jongsma (1980) did a review of the literature on cloze procedures and formed ten conclusions: (1) the cloze is a useful teaching strategy but is not more or less useful than many other widely used strategies; (2) cloze is most useful in developing some comprehension skills and least useful for developing word meaning skills; (3) there is no evidence to indicate whether cloze is more useful with narrative or expository material; (4) cloze is not more effective for any one grade or age level or for any level of reading ability; (5) even though the findings are inconclusive, cloze instruction may be more effective where discussion focuses on clues that signal appropriate answers; (6) when cloze materials are carefully sequenced according to difficulty they provide better results that material that is not organized according to difficulty; (7) the quality of instruction is more important than the duration of cloze instruction; (8) no evidence is available to indicate the minimum amount of instruction necessary to insure effective instruction; (9) when deleted words aim at a specific contextual relationship the material is more effective than when semi-random words are left out; and (10) teachers should encourage students to make semantically acceptable answers because there is no need to demand only one correct answer for instructional purposes.

Tierney and Readence (2000) state that there is not enough research that states conclusively that the cloze procedure is helpful as a test of comprehension or as a strategy for teaching comprehension skills. Johnston (1992) states that there is a debate as to whether the cloze procedure gives information about a student's comprehension of anything more than one sentence at a time. Some researchers maintain that a careful selection of the deleted words requires the student to know the entire meaning of the passage (assuming that there is only one acceptable meaning). "Of course, in order to feel a need to engage in these arguments, you have to feel it is necessary to obtain some numerical indicator of a child's ability to comprehend. If you do feel such a need then the cloze procedure remains a useful instructional technique for helping some children attend more to the use of context to figure out unknown words."

Annotated Bibliography

Blachowicz, C.L.Z. "Cloze Activities for Primary Readers." *Reading Teacher* 31 (1971): 300–302.
   Describes how to use different types of cloze materials for primary grade students.
Bloomer, R.H. "The Cloze Procedure as a Remedial Reading Exercise." *Journal of Developmental Reading* 5 (1962): 173–181.
   Discusses using the cloze procedure as a strategy for remedial college students.
Bormuth, John R. "The Cloze Procedure: Literacy in the Classroom." In *Help for the Reading*

Teacher: *New Directions in Research*. W.D. Page, ed. Urbana, IL: National Conference on Research in English and ERIC/RSC, March 1975, pp. 60-69.
    Discusses the use and scoring of the cloze procedure.
Bormuth, John R. "The Cloze Readability Procedure." In *Readability in 1968*. J.R. Bormuth, ed. Urbana, IL: National Council of Teachers of English, 1968, pp. 40-47.
    Discusses the cloze procedure as a measure of students' ability to read.
Bortnick, R., and Lopardo, G.S. "An Instructional Application of the Cloze Procedure." *Journal of Reading* 16 (1973): 296-300.
    Tells how to use the cloze procedure to improve comprehension. Emphasizes that teacher direction and help are very important for student success.
Carr, E., Dewitz, P., and Patberg, J. "Using Cloze for Inference Training with Expository Text." *Reading Teacher* 42 (1989): 340-385.
    Explains how to use cloze material to help students improve inference and self-monitoring skills.
Cunningham, J.W., and Cunningham, P.M. "Validating a Limited Cloze Procedure." *Journal of Reading Behavior* 10 (1978): 211-213.
    Describes changes in the cloze procedure format necessary for instructional use.
Cziko, Gary A. "Another Response to Shanahan, Kamil, and Tobin: Further Reasons to Keep the Cloze Case Open." *Reading Research Quarterly* 18 (Spring 1983): 361-366.
    Disagrees with Shanahan, Kamil and Tobin stating that the cloze procedure is useful as a measure of comprehension and should be used.
Dieterich, Thomas, Freeman, Cecilia, and Griffin, Peg. *Assessing Comprehension in a School Setting*. Arlington, VA: Center for Applied Linguistics, June 1978.
    Discusses using the cloze procedure as an assessment tool of reading comprehension.
Entin, Eileen B., and Klare, George R. "Some Inter-Relationships of Readability, Cloze, and Multiple Choice Scores for a Reading Comprehension Test." *Journal of Reading Behavior* 10 (Winter 1978): 417-436.
    Presents statistical data from research on reading comprehension assessment and describes how the various types of scores are interrelated.
Gove, M.K. "Using the Cloze Procedure in a First Grade Classroom." *Reading Teacher* 29 (1975): 36-38.
    Tells how to use the cloze procedure with basal readers and the language experience approach in a first grade classroom. Provides practical advice.
Grundin, Hans U., Leonard, Brother, Langer, Judith, Pehrsson Robert, Robinson, H. Alan, and Sakamoto, Takahiko. "Cloze Procedure and Comprehension: An Exploratory Study Across Three Languages." In *Cross Cultural Perspective on Reading and Reading Research*. D. Feitelson, ed. Newark, DE: International Reading Association, 1978, pp. 48-61.
    Describes the use of the cloze procedure with students who speak three different languages. The aim was to compare student progress in comprehension with the use of the cloze procedure as an instructional strategy.
Gunn, V. Patricia, and Elkins, John. "Clozing the Reading Gap." *Australian Journal of Reading* 2 (August 1979): 144-151. Also in A.J. Harris and E. Sipay, eds. *Readings on Reading Instruction*. New York: Longman, 1984, pp. 293-298.
    Describes how to adopt the cloze procedure as a useful tool for reading instruction.
Guthrie, J.T., Burnham, N.A., Caplan, R.I., and Seifert, M. "The Maze Technique to Assess, Monitor Reading Comprehension." *Reading Teacher* 28 (1974): 161-168.
    Describes the maze technique as a variation of the cloze procedure which uses multiple choice answers.
Harris, Albert J., and Sipay, Edward R. *How to Increase Reading Ability: A Guide to Developmental and Remedial Methods*. New York: Longman, **1985**, 1987, 1988, pp. 175-178; 495.
    Describes the cloze procedure for use as an assessment tool and as an instructional strategy. Research findings are presented to discuss the advantages and disadvantages of the procedure.

Hodges, Elaine J. "A Comparison of the Functional Reading Levels of Selected Third Grade Students of Varying Reading Abilities." Ph.D. dissertation, University of Northern Colorado, 1972.

Presents a useful bibliography and a comparative study of students stating that cloze test scores differ from functional reading scores on other tests.

Johnston, P. *Constructive Evaluation of Literate Activity.* New York: Longman, 1992.

This is a brief discussion of the cloze procedure with a presentation of literacy assessment theories, practices, and problems.

Johnston, Peter. "Prior Knowledge and Reading Comprehension Test Bias." Technical Report No. 289. Champaign, IL: Center for the Study of Reading, University of Illinois, September, 1983.

Discusses the importance of background knowledge for comprehension scores.

Jongsma, Eugene A. *Cloze Instruction Research: A Second Look.* Newark, DE: International Reading Association, 1980.

This is a review of the literature on the cloze procedure as a teaching strategy with suggestions for further research.

Kibby, Michael W. "Instructional Processes in Reading Comprehension." *Journal of Reading Behavior* 12 (1980): 299–312.

States that the cloze procedure is not a valid assessment of reading comprehension because it does not measure the integration of information across sentences.

Leys, Margie, Fielding, L., Herman, P., and Pearson, P.D. "Does Cloze Measure Inner Sentence Comprehension? A Modified Replication of Shanahan, Kamil and Tobin." In *Search for Meaning in Reading/Language Processing and Instruction.* J.A. Niles and L.A. Harris, eds. Rochester, NY: National Reading Conference, 1983, pp. 111–114.

A replication of research done by Shanahan, Kamil, and Tobin in an attempt to find out if the cloze procedure successfully measures comprehension.

McKenna, Michael C., and Robinson, Richard D. *An Introduction to the Cloze Procedure: An Annotated Bibliography.* Newark, DE: International Reading Association, 1980.

This is a useful tool for material available on the cloze procedure.

Peterson, J., Paradis, E., and Peters, N. "Revalidation of the Cloze Procedure as a Measure of the Instructional Levels of High School Students." In *Diversity in Mature Reading: Theory and Research.* P.L. Nacke, ed. Boone, NC: National Reading Conference, 1973, pp. 144–149.

Reports scoring results for the instructional level on the cloze procedure, stating that results were similar for students of various ages with an emphasis on high school.

Peterson, Joe, and Carroll, Martha. "The Cloze Procedure as an Indicator of the Instructional Level for Disabled Readers." In *Interaction: Research and Practices for College-Adult Reading.* P. Nacke, ed. Clemson, SC: National Reading Conference, 1974, pp. 153–157.

Presents research on the use of the cloze procedure with disabled readers.

Pikulski, John J., and Tobin, Aileen W. "The Cloze Procedure as an Informal Assessment Technique." In *Approaches to the Informal Evaluation of Reading.* John J. Pikulski and Timothy Shanahan, eds. Newark, DE: International Reading Association, 1982, pp. 42–62.

This is a detailed discussion of the research on and uses of the cloze procedure.

Rankin, Earl F. "Characteristics of the Cloze Procedure as a Research Tool in the Study of Language." In *Reading: Disciplined Inquiry in Process and Practice.* P.D. Pearson and J. Hansen, eds. Clemson, SC: National Reading Conference, 1978, pp. 148–153.

Describes the cloze procedure as a useful tool for the study of reading and language.

Rankin, Earl F. "The Cloze Procedure Results Revisited." In *Interaction: Research and Practice for College-Adult Reading.* P.L. Nacke, ed. Clemson, SC: National Reading Conference, 1974, pp. 1–8.

A reexamination of the grade level results for the cloze procedure. States that results are consistent.

Rankin, Earl F. "Grade Level Interpretation of Cloze Readability Scores." In *The Right to Participate.* F. Greene, ed. Milwaukee: National Reading Conference, 1971, pp. 30–37.

Describes how grade level scores are interpreted for cloze procedure assessment.

Robinson, Colin M. "Cloze Procedure: A Review." *Educational Research* 23 (February 1981): 128-133.
   Presents a discussion of the cloze procedure, stating that randomly deleting words provides a better assessment of comprehension than deletion of specific kinds of words.
Rush, Robert J., and Keare, George G. "Reopening the Cloze Blank Issue." *Journal of Reading Behavior* 10 (Summer 1978): 208-210.
   Discusses the importance of the use of the dash for each letter of deleted words because this method yields significantly higher scores on the cloze test.
Sauer, Freda M. "The Determination of Reading Instructional Levels of Disabled Fourth Grade Readers Utilizing Cloze Testing Procedures." Ph.D. dissertation, Oklahoma State University, 1969.
   Reports that cloze test results do not closely match functional reading levels achieved by disabled readers on several assessment measures.
Schell, Leo M. "Promising Possibilities for Improving Comprehension." *Journal of Reading* 5 (1972): 415-424.
   A detailed discussion of the use of the cloze procedure as a teaching strategy.
Shanahan, Timothy, and Kamil, Michael. "A Further Comparison of the Sensitivity of Cloze and Recall to Passage Organization." In *Search for Meaning in Reading/Language Processing and Instruction*. J.A. Niles and L.A. Harris, eds. Rochester, NY: National Reading Conference, 1983, pp. 123-128.
   Continued research investigating the relationship between the way a passage is organized, the cloze procedure and pupils' ability to recall material.
Shanahan, Timothy, and Kamil, Michael. "The Sensitivity of Cloze to Passage Organization." In *New Inquiries in Reading Research and Instruction*. J.A. Niles and L.A. Harris, eds. Rochester, NY: National Reading Conference, 1982, pp. 212-217.
   Reports that the cloze procedure is related to the organization of the passage used.
Shanahan, Timothy, and Kamil, Michael L., Tobin, Aileen Webb. "Cloze as a Measure of Intersentential Comprehension." *Reading Research Quarterly* 17.2 (1982): 229-255.
   A research study that questions whether the cloze procedure is useful as a way to assess comprehension.
Smith, William E., and Beck, Michael. "Determining Instructional Reading Level with the 1978 Metropolitan Achievement Test." *Reading Teacher* 34 (December 1980): 313-319.
   Used the Metropolitan Achievement Test to determine students' instructional level, stating the cloze procedure scores do not match the results of other measures.
Smith, William L. "Cloze Procedure [Ebbinghause Complete Method] as Applied to Reading." In *Eighth Mental Measurements Yearbook*, Vol. II. O.K. Buros, ed. Highland Park, NJ: Gryphon Press, 1978, pp. 1176-1178.
   Reports on the original cloze procedure, stating that two variables influence pupil success: (1) familiarity with the content of the passage, and (2) the ability to use language which is a combination of language development and reading ability.
Taylor, W.L. "Cloze Procedure: A New Tool for Measuring Readability." *Journalism Quarterly* 30 (Fall 1953): 415-453.
   The first discussion of the cloze procedure as a useful measure of readability.
Thomas, Keith J. "Instructional Application of the Cloze Technique." *Reading World* 18 (October 1978): 1-12.
   Describes ways to use the cloze procedure as an effective instructional strategy.
Tierney, Robert J., and Readence, John E. *Reading Strategies and Practices: A Compendium*. Boston: Allyn and Bacon, 2000, pp. 511-519.
   An overview of the cloze procedure with an annotated bibliography. A good place to start research.
Warwick, B. Elley. "Cloze Procedure [Ebbinghause Complete Method] Applied to Reading." In *Eighth Mental Measurements Yearbook*, Vol. II. O.K. Buros, ed. Highland Park, NJ: Gryphon Press, 1978, pp. 1174-1176.
   Reports that the cloze procedure can measure comprehension levels well.

Question-Answer Relationship Strategy

Question-Answer Relationship is a strategy to teach students correct ways to answer questions. Tierney and Readence (2005) state that Taffy Raphael developed the technique to help students better answer comprehension questions by providing a systematic way to analyze the demands required by different kinds of questions. According to Armbruster (1992) direct teaching and modeling the strategy are necessary for students to learn how to answer questions. Teachers need to explain how and where to locate information and how to develop the answer once the needed information is found. Applegate, Quinn and Applegate (2006) state that students may not realize that they can use prior knowledge to answer questions, may rely on background knowledge too often without using text information, or may not have adequate language ability to answer the questions.

The question-answer relationship strategy helps students learn the thinking processes involved in reading comprehension, according to Raphael and Au (2005). The strategy teaches students to use information "In the Book" or "In My Head." Raphael (1984) explains that information "In the Book" that is found stated in one sentence in a text is called "Right There." Students are to find the words in the question and read the sentence with those words to answer the question. When an answer is "In the Book" but needs information from several sentences or paragraphs, it is called "Think and Search." When the answer to the question needs to come entirely from the student's own knowledge the answer is called "On My Own." When students need to use the text information and their own knowledge, the answer called "Author and Me." Students can decide which relationship to use by learning to differentiate among the various question-answer relationships and the kinds of sources that answer each question. Direct teaching, modeling by the teacher and many opportunities to practice each relationship are necessary for students to become comfortable with the terminology of the strategy. First the two major options for finding answers are taught, then the subcategories of each are taught.

Raphael (1984) suggests that the process start with four lessons over the course of a week. The strategy should be introduced by discussing the difference between text responses and background based responses. Then a three step practice period is suggested. Raphael (1984) recommends in stage one using paragraphs with questions for which the answers and the question-answer relationship are identified. Discuss the kind of question-answer relationship that fits each question. In stage two present passages, questions and answers to the questions, with the students working as a whole class to tell which question-answer relationship fits each answer. In stage three students are required to tell answers to each question and the question-answer relationship for each answer. In stage three students work independently. Supervised practice after modeling and immediate correction to student answers is necessary. Raphael (1982) states that practice activities should involve a gradual increase in the length of passages and the difficulty of the answers required.

Research conducted using the strategy by Raphael (1984, 1986), Raphael and Pearson (1985), Raphael and McKinney (1983), Raphael et al. (1992), Raphael and Au (2005), Raphael and Wonnacott (1985), Ezell, Hunsicker, Quinque and Randolph (1996), and National Reading Panel Report (2000) report various successful findings: (1) teaching the strategy helps explain the mental processes involved in reading comprehension; (2) training helps average and below average students most; (3) primary students require more repetition to learn the strategy than intermediate students; (4) by the second grade students master "Right there" and "Think and Search" subcategories and by fourth grade students can master all the subcategories; (5) when "On My Own" questions are used before reading, students are better able to use what they know and relate this background information to the text they will read; (6) developmental differences in comprehension were found when comparing 8th graders and 5th graders, and orientation to the strategy was as useful as training in the strategy, and training helped students improve comprehension, but comprehension was not improved by reminding students to apply the strategy when they were being assessed; (7) students in grades four, six, and eight who had been taught the strategy were better able to answer questions than students who were not taught the strategy; (8) when fourth grade teachers were trained to use the strategy results were positive and similar to the results with 4th, 6th and 8th grade students; also, teachers trained to teach the strategy were pleased with the strategy and their students were better able to answer questions than groups of students who did not have a direct learning experience with the strategy.

Tierney and Readence (2005) state that the question-answer relationship strategy is a thoroughly researched strategy. Raphael has made every effort to research the use of the strategy across grade levels with students of varying abilities. Tierney and Readence (2005) express two concerns about the strategy: (1) the taxonomy Raphael uses was intended to describe question-answer relationships instead of to help students figure out a correct answer. As readers think about answering a question they could better consider the aim of the question and the point of the passage instead of whether the answer comes from categories such as text or reader; and (2) the question-answer relationship strategy might not increase comprehension in a straightforward way. Finding the kind of relationship between a question and answer appears to better follow than precede answering the question. Perhaps the strategy is better used to help students gain feedback for their answers instead of answers to questions.

Tierney and Readence (2005) note that even though these two concerns were found, the National Reading Panel (2000) stated that the question-answer relationship strategy is an effective way to improve comprehension. Roe and Smith (2012) state that many students have difficulties answering questions for a variety of reasons and need specific help that highlights their specific problems and enables them to better understand and answer questions.

Direct instruction in a specific strategy that gives students a set of guidelines for answering questions and can help improve comprehension. The research has shown that help is better than no help.

Annotated Bibliography

Applegate, Mary Dekonty, Quinn, Kathleen Benson, and Applegate, Anthony, J. "Profiles in Comprehension." *Reading Teacher* 60 (September 2006): 48–57.
    States reasons why students have difficulties answering comprehension questions.
Armbruster, Bonnie B. "On Answering Questions." *Reading Teacher* 45 (May 1992): 724–725.
    States that teachers need to provide direct instruction and modeling in order to help students learn to use the question-answer relationship strategy.
Cortese, E.E. "The Application of Question-Answer Relationship Strategies to Pictures." *The Reading Teacher* 57 (2003–2004): 374–380.
    Describes how to apply the question-answer relationship strategy to picture interpretation.
Ezell, H.K., Hunsicker, S.A., Quinque, M.M., and Randolph, E. "Maintenance and Generalization of Question-Answer Relationship Reading Comprehension Strategies." *Reading Research and Instruction* 36 (1996): 64–81.
    This study shows that training in the use of the question-answer relationship strategy can improve comprehension of explicit and implicit text questions.
McIntosh, M.E., and Draper, R. J. "Applying the Question-Answer Relationship Strategy in Mathematics." *Journal of Adolescent and Adult Literacy* 39 (1995): 120–131.
    Describes how to use the question-answer relationship strategy in mathematics instruction. A good look at the ways to adopt a reading strategy to another content area.
National Reading Panel. *Teaching Children to Read: An Evidence-Based Assessment of the Sci-*

entific Research Literature on Reading and Its Implications for Reading Instruction: Report of the Sub Groups. Washington, DC: National Institute of Child Health and Human Development, 2000, NIH Publication (No. 00-4754).
   Chapter 4 discuses the effectiveness of question answering to improve reading comprehension.
Pearson, P.D., and Johnson, D.D. *Teaching Reading Comprehension.* New York: Holt Rinehart and Winston, 1978.
   Describes the taxonomy used by Taffy Raphael for the question-answer relationship strategy. This is an overview of reading comprehension and instructional strategies. Perhaps Raphael's inspiration for developing Question-Answer Relationship strategy.
Raphael, Taffy E. "Question-Answer Strategies for Children." *Reading Teacher* 36 (November 1982): 186-190.
   Describes the strategy.
Raphael, Taffy E. "Teaching Learners about Sources of Information for Answering Comprehension Questions." *Journal of Reading* 27 (January 1984): 303-311.
   States that primary grade students need more help and repetition to use Question-Answer Relationship strategy.
Raphael, Taffy E. "Teaching Question-Answer Relationship, Revised." *Reading Teacher* 39 (February 1986): 516-522.
   Presents another look at the Question-Answer Relationship technique, providing further insight into its use in the classroom.
Raphael, Taffy E., and Au, Kathryn H. "Question-Answer Relationship Enhancing Comprehension and Test Taking Across Grades and Content Areas: *Reading Teacher* 59 (November 2005): 206-221.
   Reports the use of Question-Answer Relationship for all grade levels and its effects in various content area comprehension. Very useful for students of diverse backgrounds.
Raphael, Taffy E., Goatley, Virgina, Bentley, Jessica, Boyd, Fenice, Pardo, Laura, and Woodman, Deborah. "Research Directions; Literature and Discussions in the Reading Program." *Language Arts* 69 (January 1992): 54-61.
   Reports research using Question-Answer Relationship with literature selections and its positive effects on comprehension skills.
Raphael, Taffy E., and McKinney, J. "An Examination of 5th and 8th Grade Children's Question Answering Behavior: An Instructional Study in Metacognition." *Journal of Reading Behavior* 15 (1983): 67-86.
   Reports on research that second graders can master the question-answer relationship strategy subcategories "Right There" and "Think and Search."
Raphael, Taffy E., and Pearson, P. David. "Increasing Students' Awareness of Sources of Information for Answering Question." *American Educational Research Journal* 22 (1985): 217-236.
   Reports that intermediate students need less repetition to learn the strategy than primary students.
Raphael, Taffy E., and Wonnacott, C.A. "Heightening Fourth-Grade Students' Sensitivity to Sources of Information for Answering Comprehension Question." *Reading Research Quarterly* 20 (1985): 282-296.
   Reports on the research use of question-answer relationship subcategories stating they were learned well by the fourth grade and the training of fourth grade teachers to use the strategy.
Roe, Betty D., and Smith, Sandy H. *Teaching Reading in Today's Elementary Schools.* Belmont, CA: Wadsworth, 2012.
   A brief introduction to the QAR technique. A good place to start. Presents research.
Simmonds, D.P.M. "The Effects of Teacher Training and Implementation of Two Methods for Improving the Comprehension Skills of Students with Learning Disabilities." *Learning Disabilities Research and Practice* 7 (1992): 194-198.
   Reports a study which used the question-answer relationship strategy and tradi-

tional comprehension strategies to teach learning disabled students in grades one to nine. The results indicate that the question-answer relationship strategy helped students answer questions better than traditional strategies.

Tierney, R.J., and Cunningham, J.W. "Research on Teaching Reading Comprehension." In. *Handbook of Reading Research.* P.D. Pearson, R. Barr, M.L. Kamil, and P. Mosenthal, eds. New York: Longman, 1984.

This is a comprehensive review of research on reading comprehension strategies with a discussion of the question-answer relationship strategy. An excellent bibliography is included. This is one of the best research report sources in the field.

Tierney, Robert J. and Readence, John E. *Reading Strategies and Practices: A Compendium.* Boston: Pearson, 2005.

Provides an overview of the question-answer relationship strategy including concerns about the effectiveness of the strategy.

Alternative Assessment Techniques

Assessment, or the collection and analysis of information to better understand and recognize student learning, is a vital part of teaching. Assessment makes it possible for teachers to identify the strengths and areas in need of improvement for each student, to plan appropriate instruction, to communicate student progress, and to appraise the effectiveness of teaching strategies, according to Roe and Smith (2012). Assessment is not just testing. It is a very important part of instruction and should come from a variety of sources. When a picture of student learning is developed from more than one source it provides a more valid view of what the student is able to do, and differentiated instruction can be developed for all students, according to Walker-Dalhouse et al. (2009).

Authentic assessment or alternative assessment consists of practices that are more closely connected to the aims of instruction and assess students using activities that are close to the skills students learn. Authentic assessment uses multiple ways to find out about student progress such as activities that are real life uses of the skills. Progress is measured by growth over time. If students learn to read a bus schedule, the assessment tool is having students plan a trip to the local library by checking the time to catch the bus and the time the bus leaves the library stop to return to school.

According to Roe and Smith (2012) and Tierney and Readence (2005) the strategies for authentic assessment are: observation, anecdotal records, checklists and rating scales, rubrics, conferences and interviews, retelling, and portfolios.

Observation has been called kid watching by Goodman (1985). According to Roe and Smith (2012), Cohen and Cowen (2008) and Cooper and Kiger (2009) the teacher observes one student, a small group or the entire class to assess language use, social behavior, or a specific reading skill. The teacher may join the activity to assess it better. The teacher interacts by asking questions, holding conferences with individuals to encourage growth or responding to journal entries. The teacher engages in analysis by hearing individuals read, or reading an individual's writing. Longer observations generate more information about progress. The teacher applies principles of learning to analyze students' ability to use language. Observation and evaluation during teaching provides insight into patterns of behavior that show that students understand how reading and writing develop. Field notes help teachers analyze what was observed and form conclusions about what intervention strategies will help each student make better or faster progress. Observation takes place over time to note a pattern of progress or problems. Teachers respond to student needs with further instruction, clarification of ideas, and multiple instructional strategies.

Cooper and Kiger (2009) state that effective observation can be done when students read aloud, perform a play, write a response to a story, write a report, and talk to each other in informal situations.

Anecdotal records, Roe and Smith (2012), Harris and Sipay (1988), and Harris and Hodges (1995) state, are written statements of a specific classroom incident. The teacher writes a verbatim record of a significant language event including the time, place, students involved, the cause of the incident, exactly what happened, and the possible implication. Anecdotal records are kept for individual students, groups or the whole class. According to Parker et al. (1995) and Rhodes and Nathenson-Mejia (1992), anecdotal records provide information useful for evaluating progress, planning instruction, developing individualized instruction, reporting to parents, students and administrators about progress and problems, highlighting changes in language development, and studying student attitudes and behaviors. Baskwill and Whitman (1988) state that anecdotal records are most helpful for gathering information on the progress of students with special needs and English language learners. Teachers who keep anecdotal records on a regular basis become more sensitive to the needs and interests of students, according to Baskwill and Whitman (1988).

Checklists of the traits being observed provide a way to record what has been observed. Harris and Hodges (1995) describe such a checklist as a list of specific skills or behaviors that the observer marks as the student performs them. Checklists provide a graphic way to review student progress overtime when they are filled out periodically.

Roe and Smith (2012) state that progress reports provide more information about progress because each item can be given a number, such as 1 (lowest) to 5 (highest) according to a student's achievement level.

Rubrics provide, according to Saddler and Andrade (2004), Cooper and Gargan (2009), O'Neil (1994), and Winograd (1994), very specific standards for describing student performance at different levels of ability for several content areas. They use specific rules to describe, score and guide the performance of students. A specific number of points indicate the minimal, average and highest quality of work submitted. Students are informed what is expected before the work is completed. This informs the students how assignments will be assessed and assists teachers in the fair assessment of assignments. Students are better able to understand the grades they receive when they are able to consult the criteria by which the work will be evaluated. Students also learn what the most and least acceptable assignments must contain.

Collaboration between students and the teacher in constructing rubrics, with step by step guidance provided by teachers, helps students learn to design and use rubrics effectively. Skellings and Ferrell (2000) state students develop and practice critical thinking skills and metacognition when they learn to design rubrics. Students better understand the process of assessment when they are part of it.

Conferences and interviews provide information about skills, attitudes and interests in reading. Conferences can either be scheduled with individual students or can be spontaneous when necessary. Roe and Smith (2012) state that conferences provide information about how students interpret information and make meaning, and provide opportunities for students to explain how they reached the answers to comprehension questions.

Portfolios are used to help students and teachers to evaluate and reflect on completed work in order to assess achievement from multiple activities. Barrett (2007) and Tierney and Readence (2005) state that portfolios not only are useful as a way to assess progress, but encourage students to think about what they have done. Students can see progress over time. Artifacts should be dated and can be selected for inclusion by the teacher, the student or as a joint effort. Portfolios show what students are able to do. Criteria for artifact collection include writing samples, several activities that show use of language, culminating activities at the end of a unit, skill success in a specific content area, and the display of work for a specific period of time. A portfolio helps students self-assess progress and become active participants in their own learning. Periodic reviews of the contents of a portfolios are recommended in the form of a conference between the teacher and each student. Portfolios provide a multifaceted picture of each student's reading/writing progress over time. The portfolio provides a means to evaluate progress through actual experiences, giving a picture of progress from primary sources. Students are able to better understand their strengths and areas for improvement and to be involved in setting goals for learning. Teachers learn about what was done well, what needs more instruction, and how to better differentiate instruction.

Parents and pupils better understand how learning happens and gain a more detailed view of progress by looking through a portfolio than by looking at a letter or number grade.

Retelling happens when students retell what they have read or heard. Students can retell either orally or in writing. Roe and Smith (2012) state that retelling is useful for both fiction and nonfiction. First the student responds without teacher help. When the student completes retelling the teacher can prompt the student using open-ended questions or by having him/her complete a graphic organizer with the teacher that will encourage the student to tell more. Ellery (2010) states that retelling helps students to concentrate on story structure and sequence using a rubric will help to highlight specific criteria and standards for the retelling and become a document for the activity.

Self-assessment techniques, Au (1990) believes, are most useful to help students set goals, decide how they will achieve the goals, and view their own progress. Students, with teacher guidance, learn to become involved in the assessment process, take responsibility for assessment, become more aware of personal strengths and areas for improvement. A self-assessment checklist or a list of self-questions to answer during the assignment helps students become more aware of strengths and problem areas. Questions such as "Do I understand exactly what I have to do for this assignment? What parts of this chapter might cause my problems?" will help, Roe and Smith (2012) suggest. When students self-evaluate what they do and how often they do it, Roe and Smith (2012) suggest, students will focus on and better understand reading behaviors. Indicating how frequently "I understand what I read. I can find the main idea of a paragraph. I think about what I read. What it really means to me" provides students and teachers with specific behaviors that help improve comprehension.

Running record is another authentic assessment technique. It is a detailed description of a student's reading activity. The teacher uses a running record, Harris and Hodges (1995) state, to evaluate specific reading activity over time. No special materials are necessary. A running record is similar to how an informal reading inventory is used. While a student reads aloud the teacher notes each word read correctly by using a check mark. Miscues are coded to show the kind of miscue made such as:

SODA—Substitution
Omissions
Distortions
Additions

The teacher is able to analyze the miscues to discover why the error was made. Comprehension questions provide more information about a student's understanding of material.

A running record is practical because it is easy to use, and Lipson and Wixson (1997) believe it can be created quickly and used with any passage that the student reads aloud and the teacher has a copy of during the reading.

Salinger (1996) states that a running record provides insights into reading strategies used and how aware students are of their reading behavior by analyzing self-corrected errors.

Alternative assessment techniques can be useful tools for evaluating reading and gaining a great deal of information; however, they have limitations. Roe and Smith (2012) and Tierney and Readence (2005) list several cautions to be aware of. No method is ideal; they all have limitations.

Alternative assessment:

1. Is subjective and two evaluators might assess the same assignment differently. One evaluator may not know enough about the use of each strategy or expectations or the evaluation may or may not be realistic for a student at a specific level; therefore the assessments might not be the most just evaluation.
2. Can take too much time to complete. Writing a progress report requires more time than assigning a letter grade or a number grade from an object test score.
3. Requires teachers to be knowledgeable about how to explain and apply this information to help students read better, and
4. Requires the collection of information from several sources and the identification of differences and similarities.

Authentic assessment techniques are designed to develop methods of evaluation that are closer to the curriculum goals and are an attempt to assess progress using activities that are closer to the kind of learning the students are actually acquiring rather than other techniques that may not be considered authentic. Authentic assessment tools are used to help teachers and students gain more information and move away from using standardized test results as the only means of evaluation. They provide a broader picture of student learning over time rather than a one-time picture of a specific skill. Authentic assessment techniques, Tierney and Readence (2005) believe, better respect the complex nature of reading; are more realistic; are inter-curricular and jointly negotiated; are more concerned with student and teacher empowerment; are concerned with the relevance and purpose of the material being assessed; are concerned with the student as a partner in the evaluation of activities; and are more sensitive to the many different jobs of the teacher in ongoing assessment.

Annotated Bibliography

Au, Kathryn H. "An Overview of New Concepts of Assessment: Impact on Decision Making and Instruction." Paper presented at International Reading Association Convention, Atlanta, Georgia, May 6, 1990. Reported in Roe and Smith (2012).

Discusses the importance of students self-assessing their progress as a way of becoming part of the assessment process rather than just the recipient of a grade or evaluation.

Barrett, Helen C. "Researching Electronic Portfolios and Learner Engagement: The REFLECT Initiative." *Journal of Adolescent and Adult Literacy* 50 (March 2007): 436–439.

Discusses the importance of portfolios as a tool to help students reflect on their progress and as a motivation for improvement.

Baskwill, Jane, and Whitman, Paulette. *Evaluation: Whole Language, Whole Child*. Toronto: Scholastic, 1988.

Provides a discussion of authentic assessment in the context of the whole language classroom. A good early source.

Batzle, Janine. *Portfolio Assessment and Evaluation*. Cypress, CA: Creative Teaching Press, 1992.

A practical guide to developing and using portfolios for assessment.

Cohen, Vicki L., and Cowen, John Edwin. *Literacy for Children in an Information Age: Teaching Reading, Writing and Thinking*. Belmont, CA: Thomason/Wadsworth, 2008.

An excellent text discussing reading instruction and the best methods of assessment.

Cooper, Bruce S., and Gargan, A. "Rubrics in Education: Old Term, New Meaning." *Phi Delta Kappa* 91 (September 2009): 54–55.

Discusses rubrics as a useful tool to help students and teachers know how assignments will be evaluated in advance.

Cooper, J. David, and Kiger, Nancy D. *Literacy: Helping Students Construct Meaning*. Boston: Houghton-Mifflin, 2009.

A useful text providing an overview of assessment.

Farr, R., and Tone, B. *Portfolio and Performance Assessment: Helping Students Evaluate Their Progress as Readers and Writers*. Fort Worth, TX: Harcourt Brace, 1994.

Suggests ways to involve students in the use of portfolios to assess their reading and writing progress.

Goodman, Yetta. "Kidwatching." In *Observing the Language Learner*. A. Jaggar and M.T. Smith-Burke, eds. New York, DE: International Reading Association, 1985.

Describes the idea of Kidwatching with suggestions for observing and understanding language development. A good classic.

Harris, Albert J., and Sipay, Edward R. *How to Increase Reading Ability*. New York: Longman, 1985, 1987, 1988.

A classic text in the field with a good discussion of assessment and a good bibliography.

Harris, Theodore L., and Hodges, Richard, eds. *The Literacy Dictionary: The Vocabulary of Reading and Writing*. Newark, DE: International Reading Association, 1995.

Provides a clear definition of authentic assessment and each technique that is used.

Lipson, Mayorie, and Wixson, Karen. *Assessment and Instruction of Reading and Writing Disability*. New York: Longman, 1997.

A useful discussion pointing to the value of several techniques including running records as an easy way to assess oral reading.

O'Neil, John. "Making Assessment Meaningful." *ASCD Update* 36 (August 1994): 4–5.

A brief discussion telling how to interpret assessment data.

Parker, Emelie, Armengol, Regla, Brooke, Leigh, Carper, Kelly, Cronin, Sharon, Denman, Anne, Irwin, Patricia, McGunnigle, Jennifer, Pardini, Tess, and Kurtz, Nancy. "Teachers' Choices in Classroom Assessment." *Reading Teacher* 48.7 (1995): 622–624.

Describes several types of assessment including running records, rubrics and self-assessment. A good overview telling what teachers prefer to use.

Rhodes, Lynn, and Nathenson-Mejia, Sally. "Anecdotal Records: A Powerful Tool for On-Going Literacy Assessment." *Reading Teacher* (1992): 45, 502–509.

Tells how to use anecdotal records with examples and analysis of each example.

Roe, Betty D., and Smith, Sandy H. *Teaching Reading in Today's Elementary Schools.* Belmont, CA: Wadsworth, 2012.

    Provides a chapter on assessment. An excellent text as a starting point for an overview of assessment.

Saddler, Bruce, and Andrade, Heidi. "The Writing Rubric." *Educational Leadership* 62 (October 2004): 48–52.

    Describes the development of rubrics, how to score and use them.

Salinger, Terry S. *Literacy for Young Children.* Englewood Cliffs, NJ: Merrill, 1996.

    Suggest that running records are a useful tool for assessment and a way to adjust instruction to the needs of students.

Skellings, Mary Jo, and Ferrell, Robin. "Student Generated Rubrics: Bringing Students Into the Assessment Process." *Reading Teacher* 53 (March 2000): 452–455.

    Provides suggests for engaging students in the assessment process. A useful source.

Tierney, Robert J., and Readence, John E. *Reading Strategies and Practices: A Compendium.* Boston: Pearson, 2005, pp. 464–525.

    Provides a discussion of authentic assessment techniques describing each clearly.

Valencia, Sheila. "A Portfolio Approach to Classroom Reading Assessment: The Why's, What's and How's." *Reading Teacher* 43 (January 1990): 338–340.

    A good outline telling the importance of portfolio assessment and its uses.

Valencia, S., Hiebert, E., and Afterbach, P. *Authentic Reading Assessment.* Newark, DE: International Reading Association, 1994.

    Provides guidance for using all forms of authentic assessment. A practical source for putting authentic assessment tools into use.

Walker-Dalhouse, Doris, Risko, Victoria J., Esworthy, Cathy, Grasley, Ellen, Kaisler, Gina, McIlvain, Dona, and Stephan, Mary. "Crossing Boundaries and Initiating Conversations About RTI: Understanding and Applying Differentiated Classroom Instruction." *Reading Teacher* 63 (September 2009): 84–87.

    Discusses the use of Response to Intervention and the importance of differentiating instruction for students with special needs.

Winograd, Peter. "Developing Alternative Assessments: Six Problems Worth Solving." *Reading Teacher* 47.9 (February 1994): 420–423.

    Discusses the problems related to alternative assessment and tells why it is necessary to solve them.

Reading-Writing Workshop

Reading-writing workshop provides opportunities for students to spend more time actually reading and writing independently. Strategies are taught as needed in mini lessons.

The reading-writing workshop was organized as a strategy by Nancie Atwell originally for middle school students. Atwell (1987, 1998) states that the reading-writing workshop helps adolescents' "social relationships ... serve scholarly ends. Kids can be active, talking, and moving as part of their activity as engaged writers and readers. They can capture and channel their ideas, feelings, and enthusiasms, have more say in their learning, and assume greater independence." Roe, Smith, and Burns (2005) state that reading and writing workshops "provide opportunities for teachers to teach specific strategies directly during brief mini-lessons and for students to spend most of their time actually reading and writing."

According to Temple, Ogle, Crawford, and Freppon (2005), reader's workshop is more structured than individualized reading including small group lessons. Ornstein and Sinatra (2005) state that even though the word "workshops" makes one think of group work, the "intent of the workshop structure is to maximize individual engagement with literacy, particularly with the actual thinking process necessary for effective reading and writing.... A key aspect ... is that students take charge of what they do with their time, are able to make choices about what they read and write about, and are encouraged to take risks in their writing. The focus of the workshop structure is on the processes of reading and writing—what readers actually do while reading and reflecting on what they read and what writers actually do to accomplish a publishable highly readable piece."

The workshop model has been adopted for the elementary grades. Harvey and Goudvis (2000) describe what happens during reading-writing workshop, stating that "the teacher models a whole group strategy lesson and then gives students large blocks of time to read and to practice the strategy in small groups, pairs or independently. During this time, the teacher confers with students about their reading and about how they use a strategy to comprehend text. Sometimes the teacher meets with small, flexible groups to provide instruction in a particular strategy. Much of the time the kids read independently in books of their choice."

Atwell (1987; 1998) states that the way to help students become lifelong readers is to "approach reading from an authentic perspective...." Writing instruction, Atwell (1998) believes, must follow the writing process that professional writers use, allowing students to write about what is most interesting to them. Students need to write several drafts to polish a piece of writing before the final draft. Atwell (1987; 1998) states that readers and writers need to "REHEARSE, planning and predicting, DRAFT, discovering meaning, and REVISE, re-seeing and re-seeking meaning." Tierney and Readence (2005) state that reading-writing workshop provides the support that helps students develop "...the same kinds of reading and writing habits that good adult readers and writers have: the ability to choose books to read and topics to write about, numerous strategies used in the context of reading and writing, ways of talking about the books they are reading and pieces they are writing, and most important, a personal identity as a reader and writer."

Atwell (1987; 1998) believes that the way to help students develop the habits that adult readers and writers have is to provide opportunities to learn how to select books to read, subjects to write about, to learn many strategies to use for reading and writing, ways to talk about the books they are reading and what they are writing, and to develop a "personal identity as a reader and writer."

Atwell (1987; 1998) states that the reading-writing workshop approach is based on two underlying principles: (1) students are the owners of their reading and writing. Students make decisions about what to read and write about based on the guidelines of the approach, and (2) the teacher serves as a mentor and an expert reader-writer not as a judge of student work. The teacher participates in the reading-writing experiences and shares the results with the students.

Ross (1996) states that the theoretical foundation for the reading-writing workshop comes from many sources. The workshop is not just a set of procedures, "it is a method of implementing current views of how children learn to read and write. The developmental continuum is the foundation, and research-based concepts about language learning are the building blocks on which the workshop approach rests." Such building blocks include the importance of knowing each student's needs and abilities at many stages of development; child-centered learning determined by each student's reading interests and purposes; immersion in reading, writing or learning to read with many opportunities to use literacy skills; an integrated curriculum which helps students learn to read and write in an atmosphere that connects reading and writing to oral language and learning in the content areas; literature-based instruction using a wide variety of literature of all types, providing language skill and background knowledge essential for better reading and writing, and providing for greater social interaction through more communication with peers and the teacher about reading and writing. These concepts form the foundation for reading-writing workshop, according to Ross (1996), Goodman (1986), Atwell (1987; 1998), Cambourne (1988), Holdaway (1979), Swift (1993), Strickland (1994; 1995), Hoff (1994), and Morrow, Sharkey, and Firestone (1993).

The reading-writing workshop is made up of four procedures: mini-lessons, status-of-the-class report, workshop, and group share time, according to Ross (1996). Tierney and Readence (2005) and Atwell (1987; 1998) state that the four elements of the reading-writing workshop are: Time to read and write, forums for response, conferences with the teacher, and mini-lessons. Atwell (1987; 1998), Ross (1996), and Tierney and Readence (2005) explain each element of the approach. The mini-lesson is a short lesson that deals with an aspect of reading or writing that the students are working on. The mini-lessons are an important part of the workshop. Select a topic that can be taught in a short time or develop several mini-lessons to teach aspects of the same topic. Mini-lessons help students develop a strategy. Mini-lessons can be used to teach required curriculum topics and offer students a choice and help with authentic reading and writing tasks. Atwell (1987; 1998) suggests that mini-lessons last from five to twenty minutes. The skill selected is one the students need and the method is a quick effective way to teach it. The fast presentation of a needed skill helps students continue their reading and writing and apply the skill in a meaningful context. Select necessary skills from observing what the students need to know and from the required curriculum guide for the grade being taught. Teach only one skill in each mini-lesson so that students focus on that skill and do not become confused by too many skills presented at one time. The early mini-lessons should focus on workshop procedures until students are comfortable and understand what is expected during the workshop. Subsequent mini-lessons focus on specific aspects of reading and writing.

The status-of-the-class, Atwell (1987; 1998) states, is a report of what each student does during the workshop each day. As the student is called he or she states what has been accomplished, what is being worked on and what will be worked on. A record form with students' names and dates of activities is filled in by the teacher every day. According to Ross (1996) and Tierney and Readence (2005), the status-of-the-class report occurs at the beginning of each workshop. Atwell (1987; 1998) states that students tell what they plan to work on during the workshop. This report includes goals and completion dates. Ross (1996) states that this report helps students focus on what to do during the workshop. It helps students define their purpose and set a plan for the work. Status-of-the-class also helps teachers keep track of each student's activities each day because after the first session everyone is working on a different task. This record also makes the teacher aware of which students need help selecting a topic or finding a book. The report, Ross (1996) states, is also a valuable tool for informing parents about student progress and for computing grades.

The workshop, or time to read and write, as Tierney and Readence (2005) call it, is the time for students to read literature, write journal entries, write book recommendations, write reports on nonfiction subjects, write in literature logs to share. Students read in order to write and write in order to read. Atwell (1987; 1998) suggests that teachers spend ten minutes circulating around the room to see who needs help and then reads or writes in his or her journal. The teacher might start by writing for the first ten minutes, serving as a model. Conferences with individual students, Atwell (1987; 1998) states, should be of four kinds: (1) status-of-the-class; (2) topic conferences to help students develop ideas to write about; (3) conferences about drafts to assist students with works in progress; and (4) evaluative conferences to discuss goals, the next step or new activities to consider based on the work in progress or completed.

Students benefit from sharing their reading and writing with peers and with the teacher, and responding to that of others. This provides an audience for written work at various stages, not just for a finished work. Atwell (1987; 1988) suggests that the teacher should respond to works in progress, not only after the work is complete. Responses can be oral or written such as literature response groups, peer conferences, teacher conferences or discussing during mini-lessons. Atwell (1987; 1988) suggests that teachers do not solve the students' problems, but ask questions and listen to students to find their interests and help students find directions in which to move. Instead of offering suggestions, ask questions to help the student list options and then add other ideas to the student's ideas. Respond as a mentor, a reader and a writer, not as a teacher. Response journals between the teacher and student are suggested. The workshop model encourages everyone to be readers and writers together who learn with and from each other.

Communication is the heart of the share time. When one reads a good story or writes a funny poem there is a need to communicate what has been done with others, either with an individual or a group. Calkins (1994) suggests that listeners could write comments on cards for the author to read or focus on specific ideas being presented. The teacher often acts as an observer and is able to note areas for instruction. Focus on suggestions such as clear image, strong feelings and the strategies used, Calkins (1994) suggests, to help focus a share session. Teachers need to set guidelines about who will share, for how long, and who will respond.

Ross (1996) states that flexibility within the workshop framework is important because teachers, grade levels, and groups of students differ. Flexibility means that the teacher uses student input to monitor the workshop using what works best for the individuals and the group. Atwell (1987; 1988), Calkins (1994), and Ross (1996) offer practical suggestions for each part of the reading-writing workshop to help teachers at all levels become effective workshop mentors.

Research studies on reading-writing workshops have examined writing generated by students and peer responses to that work, according to Wade and Moje (2000). Students' written work is referred to as student-generated texts in these studies.

DiPardo and Freedman (1988) and Forman and Cazden (1985) found that providing opportunities for students to create their own written texts and to provide peer response to classmates' written work resulted in a number of positive by-products. Students who write and engage in peer response learn the social skills needed for better communication, cooperation and working with a partner. Students also experienced improved content learning as a result of the workshop model.

The workshop model, Wade and Moje (2000) state, provides "opportunities for students to build the knowledge, experiences, and skills they bring to the classroom while also developing new knowledge, experiences, and skills—and thus, new texts." McCarthey (1994) studies how students used what Bakhtin (1981) called the "authoritative and internally persuasive voices" in their original writing as a result of conferences or oral text (talk) with the teacher and peers.

Several studies raised questions and concerns about some parts of the workshop model. Lensmire (1994) studied the writing of third grade students and concluded that both published and student written texts should not only be used as models of the writing process, but should be studied for stereotypes and assumptions that they present to the reader. Lensmire (1994) states that since students' written work is a result of their own particular concept of the world, students were not challenged to think about their work or their view of the world differently. It was found that some students from non-mainstream cultural and social backgrounds were implicitly and sometimes explicitly told by peers that their writing and consequently their words were not as good as those of other students. Lensmire (1994) suggested that material in a modified writer's workshop could be used to challenge "oppression and marginalization" but students would need instruction in using suggestions from Aronowitz and Giroux (1991) on how to examine and take apart texts and how to develop counter texts.

McCarthey (1996) found that teachers using student generated writing often overlooked the importance of the student's cultural experiences and how it influences the way students react to and interpret the mainstream literature presented to them. Finders (1996), Moje, Willis, and Fassio (2000), and Willis (1995) studied how the texts written and used in workshop settings might limit or exclude more diverse material.

Willis (1995) studied how the "author's chair" and "group shares" might silence or govern diverse material which caused students in the reading-writing workshops not to include their personal writing with the rest of their classroom work. Moje, Willis, and Fassio (2000) found that seventh graders in two diverse urban writer's workshop classrooms kept their personal and social writings separate from the writing they did to meet the guidelines of the official writer's workshop. Finders (1996) studied two groups of young women in a socio-economically diverse, ethnically homogeneous midwestern classroom and found that the material they wrote and read in the readers-writers workshops was different from what they wrote and read outside of school. Wade and Moje (2000) state that the results of these studies indicate that "what is considered appropriate or acceptable text by teachers and students (in reading-writing workshops) may shape the kinds of texts students generate in both their written and oral work."

Studies by Moje, Willis and Fassio (2000) and Fassio (1998) concluded that students in diverse classrooms wrote more from their real life experiences when the guidelines of reading-writing workshops for group sharing and publication were modified.

Annotated Bibliography

Allington, Richard. *What Really Matters for Struggling Readers*. Boston: Pearson, 2001; 2006.
    Discusses strategies that help students with reading difficulties.
Aronowitz, S., and Giroux, H.A. *Postmodern Education: Politics, Culture, and Criticism*. Minneapolis: University of Minnesota Press, 1991.
    Discusses the importance of culture and politics as part of literary criticism.
Atwell, Nancie. *In the Middle: Writing, Reading and Learning with Adolescents*. Portsmouth, NH: Boynton/Cook-Heinemann, 1987; 2d edition, 1998.
    Discusses the origins and implementation of the reading-writing workshop with middle school students. Explains what Atwell did in the classroom and why the workshop model is successful. Presents stories from Atwell's classrooms to illustrate main points.
Avery, Carol. *...And with a Light Touch*. Portsmouth, NH: Heinemann, 1993.
    Discusses the procedures of the reading-writing workshop with practical suggestions for implementation.
Bakhtin, M. *The Dialogic Imagination*. Austin: University of Texas Press, 1981.
    Discusses literary criticism and the voices authors use.
Board of Education of the City of New York. *Instructional Guide: Literacy, Grades K-2; Grades 3-5; Grades 6-8*. Brooklyn: New York City Board of Education, 2000; 2000; 2001.
    Practical guides to balanced literacy procedures including how to use the reading-writing workshop.
Burns, Bonnie. *The Mindful School: How to Teach Balanced Reading and Writing*. Arlington Heights, IL: Skylight Training and Publishing, 1999, pp. 132-140, 234-254.

A practical guide to balanced reading and writing. Provides worksheets and rubrics for classroom use. Discusses the reading-writing workshop as two separate workshops.

Calkins, Lucy McCormick. *The Art of Teaching Reading*, New York: Longman, 2001, pp. 64–80.

Discusses the structure and management of an independent reading workshop. Provides support and guidance on the workshop model.

Calkins, Lucy McCormick. *The Art of Teaching Writing*. Portsmouth, NH. Heinemann, 1994.

Discusses the writing workshop as part of the writing process for teachers in all grades. This provides a guide to practice with the theory on which procedures are based. An excellent annotated bibliography is included.

Cambourne, Brian. *The Whole Story: Natural Learning and the Acquisition of Literacy in the Classroom*. Ontario: Scholastic, 1988.

Discusses student choices, ownership of work, and decision making in classroom activities as a key to child-centered learning and as a foundation for the reading workshop model.

DiPardo, A., and Freedman, S.W. "Peer Response Groups in the Writing Classroom: Theoretic Foundations and New Directions." *Review of Educational Research* 58 (1998): 119–150.

A research report of the positive effects of peer responses to student writing.

Fassio, K. "The Mexican Alliance in 2-b (on March 23, 1998): Children's Political Negotiations in a Second Grade Classroom." Paper presented at the American Educational Studies Association Meeting, November 1998. In Suzanne E. Wade and Elizabeth B. Moje, "The Roll of Text in Classroom Learning"; in *Handbook of Reading Research, Volume III*. Michael L. Kameli, Peter B. Mosenthal, P. David Pearson, and Rebecca Barr, eds., Mahwah, NJ: Erlbaum, 2000, pp. 609–627.

Reports the findings of Fassio's study of students in urban classrooms using the reading-writing workshop.

Finders, M. "'Just Girls': Literacy and Allegiance in Junior High School" *Written Communications* 13 (1996): 93–129.

Report of a study of female students who modified their writing for classroom sharing so that it was different from their work done outside the classroom.

Forman, E.A., and Cazden, C.B. "Exploring Vygotskian Perspectives in Education: The Cognitive Value of Peer Interaction." In *Culture, Communication, and Cognition: Vygotskian Perspectives*. J.V. Wertsch, ed. New York: Cambridge University Press, 1985, pp. 323–347.

Discusses the importance of peer response to students' original written work in creating better communication and social skills in the classroom.

Goodman, Kenneth. *What's Whole in Whole Language?* Portsmouth, NH: Heinemann, 1986.

Discusses integration of the curriculum as the key to language development. A standard work on whole language theory and practice.

Graves, Donald H. *Writing: Teachers and Children at Work*. Portsmouth, NH: Heinemann, 1983.

Based on a two-year study of K–6 teachers and students. Presents a valuable guide to the writing process. A classic useful for all teachers.

Harvey, Stephanie, and Goudvis, Anne. *Strategies That Work*. York, ME: Stenhouse, 2000, pp. 29–31.

Discusses the implementation of reading writing workshop briefly as part of effective strategy instruction.

Heald-Taylor; B. Gail. "Three Paradigms for Literature Instruction in Grades 3–6." *Reading Teacher* 49 (March 1996): 456–466.

Discusses three methods of literature instruction providing practical suggestions for implementation.

Hoff, Laurie. "From Omnipotent Teacher-in-Charge to Co-Conspirator in the Classroom: Developing Lifelong Readers and Writers." *English Journal* 83.6 (1994): 42–50.

Discusses mini-lessons and personal experience with the reading-writing workshop. Tells how to modify procedures based on class needs and how to move from traditional strategies to the workshop model.

Holdaway, D. *The Foundations of Literacy*. Portsmouth, NH: Heinemann, 1979.

Discusses literacy development and the importance of student interest as part of learning.

Lensmire, T. *When Children Write*. New York: Teachers College Press, 1994.

A study of third grade students' writing which raised questions about some parts of the reading-writing workshop model.

McCarthey, S. "Authors Text and Talk: The Internalization of Dialogue from Social Interaction During Writing." *Reading Research Quarterly* 29 (1994): 200–231.

A study of how students modified their writing after teacher and peer conferences. A positive part of the conferences is the improvement of writing based on oral feedback.

McCarthey, S. "Learning the Qualities of Good Writing: Literacy Practices in Elementary Schools." Paper presented at the National Reading Conference, December 1996. Reported in Suzanne E. Ward and Elizabeth B. Moje, "The Role of Text in Classroom Learning"; In Michael L. Kamil, Peter B. Mosenthal, P. David Pearson; and Rebecca Barry, eds., *Handbook of Reading Research, Volume III*. Mahwah, NJ: Erlbaum, 2000, pp. 609–627.

Reports that teachers overlook students' cultures and experiences as influences on their writing.

Moje, E.B., Willis, D.J., and Fassio, K. "Constructing and Negotiating Literacy in a Seventh Grade Writer's Workshop." In *Constructions of Literacy: Studies of Teaching and Learning in Secondary Classrooms and Schools*. E.B. Moje and D.G. O'Brien, eds. Mahwah, NJ: Erlbaum, 2000.

Reports the importance of attention to diverse material in reading and writing workshops.

Morrow, L.M., Sharkey, E., and Firestone, W. "Promoting Independent Reading and Writing Through Self-Directed Literacy Activities in a Collaborative Setting." *Reading Research Report* No. 2. National Reading Research Center, Universities of Georgia and Maryland, 1993.

Discusses the importance of freedom to choose topics, books, and approaches to activities for second graders in developing skills and responsibilities in reading and writing.

Ornstein, Allan, C., and Sinatra, Richard C. *K–8 Instructional Methods: A Literacy Perspective*. Boston: Pearson, 2005, pp. 297–298.

A brief overview of the workshop model outlining its basic parts.

Roe, Betty D., Smith, Sandy H., and Burns, Paul C. *Teaching Reading in Today's Elementary Schools*. Boston: Houghton-Mifflin, 2005, pp. 326–327.

A brief discussion of reading-writing workshop in a text for reading instruction. A good overview.

Ross, Elinor Parry. *The Workshop Approach: A Framework for Literacy*. Norwood, MA: Christopher-Gordon, 1996.

Presents the theoretical foundations and practical applications of the workshop approach at many grade levels. Provides reproducible pages and student work samples. Ross refers to the book as a handbook for teachers and provides expert guidance.

Strickland, Dorothy, S. "Reinventing Our Literacy Programs: Books, Basics, Balance," *Reading Teacher* 48.4 (1994–1995): 294–302.

Tells how to move toward balanced literacy using the workshop model. Provides common sense advice for teachers who are changing strategies.

Swift, Kathleen. "Try Reading Workshop in Your Classroom." *Reading Teacher* 48.4 (1993): 294–302.

Reports an increase in 6th grade test scores as a result of participation in reading-writing workshop. Recommends adoption of the model.

Temple, Charles, Ogle, Donna, Crawford, Allan, and Freppon, Penny. *All Children Read:*

Teaching Literacy in Today's Diverse Classrooms. Boston: Pearson, 2005, pp. 21–25; 460–461.

A brief discussion of reading workshop in this text intended for pre-service students.

Tierney, Robert J., and Readence. John, E. *Reading Strategies and Practices: A Compendium.* Boston: Pearson, 2005, pp. 87–94.

Describes the purpose, rational, and procedures of the reading-writing workshop with a list of references. This is a good resource for an overview of the workshop model.

Wade, Suzanne E., and Moje, Elizabeth B. "The Role of Text in Classroom Learning" In *Handbook of Reading Research, Volume III.* Michael L. Kamil, Peter B. Mosenthal, P. David Pearson, and Rebecca Barr, eds. Mahwah, NJ: Erlbaum, 2000, pp. 609–627.

A report on the use of student writing at various levels also providing a discussion of printed texts and teacher generated material. Discusses research findings about reading-writing workshop and other strategies.

Willis, A.I. "Reading, the World of School Literacy: Contextualizing, the Experiences of a Young African-American Male." *Harvard Educational Review* 65 (1995): 30–49.

Discusses the contributions and importance of students' culture to their written work and how the workshop setting may limit or exclude these works.

Index

alternative assessment techniques 259, 263, 265; anecdotal records 234, 239, 259–260, 264; assessment 4, 5, 30, 47, 77, 114, 120–121, 126–127, 133, 140, 143, 154, 181, 188, 192, 194, 196, 198, 212, 221, 222, 239, 242, 246, 249, 251–253, 256, 259, 261–265; authentic assessment 5, 259, 262–265; checklists 259–260; collaboration 192, 196–197, 213, 261; conferences 4, 57, 59, 101, 108–110, 112–113, 115–116, 198, 208–209, 234, 259, 261, 268–270, 273; interviews 193, 212, 214, 224, 259, 261; limitations of 26, 35, 120, 125; observation or kid watching 26, 31, 85, 111, 130, 150, 176–177, 193, 196–199, 224, 241, 259–260; portfolios 197–198, 239, 259, 261, 264; progress reports 260; rating scales 259; retelling 132, 136, 139, 169, 203, 205, 211–212, 222, 259, 262; running record 175–177, 262–265; self-assessment 262

basal reading approach 4, 41, 46, 49, 111, 162, 186; basal reading series 42, 46–47, 49; criticism of 43; Dick and Jane New Basic Readers 43; directed reading activity—DRA 42, 49; Scott Foresman series 43; strengths that basal readers 45, 48; total reading program 41, 43–44, 112, 219; weaknesses of basal readers 44; whole word approach 41, 91–92

cloze procedure 125, 246–253; advantages 25–26, 45, 48, 81, 110–111, 113–117, 153, 196, 217, 249, 251; cloze scores 247, 249; conclusions 35–36, 103, 112, 115–116, 146, 158, 240–241, 250, 260; deletions 246–248; to improve comprehension skills 171, 248; instruction In early childhood classroom 248–249; limitations 25–26, 35, 82, 120, 124–127, 138, 140, 249, 263; maze test 247; modification 79, 118, 247; psychological notion of closure 246; research studies 25–26, 50, 91, 103, 111–112, 115, 122, 137, 145, 228, 249, 270; selection of material 21, 116, 219

emergent literacy 5, 107, 164–167, 185; association of print with meaning 164; instructional strategies 165–167; learning community 164, 166, 192; reading readiness 41, 54, 164, 221; underlying principles 164–165

Fernald technique 62, 75, 77–82; analytical method 63; Bryant's principles of remediation 76–77; clinic school 62–63, 79; critique by Robinson 69–70; dyslexia 75–76, 78, 80, 85–86, 91, 93–95; Fernald's response 70–74; hand kinesthetic method 64–65, 69; partial disability 64; reconditioning method 63; remedial techniques in basic school subjects 80; stages of hand kinesthetic method 65–68; total or extreme disability 64; VAK 79, 81; VAKT 79, 81

four blocks framework 231–232, 237, 240, 241–242; ability grouping 24–26, 28, 31–32, 34–35, 38–40, 111, 116, 231, 240, 242, 245; decoding 8, 33, 38, 41, 62, 83, 139, 141, 150, 155, 186–187, 236, 243; description of each block 241; designed to 18–20, 27, 83, 116, 119, 136, 144, 191, 216, 231, 240, 244, 263; differentiation 46; first grade instruction 162, 231; first grade studies 103, 105, 162, 240; guided reading 42–43, 122, 125, 168, 170–171, 231–233, 239; instructional principles 237; letter substitution 236; mini lessons 30, 189, 192, 203, 220, 234–235, 266, 268–269, 272; multi-level instruction 38; oral reading 24, 45, 56–57, 59, 104, 109, 129–130, 132–137, 139–145, 157–158, 160–162, 178, 209, 225, 227, 230, 233, 264; phonemic awareness 167, 178, 183–187, 236; research 3, 4, 5, 13, 23, 25–32, 35–40, 44–60, 62, 65, 75, 80–84, 86–87, 91–98, 101–107, 111–116, 118–129, 131–135, 137–138, 140–143, 145–146, 153–154, 158–161, 163, 166–168, 170–174, 177–187, 190–195, 198–201, 204, 206, 210, 213–224, 228–230, 237–239, 241–244, 249–253, 255–258, 267, 270, 272–274;

275

rounding up rhymes 235–237; self-selected reading 34, 231–232, 234, 239; spelling patterns 156, 178, 181, 236; strengths 22–23, 25, 45, 48, 109, 113, 115, 135–137, 140, 142–143, 189, 207–208, 232, 238, 259, 261–262; student achievement 25, 28, 37–39, 237; success 11, 31–32, 34–37, 39–40, 51–52, 63–64, 75, 78–81, 83, 88, 91–92, 95, 102–104, 107, 115–116, 126, 128–129, 134, 153, 159–160, 179, 181–186, 191, 203, 215–218, 221, 234, 237, 240, 243, 249, 251, 253, 261; ten guiding principles 237–238; theme related books 236–237; *Understood Betsy* 242; the will and the skill 240; working with words 34, 231–232, 235–237, 239; writing 5, 7, 8, 9, 30–31, 33–34, 39, 49, 51–52, 56, 58, 60–67, 72–76, 80–81, 84, 86–90, 95, 97, 99–107, 114, 117, 119–120, 126–127, 142, 146–147, 150–151, 156–157, 161–162, 164–167, 172–173, 175–178, 180, 184–189, 191–192, 194–195, 198–200, 203, 205–206, 208, 211–213, 215–221, 224, 226, 228–232, 234–235, 237, 239–240, 242–244, 260–274

Gates, Arthur Irving 34, 43, 47, 50–57, 60, 65, 81, 92, 94, 168, 172; diagnosis of individual differences 25–26, 29, 37, 51, 110–111, 113, 116, 182, 186, 218, 231, 240, 242; First World Congress in Reading 52; improvement of reading 37, 47, 51, 53–54, 58, 81, 94, 96, 172; instructional strategies 42, 45, 48, 50, 60, 91, 127, 136, 165, 258, 260; *Interest and Ability in Reading* 51, 54–55; International Reading Association 5, 26, 36–39, 48, 52, 54–57, 59–61, 106, 114–116, 125–126, 128, 133, 140, 142–143, 146, 161–163, 166, 173, 180, 185, 187, 192–194, 200–201, 215, 218, 228–229, 251–252, 263–265; intrinsic method 50, 52–53; programmed instruction 51; reading and spelling problems 50, 53
Gillingham-Stillman Approach 83, 86–87, 91, 94–95; alphabetic method 86, 95; Bouillard 84; Broca 84; *Children Who Cannot Read* 91, 95; dominant hemisphere 84, 93; drill cards 89–90; *A Follow-up Study of 216 Dyslexic Children* 91; Galaburda 85, 93–95; Gearheart 85, 88–89, 92, 94; Gillingham Manual 87, 94; Hinshelwood 83, 85, 94–95; Kemper 85, 94; nondominant hemisphere 84, 93; patterns for the integration of associations 88; reading and the brain 84–86; spelling 7–9, 11–15, 17–20, 22, 33, 50, 53, 62, 66, 74, 79–80, 86–87, 89–94, 100–105, 107, 144–145, 149–152, 155–157, 159–160, 162, 166, 178, 181, 184, 186, 193, 234–236, 242–243; syllables 8–10, 19, 66–67, 70, 74, 84, 86, 90, 118, 148–149, 183; word-blindness 64, 83; *see also* Orton-Gillingham Approach
Gray, William Scott, Jr. 56–61, 65, 69, 82; Annual Conference on Reading 57; *Gray's Standardized Oral Reading Paragraphs* 57, 59; investigations 33, 54, 57, 59, 69, 146; *Remedial Cases in Reading: Their Diagnosis and Treatment* 57, 59; *Summary of Reading Investigations* 57, 59; *The Teaching of Reading and Writing: An International Survey* 58, 60
grouping for instruction 29, 39; achievement or ability 24–26, 28–29, 31–32, 34–35, 37–40, 111, 116, 231, 240, 242, 245; Book Club program 34; CIRC technique 33, 38; flexible 35, 39–40, 49, 113; friendship 30; interest 30, 36; multilevel teaching 34; pairs or partners 29; peer 29, 31–33, 37, 40, 130, 198, 201, 203, 213, 235, 269, 272–273; project 29–30, 198; range of individual differences 29; special skills or needs 29–30

individualized reading approach 4, 108, 110–114, 215; advantages 25–26, 45, 48, 81, 110–111, 113–117, 153, 196, 217, 249, 251; disadvantages 25, 81–82, 110, 112, 115, 116, 117, 124, 153, 251; independent work 109, 209; record keeping 108–110, 113–115, 208–209; research conducted 111–113; self-pacing 108, 208; self-selection 108, 113–116, 208; seven characteristics 108–109; sharing activities 109, 208; strategy and skill instruction 108, 208; student-teacher conferences 109, 209
Initial Teaching Alphabet—ITA 103, 144, 146; phonemically regular alphabet 144; spelling patterns 156, 178, 181, 236

Joplin Plan 24–28; homogeneously grouped pupils 24; inter-class ability grouping 24

language experience approach 4, 97, 99–107, 115, 145–146, 251; balanced reading program 99, 238; creative writing 99–100, 102, 150; directed reading thinking activities 100, 103; eclectic approach to reading instruction 99; *The First Grade Reading Studies* 102, 145–146; language acquisition 98; language production 98; language recognition 98; phonics 53, 68, 70, 78, 88–91, 99, 101–103, 124, 145, 147, 151, 153, 155, 157–162, 178–179, 181, 183–184, 186, 190–191, 232, 242; Roach Van Allen 97, 99; Russell G. Stauffer 25–27, 50–51, 53–54, 80, 99, 146; say-it, see-it 75, 101
linguistic approach 103, 145–146, 155–163;

The Basic Reading Series 156; Carl Lefevre 156, 161; Charles Fries 156–158, 160, 163; Leonard Bloomfield 155; linguistic 15, 42, 85, 99, 103, 105, 119, 124–127, 143, 145–147, 149–150, 153, 155–163, 166, 188, 199, 204, 218, 251; *The Linguistic Readers* 156; *Merrill Linguistic Readers* 156–157; *The Miami Linguistic Readers* 156; *The Royal Road Readers* 156; sound-symbol teaching 158; sounds and letters series 156; *The Structural Reading Series* 156

literature-based reading approaches 196, 210–212, 216–217, 219–221, 224; advantages 25–26, 45, 48, 81, 110–115, 117, 153, 196, 217, 249, 251; aims 123, 176, 202, 209, 259; attitude toward reading 31, 210, 214, 222; characteristics of literature-based program 34, 202–204, 209–211, 213, 216–217, 219–224; in content areas 27, 106–107, 127, 210, 215; critics 119, 209; features of 12, 75, 88, 123, 139, 179, 197; follow-up activities 205, 208; genres 109, 199, 206, 209, 229, 239; individualized reading 4, 38, 108–116, 175, 203, 208, 215, 234, 266; journals and logs 205; literature circles 196–201, 203, 205–206, 216; meaningful learning 206, 207; meta cognitive awareness 211; negative aspects 209; oral discussion 204; procedures for thematic units 207; research 3–5, 13, 23, 25–32, 35–40, 44–60, 62, 65, 75, 80–84, 86–87, 91–98, 101–103, 105–107, 111–116, 118–129, 131–135, 137–138, 140–143, 145–146, 153–154, 158–161, 163, 166–168, 170–174, 177–187, 189–195, 200–201, 204, 206, 210, 213–224, 228–230, 237–239, 241–244, 247, 249–253, 255–258, 267, 270, 272–274; science instruction and science achievement 211–212, 221; thematic literature units 206; thinking strategies 212; whole class core book reading 203; written language 4, 80, 88, 99, 104–105, 107, 147, 161, 164–165, 167, 183, 204, 211

literature circles 196–201, 203, 205–206, 216; benefits 81, 115–116, 146, 194, 199, 217–218, 229–230; collaboration 192, 196–197, 213, 261; community of readers 197; comprehension 18, 26, 32–36, 43, 45–48, 51, 53, 62, 64, 69, 71, 77–78, 81, 83, 107–109, 112–113, 117–118, 120, 124–125, 127, 129–131, 133–135, 137, 139–140, 143, 145, 152–153, 157–158, 160, 162, 168–174, 178, 180, 184, 193, 196–197, 203–205, 208–209, 211–213, 215–218, 220, 225, 228–229, 232–233, 238, 246–257, 261–262; conferences 4, 57, 59, 101, 108–110, 112–113, 115–116, 198, 208–209, 234, 259, 261, 268–270, 273; cooperative learning 31, 33, 39, 196, 198, 206; elements of 13, 91, 147, 151, 169, 185, 197, 208, 225, 268; literature logs 198–201, 204–205, 269; orientation to 176, 255; research about 93, 114, 120, 142, 171, 187; response 3, 23, 32, 35, 61, 70–72, 74–76, 82, 88, 112, 123, 138, 171, 178–179, 181–182, 196–197, 199–202, 205–207, 210, 217–220, 222–224, 230, 251, 260, 265, 268–270, 272; student led discussion 196, 199; teacher as facilitator 188, 197–198, 200, 222

McGuffey, William Holmes 17–23, 46; *The McGuffey Readers* 18, 21–23

miscue analysis 135–143; coding 136–137, 262; disabled readers 69, 78–82, 95, 139, 143, 164, 247, 249, 252–253; limitations 135–143, 262; patterns 136–138, 141, 160; Reading Miscue Inventory—RMI 136–137, 140–143

oral reading 24, 45, 56–57, 59, 14, 109, 129–130, 132–137, 139–145, 157–158, 160–162, 178, 209, 225, 227, 230, 233, 264; choral reading 130, 132, 233; circle reading 129; debates 130–131; demonstrations 130–131; interviewing 130–131; mini performances 130, 132–133; National Reading Panel 121, 127, 129, 132–133, 178, 181, 185, 255–256; positive aspects of oral reading 129–130; purposes for oral reading 130; round-robin reading 129, 134

Orton-Gillingham Approach 83, 86–88, 91–96

phonemic awareness 167, 178, 183–187, 236; blending 77, 89, 93–94, 156, 183, 184, 187, 194; research 183–187, 189–195, 199–201, 204, 206, 210, 213–224, 228–230, 237–239, 241–244, 247, 249–253, 255–258, 267, 270, 272–274; rhyming words 9, 236; segmenting 183–184, 187; symbolic hypothesis 183; use of literature 112–113, 190, 200, 213–214, 216–217, 220

question-answer relationship strategy 254–258; concerns about 49, 256, 258, 270; findings 32, 36, 45, 49–50, 52, 69, 83, 85, 94, 106, 116, 131, 140–141, 143, 146, 161, 170, 175, 181–182, 184, 213, 224, 250–251, 255, 272, 274; National Reading Panel Report 178, 255; research 93, 114, 120, 142, 171, 187; stages 255; systematic analysis 254; thinking process 152, 235, 266; use of information 190

readability 4, 117–128, 246, 251–253; Cloze procedure 125, 246–253; CWF or critical word factor 121; Dale-Chall Formula 118, 125, 127–128; Flesch Readability Formula 118; Fry Readability Graph 118, 126; levels of difficulty 209, 232; Lexiles 121, 123; limitations of readability formulas 120; literacy tasks of the digital age 123; objective estimate or prediction of reading comprehension 117; prediction 46, 98, 117, 119, 170, 204, 233; production 42, 119, 225, 227, 229; readability formulas 117, 119–120, 124–127; reading recovery levels 122; standards 34, 102, 121, 123, 126–128, 247, 260, 262; text development 121; text leveling 122–123; validity of readability formulas 127

Reader's Theater 229–230; audience 126, 130–133, 225–227, 245, 269; content area material 121, 128, 204, 228; criteria for 132, 143, 226, 249, 261; dramatize a story 227; oral interpretation of literature 132, 225; oral reading 24, 45, 56–57, 59, 104, 109, 129–130, 132–137, 139–145, 157–158, 160–162, 178, 209, 225, 227, 230, 233, 264; performance 27, 31, 34, 36, 38, 77, 130, 132–133, 139, 149, 160, 220, 225–260, 264; Sloyer outlines 226–227

Reading Recovery program 127, 175–182; admission to the program 176; at-risk students 133, 175, 217–218; diagnostic procedures 95, 115; early intervention 175, 177–179, 181–182, 187; Marie Clay 175–176, 179; one-to-one intervention 175; research 177–179; running record 175–177, 262–265; summary of the observation 176

reading-writing workshop 266–268, 270–274; author's chair 271; in diverse classrooms 271; elementary grades 4, 46, 123, 129, 211, 266; with middle school students 193, 271; principles 13, 75–76, 80, 86, 114, 145, 157, 164, 229, 243, 260; procedures 5, 25, 31, 48, 50, 66, 75–77, 81, 87, 91–93, 95, 109, 113–115, 117, 136–137, 140–143, 175, 177, 180, 189, 191, 207, 228, 239, 245, 248, 250, 253, 267–268, 271–274; questions and concerns 270; research on 5, 25, 38–39, 48, 51, 54, 57–59, 93–95, 98, 102, 104, 112, 116, 127, 131, 133–134, 141, 168, 174, 178, 182, 185, 210, 214, 217, 229–230, 237, 251–252, 257; response 269; status of the class 268-269; structure 4, 37–38, 44, 58, 78, 84–85, 88, 94, 119, 122, 124–125, 137, 150, 159–162, 168–173, 178, 180–181, 193, 196–197, 262, 266, 272; theoretical foundation 106, 216, 238, 267, 273; workshop model 234, 266, 269–274

story grammar 168–174; schema 109, 168–169, 171–174, 228; sequential questions 171; story elements 168, 171, 202, 226; story maps 169–174, 205, 233

Webster, Noah, Jr. 7–8, 10–16; *The American Spelling Book* 9, 12–14; *Blue-Back Speller* 11–12, 15; character instruction 10; *The Grammatical Institute of the English Language* 9; *New Guide to the English Tongue* 8

whole language approach 5, 32, 105, 112, 114, 161, 179, 184, 186, 188–195, 202, 210–211, 216, 218, 220–224, 264, 272; belief system 188, 191; children's literature 47, 127, 189, 192, 202, 215, 219, 220, 222, 230; concerns 49, 179, 189, 194, 256, 258, 270; disfavor of 190–191; professional movement 188

words in color 147, 149–154; aspects of language 149, 156, 231; background 42–44, 61, 64, 68, 70, 95, 103, 114, 117, 119–121, 127, 135–136, 138, 147, 150, 167, 171, 198, 201–202, 204, 209, 218, 220–221, 231, 233, 254–255, 257, 268, 270; cardboard 151; chalk 147; consonant sounds 89, 151, 158, 160; dictation 90, 99, 147, 176, 181; linguistic method 147, 163; paper 235; sequence of sounds 147; visual perception in reading 152–153; vowel sounds 77, 144, 147, 155; wall charts 147–151

www.ingramcontent.com/pod-product-compliance
Lightning Source LLC
Chambersburg PA
CBHW051212300426
44116CB00006B/537